PENGUIN BOOKS

THE NEW SPANIARDS

Born in 1950, John Hooper was educated at St Benedict's Abbey in London and St Catharine's College, Cambridge. At the age of eighteen he travelled with a television crew to Biafra during the Nigerian civil war to make a documentary for ITV. He has since worked for – among others – the BBC, Independent Radio News, the *Daily Telegraph* and the *Guardian*. *The New Spaniards* is a product of nine years as a correspondent in Spain, first from 1976 to 1979 and then again from 1988 to 1994. He is now the *Guardian*'s Southern Europe correspondent based in Rome.

John Hooper is married to a fellow-journalist, Lucinda Evans.

The forerunner of this book, *The Spaniards*, won the Allen Lane Award for 1987.

JOHN HOOPER

THE NEW SPANIARDS

PENGUIN BOOKS

PENGUIN BOOKS

Published by the Penguin Group
Penguin Books Ltd, 27 Wrights Lane, London w8 5tz, England
Penguin Books USA Inc., 375 Hudson Street, New York, New York 10014, USA
Penguin Books Australia Ltd, Ringwood, Victoria, Australia
Penguin Books Canada Ltd, 10 Alcorn Avenue, Toronto, Ontario, Canada m4v 3b2
Penguin Books (NZ) Ltd, 182–190 Wairau Road, Auckland 10, New Zealand

Penguin Books Ltd, Registered Offices: Harmondsworth, Middlesex, England

The Spaniards first published by Viking 1986
Revised edition published in Penguin Books 1987
This new and completely revised edition published under the present title 1995
10 9 8 7 6 5 4

Set in 10/12pt Monophoto Bembo
Typeset by Datix International Limited, Bungay, Suffolk
Printed in England by Clays Ltd, St Ives plc

FOR LUCY

The fight for freedom is always easier than the practice of freedom.

— Matija Beckovic

Contents

decrees' – the creation of ETA – the *ikastolas* and the revival of the language – the impact of recession – terrorists under pressure

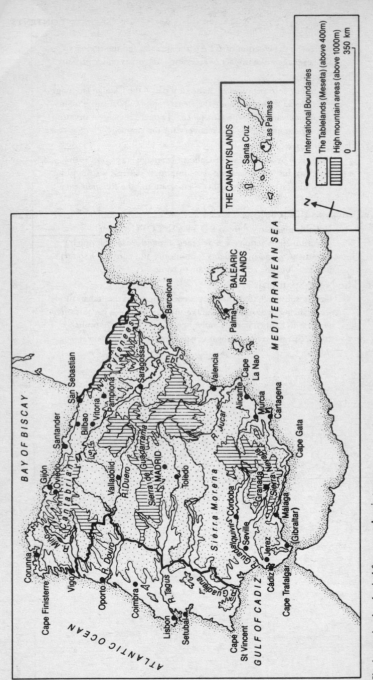

Iberian peninsula, physical features and main towns

THE CANARY ISLANDS

Santa Cruz
Las Palmas

International Boundaries
The Tablelands (Meseta) (above 400m)
High mountain areas (above 1000m)

0   350 km

N

ATLANTIC OCEAN

BAY OF BISCAY

Cape Finisterre
Corunna
Vigo
Cape Finisterre

Gijón
Oviedo
Santander
San Sebastian
Cantabrian
Bilbao
Vitoria
Pamplona
Pyrenees

Oporto
R. Douro
Coimbra
R. Duero
Valladolid
Sierra de Guadarrama
MADRID
Toledo
Zaragossa
Ebro

Lisbon
Setubal
R. Tagus
R. Guadiana
Sierra Morena
Cordoba
Guadalquivir
Seville
Jerez
Cadiz
Cape Trafalgar
(Gibraltar)
Malaga
Sierra Nevada
Granada
Cape Gata
Cartagena
Murcia
Alicante
Cape La Nao
Valencia
R. Jucar

Cape St Vincent
GULF OF CADIZ

Barcelona
Palma
BALEARIC ISLANDS

MEDITERRANEAN SEA

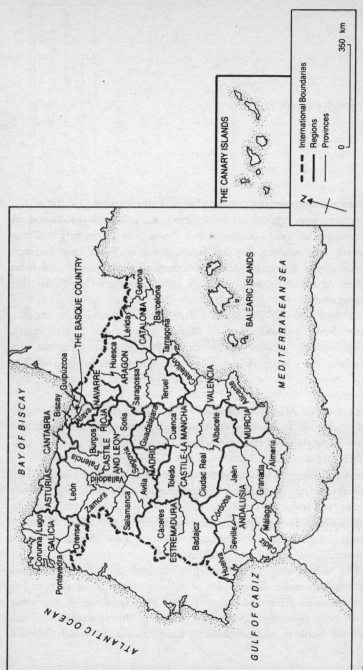

Spain, provinces and regions

Acknowledgements

My first thanks are once again due to Peter Preston, Editor of the *Guardian*, who agreed to my taking an unofficial sabbatical in the autumn of 1993, during which I was able to do much of the research and writing for this book. Paul Webster, then Foreign Editor of the *Guardian*, Ann Treneman of the *Observer* and John Parker of the *Economist* were all kind enough to agree to this arrangement.

I should also like to record a deep debt of gratitude to another editor, Pedro J. Ramírez of *El Mundo*, who in 1989 invited me to move into the offices of his newspaper, at that time not yet launched. As a result, I had access throughout the writing of *The New Spaniards* to a vast pool of specialized knowledge and information.

Various *El Mundo* journalists – Elvira Huelbes, Ana Romero and Victor de la Serna – read through sections of the book and offered suggestions and corrections. Julio Miravalls and his staff in the *documentación* section – Alicia García, Joaquín Carazo, Ana Camarero, Begoña Luaces and Isabel Mancheño – dug out cuttings, looked up dates, and ungrudgingly provided me with any number of facts and statistics. Others at *El Mundo* who gave of their time to help include Ruben Amón, Fernando Bermejo, María Carmen García, Miguel Gómez, Francisco J. López, Pilar Rubines, Carlos Sánchez, Rosa Tristan and Agustín Yanel.

The New Spaniards has been produced by a method not unlike that used to make sherry: part of what you are about to read has been retained from an earlier book, *The Spaniards*. It therefore seems only right that those who helped in the preparation of my previous book should continue to figure, in the list which follows, alongside those who made a contribution on this occasion. I should like to extend my thanks to Tesni del Amo, Joaquín Arango, Kees van Bemmelen, Nanchy Benítez, Rafael Borras, Peter Bruce, Irma Caballero, Anselmo Calleja, José Cardona of the Federación de Entidades Protestantes, Ramón Cercós, José and Jane Criado Pérez, Juan Cruz, Aubrey Davies, Amador Díaz, Juanita Eskubi, Alvaro Espina Montero, Francisco García de Valdecasas, Emilio García Horcajo, Dionisio Garzón, Pere Gimferrer, Antonio Gómez, Pedro González Gutiérrez-Barquín, José Luis González Haba, Margaret Hills, Alex Hucklesby, Amado Jiménez Precioso, Pedro Miguel Lamet, George Lewinsky, José Antonio López de Letona, Professor Aina Moll, Andrés Ortega, Campbell Page, Lluis Pasqual, Rafael del Río, Ivor Roberts, Marta Ruiz, Harry Schapiro of the Institute for the Study of Drug Dependence, Francisco Sosa Wagner, Bernard Tanter, Dr Don Tills, Jorge Tinas Gálvez, the late Professor Antonio Tovar, Francisco Velázquez, Luis Antonio de Villena, Jane Walker, Martin Woollacott and Ian Wright.

Professor Colin Smith spotted a number of errors in *The Spaniards* which I have been able to correct in this new edition, thanks to his precise and detailed observations.

Bill Lyon, formerly of *El Sol*, who has to be the only American ever to have been the bullfight critic of a Spanish newspaper, also merits a special mention. He was kind enough to read through Chapter 25 and provided me with several invaluable suggestions.

At this point, it is customary to acknowledge the 'support and encouragement' of one's spouse – a phrase which always, to my mind, conjures up the image of some woebegone figure bringing endless cups of tea and coffee. The role played by my wife, Lucy, in the preparation of this book has been very different. She persuaded me to embark on it, has made countless perceptive suggestions as to its shape and content, and brought to much of the finished text the editing skills of an ex-Fleet Street sub-editor. Thanks, in her case, is much too flimsy a word.

J.H.

Rome
June 1994

Note on the Spelling of Place Names

Wherever an anglicization exists which involves a change of spelling, I have used it. Thus Castilla has become Castile, and La Coruña, Corunna. But where the anglicized form merely involves the loss of an accent (as in Aragon or Cordoba), I have stayed with the accented Spanish version.

Note on Exchange Rates

Currency conversions have been made at the average rate for the relevant year.

Introduction: The Rediscovery of Spain

The milestones, the highlights, the great and decisive moments in the history of Spain have all been accompanied by discoveries.

They were all wrong.

The Greeks came and found what they thought was the entrance to Hell on the Rock of Gibraltar. The Romans arrived and discovered at the westernmost tip of Iberia what they took to be *finis terrae*, the end of the world. The mixed band of Arabs and Berbers who swept through the peninsula in 711 were under the impression they were conquering an island. Then, in 1492, there occurred the next great turning-point when, in a single year, Queen Isabel of Castile and King Fernando of Aragón changed for ever the ethnic and religious balance of Spain by subjugating the last Moslem kingdom on the peninsula and then giving the Jewish subjects of their two realms a choice between exile and conversion. No sooner had they done so than Columbus landed in the Americas, confident in the knowledge that he had just reached India.

In 1808 – after more than two centuries of suspicious and resentful isolation from the rest of the continent to which it belongs – Spain was invaded by France. Thus Spain rediscovered Europe. Or rather, it discovered those values which were then beginning to take hold in Europe as a consequence of the French Revolution and which would do so much to shape the modern world. The trouble was that the Spanish were forced to make their discovery from the wrong end of a musket, and many – understandably, though mistakenly – concluded they could do without the values the French had brought with them. A growing number came to feel otherwise over the next 130-odd years, with the result that during that period Spain was to undergo forty-four revolutions, counter-revolutions, and what we would nowadays call coups and counter-coups, as progressives and reactionaries struggled for ascendancy. By 1939, enough Spaniards remained unconvinced of modern ideas for them to be able to organize a successful military uprising that was to distance their country from the rest of Europe until their leader, General Franco, died thirty-six years later.

The restoration of democracy in 1977 initiated a period in which there were to be discoveries galore. Spain has since been rediscovering the rest of the world. The rest of the world has been rediscovering Spain. And perhaps, too, the Spaniards have been rediscovering themselves.

You can nowadays scarcely take a step in any of the world's major airports without hearing the penetrating strains of Spanish as it is spoken in Spain. As a result of their increased prosperity, more Spaniards take foreign holidays, speak foreign languages and read foreign publications. In the process, they are discovering a world which is not as hostile to them as they had been led to believe by their former dictator.

On the contrary, what they have found is a world in which there is immense curiosity about their country. It passed largely unnoticed in the English-speaking world, but for a brief period in the early 1980s Madrid became as fashionable among other Europeans as London had been in the Swinging Sixties. The French in particular were entranced by the phenomenon of the *movida madrileña* – an explosion of creativity among the city's young. The Middle East Peace Conference which was held in the Spanish capital in 1991, Expo '92, the Barcelona Olympics, and Madrid's stint as the European Community's Capital of Culture, all served to concentrate attention on a nation which is big enough in every sense to merit attention. Fractionally smaller than France, Spain is the second-largest country in Europe outside Russia. Its population is nearly as big as that of Canada and Australia combined. With Spanish the official language of some 300 million people, it also has the potential, as yet unrealized, to exert a truly immense cultural influence.

Freedom, meanwhile, has given the Spanish a much more clear-eyed view of themselves. The opportunity to research their history without having to make it conform to a preconceived pattern means they are perhaps closer than ever before to understanding who they really are. Their Moslem and Jewish heritages, for example, were ignored for generations. Today, Madrid has a park named after the city's founder, Emir Mohammed, and a synagogue in which King Juan Carlos donned the *yarmulka* to attend a service of reconciliation on the 500th anniversary of the expulsion of the Jews.

In spite of the fears voiced at the time, the disappearance of Franco's dictatorship has not of itself made Spain any less Spanish. It can be seen now that if Spain has come more to resemble the rest of a world that is itself becoming increasingly homogeneous, it is because of the country's economic development rather than its political liberation. And that was a process which began long before Franco died. Democracy has, if anything, arrested the loss of identity.

Franco presided over the implantation of all sorts of imported aesthetic norms. Many of the public buildings and monuments constructed under his dictatorship were inspired by a Fascist-mono-lithic style copied from Italy and Germany. His officials had a fondness for wispy little moustaches that were much less in keeping with Spanish tradition than the bushy beards so dear to his latter-day opponents. Far from conserving Hispanic values and customs, Franco repressed all those which he feared. Recent years have seen the recovery of the carnival, which he discouraged as a threat to public order and morality. They have seen a revival of languages other than Castilian, which he regarded as a threat to unity. Spain's past may have been glorified under his rule, yet little was done to conserve its legacy. Since the return of democracy, villages of historic value and entire quarters of towns and cities have been restored to their former pride with public money.

Nor has freedom made the Spanish any less idiosyncratic. They still work to a uniquely incompatible variety of timetables. They remain the only people in Europe who eat their meals in such a way that vegetables other than potatoes, or rice, if eaten at all, are usually consumed separately at the beginning. In summer, women still use fans, even when reading the news on television. In winter, men still drape their coats round their shoulders, just as if they were capes.

At the same time, though, the freedom to be themselves has removed a good many illusions. It used to be impossible to tell which of Spain's shortcomings were due to almost four decades of dictatorship, and which were symptomatic of more enduring national characteristics. Under Franco, everything that was wrong with the country – from bureaucracy to corruption – could be blamed on his authoritarian rule. Today, it can be seen that a number of these supposedly temporary blemishes are still very much in evidence and that, if they are ever to be done away with, the Spanish are going to have to look deeper into themselves and at the nature of their society.

With all this rediscovery going on, it should mean that the latest great turning-point is upon us. And that in turn means that anyone who wants, or needs, to know about Spain should take care, for if the experience of the past is anything to go by, the time is now ripe for misapprehension.

Spain is, in any case, a profoundly deceptive country. Again and again, in the pages which follow, the reader will find – as the author has found – that appearance and reality are at variance. Knowledge of it has undoubtedly grown in recent years. In the forerunner to this book,* I wrote that 'people's ideas about Spain are still based to a great extent on what was written during or about the period leading up to Franco's takeover'. Just eight years later, that is no longer the case. The majority of non-Spaniards have come to realize that Spain is not nowadays a land of conservative religious beliefs and rigid moral conventions, of vast social divisions and violent political conflicts. There is a much greater readiness to accept that it is an economically and politically advanced society with many of the problems inherent in an advanced society at the end of the twentieth century. Yet something else I wrote in *The Spaniards* remains true – that, in different ways, it is 'the best-known and the least-known of the major European nations'. Every year, some 50 million people visit Spain. Yet the vast majority are holidaymakers who spend most, if not all, of their time at coastal resorts quite untypical of the country as a whole. Flying directly to and from the *costas*, the Balearic or Canary Islands, they have little chance to see the everyday Spain of the ordinary Spaniard.

If non-Spaniards have any picture at all of the land that lies behind the *costas*, then it is probably that of the *meseta* – the

---

* *The Spaniards. A Portrait of the New Spain* (Viking, 1986; Penguin, 1987).

tableland which encompasses Old and New Castile, León, La Mancha, Estremadura, and parts of Aragón, Navarre and La Rioja. Vast and arid, stark and lofty, it has little in common with the balmy coastline the package tourists visit. Much has been written about its role in forging the character of the Spanish people, and especially that of the Castilians who have been the dominant community for much of the country's history. It may well be that the *meseta*'s testing climate – searingly hot in summer and bitterly cold in winter – has given the Castilians a stern and sober streak you will not often find among other Mediterranean people; that the immense expanses and serrated horizons of the *meseta* have made Castile a land of dreamers, of mystics and conquerors.

If Castile and the *meseta* fail to conform to outsiders' expectations of Spain, the same is true of much of the rest of the country.

Galicia, the north-westernmost region, which sits atop Portugal, is as wet and lush and mournfully beautiful as the West of Ireland. The dominant colours there are the green of its gorse and the grey of its granite. Like Brittany and Ireland, it gets a lot of rain and much of it finds its way back to the sea along valleys which have subsided over millennia to the point where their seaward ends have sunk below the level of the ocean leaving only the valley sides visible in the form of great promontories. These half-submerged valleys or *rías* are an abundant source of shellfish – crabs, lobsters, oysters and, above all, the scallops which the pilgrims who travelled to Santiago de Compostela in medieval times adopted as their emblem. The dish of scallops cooked with mashed potato and grated cheese which the world knows as Coquilles Saint Jacques is by origin a Galician delicacy copied by the French.

Further along the coast, Asturias with its wild countryside and coal-mines is more akin to South Wales than anywhere in the Mediterranean. Next door, Cantabria has soaring peaks with villages on their slopes that are cut off for weeks on end every winter, and deep potholes among which were found the famous cave paintings of Altamira. Much of the farming is pastoral and the sound of cowbells is never far away. You could be in Switzerland.

The Basque country also has an Alpine look to it. The typical Basque farmhouse with its broad eaves is virtually indistinguishable from a Swiss chalet. But whereas Switzerland is mountainous, the

Basque country – although frequently described in the press and elsewhere as 'mountainous' – is in reality a land of odd-looking, steep-sided, flat-topped hills that tower over the valleys between them. The countryside in most areas is of a uniquely intense shade of green – a green so dark that it sometimes appears unnatural. In fact, it is a result of the rain that pours down in the Basque country day in day out, week in week out, during the winter. But then, Bilbao, the biggest city in the Basque country, would be a dismal enough place even without the rain and the constantly overcast skies. To visit it is to take a journey back in time to the industrial north of Europe earlier this century. Its belching smokestacks, grimy buildings and dogged, pasty-faced inhabitants are the very stuff of Lowry paintings.

In the foothills of the Pyrenees, in Navarre and Aragón, you could almost be in the Highlands of Scotland, but in both regions the landscape changes dramatically as you move southwards away from the French border. In Navarre you go through a stretch of splendid undulating countryside around the capital, Pamplona, before entering an almost Mediterranean district where there are extensive vineyards. In Aragón you descend gradually towards the vast, flat, depopulated Ebro valley and then rise again into the bare uplands around Teruel.

Catalonia and Valencia are perhaps the regions that the majority of people regard as being most typically Spanish, although a lot would, I think, be surprised to learn that a clear majority of Catalans and a sizeable minority of Valencians do not even speak Spanish* as their first language. Nor, whatever they may think,

*The use of the word 'Spanish' instead of 'Castilian' to describe Spain's most widely spoken language is unfortunate in that it implies that the others (Basque, Catalan and Galician) are either un-Spanish or less Spanish. It is rather like calling English 'British', but with less justification since vernacular languages are far more extensively used in Spain. Hispanic Latin Americans tend to use the term *castellano* as much as, if not more than *español*. Within Spain itself, the use of the word *español* rather than *castellano* is a recent phenomenon and one which was encouraged by the nationalistic dictatorships of Primo de Rivera and Franco. The first edition of the *Dictionary of the Royal Academy* to be called 'Spanish' was not published until 1925. Both the 1931 and 1978 constitutions referred to the official language of the nation as 'Castilian'. There is now a growing tendency for Spaniards to use the two words indiscriminately. I have followed their example.

have many of the foreign holidaymakers who have visited Spain's east coast been for a holiday on the Costa Brava. The term *costa brava* means 'rugged coast' and is used by Spaniards to describe the rocky shoreline that begins around San Feliú and extends to the French border. Resorts like Lloret de Mar which tour operators habitually describe as being on the Costa Brava are on flat, sandy land further to the south.

Beyond Valencia lies Murcia – hotter, drier and flatter. But beyond Murcia lies Almería, which is sufficiently reminiscent of Arizona for it to have been used as the setting for a string of Westerns. By the coastal route, Almería forms the gateway to Andalusia – Spain's Deep South. Here again, the contrast between image and reality is considerable. The Andalusia of legend is an undulating expanse of corn fields and olive groves divided up into a small number of large estates. That is indeed true of the more northerly and westerly of the eight provinces that make up the region – Huelva, Cádiz, Seville, Córdoba and Jaén. But Málaga and Granada are hilly – and, in parts, even mountainous – provinces where smallholding has always been the rule rather than the exception. As for Almería, much of it is as barren as the Sahara.

The cities of this 'other Spain' behind the *costas* are quite unlike the jerry-built, neon-lit resorts that make up what is virtually a single city – homogeneous in character and appearance – stretching from Lloret to Marbella. Indeed, what is striking about the majority of provincial cities is how old they look. Most have extensive industrial estates and dormitory suburbs on the outskirts now, but with very few exceptions the centres have retained their historic character. Those of Pamplona, Avila and Santiago de Compostela, for example, seem scarcely to have changed since Spain's Golden Age. The same is true of parts of the great conurbations – Madrid, Barcelona, Valencia and Seville – even if they are nowadays as hectic and alive, as glitzy and seedy, as any of the big cities in Europe.

Many people are ready to accept that Spain is among the largest countries in Europe, but few would think of it as one of the highest. Yet the average height of the ground is greater than in any European country except Switzerland. If you look at a relief map you will see that, with the exception of the Guadalquivir and Ebro valleys and a relatively narrow coastal strip, the whole of Spain is upland. The *meseta* varies in altitude from two to three thousand feet as one craggy mountain range succeeds another. This gives to it one of its most distinctive characteristics – the almost painful brightness of the light. Not only is Spain a land of huge expanses, but one where you can as often as not see to the furthest limits of those expanses. 'In Spain,' wrote the author and journalist Manuel Vicent, 'there is a lot of sun and an excess of light, so that everything is all too clear. It is a country of emphatic claims and denials where historically doubt has been put to the torch – to that sinister clarity.'

This alone has made Spain seem a forbidding place to the foreigner. But then Spain is a difficult country to come to grips with from almost any angle. For a start, it contains several different cultures. What is true of most of Spain need not be true of the Basque country, or of Catalonia or Galicia. Partly for this reason, anyone who sets out to study Spanish history will soon discover that lengthy stretches of it are dauntingly complicated. Some of the country's finest artists and writers – Murillo and Calderón, for example – deal largely with themes that are peculiar to their time and place, while a lot of the popular culture derives from traditions – Arab, Jewish and Gypsy – that are alien to the experience of the majority of Europeans. Non-Spaniards appreciate the spectacle of flamenco, but few could tell good from bad. Even the cuisine, with its ardent spices and outlandish ingredients like pigs' ears and bulls' testicles, requires an adventurous spirit.

Nor is Spain a particularly easy country for the foreigner to explore. Outside the main cities you will have difficulty in making yourself understood in any language but Spanish. Road and rail communications remain inadequate, despite recent heavy investment by the government. It is still quicker to fly from north-west Europe to some of the cities on the Spanish coast than it is to drive from those same cities to the capitals of neighbouring provinces – from, say, Corunna to Oviedo, or from Málaga to Almería.

Yet it is precisely the difficulty of getting to know Spain which makes the task so appealing, for it is that which makes it so challenging and rewarding. A point which brings me, finally, to my own rediscovery of this infuriatingly, enticingly complicated nation. A string of events which owed more to accident than design returned me to Spain in the summer of 1988. What I found was a country very different from the one I had left nine years earlier and had only visited on holidays or assignments in the interval. The results of that re-encounter are set out in this book.

What I wrote at the start of the *The Spaniards* applies to this book too: apart from Part One, which briefly describes the economic trends and the political events that have moulded Spain into the nation it is today, this is not a book about economics or politics; nor does it concern itself with labour relations. Once again, my aim has been to paint a picture of contemporary Spanish society.

Ernest Hemingway thought it was 'probably a good system, if one has to write books on Spain, to write them as rapidly as possible after a first visit as several visits could only confuse the first impressions and make conclusions much less easy to draw'.

But then Hemingway didn't follow that advice. And neither have I.

PART ONE

The Making of the New Spain

Economic and Social Change: from the 'Years of Hunger' to the 'Years of Development'

Although Franco's regime was frequently referred to as a fascist dictatorship, the description was never wholly correct. Spain's fascist party, the Falange, was only one of several factions and institutions which rallied to the officers who rebelled against the elected government in 1936 and which thereby earned the right to a share in the spoils when, three years and half a million lives later, their side emerged victorious. In addition to the Falange, there was the army (or rather that section of the officer corps which had sided with the rebels), the Church and the monarchists, including both those who favoured the restoration of the heirs of Alfonso XIII – the king who had left Spain in 1931 – and those who supported the cause of the Carlist pretenders whose claims to the throne had twice provoked civil war during the previous century.

It was not unusual for membership of these 'families', as they have been called, to overlap. There were generals who belonged to the Falange, just as there were devout Catholics who wanted the restoration of the monarchy in some form. But there were also irreconcilable differences, notably between the Falangists, who wanted to set up a fascist republic, and the Alfonsine and Carlist monarchists. To ensure that their rivalries did not undermine the war effort and to assert his control over their activities, Franco – who emerged by a mixture of chance and design as *Generalísimo*, or Commander-in-Chief, of the rebel forces – fused the political parties representing these three groups into a single entity with the tongue-twisting, catch-all title of Falange Española Tradicionalista y de las Juntas de Ofensiva Nacional-Sindicalista (FET de las JONS). This odd coalition, which came to be called the Movimiento Nacional, was from then on the only lawful political entity in

Franco's Spain. Throughout his rule, there was usually at least one member of each 'family' in the cabinet and the number of portfolios held by a particular faction was usually a good indication of the extent to which it was in or out of favour with the *Caudillo*.★

The army enjoyed a brief heyday in the immediate aftermath of the war, but it was the Falange which later became the dominant influence on Franco. Neither the Church nor the army was capable of providing a programme for running the country and the monarchists of both camps stood for a solution that could only be put into effect if Franco were to give up the position which he had by that time acquired as Head of State. In any case, the Blueshirts (for blue was to Spain's fascists what brown was to Italy's and green to Portugal's) appeared in 1939 to represent the shape of things to come.

Over the next few years the Falangists took over the Movimiento and laid the foundations of Franco's regime. As soon as it became apparent that the Axis powers might not after all win the world war that had begun within months of the end of Spain's civil war, Franco reduced the number of Falangists in his cabinet by giving non-fascists the ministries which had most contact with the outside world. Nevertheless, Falangists continued to hold most of the economic and social portfolios and Falangist ideas dominated the regime's thinking.

This was partly because fascist political philosophy, with its emphasis on national economic independence and on agricultural rather than industrial development, dovetailed conveniently with the course of action forced upon Franco by events. During the Second World War, Spain had remained technically neutral while actively favouring the Axis. At the end of the war she found herself in an acutely uncomfortable position. Unlike Britain and France, she was not entitled to the rewards of victory. Unlike Germany and Italy, she was not at risk from the encroaching power of the Soviet Union. The Allies therefore had no incentive for giving Spain aid and a very good reason for denying it to her. In fact, they went

---

★This was Franco's other title, equivalent to *Führer* or *duce*. In Spain it has – or had – heroic overtones because it is the word most commonly applied to the native chieftains who led the guerrilla war against the Roman occupation.

even further than that and actually punished the Spaniards for having been taken over by a right-wing dictator. In December 1946 the newly-created United Nations passed a resolution recommending a trade boycott of Spain. Coming on top of the deprivations brought about by the civil war, which had cut real income *per capita* to nineteenth-century levels, the boycott was a disaster – not so much perhaps because of its direct effects, but because it made it unthinkable that Spain should benefit from the Marshall Plan for aid to Europe which got under way six months later.

All the European nations suffered deprivation in the post-war era, but Spain, where the late forties are known as the *años de hambre* or years of hunger, suffered more than most. In the cities, cats and dogs disappeared from the streets, having either starved to death or been eaten. In the countryside, the poorer peasants lived off boiled grass and weeds. Cigarettes were sold one at a time. The electricity in Barcelona was switched on for only three or four hours a day and trams and trolleybuses in Madrid stopped for an hour in the morning and an hour and a half in the afternoon to conserve energy. But for the loans granted by the Argentine dictator, General Perón, it is possible that there would have been a full-scale famine.

The UN-sponsored blockade was lifted in 1950, but the Falangists' insular and ineffective doctrines continued to hold sway. For this, Spain was to pay dearly. In spite of the Falangists' exaltation of the rural economy, agricultural output fell to a level even lower than at the end of the civil war. Industry, immured from the outside world by a wall of tariffs and quotas, unable to buy the foreign technology it needed to modernize or to seek out new markets for its goods, bound on all sides by government regulations, could only grow at a painfully slow pace. National income did not regain its pre-civil-war level until 1951 and it was not until 1954 that the average income returned to the point it had reached in 1936. In the early fifties an attempt was made to ease trade restrictions and stimulate private enterprise, but although it eventually succeeded in boosting industry it opened up a trade gap that rapidly absorbed the country's foreign reserves. In the meantime, bungling in other areas of the economy led to bursts of rip-roaring inflation.

To the villagers in the poorer parts of Spain – and particularly Andalusia which had been the scene of desperate poverty even before the civil war – the deprivations of the post-war era were the final straw. Individuals, families and in some cases entire villages packed up their belongings and headed for the industrial centres of the north – Barcelona, Bilbao, Oviedo and Saragossa – and for Madrid which, with the deliberate encouragement of a regime which feared the economic prowess of the Basques and Catalans, had ceased to be a purely administrative capital. Once they reached the cities the migrants settled like besieging armies on the outskirts. With nowhere else to live, they built *chabolas or barracas* (shacks) out of whatever they could scavenge – some breeze blocks from a building site, an unwanted door, a few empty cans and boxes and a sheet of corrugated iron or two to serve as a roof, weighted down with lots of heavy stones to make sure it did not blow away. The shacks were suffocatingly hot in the summer and bitterly cold in the winter. None had running water, so there was no question of sewerage. Since the shantytowns had sprung up without official permission it was usually several years before the municipal authorities got around to supplying them with electricity, let alone the more sophisticated amenities such as refuse collection or access roads. With grim humour, one of the shanty towns outside Barcelona was nicknamed 'Dallas – Frontier City'.

The whole idea of migration to the cities ran counter to the Falangist dream of a populous countryside inhabited by peasant farmers each owning a modest but adequate plot of land. At first the authorities tried to put a stop to the exodus by force. Policemen were sent to the railway stations with orders to collar anyone with a dark complexion and a battered suitcase and put him on the next train out of town. But it was like trying to turn the tide. In any case, migrants already living in the shanty towns saw in it a way of returning home for a holiday courtesy of the government – all they needed to do was put on their scruffiest clothes, travel a few miles out of town and catch a train coming up from the south.

The authorities later turned to a more sophisticated and successful approach, which was to limit the number of shacks by licensing those that had already been built and giving them numbered plaques. Those that did not have a plaque were liable to be torn down by the teams of municipal workmen – the dreaded *piquetes* which usually arrived in the middle of the morning or afternoon when the men of the shanty towns were out working, or looking for work. Although the number of licences had to be increased bit by bit, the system made the building of a shack such a hazardous enterprise that their numbers started to stabilize towards the end of the fifties.

By then Franco's regime was virtually bankrupt. The foreign exchange account was in the red, inflation was heading into double figures and there were serious signs of unrest among both students and workers for the first time since the civil war. It took a long time to persuade Franco that a radical change was required. But in February 1957 he reshuffled his cabinet and gave the Trade and Finance portfolios to two men, Alberto Ullastres Calvo and Mariano Navarro Rubio, who were representative of a new breed in Spanish politics – the 'technocrats'. The typical technocrat came from a well-to-do background, had had a distinguished career in academic or professional life and – this was the *sine qua non* – belonged to, or sympathized with, the secretive Catholic fellowship, Opus Dei.

As its title – 'Work of God' – suggests, the central belief in Opus Dei's philosophy is that of sanctification through work. Like others before him, Opus's founder, José María Escrivá, had noted with dismay that wherever and whenever there was economic progress the Roman Catholic faith seemed to lose ground. Instead of seeing capitalist development as a threat, though, he regarded it as an opportunity: if only devout Catholics could be imbued with a 'work ethic', then take a hand in the process of economic development at an early stage and use their control of it to spread their ideas through the rest of society, a rise in the GDP need not lead automatically to a fall in the numbers of the faithful.

Whether the Opus technocrats also had a political agenda is still a matter for debate. They and their admirers always insisted that its aim was to prepare for democracy. In 1966, General Jorge Vigón, who had entered the cabinet as a result of the 1957 reshuffle and was close to the technocrats in outlook, wrote that 'freedom begins as of the moment when the minimum earnings of each citizen reach $800 per annum'. However, critics of the regime and of Opus Dei have argued that the technocrats saw improving the standard of living as a way of delaying the restoration of democracy. It has been noted that in subsequent references to General Vigón's formula the target figure was repeatedly increased. But whatever the intent, the *effect* of the technocrats' reforms was wholly beneficial for Francoism, for it ensured the survival of a regime which had seemed doomed by its economic failings.

It was not until two years after their appointment that the new team began their all-out assault on the economy. Their short-term aim was to tackle inflation and redress the balance of payments. Their long-term objective was to free the economy from the restrictions that had been placed on it by the Falangists. The so-called Stabilization Plan introduced in July 1959 was intended to achieve the first of these goals. Public spending was cut, credit was curbed, wages were frozen, overtime was restricted and the peseta devalued. The Plan achieved what was expected of it. Prices levelled out and the deficit in the balance of payments was transformed into a surplus by the end of the following year. But the cost in human misery was considerable since real earnings were slashed. As a result, many Spaniards set off to find work abroad. Measures to liberalize the economy, and thus achieve the second of the technocrats' goals, were introduced over a longer period beginning at the time of the Stabilization Plan. Spain was opened up to foreign investment, much of the red tape binding industry was cut away, restrictions were lifted on imports and incentives were offered for exports.

The performance of the economy during the years that followed was dramatic. Between 1961 and 1973, a period often referred to as the *años de desarrollo* or years of development, the economy grew at 7 per cent a year – faster than any in the non-communist world except Japan's. Income per head quadrupled and as early as 1963 or 1964 – the exact moment is disputed – it passed the $500 mark, removing Spain from the ranks of the developing nations as defined by the UN. By the time Spain's 'economic miracle' had ended, she was the world's ninth industrial power and the wealth generated by her progress had led to substantial improvements in the standard of living.

Spaniards had a better diet. They ate less bread, fewer potatoes and more meat, fish and dairy products. The results can be seen on any Spanish street today – those under the age of thirty are noticeably taller and slimmer than their parents. In 1989, the Spanish bed manufacturers' association acknowledged the fact when it announced that the standard size of beds produced in Spain was to be increased by 8 centimetres to 1·90 metres.

During the sixties, the number of homes with a washing-machine rose from 19 per cent to 52 per cent, and the proportion with a refrigerator leapt from 4 per cent to 66 per cent. When the boom started only one in every hundred Spaniards owned a car; by the time it ended the figure was one in ten. Telephones ceased to be the prerogative of offices, factories and a few wealthy or influential individuals and became commonplace in private homes – a fact that had a considerable impact on relations between the sexes, which was in turn mirrored in the pop songs of the day. The number of university students tripled, and by the early seventies the infant mortality rate in Spain was lower than in Britain or the United States.

It should be pointed out, though, that one reason why the proportionate increases in all areas were so impressive was that the starting-points were so low. Even in 1973 *per capita* income was still lower than in Ireland, less than half the average for the EEC countries and less than a third of the average in the United States. Moreover, *pluriempleo*, the practice of holding several jobs, which became widespread in Spain during the boom years, meant that Spaniards had to work harder for their prosperity than other Europeans.

The principal reason why the economy was able to continue growing after 1959 in a way that it did not after the reforms at the beginning of the fifties was that ways were found of bridging the trade gap which opened up as soon as Spain's economy began expanding – a consequence of the fact that Spain had to pay more for the fuel, raw materials and capital equipment which she needed to feed her industrial expansion than she could get for the goods and produce she sold abroad. Throughout most of the period from 1961 to 1973, imports outstripped exports in a proportion of about two to one, but the deficit was amply covered by invisible earnings in the form of receipts from tourism and the money sent back to Spain by Spaniards who had found work abroad. At the same time, growing foreign investment ensured that Spain's reserves increased rather than decreased over the period.

In all these areas, the government had played an important role.

It had eased the conditions for foreign investment, provided financial incentives for Spaniards to seek work abroad and, while tourism had been growing steadily throughout the fifties, it was not until 1959 when the government stepped in to abolish the requirement for visas for holidaymakers from Western Europe that the industry really took off. It is equally true, however, that none of this cash from abroad would have been forthcoming in such quantities had the other countries of the West not been enjoying a period of growth and prosperity. It was this which created the surplus funds that found their way to Spain, which made the companies of north-western Europe thirsty for cheap foreign labour and enabled individuals in north-western Europe to contemplate holidays abroad. To this extent, Spain's economic miracle was a by-product of the sixties boom in Europe as a whole.

The way that Spain acquired her vital foreign income had an immense impact on the country's lifestyle. Oddly-spelt names which Spaniards found difficult to pronounce, like Chrysler, Westinghouse, John Deere and Ciba-Geigy, began to appear on hoardings and in the press. The young businessmen recruited by the new foreign companies picked up their employers' habits and attitudes and passed them on to their counterparts in Spanish-owned firms. Soon, a new breed of *ejecutivos* began to emerge – clean-shaven, wearing button-down shirts, casual suits and sometimes a pair of black-rimmed spectacles. Their speech, liberally sprinkled with English words and phrases, came to be known as *ejecudinglish*. The archetypal representative of these Americanized Spaniards, now entering their fifties, is the singer Julio Iglesias.

Between 1961 and 1973 well over a million Spaniards received assistance to go and work abroad. By the time the boom ended there were some 620,000 in France, 270,000 in West Germany, 136,000 in Switzerland, 78,000 in Belgium, 40,000 in Britain and 33,000 in Holland – a veritable army of Spaniards all sending back about a quarter of their earnings to swell the deposit accounts of their homeland.

Spain's Mediterranean coastline was transformed out of all recognition. It is hard to believe now that when the novelist Rose Macaulay drove along it in the summer of 1947, she 'encountered scarcely any travelling compatriots and saw only one GB car'. Her main complaint was that 'on these lovely shores as elsewhere in Spain the inhabitants stare and point'. Between 1959 and 1973 the number of visitors to Spain leapt from under 3 million to over 34 million. Land by the coast which, because it was usually either rocky or sandy, was generally regarded as virtually worthless and was frequently bequeathed to the least-favoured offspring, suddenly became valuable. On the Costa del Sol, at San Pedro de Alcántara, a plot of undeveloped land next to the beach which changed hands for 125 pesetas per square metre in 1962 was sold eleven years later – still undeveloped – for 4,500 pesetas per square metre.

The material benefits of the tourist boom were considerable – not only for property developers, but also for shopkeepers and the ordinary people of the villages near the coast who became waiters and chambermaids in the tourist hotels. But that is not to say that the tourist boom was an unmitigated blessing. The development took place in an environment which had not changed very much since the eighteenth century – a world of thrift and deprivation which had its own strict moral code. Overnight, its inhabitants were confronted with a new way of life in which it seemed as if the men had more money than they could cram into their wallets and the women walked around virtually naked. Accustomed to measuring time in hours, they were suddenly expected to think in minutes. They had to come to grips with new concepts like credit cards and complicated machines like dishwashers. The result in many cases (although, for some reason, less among women than among men) was shock. Not in the metaphorical but the literal sense of the word – the most common symptoms were insomnia, listlessness and breathlessness. In the mid-sixties, the Civil Hospital in Málaga enlarged its psychiatric wing by adding a ward specifically to cater for young patients. It immediately became known as 'the waiters' ward'. According to a study carried out in 1971, 90 per cent of all non-chronic mental illness in the rural parts of the province of Málaga was among teenage males who had gone to work on the coast.

Tourism, emigration and the arrival in Spain of multinational firms all served to bring Spaniards into contact with foreigners and in particular with other Europeans, thereby whittling away the xenophobia which had always been a characteristic of the Spanish, and never more so than in the early years of Franco's rule. But Spain did not, as the technocrats had hoped, become a member of the EEC. Her application, submitted in 1962, was ignored, although she did manage to wheedle a preferential trade agreement out of Brussels eight years later. On the other hand, her best soccer team – Real Madrid – had succeeded between 1956 and 1960 in carrying off the European Cup five years in a row (a feat which has never been equalled), and in 1968 a Spanish vocalist, Massiel, won the Eurovision Song Contest with a suitably anodyne offering entitled 'La, La, La'. These victories probably made as much of an impression on the average Spaniard as anything on the diplomatic level would have done. They showed Spaniards that not only could they gain acceptance in 'Europe' (the Spanish, like the British, often talk about Europe as if it were somewhere else) but also hold up their heads while doing so.

The 'economic miracle' changed the nature and volume of internal migration. Poverty-stricken villagers from Andalusia continued to flood into the cities, but they were joined in increasing numbers by migrants from Galicia and the regions of the *meseta* – Castile, León, Estremadura and Aragón. Whereas the typical migrant of the fifties was a landless labourer forced to move by hunger, the migrants of the sixties were likely to be craftsmen or shopkeepers whose standards of living had dropped because of the falling population in the countryside, or peasant farmers who were still able to make a meagre living from the soil but were lured to the city by the promise of a less arduous and more varied existence. An American anthropologist, Dr Richard Barrett, who carried out a field study in the Aragonese town of Benabarre between 1967 and 1968 noted that the girls there were unwilling to marry the sons of peasant farmers if they intended to stay and work their fathers' land – to such an extent that young farmers were driven to advertising in the press for brides from the poorer regions of the country. The dream of the girls of Benabarre was to marry a factory worker – or at least a boy who was prepared to leave home in an attempt to become one.

Come the sixties, the original migrants were beginning to move out of their shanty towns and into cheap high-rise accommodation. Since shack-building was by then practically impossible, the new arrivals either had to buy a shack from a family which was moving on to better things or pay for accommodation in the apartment of a family which had already done so. From the point of view of the first wave of migrants, selling a shack became a way of getting the down payment on a flat. Taking in lodgers was a way of finding the monthly instalments.

While the cities were rapidly becoming overcrowded, the country-side was equally quickly becoming depopulated. In 1971 Dr Barrett returned to Aragón and visited seventeen hamlets near Benabarre. By referring to the 1950 census figures he discovered that during the intervening twenty years they had lost 61 per cent of their population. Four were completely deserted and in some cases the depopulation had taken as little as six years. Today anyone driving through Spain who is prepared for a bumpy ride off the main road will sooner or later come across one of these deserted hamlets. Perhaps the most forlorn of all are those that are almost, but not quite, abandoned – where the last inhabitants, who are too old to leave and too young to die, keep their livestock in what were once their neighbours' cottages.

Before the civil war, the Catalan politician Francesc Cambó had described Spain as a country of oases and deserts. Migration made this even more evident. By the end of the boom, the table of population density by provinces showed a steady gradation from most to least densely populated, but what was striking about it was the size of the gap between the two extremes. At one end there was Barcelona with more than 500 people per square kilometre – which made it as crowded as the industrial centres of north-western Europe – and at the other end there were eleven provinces with fewer than 25 inhabitants per square kilometre – a figure comparable with countries like Bhutan, Nicaragua and Burkina Faso. The process of depopulation has gone so far in some parts of the country that it is difficult to see how it can be reversed. In 1973, as the flood of migration began to abate, Teruel became the first province in Spain's history in which there were more deaths than births. Since then, several provinces with elderly populations have joined Teruel. Even if migration from these areas stops altogether, they will continue to lose inhabitants.

The increasingly uneven distribution of Spain's population

encouraged an even more unequal allocation of the country's wealth. Any attempt at regional planning while Franco was still alive ran up against the problem that the areas into which the country would have to be divided for planning purposes were precisely those whose demands for recognition were anathema to the dictator and whose identity he had been at great pains to erase. The technocrats' answer was a so-called 'pole' policy. The idea was to select a number of towns in underdeveloped or semi-developed regions and offer incentives to firms to set up businesses there, in the hope that the resulting prosperity would spill over into the surrounding countryside. The criteria used for deciding which towns and firms should benefit from the scheme were never made clear and it is suspected that a good deal of corruption surrounded their selection. But the most serious flaw in the 'pole' project was that the incentives were not offered for long enough for entrepreneurs to be confident of success. By and large, investment did not live up to expectations and what investment was generated was relatively unsuccessful in creating new jobs. Of the twelve towns chosen as 'poles', only Valladolid fulfilled the hopes placed in it. By the early seventies it was well on its way to becoming a sizeable industrial centre.

With the exceptions of Valladolid and Madrid, new businesses tended to set up shop in the Basque and Catalan provinces, which had become industrialized in the last century, or in places like Oviedo, Saragossa, Valencia and Seville – big cities which had already had some industry before the civil war. In 1975 five provinces – Barcelona, Madrid, Valencia, Biscay and Oviedo – produced 45 per cent of the country's total output. Most of the prosperity was concentrated in the north and east of the country. Of the fifteen peninsular provinces with the highest average incomes, all but two lay along the River Ebro or to the north of it. The two exceptions were Madrid and Valladolid. Average earnings in the poorest provinces of Andalusia, Estremadura and Galicia were less than half those in the richest – Madrid, Barcelona and the three Basque provinces. The disparity in wealth was mirrored by a disparity in the provision of amenities and services. There were 80 doctors per 100,000 inhabitants in Jaén, but 230 per 100,000 in Madrid.

As the boom progressed, the migrants became potentially one of the most influential classes in Spain, having virtually engulfed the old highly politicized urban working class. Unlike the workers of the thirties, the militancy of whose socialism and anarchism was famed throughout Europe, the vast majority of migrants had very little interest in, or experience of, politics. In rural Spain only a tiny number of people had the time or money to take an interest in political developments outside the village, and they were the rural notables – landowners, merchants and professional people who controlled, through their economic influence, the destinies of the labourers, tenants, sharecroppers and smallholders in patron–client relationships. During the periods in which Spain was a democracy, the clients usually voted the way they were told to by their patrons (which was one of the main reasons why democracy was so widely despised and therefore so vulnerable). The migrants who arrived in the cities during the fifties and sixties were not so much right-wing or left-wing as simply apolitical, although they were highly receptive to the go-getting materialism and individualism which, to a greater or lesser extent, affected every level of society during the *años de desarrollo*. In the shanty towns, acts of great kindness co-existed with an almost total absence of class solidarity; once they had found their way out of those ramshackle purgatories the migrants were understandably reluctant to do anything, such as striking or demonstrating, that might cause them to return. Nevertheless, their initial submissiveness tended to obscure the fact that migration had broken for ever the hold that the rural upper and upper-middle classes had once exerted over the rural lower-middle and lower classes. What is more, it was clear – although not at first to the migrants themselves – that their interests were not those of their employers. Indeed, whenever they were pressed in polls and surveys to define their views, the sort of ideal society that their answers implied was distinctly more left-wing than right-wing. By the start of the seventies, they were beginning to become politically more aware and to develop an outlook that was, if not radical, then certainly progressive.

Although the 'economic miracle' changed almost everything about Spain – from how and where people lived to the way in which they thought and spoke – one of its paradoxes was that what it changed least was the economy itself. It grew, of course, but its shape and character remained virtually unaltered. When the boom ended, there were still far too many small firms (over 80 per cent of all Spanish companies employed fewer than five workers) and it was as difficult as it had ever been to get long-term credit. Between them, these two factors ensured that far too little money was spent by industry on researching new products or training skilled workers. Productivity remained low (half the EEC average), unemployment was comparatively high (certainly much higher than the official figures suggested), and the traditional gap between imports and exports was widening rather than narrowing.

The political effects of the boom were far greater, both in number and complexity. The most popular explanation of recent Spanish history goes roughly as follows. The reason why democracy did not take root in Spain in the late nineteenth and early twentieth centuries was that Spain did not have a middle class. The 'economic miracle' was responsible for redistributing the country's wealth and creating a 'new middle class'. Together, these two factors helped to remove, or rather to bridge, the gulf which had existed up until then between the 'two Spains', and which had been responsible for the civil war. By healing this historic breach in Spanish society between the upper and lower classes, the boom was thus responsible for Spain's relatively smooth transition from dictatorship to democracy.

There is an element of truth in this. Unquestionably, the 'economic miracle' in the sixties helped to smooth the way for the political transformation of the seventies. But the mechanism of cause and effect was a little more complex than is usually made out. In the first place, Spain – as we have already seen – had long had a middle class. But from the point of view of consolidating a democracy, what matters is not so much the existence of a middle class *per se* as the existence of an urban rather than a rural one. What happened during the boom years was that a substantial section of the Spanish middle classes was lured away from the countryside and into the towns for much the same reasons as the working classes. As they moved from one environment to the other, they – or more often their children – abandoned many of the conservative attitudes and prejudices which are typical of rural elites everywhere. The idea that the boom helped to level out wealth is quite simply a myth. Apart from a few radical Falangists, Franco's supporters were not ones to worry about redistributing income. The *Caudillo* himself had once cheerfully admitted that the civil war was 'the only war in which the rich became richer'. During the sixties, the technocrats were content to see the gulf between the richest and poorest in society grow even wider. It was not until the seventies, when the illegal trade unions seized the initiative from Franco's worker-employer *sindicatos* and started to flex their muscles, that the gap began to close. Even so, by the time Franco died the top 4 per cent of households accounted for 30 per cent of total income.

But although the way the cake was cut did not change all that much, the size of the cake grew enormously. Greatly increased buying power enabled just about everyone in society to jump up a class in absolute as distinct from relative terms. To that extent, the 'miracle' did indeed create a 'new middle class' from the ranks of what one might call the upper-lower class – mainly craftsmen and peasants. Far more importantly, though, the same process decimated a class which had been destabilizing Spanish society for well over a century – a lower-lower class of landless, unskilled pariahs whose misery and desperation encouraged them to throw in their lot with any messianic demagogue who promised them salvation in this world rather than the next.

On the day following the first general election after General Franco's death, the newspaper *Diario 16* published an article comparing the number of votes cast for right and left in 1977 and 1936. The percentages were almost identical. Poignantly, the article was entitled 'Forty Wasted Years'. The consolidation since then of a two-party system only serves to underline the point – to the extent that there were 'two Spains', they survived the *años de desarrollo* intact. What the boom years did was to make both of them wealthier and therefore more content and more tolerant.

The miracle ended with the same dramatic suddenness with which it had begun. The European boom had started to run out of steam towards the end of the sixties and the first people to feel the effects were the emigrants. As the expansion of the other Western European economies began to slow down, the number of jobs available declined and the need for foreign labour diminished. After

27

1970 the number of Spaniards leaving the country to work abroad dropped off. Soon, even those who were already working abroad began to find that they were no longer wanted. France, for example, offered emigrants an indemnity of 150 times their average daily wage – payable as soon as they reached their country of origin. In 1973 the emigrants began to return and in 1974 the amount of money they sent home started to fall. The same year also saw tourist earnings drop for the first time as Europeans tightened their belts and marshalled their resources. Even so, Spain's invisible earnings would have been enough to cover her trade deficit had it not been for the increase in oil prices following the war in the Middle East. Spain depended on oil – almost all of it imported – for two-thirds of her energy. The OPEC price rises doubled the size of Spain's trade gap and unleashed the inflationary pressures that had been simmering away below the surface of the economy throughout the boom years. During 1974 the cost of living rose by more than 17 per cent. The following year, an estimated 200,000 Spaniards returned from abroad in need of work. Then, on 20 November 1975, General Franco died and for the second time this century Spaniards were left with the unenviable task of restoring democracy in the depths of a worldwide recession.

CHAPTER 2

Political Change: from Dictatorship to Democracy

At first light on 21 November 1975, the day after Franco's death, a detachment of artillerymen trundled three massive cannon into a park on the outskirts of Madrid and began firing a last salute to the late dictator. The sound of the guns echoed through the city all day, heightening the sense of apprehension that had taken hold of the capital and the nation.

For thirty-six years all the important decisions had been taken by one man. His disappearance was of itself enough to justify a feeling of trepidation among supporters and opponents alike. But Franco had also left behind him a perilous gap in expectations between the people and their rulers. It was plain to anyone with eyes to see and ears to hear that Spaniards wanted a more representative form of government. Even among those who had once supported the dictatorship – and their numbers were consistently underestimated by foreign observers – there was a widespread recognition that Francoism had outlived its usefulness. Yet until his dying day, Franco had restricted the exercise of power to those who had refused to countenance change – collectively nicknamed the *bunker*, or accepted the need for change but were only prepared to introduce it slowly and conditionally – the so-called *aperturistas*. The country's illegal opposition parties, meanwhile, were united in calling, quite unrealistically, for a clean break with the past – what, in the jargon of the times, was known as a *ruptura*. However, since they had no political power, the only way that they could put pressure on the authorities was to call for street demonstrations, which invariably turned into riots as soon as the police arrived.

Of the many prophecies circulating on that chilly November morning, one of the gloomiest yet most plausible was that the government would sooner or later be overwhelmed by an outburst of popular frustration. At that point, the armed forces – which had much to lose and little to gain from the introduction of democracy – would step in to 'restore order', possibly in the name of a higher authority. From then on, so the theory went, Spain would settle into a pattern well known to the Latin American nations (and which was set in Spain during the last century) – phases of limited reform alternating with outbursts of savage repression.

If Spain were to avoid such a fate it was clear that much would depend on the role played by the young man who had succeeded Franco as Head of State. Franco had always implied that he was a monarchist at heart. Ever since 1949, in fact, Spain had in theory been a monarchy, even though Franco ensured that he was made acting Head of State for life and given the power to appoint his own successor. It was no surprise that, six years before he died, Franco should have named as his 'heir' a member of the royal family. But instead of selecting the legitimate heir to the throne – Alfonso XIII's son, Don Juan – Franco chose a young man over whom he had been able to exert enormous influence – Don Juan's son, Juan Carlos.

Juan Carlos was hardly someone in whom Spaniards who aspired to a modern, democratic state could have much faith. Ever since the age of ten, when he had come to Spain for his education, the young Prince had been projected through the media as a loyal son of the regime – passing with distinction his *bachillerato* (including a compulsory paper on the Formation of the National Spirit), going on to attend all three military academies and doing a sort of internship in the administration. In recent years he had rarely been seen except in Franco's shadow, standing behind the old dictator on platforms and podiums at official ceremonies. On such occasions he invariably looked a bit gormless, an impression which was reinforced by the awkward way in which he delivered speeches. The overall impression was of a nice enough chap but with not enough intelligence or imagination to question the conventions of his background.

Few people can have been so universally misjudged as Juan Carlos, for his rather gauche manner belied a penetrating and receptive mind. To the *Caudillo*, Juan Carlos was the son he never had. The young Prince fully reciprocated his affection – to this day he will not permit anyone to speak ill of the old dictator in his presence – but he had formed the opinion long before Franco's death that Spain could not and should not continue to be governed in accordance with the principles laid down by his mentor. Starting in the sixties, Juan Carlos made it his business to get to know as many people from as many walks of life and of as many shades of opinion as possible. By then, he was living in a small palace near Madrid guarded by police. Several of the people he wanted to meet had to be smuggled in either by the Prince's secretary or by friends. Some entered in the boots of cars. Javier Solana, then an activist in the clandestine opposition and later a Socialist minister, went in on the pillion of a banker's motorbike wearing a crash helmet that obscured his features.

Whether Franco knew or guessed what his protégé was up to will probably never be known, but he certainly restricted the freedom and influence that Juan Carlos would enjoy after his accession. On the day after he had been named as successor, the Prince was made to take an oath in front of the members of Franco's rubber-stamp parliament. Kneeling down, with one hand resting on the New Testament, he swore loyalty to Franco and 'fidelity to the principles of the Movimiento Nacional and the fundamental laws of the realm'. In a speech afterwards he hinted broadly at his true beliefs. 'I am very close to youth,' he told the ranks of elderly timeservers in front of him, 'I admire and I share their desire to seek a better, more genuine world. I know that in the rebelliousness that worries so many people there can be found the great generosity of those who want open horizons, often filled with unattainable dreams but always with the noble aspiration to a better world for all.' Nevertheless, the public oath he had just sworn meant that his freedom of movement would henceforth be severely restricted. If the apparatus of Francoism were to be demolished it would have to be done according to the rules that Franco had himself devised. This in turn meant that whoever was in charge of the government would need to be both firmly committed to the restoration of democracy and extremely knowledgeable about the structure of the dictatorship – an apparently impossible combination.

For most of his rule, Franco had been Head of Government – in other words, Prime Minister – as well as Head of State. But in June 1973 he relinquished his grip on the premiership and conferred it on one of the few men he ever really trusted – Admiral Luis Carrero Blanco. Franco evidently hoped that Carrero, a formidably able politician, would still be in the saddle when Juan Carlos succeeded to his throne. Carrero's assassination by Basque terrorists six months later was thus immensely helpful to the young Prince, because it allowed him a degree of manoeuvre which he would never have enjoyed had the Admiral still been around. The best man Franco could find to take over from Carrero was a supremely uncharismatic lawyer, Carlos Arias Navarro. Arias was the most cautious kind of *aperturista*. Dimly aware that the nation was clamouring for democracy, yet temperamentally and ideologically committed to dictatorship, Arias was incapable of moving with any determination either forwards or backwards. Even before the *Caudillo*'s death he had begun to cut a helpless figure, but not one for which anyone felt much sympathy. Juan Carlos himself had little time for Arias and their relations became still worse after Arias tried to resign during the delicate period just before Franco's death in protest at the Prince's decision to hold a meeting with the armed forces ministers without first telling him.

Under the constitutional system devised by Franco, the monarch could only choose his Prime Minister from a list of three names drawn up by the Council of the Realm, a seventeen-man advisory body consisting almost entirely of Franco diehards. Knowing that he stood no chance of getting a suitable candidate from the Council, the King reluctantly confirmed Arias in office after General Franco's death. In the eyes of the public it did him no good at all. Whenever young demonstrators took to the streets during the early days of King Juan Carlos's reign, their favourite chant was:

> *España, mañana*
> *Será republicana*

> (Spain, tomorrow
> Will be republican)

In January 1976 Arias outlined a programme of limited reforms. But it did nothing to reduce the level of violence on the streets. In

March five workers were killed in Vitoria when police opened fire on a crowd of demonstrators. The following month Arias made things worse with a broadcast to the nation in which he seemed, even more than before, to be harking back to the past. In May the government pushed through the Cortes (parliament) a law making it possible to hold meetings and demonstrations. The month after that, the centrepiece of Arias's programme – a bill for the legalization of political parties – was passed by parliament. But hours later the same assembly threw out the legislation needed to put the bill into effect. It was eventually rescued, but the incident showed that Arias could not even carry with him his old friends and colleagues in the Francoist establishment. On 1 July the King called him to the palace and told him that things could not continue like this. Arias, who had never enjoyed being Prime Minister, seized the opportunity to tender his resignation and the King accepted at once.

It was realized that the country had reached a turning-point in its history. Arias's cabinet contained three men with modestly progressive reputations – Antonio Garrigues at the Justice Ministry; Manuel Fraga, the Interior Minister; and José María Areilza, the Foreign Minister. Even the most conservative *aperturistas* had been dismayed by the effects of Arias's dithering and could be persuaded of the need for a firm policy of some kind. Most commentators were convinced that if the King, who was entitled to call for up to three lists, was prepared to hold out he could ensure that the name of at least one of these ministers would turn up.

When the King's choice eventually became known, the reaction was of stunned disbelief. The man he had chosen to succeed Arias was one Adolfo Suárez, who at forty-three was the youngest member of the outgoing government. Everything about Suárez except his youth seemed to be at variance with the spirit of the times. He had spent his entire working life serving the dictator in a variety of posts of which the most important and recent had been the General Secretaryship of the Movimiento Nacional, a post which entitled him to an *ex officio* seat in the Cabinet. Not surprisingly, he filled his first government with men of his own age whom he had met on his way up through the state apparatus. A report in the liberal daily *El País* on the composition of Suárez's first Cabinet listed the main characteristics of its members as 'an average age of forty-six, a classic Catholic ideology and good relations with certain banking institutions'. On the same day the newspaper carried what was destined to become a notorious commentary by one of Spain's leading historians, Ricardo de la Cierva. His response to the King's choice of Suárez and Suárez's choice of ministers had been the same as that of most democratically-minded Spaniards and was summed up by the headline: 'What a mistake! What an immense mistake!'. The period immediately following the change of government, the King has since admitted, was the worst of his life – 'Nobody trusted me. They didn't even give me a twenty-day margin to see if I had made the wrong choice.'

His choice of Suárez was not, as some observers had suspected, simply a matter of taking the best name on offer from the Council of the Realm. It was the culmination of months of assiduous conspiracy. During the last months of Franco's life, Juan Carlos had asked a number of politicians and officials for their opinions on how the country could best be transformed. One of the most detailed and realistic appraisals came from Suárez. The more the future king considered him, the more Suárez seemed to fulfil the apparently contradictory requirements of the Prime Minister whose job it would be to change Spain from a dictatorship into a democracy. He had an intimate knowledge of the workings of the administration, yet he accepted that its reform could not be partial or gradual. What is more, he had enough personal appeal to be able to survive once democracy had been restored – he was from an inoffensively middle-class background, he was strikingly handsome, immaculately dressed, affable and thoroughly versed in the use of the media, having been Director-General of the state television and radio network. Unknown to Suárez himself, he had only one serious rival by the time Franco died – José María López de Letona, who had been Minister of Industry during the late sixties and early seventies. It was at the suggestion of the King's former tutor and close adviser, Torcuato Fernández-Miranda, that Arias included Suárez in his team. Soon afterwards, the King made up his mind that Suárez was indeed the man for the job. He tried to forewarn him while they were watching a football match between Saragossa, which at that time had a young chairman, and Real Madrid, which was still run by the venerable Santiago Bernabeu. The King expressed the view that older men had to make way for younger ones 'because the life of the country is changing fast in every respect'. Suárez, who was perhaps too engrossed in the game, failed to take the hint. After Arias resigned, Fernández-Miranda, whom the King had manoeuvred into the chairmanship of the Council of the Realm, wangled Suárez's name on to the list of candidates as a makeweight. He received fewer votes than either of the other two and the members of the Council were as astonished as everybody else when the King chose him.

Suárez recognized that he would have to move with great speed. By November, three months after the swearing-in of his government, he had laid before the Cortes a political reform bill which would introduce universal suffrage and a two-chamber parliament, consisting of a lower house, or Congress, and an upper house to be called the Senate. His resoluteness caught the old guard in disarray. They had no leader and no alternative and only the most purblind could believe now that the nation did not want reform. In parliament, the role of the redoubtable Fernández-Miranda, who was also the Speaker of the Cortes, was once again decisive. He arranged for the bill to be sped through its committee stages so that there was no chance for it to be watered down. Outside parliament, it was made clear to the members of the Cortes – many of whom were now old men looking forward to a comfortable retirement or a remunerative sinecure – that the way they voted on the bill was bound to affect such matters as who sat on which committees and whether the administration turned a blind eye to certain untaxed accounts. Finally, the entire proceedings were to be broadcast on radio and television and each of the deputies was to be called upon by name to stand up and say either *sí* or *no* to reform.

By the time the bill came to be debated in the Cortes, it was widely expected that the government would win. Even so, when the vote eventually came to be taken on the evening of 18 November, it was difficult to believe that it was happening. As one by one the members of the Cortes – generals and admirals, ex-ministers, bankers and local bigwigs – stood up to endorse a measure that would put an end to everything they had spent their lives supporting, it became clear that the majority in favour of reform was going to be much, much bigger than anyone had imagined. In fact the vote was 425 to 59, with thirteen abstentions. On that night Spaniards began to realize that the long nightmare of Francoism really had come to an end. On 15 December the political reform bill was overwhelmingly endorsed in a referendum. Of the votes cast, the 'yes' votes totalled 94·2 per cent and the 'no' votes only 2·6 per cent. It was conclusive proof of the extent to which support for Franco's system of government had dwindled.

The speed of events dumbfounded not only the Francoists, but also the opposition. Even before Arias's resignation, some leading figures within the opposition had begun to speculate openly about the possibility of a *ruptura pactada*, or negotiated break. But, divided among themselves and mistrustful of the new Prime Minister, they failed to take up an offer from Suárez of talks until after the referendum. By that time Suárez was beginning to acquire considerable prestige as the man responsible for engineering the return of democracy, whereas the opposition politicians – most of whom had misguidedly called for abstention during the referendum campaign – had suffered a humiliating rebuff when more than three-quarters of the electorate turned out to vote. At the talks which began between the government and the opposition after the referendum on how best to hold the elections foreshadowed by the political reform bill, the government had the advantage of wielding both the moral and the real authority. Further reform measures came thick and fast. Early in 1977 the cabinet endorsed a procedure for the legalization of political parties more agreeable to the opposition than the one devised by Arias's cabinet. The Socialists were legalized in February and the Communists in April. In March, the right to strike was recognized, trade unions were legalized and the following month the Movimiento was abolished. Since by that time the government and opposition had agreed on how the elections should be conducted and votes counted, a date was set: 15 June.

The problem for Suárez and the members of his administration was that while they now enjoyed tremendous popularity, they did not belong to any of the political parties that were shaping up to contest the election. The point on the political spectrum that appeared to have most appeal for the voters was what at that time passed for the centre – the frontier between those who had worked for the old dictatorship and those who had worked against it. To the right of it were the most progressive *aperturistas*, including Suárez and his ministers. To the left of it were the most moderate opposition parties – a plethora of Christian Democrat, Social Democrat and Liberal groups, some of which amounted to little more than dining clubs. The mood of the moment was reconciliation and it was clear that whichever party could embrace supporters as well as opponents of Francoism would stand a good chance of winning the election.

The first serious attempt to create such a party was made in November 1976 when a group of *aperturistas* from inside as well as outside the government launched the Partido Popular. It was headed by José María Areilza, whose fellow-minister in the first government of the monarchy, Manuel Fraga, was busy forming the more conservative Alianza Popular (AP). In January the Partido Popular absorbed another *aperturista* group and changed its name to the Centro Democrático. From then on, like a snowball rolling down a hill, it gathered to it one after another of the minor opposition parties. As it became apparent that the Centro Democrático was the coming force in Spanish politics, Suárez approached some of its most senior figures with a deal: he would lead them into the forthcoming election, thus virtually assuring them of victory, if they would agree to two conditions. First, they must ditch Areilza, the only member of the party who could have seriously challenged the Prime Minister for the leadership. Second, they must accept into their ranks the ministers and officials whose help Suárez would need if he were to continue ruling the country. They agreed, and in March Suárez joined the party, which was subsequently renamed the Unión de Centro Democrático.

The UCD emerged from the election as the biggest party, but with only 34 per cent of the vote and 165 of the 350 seats in the lower house. By far the largest opposition party was the Partido Socialista Obrero Español (PSOE), which won 121 seats with some 29 per cent of the vote. The PSOE had been gaining strength ever since 1972, when control of the party had been wrested from its ageing and increasingly out-of-touch exiled leadership by a group of young activists inside Spain led by a lawyer from Seville, Felipe González. González was even younger than Suárez and, in a different way, just as attractive both in manner and appearance. During the run-up to the election he had managed to appear responsible and realistic while remaining aggressively anti-Francoist. Neither the Alianza Popular on the right, nor the Spanish Communist Party (PCE) on the left, did as well as they had expected, winning only 16 and 20 seats respectively.

The Spanish were already signalling a marked preference for a two-party system. But, as it turned out, what had yet to be decided was which two parties would form it.

CHAPTER 3

The Centre Falls Apart

During the final months of the dictatorship and the first years of the monarchy, Spain was gripped by what was sometimes called *fiebre autonómica* (autonomy fever). All of a sudden, it seemed, everyone wanted home rule. Not just those with a distinct language and culture like the Basques, Catalans and Galicians, but also the inhabitants of areas like Estremadura, Andalusia and the Canary Islands, whose Spanishness had never previously been questioned.

The designs of half-forgotten regional flags were unearthed and sported in defence of every conceivable cause. The regional officials of Madrid-based political parties, fearful of the rapidly growing support for regionalists and nationalists, lobbied for as much real or apparent autonomy as their headquarters would allow them. The Andalusian branch of the Communist Party thus became the Communist Party of Andalusia, almost as if Andalusia were a separate country.

Spain's medieval history, which had hitherto been depicted as a predestined process of unification, was now presented as the story of several independent nations coerced into reluctant cooperation. In fact a lot of liberally- and radically-minded young Spaniards stopped talking about Spain altogether and began referring solemnly to 'the Spanish state'. A number of organizations which came into being during this period took the phrase into their titles. Hence, the Spanish parents' body came to be called the Confederación del Estado Español de Asociaciones de Padres de Alumnos.

To some extent Spain's *fiebre autonómica* was merely the belated manifestation of a wider phenomenon. Regionalism had been having a heyday throughout Europe. The late sixties and early seventies had seen demands for self-government from the Bretons and others in France, from the Scots and Welsh in Britain and from minority groups in Germany and Italy – both countries which already offered a generous measure of decentralization. But the pressure for home rule acquired a special intensity in Spain as a result of additional, entirely domestic, factors.

The fact that Franco had been such a diehard centralist, and his most effective opponents had been separatist gunmen, created a powerful association in the public mind between regional nationalism and freedom on the one hand and between national unity and repression on the other. Towards the end of the dictatorship, dislike of totalitarian rule was frequently expressed in terms of distaste for centralism, especially among the young. It was also noticeable that, outside the three regions that had had active nationalist movements before the dictatorship, nationalist or regionalist sentiment was strongest in areas that had been particularly badly neglected by Franco. Thus there was more anti-central government feeling in Andalusia and the Canary Islands, both regions which had severe economic and social problems, than there was in, for example, Aragón or the Balearic Islands, whose claims to a distinct identity on historical and linguistic grounds were more firmly based.

Under the dictatorship, the clandestine and exiled oppositions had worked on the assumption that Franco's system of a unitary state divided into fifty provinces was unsustainable, and that when he went a measure of decentralization would be necessary. What they envisaged was the re-introduction of self-government in some form for the Basque country, Catalonia and Galicia. However, during the months between Franco's death and the holding of the first general election, it became obvious that to have granted home rule only to those regions which had had statutes of autonomy under the Republic would have been seriously at odds with the mood of the times. By the time that democracy returned to Spain the following year, there was a consensus among politicians of all parties, except Manuel Fraga's Alianza Popular and the extreme groups to the right of it, that when a new constitution was drawn up, every region that wanted it ought to have access to at least a limited degree of autonomy.

But a new constitution was still some way off; in the meantime, the unsatisfied demand for home rule in the Basque country, Catalonia, and to a lesser extent elsewhere provided a convenient pretext for agitation. Soon after the general election of June 1977 Suárez decided that the regions with the best claims to separate treatment needed something to be getting on with. He began with Catalonia, an area for which he always felt a special affinity and from which several of his closest advisers hailed.

Unlike the Basques, the Catalans had abolished their government-in-exile as soon as it became apparent that the victors of the Second World War had no intention of invading Spain and overthrowing Franco. They did, however, keep alive the title of President of the *Generalitat*, Catalonia's former home-rule government, as a single, symbolic link with the past. In 1954 the mantle of that office settled on the broad and lofty shoulders of one Josep Tarradellas, an exile and once a minister in Catalonia's republican administration. He was still the incumbent when democracy was restored to Spain twenty-three years later.

A high-handed, self-opinionated but charismatic old man, Tarradellas refused to return to his native land until the *Generalitat* was re-established. Yet he was stubbornly opposed to the efforts being made by younger nationalists to negotiate its restoration on the grounds that by doing so they were usurping the *Generalitat*'s rightful powers. Sensing an opportunity to put himself in control of the situation, Suárez made contact with the ageing exile and at the end of June 1977, in a spectacular *coup de main*, flew him back to Spain to take over a 'provisional' *Generalitat* set up at the stroke of a pen. The younger nationalists were furious, but there was little they could do.

Tarradellas, whom even they regarded as the very embodiment of Catalonia's survival as a nation, arrived back in Barcelona to an ecstatic reception. For a man who must often have wondered whether he would see his homeland again and who only managed to do so by outwitting an array of political opponents half his age, his first words on Catalonian soil were splendidly appropriate – '*Ja soc aquí*', which roughly translates as 'I made it!'.

The provisional *Generalitat* was the first of a succession of 'pre-autonomous governments' set up in the regions, most of which were made up of local deputies and senators. They had no real power, but they helped to get people used to the idea of regional government before it became a reality after the introduction of a constitution.

Since the UCD had emerged from the general election without an overall majority in the lower house, it looked as if Suárez would have to negotiate individual, *ad hoc* alliances with the parties on either side of him to win a majority for each of the items in his legislative programme. Instead, he opted for a comprehensive agreement. The Moncloa Pacts, named after the Prime Minister's official residence where they were signed in October, covered not only a substantial part of the government's legislative programme but also such matters as prices and incomes, government spending and regional policy. The worst thing about the Pacts was the effect they had on public opinion. Spaniards were all in favour of reconciliation, but after so many years of contrived unanimity they were equally hungry for debate. Yet here were the four main party leaders, who only a few weeks before had been ridiculing one another's programmes on the electoral hustings, apparently seeing eye to eye to the extent that they were able to come up with a comprehensive plan for running the country. There was a widespread feeling that the politicians, having taken the electors' votes, were now deciding what was good for them. The Pacts created a mild feeling of scepticism about democracy in Spain which lodged itself in the body politic like a tumour, where it remained for some years contracting and expanding according to circumstances. The great merit of the Pacts was that they allowed the politicians to concentrate on the most important task before them – the drawing-up of a new constitution.

Since the beginning of the previous century, Spain had had no fewer than eleven constitutions. The main reason why none had worked was that each had been drafted and imposed by one particular group with little or no regard to the views of anyone outside it. As far as the constitution was concerned, the case for consensus was unanswerable. The work of preparing one was entrusted to a parliamentary commission representing all the major national parties and the more important regional ones. The document which they produced, which was passed after amendments by the Cortes in October 1978, was exactly what one would expect of a committee made up of people with very different political outlooks. It is far too long, often vague and sometimes contradictory. But it is nevertheless something in which all the major parties have a vested interest and which they have so far shown little sign of wanting to amend, let alone replace. The new Spanish constitution is arguably the most liberal in Western Europe. Spain is defined as a parliamentary monarchy, rather than just a constitutional monarchy. There is no official religion. The death penalty is forbidden and the voting age fixed at eighteen.

However, the outstanding innovation of the 1978 constitution was the sharing of power with the regions, which occupied almost a tenth of its length. The basic unit of the state envisaged by the constitution was the Autonomous Community, which could be made up of a single province or several neighbouring provinces.

Each Autonomous Community was to have its own President, government, legislature and Supreme Court. The exact powers of the Autonomous Communities were to be defined later in their respective statutes, but the constitution laid down certain guidelines, albeit somewhat ambiguous ones. Firstly, it specified the areas of government which could be handed over to the Autonomous Communities, of which the most important were housing, agriculture, town and country planning, sport, tourism, and health and social services (although with the proviso that in several of these areas the actions taken by the regional governments would have to fit into a framework constructed in Madrid). Secondly, the constitution listed the fields for which the central government held 'exclusive responsibility', among which were foreign affairs, external trade, defence, the administration of justice, merchant shipping and civil aviation. However, in several cases the constitution added that this or that sphere of activity was given to Madrid 'without prejudice' to whatever powers might be granted to the Autonomous Communities. These grey areas, together with those such as education which were not specifically allotted to either central or regional government, and those such as the environment which were rather vaguely divided between the two, provided a means whereby the statutes of the various Autonomous Communities could be varied substantially.

Except in the cases of the Basque country, Catalonia and Galicia

– the so-called 'historical nationalities'* – where all that was needed was for the existing pre-autonomous governments to notify the central government, the process whereby a region achieved home rule began when a provincial council (*diputación*) decided that it wanted the province it represented to become an Autonomous Community in its own right or join with others to form one. Thereafter, the constitution set out two paths by which a region could attain self-government. The normal procedure was laid down in article 143.

The second route offered by the constitution was available to the 'historical nationalities' and any other region where the proposal for home rule was capable of securing the endorsement of more than half the votes in a regional referendum. Regions seeking home rule under this option, which was mapped out in article 151, could lay claim in their draft statute to the powers which the constitution deliberately refrained from allotting to either the central or regional governments. However, the constitution also stipulated that the text, once approved by the Cortes, had to be endorsed by the regional electorate in a further plebiscite. The challenges involved in pursuing this route may have been greater, but then so were the powers to be gained. Unwittingly, what the authors of the constitution had done was to create a sort of regional virility test and, as will be seen, this was to have a dramatic effect on Spain's fortunes over the next few years.

In December 1978 the constitution was overwhelmingly approved by the public in a referendum. Then, early in the New Year, Suárez dissolved what had in effect been a constituent Cortes and called another general election for 1 March. It produced a result almost identical to the previous one.

Immediately after the 1979 election, Suárez set up a new Ministry

---

*This is, to my knowledge, the only way of translating the phrase '*nacionalidades históricas*', which was first heard soon after Franco's death and has since become common usage. It needs to be pointed out, however, that the word '*nacionalidad*', like its counterpart 'nationality', had always previously been used to describe a condition rather than an entity. It started to be used out of context in an attempt to satisfy the claims of the Basque country and the other regions to national status without actually having to call them nations. 'Historical nationality' may not be English, but then '*nacionalidad histórica*' is not Spanish.

of Territorial Administration whose principal task was to oversee the transfer of power to the regions. The granting of home rule to Basques and Catalans was achieved with speed and generosity. Both communities gained control of education and won the right to set up their own police forces and radio and television stations. The first elections to the new Basque and Catalan assemblies were held the following year. The two statutes, known as the statutes of Guernica and Sau, were overwhelmingly endorsed at referendums held in October 1979 and came into effect two months later.

Galicia's home-rule statute, the statute of Santiago, gave the Galicians powers that were almost as extensive as those granted to the Basques and Catalans. However, when it was submitted to a referendum in December 1980, less than 30 per cent of the Galician electorate turned out to vote and of those who did so almost one in five voted 'no'. It was a moral victory for those, especially on the right, who regarded the process of decentralization as unnecessary as well as dangerous.

By and large, though, it was not the 'historical nationalities' but the other regions which presented the government with its worst headaches.

For local politicians, the pressure to demonstrate their loyalty to, and faith in, their region by supporting home rule under article 151 was immense. By the end of 1979 only two of the seven regions where the issue had been decided had opted for the normal route.

At the beginning of the following year, Suárez ill-advisedly tried to deter the Andalusians, who had been the first to opt for the more demanding but rewarding path to self-government and whose enthusiasm for autonomy gave them a genuine claim to preferential treatment, from going ahead with their plans. The attempt backfired on him when they overwhelmingly endorsed the autonomy initiative in the referendum called for by the constitution.

The government was beginning to get the distinctly uncomfortable feeling that the experiment was getting out of hand, and it was in the hope of bringing some order and discipline into the proceedings that in September the Ministry of Territorial Administration was handed to the hard man of the Suárez team, Rodolfo Martín Villa. A few months later he proposed that the major parties ought to reach an agreement on devolution similar to the Moncloa Pacts and welcomed an idea floated by Felipe González that there should be a special law to clarify, once and for all, the ambiguities in the section of the constitution dealing with home rule.

The other outstanding challenge facing the government was to ensure that the transition from dictatorship to democracy was reflected in people's daily lives. Divorce and abortion were still forbidden; the administration, the army, the police, the judiciary, the health and welfare services, the state broadcasting network, and the schools and universities were all imbued with the spirit of a totalitarian regime. A thoroughgoing reform programme was needed to sweep away the authoritarian institutions and practices that had survived in every corner of society. But it soon became apparent that Suárez and his party were incapable of meeting the challenge. To some extent, this was a consequence of the Prime Minister's own personality. All politicians are a blend of ambition and conviction. In Suárez's case, however, the element of belief seemed to be limited to a single premise – that democracy was preferable to dictatorship. Once the transition from one to another had been completed, he appeared to have no aspiration to inspire him or any ideology to guide him. By contrast, the problem for the UCD was an excess of aspirations and ideologies, many of which were in conflict with one another. The parties which had formed the basis of the union ranged on the conventional European spectrum from a point just to the left of centre to one quite a long way to the right, and contained an ill-assorted mix of the secular and confessional. By the summer of 1980, a gap that was to prove unbridgeable had begun to open up between the Social and Christian Democrats within the UCD over the government's plan to legalize divorce. As for the men and women who had been inserted into the union at Suárez's insistence in early 1977, it was not their differences but what they had in common that proved to be the problem. Having come up through the old Francoist administration, most of them found it genuinely difficult to see the need to do more than tinker with Franco's legacy, and true to their political origins, their first impulse, whenever an apparent misdemeanour or injustice came to the surface, was to cover up rather than investigate. Within the party, they found it difficult to come to terms with the idea that in a democratic institution policy initiatives can come from the rank-and-file as well as from the top brass.

It was only in the very last months of Suárez's premiership that he began to reveal – or perhaps discover – his true sympathies. But far from making things better, it only made them worse; the Prime Minister was seen to be siding with the most liberal wing of his party and to lead a coalition as diverse as the UCD from anywhere but close to the centre was virtually impossible. Not surprisingly, therefore, the revolt against Suárez's leadership, when it came, was mounted by the Christian Democrats. But it drew considerable strength from the discontent in every sector of the party over lack of consultation. In January 1981 Suárez resigned from the premiership and in recognition of his services the King bestowed on him the highest honour in his gift: a dukedom.

One of the least satisfactory aspects of Spain's new constitutional arrangements is that an unusually lengthy period is allowed to elapse between governments. It was during the uncertain month between Suárez's resignation and the swearing-in of his successor, Leopoldo Calvo Sotelo, that all Spain's nightmares came true.

From the very beginning, the most serious threat to democracy had come from the predominantly reactionary officers of Spain's armed forces. In 1978 a conspiracy was found to have been hatched in a Madrid café and on more than one occasion the UCD's defence overlord, Lieutenant-General Manuel Gutiérrez Mellado, was openly insulted by fellow-officers. By early 1981 a group of senior officers had persuaded themselves that the country faced political and economic turmoil and that the unity of Spain, whose preservation had been entrusted to the armed forces by the constitution, was at risk from the government's regional policy.

On the afternoon of 23 February, a lieutenant-colonel in the Civil Guard, Antonio Tejero Molina, who had been demoted for his part in the 1978 plot, marched into Congress with a detachment of his men and proceeded to hold almost every politician of note in Spain at gunpoint for the best part of twenty-four hours. Tejero was what he appeared to be – a naive fanatic. But he was merely the puppet of more senior officers – in particular, the commander of the Motorized Division at Valencia, Lieutenant-General Jaime Miláns del Bosch, and a former military instructor and personal secretary to the King, Major-General Alfonso Armada. The coup was cut short mainly because of Juan Carlos's quick wits and steady nerve. Using a specially designed communications centre which he had had installed at the palace to enable him to talk directly to the country's eleven captains-general, he assured them that Tejero's action did not – as the plotters were claiming – have his backing. Any captain-general who showed signs of wavering was commanded to obey.

The abortive coup persuaded the incoming government to try to appease the military. The army was given a token role in the troublesome Basque country and plans for reform in a number of areas were either diluted or abandoned. Perhaps inevitably, regional policy was the principal casualty.

In April the government and the PSOE began talks aimed at producing a pact of the sort that Martín Villa had suggested. After a brief and not particularly serious attempt to involve the other two major parties, the UCD and the PSOE signed a formal agreement in July in which they set a deadline for the completion of the decentralization process (1 February 1983) and set out a strategy for generalizing and homogenizing it.

The agreement stipulated that, with the exception of Andalusia, which was already so far down the road mapped out by article 151 that it was pointless to try to do anything about it, the regions which had yet to be granted a statute should attain home rule in the normal way. What is more, it was agreed that none of them should get more than the minimum powers set out in the constitution. Any other powers granted during the negotiation of the statute would have to be listed under a separate heading and put into cold storage for at least three years from the date the statute came into effect. The only exceptions to this rule were the Canary Islands and Valencia, for which special laws would be passed giving them rather greater powers than the others, and Navarre which – uniquely – had enjoyed a kind of autonomy under Franco and merely required a law to update its existing arrangements.

In just over four years, one of the most centralized nations on earth had been carved into seventeen self-governing administrative units, each with its own flag and capital.

How to describe the resulting set-up was a problem. Although the powers granted to some of the Autonomous Communities were greater than those enjoyed under a number of existing federations, there had not been that ceding of sovereignty which typifies a federation. Nor was the British word 'devolution' appropriate. In many cases, authority had not been handed back to the Autonomous Communities in the way that it might have been to Scotland or Wales, but had been given to a new entity for the first time.

Eventually, therefore, the new arrangement came to be known by another of those grammar-bending phrases in which the process of its creation had been so rich. It was deemed to be an *estado de las autonomías* (state of autonomies).

Despite the drive towards homogeneity after the coup, the most striking aspect of the new system was the degree to which the powers granted to the autonomous governments varied from region to region. Yet if one were to award points to each of them on the basis of their historical, cultural and linguistic singularity as well as their degree of enthusiasm for home rule in recent years, the result might well be a ranking which would correspond to that of their relative autonomy – the Basques and Catalans pre-eminent, followed at a short distance by the Galicians and Andalusians, and at a longer distance by the Canarians, Valencians and Navarrese, with the rest an equal last.

Somewhat, I think, to their own surprise the Spaniards had provided themselves with a system of regional government which reflected comparatively accurately not only Spain's diversity, but also the degree of variation from the mean in each of its component parts.

Within the UCD the coup initially had the effect of forcing the warring factions to close ranks. But the truce was short-lived and as soon as the government had to face an important policy decision the familiar divisions reappeared. Each time, during the eighteen months between the coup and the next general election in November 1982, the new Prime Minister Calvo Sotelo tried to shift the balance of his programmes to left or right in an attempt to accommodate a rebellious faction on one wing of his party, he would invariably provoke defections from the other. In this way, the UCD spawned a Social Democratic Party (which linked up with the PSOE), a Christian Democratic Party (which linked up with

49

the AP) and a Liberal Party. In 1982, the Duque de Suárez delivered what many saw as the *coup de grâce* to the party he had founded, when he himself left it to found the Centro Democrático Social (CDS). By the time a general election was called, the UCD had lost a third of its deputies in Congress. The loss of its support in the country was even more dramatic and this was in part because of the coup. The Centrists had topped the poll at two elections by selling themselves in much the same way as one might sell a contraceptive – by persuading the electorate that they represented 'the safe way' to democracy. If, voters reasoned, you got a coup even with the UCD in power, what was there to lose by going for broke with a party that had a much more genuine commitment to reform? The door was thus open at last for Felipe González and the PSOE.

Ever since the 1979 election González, like Suárez but with greater success, had been trying to drag his party towards what the polls indicate is the political fulcrum of Spain – the centre-left. At one point he went so far as to resign the leadership in a bid, eventually successful, to force his supporters to drop Marxism from the party's definition of itself. At the 1982 election, standing on a platform of exceptional moderation, the Socialists won over 10 million votes – 4 million more than the Centrists in 1979. Their 201 seats gave them an ample majority in Congress. To the PSOE's left, the Communists' share of seats fell dramatically and humiliatingly from 23 to 5. On the right, the Alianza Popular emerged as by far the biggest opposition party, with 105 seats. But the UCD, which had run the nation for five years, picked up only 11. And as for Suárez – the mastermind of the transition, the man who had led the nation for much of its eventful journey along the path from dictatorship to democracy – his Centro Democrático Social won precisely 2 seats.

CHAPTER 4

Socialist Spain

On the night of the Socialists' landslide, I was chatting about the result to a Spanish journalist, and at some point I must have described it as a victory for the left or a defeat for the right. 'Careful,' she said. 'This isn't a victory by the left over the right. It's a victory by the young over the old.'

It was an observation that went a long way towards explaining the curious nature of the campaign that had just ended. The Socialists' slogan had been simply '*El cambio*' ('The change'). But they had not explained, except in the vaguest terms, what it was they intended changing, or how. Virtually their only substantial commitment was to create 800,000 new jobs.

For the most part, the PSOE's moderation was explained to the rest of the world by foreign correspondents reporting the campaign as a purely tactical and pragmatic move. Spanish democracy had just survived an attempted *coup d'état* and the Socialists were keen not to upset reactionary officers in the army. In any case, the economy was in deep recession and the incoming administration would need to generate wealth before it could redistribute it. Thanks to Francoist corporatism, it was already heavily nationalized, so a conventionally socialist programme to extend state ownership was unnecessary.

All this was true. But it missed the point. The PSOE did not need to promise to change anything because its voters were already convinced that they were going to change everything. Just by being who they were – young men and women unencumbered by the intellectual baggage and ballast of a totalitarian past – they would be able to bring about a revolution in Spanish society when they applied to the nation's affairs attitudes regarded as normal in the rest of democratic Europe. Alfonso Guerra, Felipe González's lifelong friend who became his deputy Prime Minister, caught the spirit of the moment when he promised the Socialists would change Spain 'so that even its own mother won't recognize it'. For a while it seemed as if they would.

The Socialists swung into office with dazzling energy and set about implementing reforms in almost every area over which the government exercised control. It was a 'first hundred days' in the style of John Kennedy and his team. They soon demonstrated that they had learnt the lessons to be read from the UCD's failure to cope with the military: that the soldiers would tolerate, even admire, toughness. When a general publicly justified the 1981 coup attempt, he was sacked within the hour. They tackled with vigour and resolve the challenge posed when Spain's largest privately-owned group, RUMASA, threatened to collapse and bring down much of the banking system with it. In a controversial move, the new government expropriated the group and sold off its component parts.

The promise – and evidence – that the Socialists could give Spain a bright new future helped them to get away with a much-needed shake-out of Spain's older industries. But the job-shedding caused by what was euphemistically known as 'industrial reconversion' led to outbreaks of street violence like that which took place round the doomed Sagunto steel works in Valencia. And instead of creating new jobs, the austerity policies applied by the Socialists pushed up the unemployment rate inexorably – from 16 per cent when the PSOE came into office, to over 22 per cent when it peaked at the beginning of 1986. In a society with virtually no tradition of saving and in which entitlement to unemployment pay was severely limited, the effects were dire. The fall from relative prosperity to utter deprivation could take months, or even weeks.

An important reason why the government was able to hold to its course was the cooperation it received from the country's labour leaders. Recognizing that Spain's ability to compete had to be improved ahead of Common Market entry, the trade unions, sometimes with the employers' representatives, signed a number of agreements in the early years of Socialist rule in which they accepted wage restraint and job losses. But it was on the implicit (and sometimes explicit) understanding that when the economy began growing again the administration would ensure the wealth generated was more evenly distributed. In particular, the government pledged an increase in the proportion of jobless workers eligible for unemployment pay. The target figure, modest enough by the standards of the rest of Western Europe, was 48 per cent.

The Spaniards who had cast their votes for Felipe González and his team in 1982 had not opted for red-blooded socialism, and it would be unfair to judge their performance in government on that criterion. What the electorate wanted was modernization. But they expected it to be modernization infused with a progressive spirit. During the Socialists' first term of office, painful measures of economic adjustment were effectively counterbalanced by an energetic programme of social reform. They also benefited enormously from the fact that Spain's application to join the European Community came to fruition during their mandate. The prospect of entry was – quite rightly, as it turned out – a cause for hope that things would get better. But by the time Spain became a member of the EC at the start of 1986, there was a growing realization that the Socialists had brought with them into office a number of attitudes and practices at variance with what many of those who had voted for them had assumed they represented.

When power passes from one party to another in Spain, it is the signal for a clear-out even more comprehensive than that prompted by a change of president in the United States. In the last century, incoming Spanish governments swept clean the administration down to the level of clerk. The practice went into abeyance under Franco because, having packed the bureaucracy with loyalists at the outset, he saw no reason for change every time he reshuffled his cabinet. Nor did it attract much debate under the UCD because to a large extent the Centrists were content to work with men and women who had served Franco. Yet by the time the Socialists came to office, the degree of patronage available to a government had grown enormously. Franco had set up quasi-independent government organizations galore, and had founded a multitude of state-owned enterprises, all run by political appointees. After the return of democracy, the granting of autonomy to the regions created an additional layer of executive activity between central and local government, and the duplication it caused has yet to be eliminated.

According to *España 2000*, a working policy document published by the PSOE in 1988, 40,000 party members – almost one in every three of the membership – took up 'institutional posts' following the Socialists' victory. More than 26,000 were elected to office as mayors or councillors when the PSOE went on to sweep the board at the 1983 local elections. But most of the rest were appointed.

By giving in to the temptation to put party members in charge of everything from the state holding company to the smallest city museum, the Socialists perpetuated a tradition which diminished their claim to be the party of change. Indeed, it was not long before their critics were drawing pointed comparisons between the PSOE and the old Movimiento Nacional.

With so many of the party's members dependent for their livelihood on the goodwill of its leadership, few were ready to challenge directives from the top. This was particularly significant in view of the immediate past. The Socialists had just seen how in-fighting had wrecked the UCD (which was in fact wound up altogether during the PSOE's first term of office). The lesson they drew was that unity was paramount. Over the next few years the PSOE was to change into one of the most secretive and disciplined parties in Western Europe. The media began to be excluded from all but the opening and closing sessions of its Congresses. Members who spoke out against government policy were speedily and effectively removed from public life. If they had been appointed, they were dismissed. If they were elected, their names were struck off the list of candidates for the next election.

The most striking thing about Spain's new oligarchy was its youth. The Socialists' victory signalled the rise to power, for the first time in Europe, of the 'Generation of '68'. A junior minister at the Interior Ministry found himself giving orders to a policeman who had arrested him for rioting against Franco. Very few of the PSOE's older members had survived in positions of responsibility after González had wrested power from the exiled leadership. The average age of the ministers in his first Cabinet was forty-one. One of the directors of the telecommunications monopoly, Telefónica, took his seat on the board at the age of thirty-two.

Another characteristic of Spain's new rulers was the high percentage who came from the educational world. A survey of the delegates to the PSOE's 32nd Congress in 1990 was to show that more than one in five had been teachers at school or university. But many were so young that they had not had time to acquire a reputation before entering full-time politics.

Spain had certainly the youngest, and arguably the cleverest, ruling class in Europe. But it was also the least employable outside politics. A worrying number of Socialist office-holders who subsequently left government went on to set up consultancies and the like which were primarily dependent on official contracts. The effect was to create an old boy, and girl, network which extended far beyond the administration itself.

The power of this new Socialist establishment was considerably reinforced by the absolute parliamentary majority it had just won, and which it was to enjoy for another eleven years. It had always been assumed that a system of proportional representation would give rise to a succession of 'hung' parliaments. So the commission which drafted the 1978 constitution decided that it would be safe, as well as fair, if membership of all sorts of new institutions were determined by the balance of forces in parliament. The Socialists' outright majority thus gave them automatic control over such key bodies as the council which runs the judiciary and the board in charge of the state-owned radio and television network.

The arrival of the Socialists also tilted the balance of influence from north to south in a country where regional differences are profound. Both González and Guerra came from Seville. Several other ministers and numerous officials were drawn from Socialist strongholds in Spain's poor south. It is perhaps no coincidence that southern values should have seized hold of Spain after 1982. Bullfighting began to regain favour. And within a few years of a Seville-born Prime Minister taking office, there was a craze for dancing *sevillanas*.* Seville is to Spain what Naples is to Italy. The Andalusians contributed verve, flair and eloquence to public life.

---

* The *sevillana* is the dance most often presented to non-Spaniards as flamenco. It is actually on the fringe of the flamenco canon and many authorities consider it not to be flamenco at all.

But they also imported a tendency to clannishness and an outmoded concept of honour, in which admitting to mistakes is considered a sign of weakness rather than strength.

For many Spaniards, the watershed of Socialist rule was the referendum on NATO membership. Spain had joined the alliance, with a minimum of debate, under the UCD in 1982. The Socialists, who had been critical, had pledged in their electoral manifesto to hold a referendum on withdrawal; but before long they were persuaded that Spain's continued membership was a necessary condition of belonging to the Western 'club'. In the event, the electorate was offered a choice between pulling out of NATO and continued membership outside the integrated military command. But ahead of the referendum, held on 12 March 1986, the full weight of party discipline was brought to bear on members to change their minds – or at least to keep quiet if they were opposed to government policy. The fact that so many Socialists did so disillusioned pro- and anti-NATO voters alike. The poll, though, came up with the result the government wanted. The vote in favour of membership was more than 9 million to less than 7 million.

Against such a background, it was hardly surprising that when a general election was held in June the PSOE lost more than a million votes. The results could well have been worse but for evidence that a leaner, fitter Spanish economy was already benefiting from entry into the EC. Foreign investment had been pouring into the country since the previous year, and unemployment began to fall just a few months before polling.

The Socialists' tally of seats in Congress dropped to 184, but that still left them with a comfortable outright majority. Manuel Fraga's Alianza Popular, standing with allies under a new label, the Coalición Popular, held on to 105 deputies, but failed to pick up any of the seats left vacant by the collapse of the UCD. These, and more, went to Suárez's CDS, whose representation in Congress soared from 2 to 19. The United Left, an alliance which included the Communist Party, but also a number of non-Communist groups and individuals, won 7 seats.

It was appropriate that a year of turning-points should also have seen the death of a Socialist who embodied many of the values that had brought the PSOE to power. None of the academics who struggled during the Franco years to impart forward-looking ideas to their students inspired quite as much devotion as Professor Enrique Tierno Galván. By the end of the dictatorship, he was affectionately known throughout Spain as 'the old teacher'. The small party of intellectuals which he had once led merged with the PSOE before it took office. Although some of his acolytes went into government after 1982, he himself remained mayor of Madrid, a post to which he had been elected three years earlier. The record of his administration was exemplary – efficient, imaginative and caring. A million people, one in three of the city's population, turned out for his funeral. It has sometimes been remarked since, in the knowledge of what was to come, that on that day Spain's Socialists buried the spirit of their young ideals along with the body of their old teacher.

During 1986, the rate of growth in the economy averaged 3·3 per cent, and it was accelerating as the year drew to a close. Spain had embarked on a typical post EC-entry boom. Between 1986 and 1991, the Spanish economy was to grow faster than that of any other country in the Community.

CHAPTER 5

Not-so-Socialist Spain

Throughout the developed world in the 1980s, the creation and enjoyment of wealth shed the distinctly unfashionable air that had attached to it in the serious seventies. In Spain, social attitudes towards money underwent a revolution. A nation whose historic poverty had led it to build an entire value system around non-materialistic virtues – dignity, austerity and sobriety – all of a sudden flung itself into the business of earning and spending money with, it seemed, scarcely a backward glance.

Things rarely happen by halves in Spain, but it is worth remembering that its recession had been deeper and longer than any in Western Europe. It had cut deeper because the country's previous leaders, beset by the problems of the transition, had failed to react vigorously enough to the challenges presented by the OPEC oil 'shocks' and the information technology revolution. It had lasted longer because the Spanish economy was still being restructured in the early eighties and was thus in no fit state to benefit from the first post-recessional upswing in world growth: by 1984 average real incomes in Spain were fractionally lower than they had been in 1975 when Franco died. After so many years of deprivation, it is not surprising that Spaniards were in a mood to celebrate prosperity.

What made Spain's eighties boom exceptional, and more entertaining than in many other countries, was the degree to which serious money became associated with style, glamour and, ultimately, scandal. The recently completed Torre Picasso office block on Madrid's Paseo de la Castellana provided Spaniards with a suitably phallic symbol of thrusting eighties values. Mario Conde, the elegant son of a customs official, who became Chairman of Spain's most aristocratic bank, Banesto, offered them an immaculately groomed archetype of the new, classless financier.

Conde, his associates and rivals were soon taking pride of place in the gossip magazines over the familiar cast of starlets, entertainers and exiled royalty. Readers were to discover that the financial elite provided much more racy entertainment, in fact.

Among the oddest characters to emerge from among the balance-sheets were the 'two Albertos'. Cousins, brothers-in-law, namesakes and neighbours, Alberto Alcocer and Alberto Cortina delighted in highlighting the similarities between them by wearing identical raincoats. They were also business associates, being Chairman and Vice-Chairman respectively of ConyCon, the centrepiece of a £1·5 billion conglomerate which was to play an active role in the restructuring of Spanish banking. In 1987, ConyCon linked up with the Kuwait Investment Office, which had already bought heavily in Spain, to form an investment management company that took stakes in both Banesto and another powerful financial institution, Banco Central.

Unfortunately for the 'two Albertos', ConyCon was almost wholly owned by their wives, Esther Koplowitz, the Marchioness of Casa Peñalver, and Alicia Koplowitz, the Marchioness of Real Socorro. Their empire was first rocked in 1989 when Alicia Koplowitz broke up with her husband after publicity given to Cortina's relationship with one Marta Chávarri, the daughter of the government's Chief of Protocol and herself a marchioness by marriage. At the height of the scandal, the magazine *Interviú* published a photograph of Marta Chávarri in a nightclub which showed she was wearing nothing but tights under her mini-skirt. Subsequently, Alcocer's name was linked to that of his secretary and he too separated from his wife, Esther Koplowitz. The sisters then took spectacular revenge by ousting their estranged husbands and taking their places in a boardroom revolution.

Wealth exerted a fascination on every section of society, including the government. One of the Socialists' earliest tasks had been to enlist the support – or at least encourage the tolerance – of the Madrid banking community. In Spain, as in Germany, the banks own and run vast swathes of the rest of the economy. A lot of early introductions were effected by Miguel Boyer, the Socialists' first Economics and Finance Minister. After resigning his job in 1985, he divorced to marry one of the country's foremost socialites, the Philippines-born beauty, Isabel Preysler. It was her third marriage. She had already been the wife of the singer Julio Iglesias, and then of a marquess.

Boyer and his new wife; Boyer's successor, Carlos Solchaga, and his wife, together with a number of other Socialist luminaries, came to be photographed regularly at high-society parties in Madrid and in the jet-set Costa del Sol resort of Marbella. The press snidely dubbed them 'los beautiful people'.

The reaction would have been less sour if it had not been Boyer who had demanded such sacrifices of the rest of the population during his three years in charge of the economy, or if, under Solchaga, the benefits of growth had been spread more evenly. But the 800,000 jobs promised by the Socialists in their first manifesto were not created until the middle of 1988; by then, because of a steep rise in the number of job-seekers, unemployment was still running at well over 18 per cent.

It became clear, moreover, that a lot of the wealth so flamboyantly on display was, to a greater or lesser extent, unearned. Much of it stemmed from the sale of family businesses to overseas investors. Much of it derived from speculation in stocks and shares which throughout the period was a much more profitable activity than trying to run a business, because the Socialists kept interest rates high and the national currency strong in order to attract foreign investment. A lot more of the money came from a boom in land and property prices that was also, in large part, attributable to government action. A law passed in the early years of Socialist rule intended to encourage rentals had had the effect of attracting to the housing sector vast sums kept secret from the tax authorities. When this so-called dinero negro (black money), invested by tax-dodging upper-middle-class Spaniards, met the ready cash being flourished by foreigners keen to establish themselves in Spain after it entered the EC, prices soared – first in Madrid, then in Barcelona, and finally in Seville and the other major regional capitals. In a country with a high level of owner-occupancy, the effect was not as socially disastrous as it might have been. Indeed, it enriched a broad swathe of the new middle class. But it also meant that those who lived in the bigger cities and did not have savings invested in bricks and mortar at the start of the boom ended it with precious little chance of ever owning their own home.

What really inspired outrage, though, was the fact that a number of Spain's new rich owed their wealth to straightforward graft: civil servants who had accepted bribes in return for awarding public contracts, elected representatives who had managed to divert public funds into their own pockets. It would have been surprising if such an abrupt surge in the country's economic fortunes had not been accompanied by increased corruption. But other factors made Spain especially vulnerable: the overriding importance of family ties; the size of its public sector; the rapid growth in government revenue – and therefore spending – because of tax increases ordered by the Socialists; and perhaps most importantly, the paucity of anti-corruption legislation. Initially, this could be excused as an inheritance from Franco. But the Socialists showed little interest in changing things, and there were even hints that the omission was deliberate: that some in the Socialist leadership believed corruption could actually promote economic growth in Spain by getting round the bottlenecks created by its antiquated bureaucracy. In 1991, the World Economic Forum concluded that, among the developed countries, Spain was second only to Italy in the inadequacy of its anti-corruption measures.

From the very beginning, González entrusted control of the economy to his party's most conservative faction. Boyer, Solchaga and most of the junior ministers given economic portfolios were drawn from among the so-called 'social democrats'. In the sense that they followed a policy of deficit financing and consented to the use of government spending for job creation by means of public works, they were neo-Keynesians. They allowed more money to be spent on health and education. They pursued tax evasion with more vigour than their UCD predecessors. And they did not go in for true privatization (under the Socialists, although shares in public enterprises have been sold off, the government has almost invariably retained effective control).

What distinguished Spain's 'social democrats' from their counterparts in the rest of Europe, was their reluctance to countenance a policy aimed at the deliberate redistribution of wealth. The consistent goal of economic policy under González's governments has been absolute growth, in the expectation that wealth will spill down the social pyramid without the need for government intervention.

But for several years, growth – and growth on an impressive scale – is what the Socialists managed to deliver. By 1992, Spain had become about 40 per cent richer in real GDP terms than it had been in 1980. The result was that the majority of its people were considerably better off than they had ever been before.

The tough-minded economic policy adopted by Spain's 'social democrats' was similar to that in many other parts of Western Europe in the late eighties. Elsewhere, though, free-market doctrines were being applied to countries which already had comprehensive systems of welfare provision. González's team began pursuing similar policies in a nation where only slightly more than a quarter of the jobless were entitled to full unemployment pay. The promises made to the trade unions in this respect were forgotten after the growth rate leapt. A glance at the statistics relating to other aspects of welfare provision will show that in most cases the rate of improvement slowed down, notably after 1986.

The highest priority in government planning was given to enhancing the country's infrastructure. This was partly to create new jobs, partly to enhance Spain's competitiveness, but also partly to meet the demands imposed on the country by the events planned for 1992. Seville was to be the venue for the world fair, Expo '92. Barcelona was due to host the Olympic Games. Madrid was going to be the EC's Capital of Culture. And events in various parts of Spain were scheduled to mark the 500th anniversary of Columbus's voyage to America.

The 1992 jamboree always had an air of 'bread and circuses' about it. But when accompanied by prestige projects of such dubious necessity as the Madrid-to-Seville high-speed train line, the Socialists' approach became reminiscent of one that was common in Third World nations immediately following decolonization. Spain also feels itself to be a 'young nation', and is prone to overreach itself in its efforts to impress.

In mid-1988, the González government was confronted with a potentially catastrophic scandal. Soon after the Socialists came to power, an organization calling itself the Grupos Anti-Terroristas de Liberación (GAL) had made itself known and gone on to claim responsibility for the murder of 24 people in the south-west of France. Most were exiled members or supporters of the Basque terrorist movement, ETA. But some were not.

Subsequent press investigations, notably that carried out by the newspaper *Diario 16*, accumulated a wealth of evidence to suggest that GAL had been organized by two Spanish detectives, Chief Superintendent José Amedo and Inspector Michel Domínguez. As a result of court proceedings inspired by the press revelations, both men were committed to prison to await trial. But the key question of whether they were acting on their own initiative or on orders from above remained a mystery. The chief of the Spanish police testified that a trip on which they were alleged to have recruited mercenaries had been paid for out of secret government funds. But attempts by the investigating magistrate to find out more about these funds were blocked by the Interior Ministry. The result was a showdown between the judiciary and the executive of a kind never before seen in democratic Spain. In the end, though, the council which administers the legal system backed down, and the government's claim to executive privilege was upheld.*

The GAL affair came in the wake of a succession of petty scandals involving Socialist politicians and officials. In all of them, the issue at stake was the Socialists' inability, or unwillingness, to draw a line between what they were entitled to in their private and official capacities. Concern had first been voiced as early as 1985 when Felipe González took his family holiday on board Franco's old yacht, the *Azor*. It surfaced again when his deputy, Alfonso Guerra, commandeered a military jet to avoid a traffic jam on the way back from his Easter holidays. Then in October 1988 the government-appointed head of the state radio and television monopoly, Pilar Miró, was accused of using the corporation's money to buy clothes and jewellery for herself and presents for her friends.

Ms Miró was later acquitted of all the charges against her, but it

---

*In September 1991, the two officers were each sentenced to more than 100 years for their involvement with the GAL 'death squads'. Crucially, the judges acquitted the state of any responsibility for, or involvement in, the detectives' activities.

was against a background of rising public anger that the trade unions, having made numerous unsuccessful attempts to get the government to honour its earlier pledges, called for a one-day general strike on 14 December 1988. The outcome exceeded all forecasts, including the trade unions' own. Some two-thirds of the nation's work-force stayed out. The government's response was to allow a special debate to be held in the Cortes at which González explained why it was impossible to satisfy most of the unions' demands. A youth employment scheme which they had objected to was withdrawn. And that appeared to be that.

However, after allowing a decent interval to elapse, Felipe González's ministers very slowly and cautiously resumed contact with the unions and, over a period of many months in lengthy and tangled negotiations, the government gave in to many of their demands. The results of these talks, which substantially improved welfare provision in Spain, were given a minimum of publicity. The 1988 general strike and its semi-clandestine aftermath provided a fascinating insight into the government's outlook. What mattered most to González and his ministers – and what they assumed would matter most to the voters – was not that they should be seen to be responsive to public opinion, but that they should not lose face in the eyes of the electorate.

The Socialists judged – correctly – that the growth in the economy would soon start to reduce the numbers of jobless. In any case, dissatisfied voters had no obvious political alternative. At a time when Communism was being discredited and dismantled elsewhere in Europe, it was assumed they would be reluctant to support the Communists and their allies in the United Left. Notionally to the right of the PSOE, though often at that time arguing for policies more left-wing than those of the government, were the CDS and the AP.

Both parties, however, suffered from being led by men whose prospects were undermined by their Francoist past. Adolfo Suárez's role in the transition had convinced the electorate that he was a genuinely committed democrat; but he seemed unable to act on the notion that a democratic politician must do more than go to the hustings at election time. His public appearances between elections had become so rare that one cartoonist took to drawing him as a snail.

Manuel Fraga's contribution had played an almost equally valuable part. By throwing himself into the democratic game with such evident gusto, he had persuaded most of the more reactionary elements in society that they had nothing to fear from it. But his authoritarian manner was a constant reminder of his totalitarian past.

After the 1986 election, he and his party had come to the reluctant conclusion that they would never win power under his leadership. Early the following year, Fraga stepped down in favour of a youthful Andalusian lawyer, Antonio Hernández Mancha. But Mancha's lightweight manner and appearance failed to earn him respect, and the AP was soon racked by squabbling. At the beginning of 1989, Fraga returned to pave the way for a more permanent successor.

His first choice was Marcelino Oreja, a former UCD minister and Secretary General of the Council of Europe, who had the additional attraction of being able to bring with him a number of dispossessed Christian Democrats. Although more of an alliance than ever because of their inclusion, the Alianza Popular was perversely renamed the Partido Popular (PP). Oreja became its candidate at the elections to the European Parliament in June, but in spite of his impeccable Euro-credentials the party lost ground. The Socialists were known to want a mandate that would ensure they stayed in government throughout 1992. Fraga had thus to cast around for an acceptable candidate for the premiership with a general election likely to be called any day. He opted for José María Aznar, a young former tax inspector who had put in an impressive performance as head of the regional government in Old Castile and León.

In the run-up to the general election of October 1989, the Socialists' appeal to the electorate was unchanged. Felipe González told a rally that Spain was enjoying greater international prestige than at any time since the reign of the Emperor Charles V in the sixteenth century. His claim was possibly true, but it brought criticism that he and his ministers were becoming prey to delusions of grandeur. In a newspaper interview, the Communist leader Julio Anguita also resorted for inspiration to Spain's Golden Age, but compared the state of the country to a Habsburg caravel – its glitteringly decorated façade concealing the rottenness within.

His critique of the government seemed to strike a chord with voters, for when the results started coming in it was clear that the United Left had defied a Europe-wide trend away from Marxism. It doubled its share of the vote and increased the number of its seats in Congress from 7 to 17, overtaking the CDS whose representation fell from 19 to 14. The United Left's success robbed the Socialists of an overall majority.* The PSOE was left with exactly half the seats in Congress, although it remained able to pass legislation without support from the opposition.

On share of the vote, the Partido Popular under Aznar did slightly worse than the Coalición Popular had done under Fraga in 1986. But it picked up an extra seat and the result was seen as reflecting well on a candidate who had only been confirmed after the campaign began. When Fraga was elected head of the regional government in his native Galicia in December, he was able to bow out again in the knowledge that his party had at last found a leader who could credibly offer moderate conservatism to the electorate.

Polling was scarcely over when the Socialists found themselves faced with a scandal of quite different dimensions to the Miró affair. Alfonso Guerra's younger brother, Juan, was shown to have occupied a government office in Seville for several years, during which he at no time held a government appointment. Allegations were also made that he had used his links with the administration to amass a personal fortune by peddling influence. His brother stepped down as deputy Prime Minister – though not as deputy General Secretary of the party – at the start of 1991. His departure deepened a rift which had been growing for some time between the Socialist party machine, which remained loyal to the rhetoric, if not the practice, of orthodox socialism, and a Socialist government increasingly seduced by neo-liberalism.

The growth of a new class of intermediaries had been rumoured for some time and earlier in 1989 a deputy in the Madrid regional parliament had claimed he had been offered 100 million pesetas to

---

*The outcome was not decided until almost five months later. The poll was clouded by numerous allegations of irregularity which had to be settled in the courts and then, in some cases, by fresh ballots. The last re-run was not held until the following February in the North African enclave of Melilla.

change his allegiance by just such a 'Mr Fixit' operating on behalf of the PP. Juan Guerra, though, was so intimately linked to the highest level of the ruling party that questions began to be asked about whether he was in fact acting on his own, or the PSOE's, behalf.

Anyone who had attended its election rallies, equipped with state-of-the-art sound and lighting effects, could be forgiven for wondering how a party ostensibly belonging to the workers could possibly afford them. Part of the answer was that the PSOE, in common with other Spanish parties, was running up huge debts. But there were growing suspicions that it was not the whole answer.

In theory, the PSOE was bound by the provisions of a law on party financing which had come into effect in 1987 and which made it illegal for political parties to draw funds from any source other than public subsidies, members' dues and strictly limited donations. In practice, the only check on it was a tribunal whose members were appointed by a parliament in which the PSOE enjoyed an overall majority.

In the event, though, it was the PP, and not the PSOE, which was first caught up in a cash-for-favours scandal. Early in 1990, transcripts of telephone conversations recorded by the police – the by-product of an investigation into drug trafficking – were leaked to the press. They depicted senior officials of the PP, including two successive national treasurers, discussing in language more appropriate to the Mafia how they 'collected' from property developers for the privilege of not having their projects obstructed at local and regional council level.*

It was inevitably suspected that the affair had been brought to light at the instigation of the Socialists. If that was the case, then the edge they gained was short-lived, for in April 1981 the so-called FILESA affair burst on to the front pages of the newspapers. It arose when an aggrieved Chilean accountant by the name of Carlos Alberto van Schouwen took out a case for wrongful dismissal against the owners of a Barcelona-based group of companies of which FILESA formed part. In the documents he presented to the

---

*The case against them was subsequently dismissed after the tapes were ruled to constitute inadmissible evidence.

court, he asserted that the real business of the group was to raise funds by charging big companies for non-existent consultancy work.

By the time the Socialists had to go to the country again in the local elections of May 1991, the opinion polls carried two alarming messages for them. One was that the right-wing vote was consolidating behind Aznar and his remodelled PP. The CDS put up a disastrous showing at the local elections, and immediately afterwards the party's leader, Adolfo Suárez, resigned. He has since disappeared from the political scene.

The other warning sign was that the PSOE's supporters were increasingly to be found among the least politically aware sections of the population. More and more, the Socialists found themselves reliant on elderly, rural voters, especially those in the poor south. Their vulnerability was underlined when they were ousted from power in Seville, the home town of González, Guerra and several of their closest associates, and a city on which the Socialists were lavishing cash in order to prepare it for its role during 1992.

'Spain's year', as it began to be known, had come about almost by accident. Although Expo '92 was identified with the Socialists because of their leaders' links with Seville, it was first conceived – before they came to power – as one half of a unique twin-based world fair, the rest of which was to have been held in Chicago. When the Americans backed out, the Spanish decided to press ahead.

At the same time, the authorities in Barcelona were pursuing an entirely separate initiative to host the Olympics. When they succeeded, it seemed only fitting that the EC should offer Madrid the consolation prize of being EC Capital of Culture during 1992.

Thus Spain found itself responsible for staging a unique extravaganza. When trying to rationalize the situation, the authorities put forward various arguments: that it provided the country with a deadline to work to, an excuse to develop its infrastructure, and an opportunity to get back on to the world stage in style.

On all three counts, 1992 can be judged a partial, though only a partial, success. A number of the projects that had been envisaged were either abandoned, like the extension of the Barcelona metro, or not finished on time, like the restoration of Madrid's Teatro Real. Considerable improvements were made to Spain's communications network, but they were often skewed by the specific requirements of the 1992 events. Seville, for example, acquired an immensely expensive airport terminal of which it will not be able to make full use until well into the next century.

Certainly, 1992 allowed Spain to make a spectacular re-entry after the isolation of the Franco years. But I think it is fair to say that had it not been for the resoundingly successful Barcelona Olympics, Spain might have been judged to have tripped and stumbled a bit as it stepped back on to the platform. The best that can be said of Madrid's stint as EC Capital of Culture is that it was unexceptional. Both Expo '92 and the Quincentenary proved extraordinarily accident-prone. A specially commissioned replica of the first vessel to circumnavigate the world sank as it left the slipway. The flotilla which retraced Columbus's voyage to the New World suffered a mutiny. Expo '92's centrepiece pavilion was burnt to the ground. And on the night before the exhibition opened, police opened fire with live ammunition on demonstrators in Seville, thereby recalling precisely the image of Spain that the events of 1992 were meant to dispel.

The Prime Minister, Felipe González, said when it was all over that the Spaniards had laid the ghost of Spanish inefficiency and shown they were as capable as anyone of staging major events. In fact, I suspect that Spain's success the year before in hosting the Middle East peace conference at frighteningly short notice did far more to convince the world of the Spaniards' abilities as organizers.

What did come as a revelation was the abruptness with which Spain's *fiesta* ended. Even before 1992 was over, the country was plunging into recession. As if symbolically, the Kuwait Investment Office, the biggest single foreign investor in Spain's eighties boom, closed down its operations. GDP in the opening quarter of 1993 was 1·2 per cent lower than in the first three months of the previous year. By the end of the following quarter unemployment had reached 22·5 per cent, the highest rate in the EC. The peseta had meanwhile been devalued for the third time in eight months.

In fact, the boom had run out of steam much earlier – some would argue as early as 1989. What the government then did was to pass a couple of expansionary budgets designed to get the country ready for 1992. A lot of building was done, which helped to generate economic activity in general and keep people off the dole queues in particular. But the collapse, when it came, was correspondingly more abrupt.

What I wrote in an earlier chapter about the rapid growth between 1961 and 1973 was also true of the brief but giddy boom of the eighties: what it changed least was the shape of the economy. By the early nineties, Spain still suffered from the traditional problems of high unemployment and costly borrowing. Investment had been considerable, but a lot of it had been speculative rather than productive. In fact, after Spain joined the European Community's Exchange Rate Mechanism in mid-1989, holding pesetas became a one-way bet – the real rate of return on deposits was greater than the maximum depreciation allowed by the ERM. A lot of firms were modernized, often after being taken over by foreigners, but industry as a whole had not resolved the problem of how to compete effectively with European rivals.

In many areas, improvements in the quality or quantity of output had been offset by a rise in the cost of labour. Spain was no longer a cheap place for manufacturing, certainly not compared with the new democracies of eastern and central Europe. Nor, by and large, could it offer products to match those of the more advanced nations of the EC.

The government's travails were compounded by the continuing investigation into FILESA. In March 1993, government auditors submitted a 500-page report to the Supreme Court which upheld all the main charges and detailed irregular payments totalling 997 million pesetas (£5 million or $7.5 million). González reacted by threatening to resign unless someone in the party agreed to take responsibility. When the party bosses led by Guerra refused to oblige, the Prime Minister called an election instead.

The 1993 general election campaign had everything. Polls showed the lead being swapped almost daily between the two main contenders. Such was the pace on the hustings that the leader of the Communist-dominated United Left, Julio Anguita, ended the campaign in a hospital bed. It was also the first general election contest in Spain to see American-style television debates. In the first of them Felipe González, who had been thought unbeatable in any sort of face-to-face confrontation, was thrown into confusion by a better-prepared José María Aznar. It was only in the second of their two encounters that the Prime Minister regained the upper hand.

What seemed to tip the balance in the last few days before polling, though, was the Socialists' resort to blatant scare tactics. At various times, they compared Aznar with Hitler, Franco, and the leader of the abortive 1981 coup. Their constant emphasis on the need to support the 'left' against the 'right' stemmed the loss of votes to Anguita's alliance.

In the event, the PSOE won 159 seats in Congress against the PP's 141. The United Left, with 18, gained only one seat more than in 1989. The CDS did not win any.

In different ways, Spain's young democracy emerged both strengthened and weakened from the ballot. The excitement of the contest gave a shot in the arm to a political culture that had seemed in danger of atrophy. But what a youthful democracy needs above all is the experience of power changing hands, and that did not happen. By the time the next general election is held, the PSOE and González will have been in power for up to fifteen years.

On the night of the election, the Prime Minister promised his jubilant supporters 'un cambio sobre el cambio' ('a change on top of the change'). It was a conscious invocation of the spirit of '82, and indeed the psephological arithmetic showed he had already succeeded to some extent in summoning it up. The figures implied the PSOE had won the support of a lot of erstwhile abstainers who had voted for the PSOE eleven years earlier in order to prevent a return to right-wing dictatorship and were persuaded they ought to do so again.

However, everything González did afterwards suggested that, having solicited and secured the left-of-centre vote, he was determined to stick to right-of-centre policies. The election left the Socialists seventeen seats short of an absolute majority. González offered places in a coalition cabinet to the main Catalan and Basque nationalist groups, which stand to the right of centre. Yet despite being turned down by both, he ruled out a pact with the United

Left. When he eventually announced a reshuffled, minority Cabinet, it was one purged of the more orthodox faction loyal to his erstwhile friend and deputy, Alfonso Guerra. A third of the members of the new Cabinet did not even belong to the PSOE.

But then it can be argued that far from underlining the Spanish voters' desire for change, the outcome of the 1993 elections showed their profound mistrust of it.

Despite, or perhaps because of, their history, Spaniards have traditionally been suspicious of radical or sudden transformations. And their attitude was inevitably reinforced by thirty-six uninterrupted years of rule by Franco. It can, I believe, be discerned in the way that the Spanish reassure each other by using phrases denoting a lack of change. Whereas the English, French and Italians all use positive expressions – 'All right', '*Ça va*', '*Va bene*' – Spaniards have long used negative ones. It used to be '*sin novedad*' ('without novelty'). Nowadays, it is '*no pasa nada*' ('nothing happening'). Newcomers are struck by the way that a cabinet reshuffle in Spain is invariably described as a *crisis gubernamental*.

It is one of numerous ways in which, almost two decades afte Franco's death, the new Spain still bears witness to his lengthy dictatorship and the subsequent developments which were made inevitable by it.

CHAPTER 6

The Spirit of the New Spain

Spain's year, its 'year of years', turned out to have so many anniversaries that it began to seem almost contrived. Apart from the quincentenary of Columbus's journey to America and the anniversaries of the conquest of Granada and the expulsion of the Jews, 1992 also happened to be the 100th anniversary of the birth of General Franco.

In Spain itself, not a great deal was made of it. A few new books on the *Caudillo* were published. Some original film footage of him was discovered and televised. And on the day itself, 4 December, most of the newspapers published a supplement or an editorial, or both.

Possibly the sentiment most often expressed about Franco around the time of his centenary was that he had become an irrelevance. 'Spaniards,' in the opinion of an *El Mundo* editorial, 'look at the Franco era as if from an enormous distance . . . his memory has been blotted out of the collective present. It now serves as a point of reference for almost no one.'

In a sense, that is true. Francoism has not survived as a political movement. And since the history taught in schools usually ends with the civil war, a lot of younger Spaniards have only the haziest idea of who he was. A number of schoolchildren interviewed on radio for a programme to mark the centenary were under the impression that Franco had belonged to the PSOE. Those who have grown up since the end of the dictatorship are baffled, and even annoyed, by the way in which foreigners continue to refer to the country in which they live as 'post-Franco Spain' almost twenty years after his death.

But then foreigners can often see more clearly than Spaniards what it is about Spain that is distinctive. And they know, or sense, that many of its distinguishing traits are the result of its having been ruled by one man, not for five or ten or even twenty years, but for thirty-six. Whether Spaniards care to recognize the fact – and for the most part they do not – Franco's signature continues to be written all over the country he ruled. Its inflexible labour market, its huge, largely inefficient and unprofitable public sector, and the corporatism to be found in the civil service and the liberal professions, are all legacies from Spain's Francoist past.

So too are many of the instincts and attitudes most characteristic of the new Spain. Paradoxically, his most obvious legacy is one which, all the evidence suggests, he had no intention of bequeathing: a generous tolerance which has become the hallmark of modern Spanish society.

Franco himself was obsessively vindictive. Several months before the end of the civil war, he promulgated a Law of Political Responsibilities which made it an offence not only to have fought against the Nationalists but also to have refrained from joining their rebellion; and not only to have been on the wrong side during the civil war but also to have been on the other side before it even broke out.

Tens of thousands of 'reds' were executed in the years which followed the conflict. The inhabitants of the two most populous Basque provinces had a 'punitive decree' passed against them. The leader of the Catalans was shot. And though Franco's regime was to become progressively less active in the persecution of its opponents, some remained unconvinced that it was safe to emerge from hiding. One of the most remarkable developments in the years immediately following Franco's death was the reappearance of a string of so-called *topos* (moles) who had stayed in hiding within Spain for more than three and a half decades. By ensuring that the wounds left by the civil war remained open so long, though, Franco seems to have inoculated his fellow-Spaniards against the very intolerance he came to symbolize.

At the same time, he – or rather his lieutenants – imbued Spanish society with a distinctive mixture of conservative and corporatist attitudes. Spain is unique in being the only country in Europe which developed into a technologically advanced society under the aegis of an ultra-right-wing dictatorship. Most Spaniards, as we shall see, acquired their first taste of prosperity in a society in which taxes were low, but in which they were expected to buy their own houses, provide for their own futures and pay for their own health care; a society in which overtime was available, but where trade unions, collective bargaining and strikes were all illegal.

The Opus Dei technocrats who masterminded Spain's economic 'take-off' did not perhaps succeed in replacing altogether the Spaniards' traditional disdain for labour with a new – Catholic, rather than Protestant – work ethic. The two attitudes can be seen in daily conflict. But they certainly did succeed in superimposing the one on the other, and in infusing society with an element of the 'stand on your own two feet' ethos.

Spaniards tend not to expect from the state the sort of cushioning which is regarded as normal in the rest of Western Europe. Government campaigns to stop people from killing themselves on the roads, or with tobacco, or putting themselves at risk from AIDS, are mounted from time to time, but they remain quite rare. Welfare provision has become more generous under the Socialists, but it is still regarded by them as subject to withdrawal as soon as times get tough. On at least three occasions since coming to power, the Socialists' response to a downturn in the economy has been to cut entitlement to unemployment pay. Spaniards look astonished when you say it, but of all the societies in Europe, theirs is the one where attitudes to the role of the state are closest to those in the United States.

Closest yet furthest, for the technocrats were not writing on a blank slate. They were imposing their liberal ideas on a society which had already been profoundly affected by the fascism of Franco's earliest days. One of the ideas which characterized fascism, as it did communism, was a belief in the benefits of state ownership and intervention. Its legacies can be seen in many aspects of life in Spain today, and in that respect Spain is more akin to some of the nations of the former Soviet bloc.

Nobody in Spain, for example, challenges the government's invariably unsuccessful attempts to negotiate three-way pacts on social and economic policy with the trade unions and the employers' federation. There are undoubtedly arguments why it should wish to

75

have them. They are in line with socialist thinking. They are the norm in several European countries. They are implicitly recommended in the constitution. But what makes Spain remarkable is that despite the fact that the rest of the world has been undergoing a free-market revolution over the past decade and a half, nobody – least of all the employers – even poses the question of whether such matters might not be left to market forces.

But then rarely does anyone query the government's right to fix petrol prices. Or help itself to billions of pesetas by forcing the clearing banks to lodge part of their deposits with the Bank of Spain. No one seems to think it odd that there should still be an official news agency. Or that the government should use the taxpayers' money to finance opinion polls, the results of which are given to the government first and to the opposition party later, if ever.

Franco's rule made Spaniards more reliant on themselves and on the state. But not on each other. Their reluctance to associate had been noted long before Franco. 'The Iberians,' declared the nineteenth-century traveller, Richard Ford, 'never would amalgamate, never would, as Strabo said, put their shields together – never would sacrifice their own local private interest for the general good.' Spanish thinkers reached similar conclusions. For Ortega y Gasset, writing in 1921, Spain was 'invertebrate'.

What is undoubtedly true is that it has traditionally been deficient in the voluntary associations – trade unions, mutual societies, political clubs, pressure groups, charitable foundations and the like. The origins of the phenomenon may indeed lie in the nature of Spanish society or the personality of the Spanish people, but by making it difficult – and in many cases illegal – to create such groups, Franco's dictatorship ensured its persistence. Ironically, Spain's continuing 'invertebration' may be one reason why it has proved so easy to change. The authorities have not had to contend with the normal array of well-organized interest groups which in other countries might have questioned and obstructed their reforms.

One way of judging Franco is to compare his record with that of Salazar, his fellow-dictator in neighbouring Portugal. Two differences stand out, and they have both had a far-reaching influence on the way that Spain has developed. In the first place, Franco did not, like Salazar, resist attempts to improve the material wellbeing of his people. Nor, unlike Salazar, was he lured into colonial warfare, thereby succeeding where his Portuguese counterpart failed, in keeping his army loyal.

That ruled out a revolution of the kind that disgruntled officers launched in Portugal in 1974. In fact, it ruled out a revolution of any kind, because the army – still broadly loyal to the memory and ideals of its *Generalísimo* – would have seized on any evidence of a return to pre-Francoist chaos as a pretext for intervention. Spaniards, predisposed by their folk memory of the civil war towards evolution rather than revolution, were thus given an extra incentive for bringing about change in a more conciliatory way. The word they invented to describe the process was 'transition'. Though the fact is rarely noted, this was a special – perhaps unique – process. And it has endowed the country which emerged from it with special, and perhaps unique, characteristics. Yet while it may be that transition was the only sensible course to be taken after Franco's death, its advisability should not obscure the fact that negative as well as positive effects flowed from it.

It has become customary to talk of Spain's 'peaceful transition' from dictatorship to democracy, as if peacefulness were its defining characteristic. It was not. Politically motivated violence took the lives of more than twenty people between Franco's death in November 1975 and the first democratic general election in July 1977. Since then the toll has risen to over a thousand, principally because of the activities of the Basque separatist group, ETA.

What made Spain's transition special was the lack of a clean break with the past. In essence, the transition was achieved by an unwritten, and for the most part unspoken, pact. The Francoist establishment acknowledged that the time had come for a change and undertook to wind up its operations on condition that reprisals were never taken against any of its members.

In the event, those who had served Franco escaped, not just retribution, but refutation. In the years immediately following Franco's death, politicians were eager to extol the virtues of the new arrangements. But because of the continued threat from the armed forces, they were not so keen to recall the evils of the old ones. Spaniards were often told that democracy was good, but only rarely that dictatorship was bad.

The virtual absence of a far right in Spanish politics can be construed as proof that the point did not need to be made: that the experience of Francoism has acted as a kind of aversion therapy. Not all the evidence points in that direction, though.

Among the polls published at the time of Franco's centenary was one conducted among 18- to 29-year-olds, whose views would have been based on what they had been told by their parents and read in books: the oldest would have been no more than eleven when Franco died. Their verdict on him was pretty ambiguous. Asked whether his rule had been good or bad for Spain, 14 per cent did not know, 14 per cent said 'very bad' and 33 per cent 'bad', but 22 per cent chose 'fair' and 17 per cent 'good' or 'very good'. To put it another way, less than half of young Spaniards considered that Francoism had been a mistake. It is also noticeable that Spaniards sometimes seem to find difficulty in understanding the degree of censure which collaboration with a dictatorship can inspire elsewhere. In the run-up to the Barcelona Olympics, the head of the IOC, Juan Antonio Samaranch, was attacked in a book by two British journalists who dwelt heavily on his Francoist past. Spaniards were disconcerted, and tended to give credence to Samaranch's protestations that it was all part of an anti-Latin plot hatched by unidentified Anglo-Saxon enemies.

The spirit of transition is sometimes described as being that of 'forgive and forget'. That is not entirely correct. Since no one in Spain was ever judged, no one was ever deemed guilty. And since no one was ever deemed guilty, forgiveness never entered into it. It was just a matter of forgetting.

Franco's relatives have not simply been allowed to live out their lives in peace. They have been turned into celebrities once again by the gossip magazines. Notorious torturers from the Franco era have not only not been made to pay for what they did. They have been allowed to remain in the police and, in some cases, raised to the highest levels. Journalists who once profited handsomely from their collaboration with the Franco regime have not just been allowed to continue with their careers. Some have re-emerged as respected commentators whose views on how best to run a democracy can be read or heard on any day of the week.

But then there are times when it seems as if having shifted your ground, having changed your views, is not something to be over-looked, but to be admired. Of all the public figures whose lives have ended in recent years few have been accorded such fulsome praise as Francisco Fernández Ordóñez. A former chairman of Franco's state holding company, INI, Mr Fernández Ordóñez spent four years in the right-of-centre governments of Adolfo Suárez before joining the PSOE just in time for the Socialists to win power. As a result he was able to resume his extraordinary political career and eventually rise to become Foreign Minister under Felipe González. Now, Mr Fernández Ordóñez was a kindly and likeable man and I have no wish to tarnish his memory. Yet I doubt whether in any other country but Spain would someone who had changed sides as often have been accorded such an uncritical farewell.

Against this background, it becomes easier to understand some of the peculiarities of contemporary Spanish politics. How, for example, Spain's nominally Socialist leaders have found it so easy to leave behind their ideological commitments. And why both the parties to have ruled Spain since Franco's death, the UCD and the PSOE, evolved so rapidly into catch-all alliances.

The UCD embraced everything from social democracy to right-wing conservativism; the PSOE includes free-marketeers and Marxists alike. Since coming to power, moreover, the PSOE – like the UCD – has drawn to itself a quite extraordinary range of former critics and opponents. Those who have joined the Socialists and currently hold a seat in parliament or a job in government include ex-leaders of the Maoist and Trotskyist movements, numerous former communists, and someone who was Fraga's right-hand man when Fraga led the then People's Alliance.

Concern over the centripetal force exerted by the authorities, by *el poder* ('the power'), as it is graphically described in Spain, reached a climax shortly before the 1993 election when it was announced that Judge Baltasar Garzón, who had made his name by defying the government over the GAL case,* would be standing alongside the Prime Minister in the PSOE list for Madrid.

---

*See above, pp. 62-3.

The fact that Spain underwent a transition rather than a revolution or anything of the kind is another important reason why tolerance should have emerged as the supreme value in contemporary Spain. But it is also, I believe, one of the causes of something which goes beyond mere tolerance: a sort of ethical emptiness which is equally characteristic of today's Spain.

A survey in *Cambio 16* carried out at the time of the Gulf crisis found that only 8 per cent of Spaniards would give their life for their country; only 3 per cent thought it worth dying for love or liberty; and a mere 2 per cent would sacrifice themselves for an ideal. The results clearly astonished the magazine's proprietor, Juan Tomás de Salas, who wrote an impassioned editorial saying that it was time 'Spaniards stop believing that our destiny on this planet is to enjoy, enjoy, enjoy and that our problems will be taken care of by others'. As a description of the spirit of post-Franco Spain it could scarcely be bettered.

'Enjoy, enjoy, enjoy.' Not at all an unsuitable motto for a nation which, according to a government survey conducted in the winter of 1989–90, had 138,200 bars – only slightly fewer than in the whole of the rest of the European Union. No other people I have ever encountered put as much effort as the Spanish into having a good time. Whatever its political and economic problems, their country is an immensely entertaining place. After Spain's 1992 extravaganza, the tourist authorities started an advertising campaign intended to capitalize on it with the slogan, 'Spain – passion for life'. It is not one with which I would quibble. Today's Spaniards do have a passion for life that matches their traditional fascination with death. Indeed, the two are almost certainly linked – thinking so much about death gives them a heightened appreciation of life. An explosion of carefree hedonism was doubtless inevitable after so many years of repression under Franco. What seems to have delayed it was the lack of real economic growth between 1975 and 1985. But if you look back over Spain's recent past what you see is a pattern of civil war followed by military dictatorship, not unlike that which characterized seventeenth-century England. It is perhaps not surprising therefore that Restoration Spain should have much the same frivolous air as Restoration England. Almodóvar as Congreve? There are worse comparisons.

That irresponsible edge which De Salas rightly identified is also, I think, attributable to Spain's recent history, though not directly to either Franco or the transition. The fact is that those Spaniards who chose to assume that their problems would be taken care of by others have not been proved all that wrong. In differing degrees, both their prosperity and their freedom have been handed out to them.

The boom of the 1960s was made possible thanks largely to an influx of foreign tourists; that of the 1980s was sparked off by Spain's entry into the European Community. Spaniards were able to take advantage of these opportunities only by putting in a considerable amount of hard work, it is true. But in both cases the role played by external factors was crucial. And the consequent rapid growth depended heavily on overseas investment.

As for liberty, the harsh reality is that Franco died in his bed. A lot of Spaniards, students and workers particularly, risked terrible beatings – and worse – to protest against the dictatorship. Their courage helped to create a consensus for change. In the event, though, it was not the opposition to Franco which devised and applied the formula which turned Spain into a democracy, but a young man who had been standing in the dictator's shadow all along.

PART TWO

The Pillars of Society

CHAPTER 7

A Modest Monarchy

The tone of King Juan Carlos's reign was set before it began. Some months before Franco's death, the Prince – as he then was – decided that when he took the throne he would not move into the residence of his ancestors, the eighteenth-century Palacio de Oriente in Madrid, but would remain in the house where he had lived since 1962.

Although extensions have been added in recent years, the Palacio de la Zarzuela, a few miles to the north-west of the capital, is no bigger than many a company chairman's home. The drawing-room can only just take a hundred people standing, so the grander official receptions have to be held in the Palacio de Oriente. Yet the Zarzuela houses not only the royal family itself but also the offices of the royal household and the living quarters of some of the people who work for it. Apart from the Zarzuela, the King and Queen also have the use of the Palacio de Marivent, a former museum overlooking a bay just outside Palma de Mallorca, where they spend August and some of their weekends during the summer. During the winter, the royal family occasionally goes skiing at Baquiera Beret, a resort in Catalonia.

To the disappointment of some of the aristocracy, they have not re-established any sort of court. The Spanish monarchy costs about half as much as Britain's and less in fact than any in Europe.

The modesty of his claims upon the nation nevertheless reflects a realistic assessment of the position in which the King finds himself. He knows that if he is to retain the respect of the Spanish people and ensure the survival of the monarchy, he needs to be seen to be putting in more than he takes out.

This may seem an odd conclusion to reach about the man who

both gave the Spanish people their democracy and saved it for them in 1981. Polls suggest the Spanish are as appreciative as you would expect them to be of the King's contribution. Three surveys by the government-run Centro de Investigaciones Sociológicas (CIS) between 1987 and 1989 all found that about two-thirds felt that, without him, 'democracy in Spain would not have been possible'.

Paradoxically, a minority still have their doubts about his role during the abortive coup. In those parts of the country with strong regional nationalist traditions and among some radical Spaniards of both right and left, there lingers a suspicion that General Armada, who had been one of Juan Carlos's few confidants, would not have acted without the King's complicity. A milder variation on the same theme is that the King waited until it was clear the coup would fail before committing himself. However, it needs to be stressed that both these are minority views. The vast majority of Spaniards – four out of five, according to one of the CIS polls – felt his handling of events on the night of the coup attempt only served to enhance his reputation as a champion of democracy.

Ever since then the King's personal popularity has been considerable, and it reached new heights during the 1992 Barcelona Olympics when it seemed as if his mere presence was sufficient to guarantee success for Spanish competitors. His enthusiastic support for the Spanish team – indeed, that of his whole family – did much to bind them more closely to the people over whom he reigns. But as the Spanish themselves often remark, they are *'muy Juancarlistas, pero poco monárquicos'*, which roughly translates as 'keener on Juan Carlos than on royalty'. More than four out of ten of those questioned by the CIS thought the institution of monarchy was 'outdated'.

Clearly, the absence of a monarchy in Spain for almost half a century is largely to blame. But it is also the case that in modern times the Spanish have been poorly served by their royals. With few exceptions, Spain's Bourbon monarchs, of whom Juan Carlos is the latest representative, have been a pretty feckless lot whose role all too often was to divide the nation they ruled. Of the three institutions that have traditionally held Spain together, the 'three pillars' as they have sometimes been called – monarchy, army and Church – it is the monarchy which has invariably looked the shakiest.

The Bourbons came to rule Spain, not by invitation but through a war – the so-called War of the Spanish Succession – which broke out among the European powers over who should inherit the Spanish throne after the previous (Habsburg) monarch had died without an heir. The war not only split Europe; it divided Spain too. A sizeable number of Spaniards – principally the Catalans, Valencians and Aragonese – supported the Bourbons' opponents and when the war was over they were punished for having picked the wrong side.

It was a Bourbon, moreover, who abjectly surrendered to Napoleon's forces in 1808, and although his son was restored six years later his descendants never really lived down the fact that a monarch had shown himself to be less patriotic than his subjects. During the 123 tumultuous years that followed, dissatisfaction with the monarchy twice reached such a pitch that the ruler of the day was forced to leave the country.

The first occasion was in 1868 when an alliance of liberal generals and admirals got rid of the nymphomaniac Queen Isabel and the Cortes invited a member of the Italian royal family to take her place. But he abdicated soon afterwards, ushering in a brief and disorderly period of republican rule. After the failure of the First Republic the Spaniards decided that there was nothing left to try and restored the Bourbons in the person of Isabel's son, Alfonso XII. It was his son, Alfonso XIII, who lost the throne once again.

In 1923 he connived at the seizure of power by a group of senior officers led by the flamboyantly eccentric General Miguel Primo de Rivera. By putting up with Primo de Rivera's dictatorship the King flouted the very constitution from which the restored monarchy derived its legitimacy, and tied its standing to the success or failure of Primo de Rivera's experiment. After seven years, the experiment failed. The King survived for slightly more than a year until he allowed the local elections of 1931 to become a trial of strength between pro- and anti-royalists. As the results came in from the towns and cities, which were the only areas where a fair ballot had been held, it became clear that the King's opponents were going to sweep the board. A republic was declared in the Basque industrial centre of Eibar and it seemed certain that unless Alfonso stepped down there would be bloodshed. On the evening of 14 April he issued a statement in which he carefully avoided abdicating but said that he did not want to be held responsible for the outbreak of a civil war. 'Therefore,' he added, 'until the nation speaks I shall deliberately suspend the use of my royal prerogative.' That night he left Madrid for exile. Spain became a republic, but the tensions between right and left that had been articulated for a brief period as support for and opposition to the monarchy merely resurfaced in other guises; the internecine conflict that Alfonso had been at pains to avert broke out five years later.

Alfonso died in Rome in 1941, a few weeks after his failing health had persuaded him to abdicate. His eldest son, also called Alfonso, had already given up his claim to the throne in 1933 to marry a Cuban woman. He died in a car crash five years later without leaving any children. Shortly after his renunciation, his brother Jaime, who was next in line but being deaf was thought incapable of assuming the responsibilities of kingship, also renounced the succession. He subsequently married and had two children, Alfonso and Gonzalo. The legitimate heir was therefore Alfonso XIII's third son and fifth child, Juan, Count of Barcelona.

Don Juan, as he came to be known, had left Spain with his father in 1931 and had been sent to the Royal Naval College at Dartmouth. In 1935 he married another Bourbon, María de las Mercedes de Borbón y Orléans, Princess of the Two Sicilies. The military uprising against the republic the next year seemed to the young Prince as if it could be the means by which he might recover his throne and that he ought to be a party to it. A fortnight after the start of the rebellion he crossed secretly into Spain to join the Nationalist forces, but the rebels – reluctant to risk the life of the heir to the throne – put him back over the Pyrenees. Perhaps they were sincere in their motives, but it was nevertheless a singularly convenient decision for General Franco, who was proclaimed Head of State later that year.

Once the war was over the *Caudillo* showed no intention of giving up to Don Juan his position as Head of State. The principal reason was of course that he thoroughly enjoyed the exercise of power, but it is only fair to point out that had he, say, become a mere Prime Minister under Don Juan, he might have wrecked the tenuous alliance of forces that had won the war – the accession of a monarch, any monarch, would have upset the anti-royalist Falange, while the accession of one of Alfonso XIII's sons would have alienated their Carlist rivals. Equally, Don Juan's subsequent disenchantment with Franco, although it had its roots in the *Caudillo*'s refusal to surrender power, grew in conviction as the Count, who saw the monarchy as an instrument of reconciliation, had to stand by while Franco used his power to humiliate his former opponents.

The Law of Succession to the Headship of State, which the Cortes passed in 1949, restored the monarchy in name but made Franco acting Head of State for life and gave him the right to name his successor 'as King or Regent'. Spain became, in the classic phrase, 'a monarchy without a monarch'. The law split Don Juan's followers down the middle. To some – the more liberal – it proved that Franco intended hanging on to power for as long as he could and that the only sensible course was to side with the proscribed opposition. To others – the more conservative – it showed that the only way the monarchy would ever be restored was through Franco's offices and that if the royalists were to get their way they would have to collaborate with Franco's regime. The sometimes bewildering changes of tack by Don Juan over the years that followed, which succeeded in antagonizing the majority of both pro- and anti-Francoists, can to some extent be explained by the conflicting advice he received from 'purists' and 'collaborationists' on his 93-member Privy Council. Shortly after the Law of Succession was passed, for example, his representatives entered negotiations with the exiled socialists and communists. These negotiations ended in the so-called St Jean de Luz Agreements whereby, if Franco fell, there would be a referendum to decide the form of state. Yet before they were signed Don Juan had met Franco on board his yacht to discuss the dictator's suggestion that Don Juan's sons should be educated in Spain.

Don Juan's heir, Juan Carlos, was born in Rome on 5 January 1938. He was Juan and Mercedes' third child; they already had two daughters, Pilar and Margarita. In 1942 the family moved to Lausanne in neutral Switzerland and it was there that Juan Carlos began school. In 1946 when his parents moved to Portugal, so as to be as close as possible to Spain, they made arrangements for Juan Carlos to stay as a boarder at the Marian Fathers' school in Fribourg.

Franco's offer put the Count of Barcelona in an extraordinarily difficult position. On the one hand, he was being asked to surrender control over the upbringing of his son and heir to a man he mistrusted. Moreover, to do so would give credibility to the dictator's claim to have restored the monarchy. On the other hand, Franco undoubtedly had a point. If the monarchy were ever to be restored it would have to have a credible representative and if Don Juan were to die before the *Caudillo* his son would need to be up to the challenge. As it was, Juan Carlos – who had never seen Spain – spoke Spanish with a pronounced French accent. After several weeks' deliberation Don Juan decided to accept Franco's offer and on 8 November the ten-year-old Juan Carlos, accompanied by his younger brother, Alfonso,★ boarded the Lusitania Express at Lisbon for a train ride that would eventually take him to the throne.

The first few years of the Princes' stay in Spain, during which they studied in Madrid and San Sebastián, saw something of a reconciliation between the Count and the *Caudillo*. But after Juan Carlos passed his *bachillerato* in 1954 it became clear that the two older men had very different ideas about his higher education. Don Juan wanted him to go to a foreign university where he would receive a liberal 'European' education. Franco, on the other hand, wanted him to study at a military academy before entering a Spanish university. In December 1954, Don Juan and General Franco met once more, this time at a hunting lodge near the Portuguese border, and Franco once again won the day.

The following autumn Juan Carlos began a four-year military training – two years at the army college in Saragossa to be followed by a year each at the navy and air force colleges under the overall supervision of General Carlos Martínez Campos, Duque de la Torre. In 1959 Juan Carlos passed out as a lieutenant in all three services and returned to his parents' home in Estoril. Franco had decided, in consultation with the Duke, that the next phase of Juan Carlos's education should take place at the University of Salamanca,

---

★ Like his namesake in the previous generation, Alfonso died in tragic circumstances. In 1956, at the age of fifteen, he was shot while playing with a loaded gun at the family home in Estoril. Juan Carlos, who was with him at the time of the accident, was profoundly affected. Childhood friends say that the incident turned him from a bit of a bully into an altogether more thoughtful, sensitive boy.

and it was only after his rooms had been chosen and his tutors selected that Don Juan seems to have realized the implications of his son being sent to an institution that had remained intellectually fossilized for centuries. He refused to sanction the idea and the Duke resigned his post. Don Juan and General Franco returned to the hunting lodge in March 1960 and this time it was the Count who got his way. The Duke's place was taken by a panel of six eminent academics who designed a special two-year course in liberal studies for Juan Carlos. He was to take the course in Madrid, but would be taught by the academics on the panel and the lecturers and professors they selected.

The Prince's engagement to Princess Sofía of Greece was announced while he was at university. They had first met in 1954 aboard the Greek royal family's yacht during a cruise in the Aegean, but it was not until the Duke and Duchess of Kent's wedding seven years later that their romance began.

'We were alone. We were without our parents. And we more or less got engaged in London,' she later told an interviewer. 'In fact, my parents had never contemplated the possibility of my marrying into the Spanish royal family. There was a difference between the religions of our two countries.' The problem was solved by Juan Carlos's grandmother, Victoria Eugenia, who travelled to Rome to secure the Pope's personal permission for a double ceremony.

Princess Sofía, the eldest daughter of King Paul and Queen Frederika, had been born on 2 November of the same year as Prince Juan Carlos. They shared a passion for sailing. The Princess had been her brother Constantine's reserve at the 1960 Olympics, when he won a gold medal. The Prince was later to sail for Spain in the 1972 Olympics. But initially their common interest did more to separate than unite them. 'I once went sailing with him when we were still engaged,' Sofía later recalled, 'and I shall never understand how I was able to marry him after that.'

More importantly, perhaps, the earliest memories of both were of exile. In 1940, Sofía's parents had fled Greece ahead of the Nazi invasion and settled in South Africa. When she returned to her native country at the age of eight, she had no memory of it. Like Juan Carlos, she had been packed off to boarding-school – only in her case she went later but stayed longer.

On 14 May 1962 Juan Carlos and Sofía were married at the Catholic cathedral in Athens before a constellation of kings, queens and presidents. Over the next few years, Sofía gave birth to three children – Elena in 1963, Cristina in 1965, and Felipe, who was born on 30 January 1968.

After university, Juan Carlos spent a few weeks in each of the ministries to understand how they worked. In December 1962 Franco had celebrated his seventieth birthday and the question of who should succeed him appeared increasingly urgent. But it was not easy to see how he could put into effect his apparent intention of restoring the monarchy.

The Carlists were a spent force. In the first place, their claim to the throne was now exceedingly tenuous. The original pretender's last direct male descendant, Alfonso Carlos, had died in 1936 without leaving a son. His closest male relative and therefore the successor to the Carlist claim was none other than Don Juan, so to keep alive the cause Alfonso Carlos had before his death adopted as his heir a remote cousin, Prince Javier de Borbón Parma. In spite of this, in 1958, several leading Carlists publicly acknowledged Don Juan's entitlement to the pretendership. Javier subsequently abdicated in favour of his son, Carlos Hugo. Eight years older than Juan Carlos, Carlos Hugo was young enough to be an eligible successor to the throne and in 1964 he enhanced his credentials still further by marrying Princess Irene of the Netherlands after a runaway romance. But the Carlists' dream of a return to absolutist monarchy seemed even to Franco to be impracticable in the latter half of the twentieth century and throughout his rule the Carlists never had more than a token presence in the government.

The problem was that the other branch of the family was represented by a man whom he neither liked nor respected. In view of Franco's disdain for Don Juan, an increasing number of Don Juan's more reactionary supporters, who had always felt that it would be better if Franco were to outlive the Count so that he could hand over to a king brought up under the dictatorship, began to toy with the seemingly outlandish notion that, even if the Count outlived Franco, Juan Carlos might succeed to the throne. The most committed proponents of the 'Juan Carlos solution' were the Opus Dei 'technocrats' who had been responsible for initiating Spain's 'economic miracle' and whose popularity with Franco was rising at about the same rate as the GNP. Their patron was Franco's old friend, Admiral Carrero Blanco.

A lot of Spaniards, though, were convinced that, given the problems, Franco would never bring himself to name a successor. The Falangists in particular hoped that he might fudge the issue by bequeathing power to a regent. The man they had in mind for the job was another old friend of Franco's, Lieutenant-General Agustín Muñoz Grandes. A lifelong Falangist, he had led the Blue Division – Franco's contribution to the Axis war effort – and served as a minister in two cabinets. In 1962 Franco appointed him deputy Prime Minister, the first time he had created such a post.

Muñoz Grandes's elevation thoroughly alarmed royalists of all hues and it was at about this time that the technocrats and Admiral Carrero Blanco launched a campaign, which came to be known as *Operación Lucero*, aimed at promoting Juan Carlos's candidacy both to Franco and to the nation. In retrospect, it can be seen that Franco needed very little persuading – at about this time he remarked to Juan Carlos that he had 'more chance than your father of becoming King'. Selling Juan Carlos to the country was a more difficult task. The technocrats had considerable influence in the media, business and the universities, but the Falange – through their control of the Movimiento – held sway over much of local government. When Juan Carlos and Sofía visited the provinces, as they did a lot at about this time at the prompting of their supporters, they were often met with either total indifference – or rotten fruit. Juan Carlos, who had been jeered by Falangists in the streets of San Sebastián when he was at school and had had to face a demonstration by Carlists when he was at university, knew how to cope. He subsequently recalled how on one occasion when he was being shown round by a local bigwig, 'I sensed that something was going to happen – something disagreeable, naturally. We were walking along, with me on the alert, looking out for the place where I thought the trouble might occur, when suddenly I took one step forward and two steps back and a tomato imprinted itself on my companion's uniform.' For Sofía, it must have been quite a trial.

The extent to which Juan Carlos sympathized with the ulterior motives of *Operación Lucero* remains a mystery. As late as January 1966 he told a visiting correspondent, 'I'll never, never accept the crown as long as my father is alive.' The first public indication that the plan was succeeding came the following year when Franco summarily dismissed Muñoz Grandes and gave his job to Carrero Blanco. The accession of Juan Carlos now began to look like more of a probability than a possibility. Feeling that regency was a lost cause, a number of Falangists reconciled themselves to the idea of a monarchy and began promoting the candidacy of Alfonso de Borbón-Dampierre, the son of Don Juan's deaf elder brother who had renounced his claims to the throne in 1933. Carlos Hugo, meanwhile, moved rapidly from the right to the left of the political spectrum in an attempt to secure the support of the democratic opposition – a move that appalled many of the traditional supporters of his cause. In December 1968 he made a speech openly attacking Juan Carlos and five days later the police gave him and his wife twenty-four hours to leave the country.

With the Falangists and the Carlists both now clutching at straws, the succession was Juan Carlos's for the asking. In January 1969, he asked. 'I am ready,' he told the official news agency, 'to serve Spain in whatever post or responsibility may be of most use to her.' The Prince's remarks took his father completely by surprise, but there was nothing he could do to stop the giddy progress of events.

On 12 July Franco called Juan Carlos to see him and in the course of a forty-five-minute conversation told him he intended naming him as his successor. Ten days later Franco announced his choice to the Cortes which endorsed it by 491 votes to 19 with 9 abstentions. To drive home the point that Juan Carlos's title to the throne derived from his being Franco's protégé rather than Alfonso XIII's grandson, he was henceforth to be known as Prince of Spain, not as Prince of Asturias, the title traditionally accorded to the royal heir.

The next day Juan Carlos swore his oath of loyalty to Franco and to the Movimiento Nacional. Don Juan, who had let it be known that he was at sea in his yacht, put in that afternoon at a little village on the Portuguese coast so that he could watch the proceedings on television in a fishermen's bar. His only comment when his son had finished speaking was, 'Nicely read, Juanito, nicely read.' Back in

Estoril, he disbanded his Privy Council and issued a statement bluntly pointing out that 'I have not been consulted and the freely expressed opinion of the Spanish people has not been sought.' From then on he maintained increasingly friendly contacts with some of the leading figures in the democratic opposition, including some who had once been openly republican. Then in June 1975 he made a speech at a dinner in Barcelona lambasting Franco and his regime and was banned from re-entering the country.

As for Juan Carlos, his problems did not end with his being named successor. Neither the Carlists nor the Falangists were prepared to give up their aspirations. Carlos Hugo decided that his cause would best be served by forming a political party which espoused left-wing socialism and workers' control. The most extreme traditional Carlists subsequently rallied to his younger brother, Sixto Enrique.*

A more serious threat to Juan Carlos emerged when, in 1972, Alfonso de Borbón-Dampierre married Franco's eldest granddaughter, María del Carmen Martínez Bordíu. As a consequence several members of Franco's family – in particular his wife, Doña Carmen – threw their weight behind the conspiracy hatched by Alfonso's Falangist champions to put him on the throne of Spain. Doña Carmen tried to have their marriage declared a Royal Wedding and it was proposed that Alfonso should be addressed as 'His Royal Highness'. Both ideas were scotched only by Juan Carlos's personal intervention. Franco's royalism had always been in part a reflection of his own kingly pretensions,† and throughout the last years of his life there was some apprehension among Juan Carlos's supporters that the *Caudillo* might change his mind and transfer the

---

*In 1976 when followers of Carlos Hugo made the Carlists' traditional annual pilgrimage to the top of Montejurra, a high hill near Pamplona, they were set upon by a band of armed right-wingers led by Sixto Enrique. One man died and several were wounded.

†Among other things, Franco felt empowered to hand out titles of nobility. Today more than thirty Spanish families owe their peerages to the munificence of the son of a naval supply officer. One of the aristocrats he created, Pedro Barrié de la Maza, head of the Galician hydroelectricity concern, Fuerzas Eléctricas del Noroeste Sociedad Anónima (FENOSA), was allowed to take his title from the name of his firm, becoming the Count of Fenosa.

succession to Alfonso in order to make himself the founder of a dynasty.

Juan Carlos's astute conduct of affairs during the first year of his reign did much to heal the breach between him and his father. In early 1977, as it became clear that Suárez's government was heading towards the setting-up of a fully-fledged democracy, Don Juan decided to give his son the public endorsement he had so far withheld. On 14 May at the Palacio de la Zarzuela he renounced his rights to the throne in a speech reiterating his faith in democracy. At the end of it he stood to attention, bowed deeply and declared, 'Majesty. Spain. Above all.' Don Juan will, I suspect, go down in history as one of the tragic figures of the twentieth century – the king who never was, a simple man who always said that his happiest years were spent as an ordinary naval officer, an indecisive man caught between his distaste for a parvenu dictator and his responsibility for the survival of his dynasty, he nevertheless proved himself in the end to be wise enough and humble enough to recognize that, having lost a throne, he need not lose another son.

The same year also saw the beginning of the end of another, far more momentous, division within the Bourbon family. In October Carlos Hugo returned to Spain after nine years in exile and made it clear in his very first speech that he saw himself as the leader of a political party rather than the head of a rival dynasty. Five months later he and Juan Carlos met and in 1979 Carlos Hugo was granted Spanish citizenship. Since then, his party has virtually disappeared from the political scene.

On big occasions, Juan Carlos can still look a little awkward, and he has never truly acquired the knack of delivering a prepared speech with ease. It is in the slightly more informal atmosphere of audiences and receptions that the King is at his best. Outgoing and casual, he is blessed with a good sense of humour and a prodigious memory for names and faces. His easygoing, back-slapping manner goes down well in an unstuffy country.

The King drinks and smokes little – the occasional whisky and a cheroot now and again. He keeps fit with regular exercise and remains an active sportsman. Apart from sailing, he is keen on, and reputedly good at, skiing, squash, tennis and karate.

He also seems to have a boyish enthusiasm for technological

gadgetry. His office has a videotelephone connected to the Moncloa Palace, the Prime Minister's official residence, and an adjoining room is stuffed full of audio and video equipment, cameras, lenses and his short-wave radio set. But the videotelephone has a strictly practical justification and it could be that the King's expertise as a radio 'ham' was acquired for reasons of prudence. A number of monarchs have the same hobby, including King Hussein of Jordan, with whom Juan Carlos sometimes links up. Both no doubt recall that King Hassan of Morocco's ability to operate a two-way radio saved his life — and his throne — during a coup in the early seventies.

Queen Sofía has undergone a noticeable change over the past few years. In early middle age, the retiring daughter of a formidable mother has become a woman of confidence and poise. As with her husband, the less formal the occasion, the more favourable the impression she creates. She herself has recognized that she has a distinctly forbidding 'ceremonial expression', like that of Queen Elizabeth of England. But she is capable of breaking into a dazzling smile which implies a likeable personality behind it.

There is a lot of uncontrived evidence to suggest that this is indeed the case. The reporters who follow her on official visits abroad think the world of her. In a characteristic gesture, she and her eldest daughter, Elena, carried out baskets of food to the journalists 'doorstepping' them on holiday in Mallorca a few years ago.

But Sofía's charms are discreet ones and in a country where forceful personalities are appreciated, reserve is all too often mistaken for coldness or slyness. It is probably fair to say that, instinctively, the Spaniard in the street takes to the Queen less than to her husband. She has said that she now feels that Spain, not Greece, is her homeland, but she has undoubtedly had problems in adapting. In an interview on her fiftieth birthday, she was asked what she most liked and disliked about the Spanish. Her response was frank: 'I admire [their] generosity, courtesy, gaiety — and pride when it is kept within bounds. I admire less — not to say detest — the exaggeration of that pride, and also covetousness.'

The Queen's enthusiasms are wide-ranging. With one idiosyncratic exception, they are all in some way intellectual, humanitarian or artistic. Appropriately enough for a Greek, she is keen on archaeology. When she was younger, Sofía took part in several excavations and wrote two books on her discoveries in collaboration with her sister, Irene. She is also known to have taken an interest in subjects as varied as UFOs and the Sephardic Jews, whose history and culture she was studying at the Universidad Autónoma in Madrid when Franco died and she had to give up her course.

She has a passion for classical, and especially Baroque, music. She plays the piano and is a regular concert-goer. She has also done a lot to promote the cause of Spanish performers and composers both inside and outside the country, and in recognition of her contribution, the national chamber orchestra is named after her. Montserrat Caballé and Mstislav Rostropovich are among the Queen's personal friends.

Sofía, who was once a children's nurse back in Greece, is on record as saying she would like to have gone on to be a paediatrician. Today she is the active head of two organizations dedicated to children's welfare. But she has also said that if she had not been born a royal she would not have minded being a hairdresser. Above all, Queen Sofía gives the impression of wanting to live as ordinary a life as her circumstances will allow. 'There's only one thing I really hate about my work,' she once said, 'and that's having to try on dresses.' Ironically, since she is said to be the most prudent of her family, the Queen is the only one who has been fined for speeding, one summer on Mallorca.

She is reputed to be deeply religious but it is noticeable that she arranged for all her children to be sent to secular schools. Nothing is known for certain about her political attitudes, but her views on other subjects suggest a woman of liberal leanings. She objects to the wearing of furs, as well as to bullfighting, and is something of a vegetarian. The schools she chose for her children are known for their progressive methods and one of the most telling anecdotes about her concerns the primary school which Prince Felipe attended. Some of the parents, who felt that the cost of meals was too high, decided to boycott them and send their children to school with packed lunches. Queen Sofía took their side and thereafter the heir to the throne turned up every morning with sandwiches in his satchel.

There is a school of thought which holds that Sofía, whose gentle looks are said to belie a will of iron, may have had as much of an impact on recent Spanish history as her husband. The young Princess, so the theory goes, was horrified by the hold that Franco and his wife exerted over Juan Carlos and set about making him into his own man, converting him to the view that no monarchy supported by the followers of a totalitarian regime could survive in the late twentieth century. How much truth there is in this will not be known for many a long year, if ever. But it is noteworthy that the future King began his secret meetings with politicians and others shortly after marrying Sofía.

As a couple, their closest friends are Sofía's brother, ex-King Constantine, and his wife Anne-Marie, who often spend time at Marivent during the summer. Among reigning royalty, they are probably closest to the British royal family, to whom they are both related. For more than a decade, however, contacts between the two monarchies were limited by the continuing dispute over Gibraltar. It was not until 1985, when the Spanish government lifted the restrictions imposed on the Rock by Franco, that the way was cleared for a state visit to Britain by the King and Queen the following year.

In recent years, growing interest has inevitably focused on the royal couple's children. The eldest is paradoxically the least well known to the Spanish public. Although friends say she has a lively sense of humour, Princess Elena is a shy person. Of the three children, she appears to be the most uncomfortable at official functions. She trained as a primary-school teacher and taught for a short while at her old school, but has since ceased to work. She is a keen horsewoman and is said to be by far the best rider in the family. At the opening ceremony of the Barcelona Olympics in 1992, she touched a lot of hearts when her brother – bearing the Spanish flag – led the national team into the stadium and the TV cameras picked out Elena doing her best to smile as tears gushed down her cheeks.

Of all the younger members of Europe's royal families, her sister Cristina has to be counted one of the most attractive – blessed with pleasant looks, easy charm and brains. She has also won considerable distinction for herself as a yachtswoman. In 1988, she qualified as a reserve for the Spanish team at the Seoul Olympics and carried the

Spanish flag at the opening ceremony. Four years earlier, she had entered the Universidad Complutense in Madrid to study politics. Since graduating, she has gone to work in Barcelona for the cultural foundation set up by Spain's biggest savings bank, La Caixa.

As a Spanish journalist once wrote, to address the heir to the throne as 'Your Highness' is merely to do honour to the truth, for Prince Felipe has grown to almost two metres (6' 7"). His height gives him an immediate advantage over all but a handful of his future subjects, though it means he can scarcely move around incognito.

Felipe made his first official appearance in 1975 when his father was proclaimed King. Two years later he was given the title of Prince of Asturias, which is traditionally bestowed on the heir to the Spanish throne. In 1980, a Prince of Asturias Foundation was set up to give awards for distinction in the arts and sciences. Its annual prize-giving ceremony, at which the Prince presides, provided an early opportunity for him to become accustomed to formal occasions. It was to one such that he gave his first public speech when he was thirteen.

By then, though, he had already had a harsh lesson in the realities of his position. At his father's insistence, he spent the whole of the night of 23 February 1981 at the King's side watching him foil the coup attempt. Since then, the Crown Prince has been none-too-gradually introduced to the duties of an heir. In 1985 he was sent to a school in Canada for a year before returning to Spain to do one-year courses at each of the three military academies. In 1988 he entered the Universidad Autónoma in Madrid to study Law and Economics, and five years later he began a course in international relations at Georgetown University in Washington DC.

His personal preference at school had been for the sciences, though he also appears to have inherited his mother's fondness for music. Those who have worked with him say he is both affable and thorough.

In the long term, the challenge he faces will be to find a useful role with which to fill the years until he succeeds to the throne. In the short term, it will be to find a wife who can be Spain's future Queen. The Prince's love life has already been at the centre of a controversy with potentially far-reaching implications.

In 1989, he began to go out with a young aristocrat, Isabel Sartorius. Rumour soon had it, firstly, that the Prince was deeply in love and, secondly, that his parents disapproved. Isabel certainly had a lot more experience of life. Three years older than the Prince, she had had a sophisticated and cosmopolitan upbringing, as her twice-divorced mother moved in and out of the international jet-set. The following year, though, things took an altogether more serious turn when the press linked some of her mother's friends to allegations of cocaine smuggling. But no proof was ever supplied to support the claims, and attention switched to another explanation for the royal couple's supposed hostility.

It was pointed out that one of the 'house rules' of the Spanish royal family, laid down by Charles III in the eighteenth century, is that if any of its members wish to marry a commoner they must first renounce their rights to the throne. What made the situation all the more difficult, according to this view, was that King Juan Carlos's own claim to the throne rested on just such a renunciation – that of his uncle Alfonso.* Since Alfonso subsequently died without issue, the point would seem to be academic. What is more, the Queen, who was supposed to be firmest in her objections to the liaison, had appeared to dismiss Charles III's ordinance in an interview she gave in 1989. 'All that we ask,' she said of her children, 'is that they marry someone nice and decent who looks after them.'

Spanish public opinion was consistently, and overwhelmingly, in favour of an eventual marriage between Felipe and Isabel. But that now looks most unlikely. In 1993, after months of on–off speculation, Isabel Sartorius (who had left to live in London) gave an interview to *El Mundo* in which she made it plain that the relationship was finished, though she gave no reason.

A damaging legacy of the affair may have been its effect on the Prince's attitude to the press, which had shown an insatiable appetite for details of the state of the relationship and had indulged in much speculation. 'If there really had been anything in it,' he once remarked bitterly, 'the press would have fouled it up.' This is very different in tone from anything said in public by either of his

* See above, p. 88.

parents. But then, coverage of the private lives of the King and Queen, and even comment on their public roles, has until recently been taboo. The King, it must be remembered, has been viewed not only as the architect but also the guarantor of Spanish democracy, and for as long as the survival of democracy was felt to be at stake he was protected by the voluntary restraint of editors. The most they permitted themselves was a murmur of disapproval whenever the King's enthusiasm for dangerous sports brought him to grief.

They did not, for example, focus on the fact that relations between the royal couple often seem cool. Asked about them in an interview published on her fiftieth birthday, the Queen merely replied, 'Fine, given the differences that can exist between two people.'

But in the summer of 1990, the pact began to crumble. *Tribuna* published a detailed report on the gaudy jet-set which follows the King to Mallorca, and *El Mundo* chided him in an editorial for not breaking off his holiday because of the Gulf crisis. In different ways, the two articles highlighted the same problem.

The images of the King to which his subjects had become accustomed showed him aboard a yacht or otherwise enjoying himself. In fact, he does a lot on their behalf. He travels abroad frequently. He holds weekly civil and military audiences to keep himself in touch with the country, talks to the Prime Minister at least once a week, and attends the various ceremonial functions his job demands. But he is less involved than Queen Elizabeth, for instance, in the sort of activities which would make his endeavours more obvious to his people. Unlike her, he is not constantly opening hospitals and touring factories.

A passage that year in King Juan Carlos's Christmas address stressing the need to balance press freedom with responsibility prompted renewed criticism from the media, who felt that, after a year in which they had helped to uncover several scandals, it was a reminder they did not need. Unhappily for the King, just two days later the most frequently aired criticism of him again drew media attention when he crashed his Porsche while driving to a ski resort in the Pyrenees.

Then in July 1992 it emerged that the King had made two

unannounced visits to Switzerland without the Queen in less than a week. The official explanation, that he had gone abroad for a rest, only served to prompt fears for his health while at the same time generating a certain degree of scepticism. The following month, *El Mundo* reported that an Italian magazine had linked the King with a Mallorcan woman who was also named at about this time in reports in the British and French press. The article caused a storm of protest, not least from rival newspapers. There was talk of an 'orchestrated campaign', and even Felipe González weighed in with a claim that it was all the result of foreign jealousy over Spain's international success. *El Mundo* dropped the subject, and has never returned to it. For the time being, the taboo on references to the royal couple's private life has been reasserted.

The speculation about the King, the Queen and their son all took place during a period of about three years; with hindsight, this may be seen as a make-or-break phase in the evolution of the monarchy. The same period, lasting from 1989 until 1992, also revealed evidence of considerable upheaval at the palace. In 1991 the head of the King's secretariat, a distinguished former ambassador, José Joaquín Puig de Bellacasa, left the Zarzuela after less than a year in the job. Puig de Bellacasa, who had served the King before he came to the throne, had been instrumental in introducing him to members of the opposition before Franco's death. Energetic, cosmopolitan, forthright and open-minded, he had been thought to be precisely the kind of person needed to steer the King towards a new role. Then, two years later, General Sabino Fernández Campos, the Head of the Royal Household, also departed in circumstances and for reasons that were equally unclear. One theory, which he denied, was that there had been a clash over a film made for British television. Another was said to be the General's opposition to the King's cooperation in a book about him written by the Marquis of Vilallonga.*

What appears to have worried General Fernández Campos was the degree to which the King's true opinions were allowed to emerge – both in the book itself, which was based on a series of

---

*Ironically, it was Vilallonga who had predicted years before that the King would go down in history as 'Juan Carlos the Brief'.

lengthy tape-recorded conversations, and in the interviews given by the author in the run-up to publication.

Perhaps the most striking of these was what the Marquis of Vilallonga called 'a sort of obsession about not saying anything that might be regarded as offensive' to the instigators of the 1981 coup. He told interviewers that the King had struck out or toned down a number of the passages which dealt with the coup, and even objected to its leader, General Armada, being described as a 'traitor'. As their Commander-in-Chief, though, the King probably understands better than anyone the sensibilities of his officers. His own reported sensitivity is worth bearing in mind when weighing up the assurances, which Spaniards of all kinds will give you, to the effect that the threat of military intervention has gone and will never return.

CHAPTER 8

The Army: Back in Step?

The reaction of Spaniards to Iraq's invasion of Kuwait underlined an important difference between the new Spain and the old one. A country with one of the most formidable military traditions on earth – birthplace of El Cid and cradle of the *conquistadores* – had become a nation of pacifists.

The media's treatment of the sailors who made Spain's modest contribution to the UN-enforced blockade of Iraq and Kuwait ranged from the appalled to the mawkish. It was rarely pointed out that none of Spain's three ships was actually in the Gulf, or that the government had ruled out their engaging in hostilities.

'A lot don't know how to swim and others get seasick,' ran the headline on *Diario 16*'s report of their departure. An *El Mundo* cartoonist depicted a sailor weeping over a letter to his parents as he informed them that he was going into battle the next day. Extensive coverage was given to the protests of relatives left behind. Often the report was illustrated with a photograph of a mother holding up a picture of her son, just as if he had died.

The government railed at the media for spreading gloom and alarm. But the evidence suggested that they were reflecting faithfully the mood of the nation. Spain saw some of the biggest anti-war demonstrations in Europe. Polls suggested that over two-thirds of the population was against the war – the highest proportion among the bigger European nations after Germany – and that a clear majority was against sanctions as well, presumably because Spain was involved in the blockade required to enforce them. One survey, in the magazine *Cambio 16*, indicated that the course of action favoured by the largest number of people was simply to 'keep out of a conflict between Arab countries'.

There were, it is true, special circumstances surrounding the Gulf crisis. It was the first time since the 1920s that Spain had been embroiled in an overseas conflict, and part of the reaction was no doubt caused by the shock of getting caught up in world affairs after so many years of isolation. The Spanish, moreover, had always taken the Arab side in the dispute with Israel, and public opinion was sympathetic to the Iraqi argument that Desert Shield, and later Desert Storm, were anti-Arab initiatives. Of crucial importance was the fact that the Spanish ships which took part in the blockade were partly manned by conscripts. The public's reaction to the decision two years later to commit to the UN force in Bosnia a contingent made up exclusively of professionals and volunteers was noticeably more muted. But it is possible that another reason why the Spanish were so ready to support the Bosnian initiative was that it had been sold to them as peacekeeping; numerous surveys have highlighted that a strong streak of pacifism runs through contemporary Spanish society.

The reasons can only be guessed at. Resentment at enforced military service is doubtless one. The communal memory of civil war and dictatorship are perhaps others. But it could also be because it was soldiers – Spanish soldiers – who gave most of today's Spaniards the biggest shock of their lives.

Just as all Americans remember where they were when they heard the news of President Kennedy's shooting, no Spaniard will ever forget what he or she was doing on the afternoon of Monday, 23 February 1981. That was when a detachment of Civil Guards led by the elaborately moustachioed Antonio Tejero burst into Congress, interrupting a broadcast debate on the appointment of the new Prime Minister. The millions of people listening to the proceedings on the radio heard, first, a series of confused shouts and then a sustained burst of gunfire. The intention was to force the assembled deputies on to the floor, but to everyone listening it sounded as if a madman had wiped out the entire political class of Spain.

How many army units were meant to have risen against the government during the hours that followed will probably never be known. In the event only the Motorized Division under Lieutenant-General Miláns del Bosch, based near Valencia, actually took to the streets. Cristina Soler Crespo, a resident of Valencia, scribbled down what she saw and heard as it happened. Her account, published some days later by the newspaper *El País*, evokes something of the terror and uncomprehending outrage of that night.

As I write these lines at 2 o'clock on a cold February morning, I can see a few metres from my window on the third floor of the Gran Vía in Valencia a tank – a huge, terrifying, green tank – parked calibrating its guns . . . aiming at thousands of windows, behind whose net curtains one can glimpse the terrified faces, the terrified eyes of peaceful citizens, of families with children, of old people who have seen these scenes before and are reliving the deaf, dumb, impotent panic of those who don't understand . . . Lorries full of soldiers arrive. Army jeeps and police cars occupy every corner along the wide avenue and the birds take to the air, as startled as the humans. Now the lights in the garden that runs down the centre have been put out and the scene takes on the appearance of a nightmare. I can see that the three young men in the nearest tank are no more than twenty years old. Their gun is now definitely aimed at the PSOE office with its red flag opposite my window. The people at the windows above it draw their curtains and put out the lights.

The events of 23–24 February made real something that the majority of Spaniards had dreaded ever since Franco's death. The threat of military intervention had distorted almost every aspect of Spanish life, conditioning the way that politicians approached a range of issues and, in particular, regional policy, making them much more wary than they would otherwise have been. There again, by the standards of Spain's history, involvement by the army is the norm rather than the exception.

The origins of the army's enthusiasm for meddling in the affairs of state have been traced as far back as the eighteenth century, when senior officers were called upon to play an unusually prominent role in the administration. But it was the Napoleonic invasion in 1808 which created the preconditions for that persistent military intervention which became the hallmark of Spanish politics during the last century.

One of the paradoxes of the War of Independence which followed the invasion was that while the middle-class administrators and officers who filled the vacuum left by the King and his court were busy fighting the invaders, they adopted many of the ideas that the French were bent on propagating. Of these the most basic was that the monarch should be subject to the constraints of a written constitution. However, Fernando VII, who was put back on the throne in 1814, refused to acknowledge that times had changed; the result was that his reign was punctuated at frequent intervals by uprisings led by officers who had served in the War of Independence and who sought to impose a constitution. The upheavals under Fernando gave the world two new words. One, which was coined to describe the opponents of absolute monarchy, was *liberal*.* The other, first used by Major Rafael de Riego to describe his declaration of a rebellion against the crown in 1820, was *pronunciamiento*. At first, *pronunciamiento* was used to describe only an initial call to arms, but it subsequently came to mean an uprising in its entirety. By 1936 there would have been no fewer than forty-four of them.

Fernando died in 1833 at a time when his heir, Isabel, was not yet three years old, and Spain came to be ruled by that least authoritative form of government – a regency, exercised in this case by Fernando's widow, María Cristina. Her shaky authority was still further undermined by the dynastic wrangle that had led Fernando's brother, Carlos, to declare war on the government and recruit to his cause all those who had a vested interest in the perpetuation of absolutism. The Carlist war made María Cristina exceptionally dependent on her army, so that when her two leading generals demanded that she agree to a constitution she was in no position to refuse.

In one sense, Spain was well-suited to a two-party parliamentary democracy. From the very beginning the *liberales* had been split into two groups, which came to be known as the Moderates and the Progressives. Unfortunately, Spain's economic backwardness and political inexperience were such that the idea of one party voluntarily surrendering power to another by means of fair elections never really took root and the politicians soon got into the habit of getting the army to oust the government instead. In a society where

---

* Although the word has since come to denote someone to the left of the centre of the political spectrum, it is important to understand that the nineteenth-century Spanish *liberal* would be considered a conservative in the twentieth century. To distinguish them from modern liberals I shall continue to use italics whenever I refer to the original Spanish variety.

it was demonstrably impossible to assess public opinion through the ballot box, the generals and colonels acted ostensibly as interpreters of the will of the people. Throughout Isabel's reign, power usually changed hands by means of *pronunciamientos* by officers allied to one or other *liberal* camp – men like Espartero, O'Donnell and the indomitable Ramón María Narváez who, when asked by his death-bed confessor to forgive his enemies, is said to have refused on the grounds that, 'I have killed them all.'

Perhaps inevitably it was a *pronunciamiento*, led by an alliance of Progressive generals and admirals, which finally robbed Isabel of her throne in 1868. Unfortunately for the Progressives, however, their idea of importing a more amenable ruler from abroad did not work and the initiative passed outside the *liberal* camp to those who did not want a monarchy of any kind, constitutional or absolute. The politicians who ruled Spain during the short-lived First Repub-lic were not only anti-monarchist, but anti-militarist. They espoused several ideas which the officer corps abhorred. In particular, a significant number of them favoured turning Spain into a federal state. In this respect they had something in common with the Carlists, whose dream of putting the clock back to the eighteenth century included restoring traditional local rights and privileges. To the officer corps, whose principal task had been the suppression of Carlism, the devolution of power in any form was anathema and it was altogether appropriate that the Republic should have been overthrown by a general seeking to forestall the introduction of federalism.*

The experience of the First Republic persuaded the *liberales* that they had to make a two-party system work, and the restoration of the monarchy in 1874 ushered in a period of contrived democracy in which the opposing *liberal* factions, re-christened Conservatives and Liberals, swapped power by means of rigged elections in an effort to keep the Republicans and other radicals at bay. Almost incidentally, this system succeeded in putting an end to the *pronun-ciamientos*. Its failing was that the only sections of society whose

---

*General Pavía's coup which brought down the First Republic in 1873 almost certainly provided the inspiration for Tejero's intervention. Like Pavía, Tejero led his men into the Cortes and ordered them to fire in the air.

interests were represented were the upper and middle classes. As parts of Spain became industrialized over the next fifty years, an ever larger and stronger urban working class was left without a voice in parliament. Therefore it frequently took its grievances on to the streets and successive governments had to call on the army to restore order.

The same period also saw a string of humiliating defeats overseas. It started with a forlorn struggle to hold on to Cuba, which ended abruptly in 1898 when the United States declared war on Spain, wiped out her fleet and deprived her not only of Cuba but also of Puerto Rico and the Philippines. Six years later Spain received compensation of a kind when she secured two small chunks of Morocco. But almost immediately she was faced with resistance in the northern sector. From 1909 until 1925 she had to contend with a full-scale war there, waged by the tribes of the Rif mountains,* which, although it was eventually won by the Spanish, was blighted by a succession of disasters for them. In the worst of these, caused by the defeat at Annual in 1921, they lost 15,000 lives and 5,000 square kilometres of territory in a matter of days. Like the leaders of many a defeated army before and since, Spain's officers sought to explain their lack of success in terms of the alleged incompetence or indifference of the politicians 'back home'. In the process, they became excessively sensitive to criticism. After the 1905 local elections, for example, the victorious party in Catalonia held a massive banquet that inspired the humorous weekly *Cu-Cut* to publish a cartoon showing a soldier asking a civilian about a group of people he saw gathered in front of a door.

---

*The Moroccan war saw the creation of what was to become the most renowned unit in the Spanish army – the Legion, founded in 1920 by Lieutenant-Colonel José Millán Astray. Like the French Legion, upon which it was modelled, the Spanish Legion was meant to have been composed of foreigners and was originally called the *Tercio de Extranjeros*. In fact, foreigners never accounted for more than a minority. But the Legionnaires, with their distinctive quick march, exotic mascots and tasselled forage caps, soon became a formidable combat force with a strong *esprit de corps*. Their most distinctive characteristic was an attitude towards death that bordered on the affectionate and which perhaps owed something to the Moslem tradition of enthusiastic martyrdom that so inspired their earliest enemies. Millán Astray called them *los novios de la muerte* (the fiancés of death).

'The victory banquet,' the civilian explained.

'Victory! Ah, then they must be civilians,' said the officer.

This cartoon so enraged the military that to appease them the Cortes passed a law that was to bedevil relations between the armed forces and the rest of society until only a few years ago – the *Ley de Jurisdicciones*, according to which any offence against the army or its members could be tried by a court martial.

By 1923, when General Primo de Rivera seized power and set up a dictatorship, the Spanish army officer had begun to play the roles of both policeman and judge. And whether he was serving in the hills of Morocco or behind a desk in Madrid it was obvious that the distance between him and his fellow-citizens was growing. This posed a special problem for a body of men accustomed to regard themselves as instruments of the collective will and they began to evolve the curious belief that, even though they might not reflect the circumstantial preferences of the electorate, they none the less embodied the eternal values of the fatherland. A distinction was beginning to be drawn between Spain and the Spanish which in 1936 would serve to justify a war against the majority of Spaniards as a war in defence of Spain. Even so, it required a prolonged bout of near-anarchy under the Second Republic to create the conditions for a successful uprising.

What is so striking about the army's role during the century that elapsed between Isabel's accession and the outbreak of the civil war is not that its political outlook changed so much, but that it changed so little. At first sight, it appears that an officer class fervent in its defence of liberalism during the nineteenth century was somehow transformed into a potent force for reaction in the twentieth. But that is more than anything the result of confusion over the changing meaning of the word 'liberal'. What in fact happened was that as the centre of gravity of political life moved steadily to the left, as it did throughout Europe during this period, the officer corps stoutly continued to occupy the same area of the political spectrum, clinging to a view of politics which may have seemed radical by comparison with the absolutism of Fernando VII, but which was beginning to look somewhat conservative by the time of the First Republic and positively reactionary by the time of the Second Republic.

Having said that, it is important to stress that the area of the political spectrum occupied by the officer corps was always quite a broad one. When, as occurred under Isabel, the focus of political life fell more or less in the middle of it, its members could appear severely divided. Events during the First Republic served to make the views of the officer class somewhat more uniform than they had been, but they continued to vary significantly, as the 1936 uprising showed. By no means every officer joined the revolt and a sizeable minority – including the majority of senior officers – stuck by the Republic.

What really changed things was the outcome of the civil war. The 3,000 officers who had remained loyal to the Republic and survived the war were purged from the army, and about 10,000 young men who had joined the Nationalists as *alfereces provisionales* (temporary subalterns) and been put into the field after a brief training course were allowed to stay in. As a result the officer corps became considerably more homogeneous and reactionary, and this process continued as, with the passage of time, an increasingly large proportion of the officer class came to be made up of post-civil-war recruits – young men who had actively chosen to serve a dictatorship and were more inclined to define themselves simply as 'Francoists' than as supporters of a particular 'family' within the regime.

Knowing he could count on their loyalty, Franco encouraged them into spheres of activity that in other countries would be regarded as pre-eminently civilian. Officers were prominent in politics, for example – not only did each of the three services have a minister of its own drawn from among its serving officers, but the *Caudillo* often appointed generals, admirals and air marshals to head ministries quite unconnected with defence. Of the 114 ministers who served in his cabinets, 32 were military men and 11 of them were given non-defence portfolios.

The military also played an important role in the economy. From quite an early stage – long before *pluriempleo* was common in society as a whole – Franco followed a policy of using officers as executives in companies owned by the Instituto Nacional de Industria (INI). The navy and air force were given extensive control over merchant shipping and civil aviation, so that port administration and air traffic control, for example, both came under the control of the armed services. Most of the officers in the two paramilitary police forces were drawn from the armed forces, as were most of the members of the intelligence services. In addition, officers were often called upon to try terrorist suspects at courts martial. All this inevitably created an impression among officers that their job had as much to do with controlling society as with defending its interests with the use – or threat – of force.

The Institutional Law of the State, passed in 1967, which was the nearest thing that the dictatorship had to a constitution, made the armed forces responsible for guaranteeing 'the unity and independence of the country, the integrity of her territory, national security and the defence of the institutional system'. In other words, the armed forces were charged with protecting the regime from its internal as well as its external enemies.

When Juan Carlos ascended the throne, probably the largest ideologically committed faction among army officers was made up of monarchists. But they were almost certainly outnumbered by those who simply regarded themselves as Francoists and were content to accept as their ruler and commander-in-chief anyone chosen by Franco. However, they regarded Juan Carlos as King by virtue of the oath he had sworn in 1969 rather than by virtue of his Bourbon blood. The question that soon emerged was whether the armed forces would regard the introduction of democracy as a betrayal of that oath. If they did, it would, in their eyes, negate the legitimacy of the government appointed by the King and give them a pretext for intervention.

A month after his first government took power, Suárez held a meeting with Spain's most senior officers at which he set out his plans and asked for their support. The outcome was a florid communiqué, the gist of which was that the armed forces would put up with the government's reforms provided they were approved by the Cortes (which at that time was still filled with Franco's supporters). During the meeting, however, it appears that the officers got the impression that he would consult them before legalizing the Communist Party. When, the following year, Suárez was prompted by events and – it would seem – the King to legalize the PCE, the reaction within the officer corps was one of outrage. Only one of the three armed service ministers actually handed in his resignation, but the damage done to Suárez and the government's standing in the eyes of the military was immense. Thereafter, there was always a mutinous undercurrent bubbling away just below the surface of army life.

The Centrists responded by virtually abnegating responsibility for discipline within the armed forces. In the five years between 1977 and 1982, there were several occasions on which officers were punished by the military authorities for expressing support for the Constitution while others who openly abused it were let off. The 1981 coup was itself a consequence of the UCD's timidity. Both Tejero and Miláns del Bosch had been caught plotting against the government, yet were allowed to continue in positions of responsibility.

The torrent of indignation unleashed by the coup must have proved to all but the most quixotic officers that, had Tejero and his masters succeeded, they would not have been able to count on a significant measure of support from the population, as Franco had done. That, as much as anything, explains why the danger of renewed military intervention has receded so quickly in the years since 1981. That, and the fact that the political attitudes embraced by most of the rest of society in the seventies spread further through the army during the eighties.

However, it is also the case that it was not until after the Socialists took power that the public's fear of another coup abated or that evidence of plotting in the army receded.* For this the Socialists deserve full credit – particularly the bearded and bespectacled former mayor of Barcelona, Narcís Serra, who served as Defence Minister from 1982 until 1991, when he was promoted to become Felipe González's deputy Prime Minister.

Without compromising their undertakings to the electorate, the Socialists settled many of the issues which had been causing such anxiety in army messes. They gave the country the firm government

---

*For some time it was assumed that the last attempt by army officers to overthrow the elected government was one known to have been foiled in October 1982, shortly before the Socialists came to office. But in 1991 a detailed, though unsourced, report in El País said a plot to kill the King and Queen, the Prime Minister and the heads of the armed forces had been detected in 1985. The report did not make clear whether the conspirators were identified or, if so, whether any action was taken against them.

it had been lacking ever since the UCD started to fall apart. They made it clear that the granting of additional powers to the regions would not be allowed to endanger Spain's unity. And above all, they applied to the army itself the strict discipline whose absence had so disconcerted its officers since Franco's death.

The Socialists have also taken Spain into the European Union. Anyone plotting a coup in the future would do so in the knowledge that if it succeeded it could bring about Spain's expulsion from the EU and the dire consequences that that would cause.

But has the army's fondness for dabbling in politics been cured for ever? The majority of Spaniards – more than 70 per cent, according to an *El País* poll in 1991 – would say 'yes'. Certainly, the possibility of another military intervention appears remote. Spain looks more and more like one of those stable, prosperous nations in which tanks just do not come rolling down the street.

But 'for ever' is still a long time, and Europe is becoming a more turbulent continent. As has been remarked, today's Spaniards are profoundly reluctant to look back. They already talk about the coup attempt as if it had taken place in the last century. But it did not. The period which has elapsed since is still a good deal shorter than the 161 years of intermittent military involvement that came before. More to the point, it is also a good deal shorter than the longest period within those 161 years during which Spain was free of coups and *pronunciamientos*.

Evidence of the sort of views which still exist in the armed forces surfaced in 1993 when the defence staff college published the proceedings of a seminar on relations between society and the armed forces. 'The government, the trade unions and the employers' federations are too busy brawling to give a damn about the economy or the welfare of the people,' declared an artillery colonel. Opposition to the armed forces, he believed, was the result of a 'well-orchestrated disinformation campaign generated fundamentally in Marxist circles'.

The greatest concern, though, which was shared by officers less evidently reactionary than the colonel, had to do with Spain's regional nationalist movements. As we have seen, the unity of Spain has been the overriding preoccupation of its armed forces since the First Republic. A factor scarcely referred to in Spain these days, but which is of the utmost potential importance, is that the 1978 constitution makes the armed forces responsible for preserving that unity. They 'have as their mission to guarantee the sovereignty and independence of Spain, defend its constitutional arrangements *and its territorial integrity*' (my italics). It is difficult to read that passage without concluding that they not only have a right but a duty to step in if Spain's unity is threatened. But who is to decide when that is the case? The King? The government? The Chiefs of Defence Staff? The constitution does not say.

Its reference to the armed forces' responsibility for territorial integrity would almost certainly have been used by Tejero and his backers as justification for their coup if it had succeeded. That, though, would have involved them in a logical inconsistency, because the very constitution which appears to empower the armed forces to intervene also creates the system of regional government to which the conspirators so objected. No such problem arises if the arrangements can be depicted as exceeding the limits of that constitution. But as we shall see in greater detail later, the debate between the central and regional governments is increasingly focusing on areas where it will be a matter of opinion as to whether the deal struck is in fact constitutional.

One could feel more confident that the Spanish armed forces would never again meddle in politics if they had an obvious mission and the means with which to perform it.

Under Franco, the only fighting the army had to do was against Spain's colonial subjects in North Africa – and there was precious little of that. The *Caudillo* was nothing if not a realist and for all his talk of reviving Spain's empire he realized that the tide was turning against colonialism. One after another, Spain's colonial possessions were relinquished at the first whiff of trouble. Spanish northern Morocco went in 1956. Spanish southern Morocco went in 1958 along with Ifni, a territorial enclave opposite the Canary Islands which had been ceded to Spain in 1868. Río Muni and Fernando Po jointly gained their independence as Equatorial Guinea in 1968. Back home, Franco re-instituted the division of the country into captaincies-general, each commanded by a lieutenant-general with significant civil as well as military powers. But unlike many of his predecessors he did not use the army on the streets to break up demonstrations.

The obvious role for the Spanish army after Franco's death was to join the fighting forces of the rest of the West in the confrontation with communism. But within three years of Spain's NATO membership being confirmed by the 1986 referendum, the Berlin Wall came down and the Soviet Union's influence crumbled, undermining NATO's original purpose. Since then, the Socialists have tried to provide the soldiers with an additional role by involving them heavily in the UN's peacekeeping activity. In 1989, the army got its first experience of such an operation when seven of its officers donned sky-blue berets to join the mission supervising the withdrawal of Cuban troops from Angola. Just three years later, Spain had more officers serving under the UN flag than any other country in the world. They were to be found not only in Angola but in Kurdistan, Bosnia, Namibia, Equatorial Guinea, Haiti, and various parts of Central America.

The fact that a unit with such a bloodcurdling reputation as the Legion should be found peacekeeping in ex-Yugoslavia is often cited by Socialist politicians as evidence of the extent to which Spain has changed under their rule. On the other hand, the speed with which the politicians have rushed so many of Spain's soldiers into this new role may show that they continue to harbour doubts about what the military could get up to if not kept busy.

What is clear is that the Spanish army still has some way to go before, in the jargon of the military sociologists, it completes the transition from an 'institutional' model, in which the military is held to be the instrument of national values or the collective will, to an 'occupational' one, in which its sole aim is to be an efficient military force. It is a change which will require the undoing of almost two centuries of institutionalized ineffectiveness.

The War of Independence saw the recruitment of a large number of officers who were allowed to remain in the army afterwards. Throughout the nineteenth century there were usually about 10,000 of them – an acceptable enough figure in wartime when the army swelled to around 100,000, but a grotesque one in peacetime when there were fewer than half that number of men to command. In addition, politically inspired promotions ensured that the officer corps was absurdly top-heavy. The number of generals during this period rarely fell below 500. It seemed that the problem had at last been solved with the measures that were introduced under the Second Republic. But between 1936, when the normal officer-training programme was interrupted by the war, and 1946, when it was resumed, the army's net intake of officers was about 7,000. Before the civil war, the rate of commissions had been around 225 a year. So in ten years the army absorbed more than thirty years' worth of new entrants.

Laws were passed in 1953 and 1958 under which officers who wished to retire early were offered generous gratuities and pensions, but by the time the laws were passed, the civil war veterans were about thirty-five and forty respectively and they were understandably reluctant to embark on a new career in 'civvy street'. Moreover, the intake of the reconstituted Academia General Militar at Saragossa, small at first, was incomprehensibly allowed to grow as the years passed until in 1955 well over 300 new officers were commissioned.

Franco's way of reducing the ratio of officers to men was to keep a far larger number of men under arms than was needed. Immediately after the civil war, the army's strength was cut by about two-thirds (from a million men to about 340,000). By 1975 the number had fallen to 220,000, of whom more than 24,000 were officers. But this was still far more than was needed for Spain's defence and it was also out of all proportion to the size of the other armed services. In 1975 the strength of the navy was 46,600 and that of the air force was 35,700.

The whole of the first class to pass out of the reconstituted Academia General Militar became generals and although a degree of selectivity had to be imposed on their successors there was no selection of any kind until they reached the rank of colonel. Promotion up to the rank of colonel was dependent solely on length of service. Before any of the officers who had graduated from Saragossa in, say, 1960 could be promoted to a particular rank, *all* officers who passed out in 1959 had to have reached that rank. An officer's ability was reflected in the commands he was given, but there again his ability was assessed on the basis of the class list or *escalafón* drawn up at the end of each officer training course. On the day that he left Saragossa, therefore, an officer not only knew what rank he would hold thirty years later, but he also had a good idea of what sort of job he would be doing.

Ironically, Franco himself was an outstanding example of the shortcomings of the *escalafón* system. After passing out 251st in a class of 312, he rose faster than any officer before or since by dint of sheer bravery and skill in the field. Promoted to brigadier-general at the age of thirty-three, he is believed to have been the youngest general in Europe since Napoleon.

In the years following the end of the civil war the army, navy and air force ministries together accounted for about a third of government spending. All three services were well armed and equipped, and the pay of regular officers and NCOs compared favourably with that of other Spaniards during the forties. But once the threat of an Allied invasion had passed, Franco realized that there was no real need to invest heavily in the armed forces and he calculated, correctly, that he enjoyed sufficient prestige among his fellow-officers not to have to buy them off. From then on, defence spending as a proportion of total government expenditure fell steadily. Pay did not keep pace with the rise in the standard of living of the rest of society – especially during the *años de desarrollo* – and since the hours that Spanish army officers worked were not exactly demanding many took to doing another job in their spare time. Some worked as executives. Those from the more technical branches often held teaching posts in schools and universities.

Nevertheless, there were so many officers that paying them even a modest salary used up a large share of the defence budget. This in turn meant that proportionately less cash was available for buying and maintaining arms and equipment. 'Spanish officers,' wrote Juan Antonio Ansaldo, a distinguished Nationalist flier who became one of Franco's bitterest critics, 'suffer in silence like poor lads in front of a shop window on Christmas Eve.'

Franco's agreement with the United States whereby the Americans were allowed to set up bases in Spain required the Americans to give, loan or sell Spain outdated equipment at favourable prices. The air force got the best deal, acquiring their first jet fighters. But the army and navy remained woefully ill-equipped.

Shortly after Franco's death the authorities at the Academia General Militar conducted a survey of the cadets' attitudes and beliefs. The survey suffered from serious defects (for example, only four responses were available for each question). But nevertheless the results were intriguing. When asked, 'What is the most valuable factor for the efficiency of an army?', less than 6 per cent chose 'the quality of its equipment and the technical proficiency of its regular soldiers'. The most popular reply was 'the patriotism of its members'.

It was clear that, if the army was to be fit for any task other than overthrowing governments, it would need a thorough shake-up.

Barely a month after Suárez took office, Lieutenant-General Santiago y Díaz de Mendívil, the deputy Prime Minister with responsibility for Defence, resigned in protest at the government's plans for the legalization of trade unions and Suárez asked Lieutenant-General Manuel Gutiérrez Mellado, Chief of the General Staff, to take over.

With his pinched face, closely cropped moustache and heavy-rimmed spectacles, 'Guti', as he was nicknamed, looked the very image of a Francoist general. Indeed, he had spent most of his adult life in the service of the *Caudillo* – first as an undercover agent for the Nationalist side in the Republican zone during the civil war and later as a talented staff officer and unit commander. But his views were not those of a Francoist. 'The army,' he declared in a speech shortly after Franco's death, 'is there not to command but to serve.'

The general threw himself into the job with Herculean gusto. Working with only a modest staff, sleeping as little as three hours a night, he drafted a string of decrees that reformed the pay system, laid down the limits of political activity in the armed forces and abolished their jurisdiction over terrorist offences. Most important of all, he transformed the armed forces' command structure so that it began to resemble that of a democratic nation. Under Franco, the armed forces' most senior representatives – the head of the Alto Estado Mayor and the three armed forces ministers in the cabinet – all had direct, routine access to the head of government. The armed forces did not come under the control of the government. They were part of it.

Gutiérrez Mellado rendered superfluous the armed service ministers by making the Chiefs of Staff the commanders of their respective services, and then did the same to the head of the Alto Estado Mayor by transferring his powers to a newly-created joint chiefs of staff committee, the Junta de Jefes del Estado Mayor (JUJEM), comprising the three service chiefs and a chairman. By early 1977 the lines of command were quite clear. They led from the three services to the JUJEM, from the JUJEM to Gutiérrez Mellado and from him to Suárez. The armed forces had been put firmly under the thumb of the government and the way was open for the abolition of the three armed forces ministries and their replacement by a single Defence Ministry immediately after the general election of June 1977.

Gutiérrez Mellado became the first boss of the new ministry, but his eventual aim was to work himself out of a job by preparing the way for the appointment of a civilian Defence Minister. After the 1979 elections direct control of the armed forces was handed, for the first time in forty years, to someone who was not, nor ever had been, an officer: Agustín Rodríguez Sahagún. Even so, Gutiérrez Mellado retained a seat in the cabinet as deputy Prime Minister with responsibility for security and defence. It was not until 1981 when Suárez threw in the towel that Gutiérrez Mellado also withdrew from the government, thus enabling Calvo Sotelo to form a cabinet devoid of military ministers.

But by that time Gutiérrez Mellado had initiated a host of other reforms. One which came to fruition while he was still in office was a revision of the *Reales Ordenanzas*, the armed forces' standing orders which were drafted under Carlos III in the eighteenth century and which had never been altered since. The new, eminently modern, *Reales Ordenanzas* came into effect at the beginning of 1979. The same period also saw the introduction (belatedly, and under pressure from the Socialists and Communists, who made it a condition of their signing the Moncloa Pacts) of a law on military justice. The new act, which took effect in 1980, limited the jurisdiction of courts martial to the purely military sphere. The period following the coup saw the freezing of a whole series of laws, drawn up on Gutiérrez Mellado's orders, dealing with deployment, mobilization, training, military service and the defence industries.

Only two military reform bills got through the Cortes during Calvo Sotelo's premiership. However, they were both measures of cardinal importance. One gave the military authorities the power to remove officers from the active list for 'physical, psychological or professional incompetence' and changed the arrangements for retirement in such a way that the lower an officer's rank the sooner he was forced to retire. The other made promotion dependent in part on merit by stipulating that officers had to go through selection processes before being promoted to major and brigadier. The combined effect of these two laws, which came into force in 1981, was to allow the authorities to reduce the number of officers on the active list by removing the least talented among them – the longer it took an officer to get over the hurdles created by the second law the more likely it was that he would reach the age of retirement set for his rank by the first. Even so, every officer was guaranteed to reach the rank of colonel. But the two laws were deeply resented by those officers who had come to regard the army as a meal ticket for life. Their fears were played on by the ultra-right-wing press and the campaign against the officers responsible for drafting the reforms reached such a pitch that one of them – General Marcelo Aramendi – shot himself.

The 1981 reforms fell a long way short of what was logically required – to match the number of officers in each rank to the number of posts of corresponding importance. Although the annual intake of cadets had fallen steadily since Franco's death from a peak of more than 400 to just over 200, by the time the Socialists came to power there were still 21,800 officers – one for every eleven other ranks – of whom no fewer than 300 were generals. The Spanish army's officer corps was not only very large, but also very old. The average age for a general was sixty-two, that of a colonel fifty-eight and that of a captain thirty-eight.

The approach taken by the Socialists was based on an estimate of the number of officers that the army would need by the end of 1990. What it showed was that more than 5,000, almost a quarter of the total, would be superfluous.

A law was introduced which carefully avoided tampering with the system of promotion. Officers were allowed to continue working their way up the scale of ranks largely according to age, but were not guaranteed a posting. Those who failed to qualify for one were offered the chance, in effect, of retiring on full salary. And not only that; as members of the so-called 'transitory reserve', they continued to qualify for promotion and the salary increases that went with it.

By the start of 1990, more than 4,400 officers had taken up the offer, although the numbers varied considerably according to rank. The army still had almost twice as many colonels as it needed – a result of the rising numbers admitted to the Saragossa academy until the mid-fifties. The pay of the fortunate pensioners in the transitory reserve was already costing the Treasury more than 20,000 million pesetas ($200 million or £110 million) a year, but that will have been a small price to pay if the outcome is a more efficient army.

That, though, will also depend on a much more controversial reform which did not come into effect until the start of 1990. This divides the officer corps into 'fast' and 'slow' tracks according to their performance in training. Those on the 'fast track' are assured of reaching the rank of major and those on the 'slow track' that of captain. But after that, their promotion is determined by selection. And if they have not made the rank of brigadier after thirty-two years in the service, they are out, though with a generous pension. A figure not unlike the typical English major, retired at fifty with enough money to live in modest comfort, can be glimpsed on the horizon of Spanish society.

The reform of the officer corps begs the question of the quality of Spain's rank-and-file soldiery. The army's NCOs are professionals. So are most of its technicians and the troops in elite units like the Royal Guard, the Parachute Brigade and the Legion. But the bulk of the army is made up of conscripts. More than 200,000 are currently being called up each year.

The shift in attitudes towards military service is as good an illustration as any of the changes which have overtaken Spain in the past thirty years. There was a time when a lot of youngsters looked forward to the *mili*. It gave them a chance to see the world outside their *pueblo* and provided some with a last opportunity to learn to read and write. For today's young Spaniard, it is simply a waste of time. It teaches him nothing he is likely to need to know during the rest of his life. And for early school-leavers, it can mean the loss of a hard-won job.

One symptom of growing discontent with the present arrangements has been a rise in conscientious objection. Franco's governments simply refused to recognize it.* In fact it was not until 1984

---

*One poor soul, a Catalan Jehovah's Witness, spent eleven years in gaol for refusing to do military service before being pardoned in 1970.

that legislation was passed by the Cortes that did. Since then, the number of youngsters applying for recognition as conscientious objectors has soared. In 1993, it was expected to represent about a third of the total call-up. More than 90 per cent of those who apply are recognized.

It is one of Spain's peculiarities that laws are frequently put into effect before arrangements have been made for their implementation, and the Conscientious Objection Act was a case in point. It stipulated that recognized conscientious objectors should do community service (*prestación social*). But nothing like enough work had been sorted out for the 20,000 or so whose cases had been put on ice while the law was going through parliament, so the authorities were eventually forced to exempt them. Since then, they have been unable to provide work for more than about one in twenty.

Though they are unlikely ever actually to have to do it, some radical conscientious objectors, the so-called *insumisos*, refuse to agree to the *prestación social* either. By law, this should earn them a spell in gaol. But here too the authorities have been unable to cope. At the end of 1992 there were more than 3,500 *insumisos*, yet only eight were behind bars.

Small wonder, then, that the whole system of military service has come under critical scrutiny from soldiers and politicians alike. Their main concern was whether, if it came to a war, conscripts with just a few months' experience would be of any use in the field. Colonel Amadeo Martínez Inglés, a general staff officer with a distinguished service record, was in no doubt. 'The Spanish army,' he told *Cambio 16* in 1989, 'is useless.' By the end of the year, his refusal to stop advocating a volunteer army had landed him in prison. It eventually led to his removal from the army.

In the meantime, military service had become an issue in that year's general election. Its abolition had first been mooted by Adolfo Suárez's CDS in the 1986 election campaign. It took some time for the other opposition parties to realize that the idea held considerable appeal for young voters. But by the time the 1989 campaign began, they were all offering reductions of various lengths. The result was that the Socialists, who had already cut the period of military service from fifteen months to twelve, were stampeded into promising a further cut to nine.

To compensate for this, the government's plan is to increase the number of volunteers in all three services. By 1997, it is intended to have some 40,000 professionals in the ranks in addition to a projected 50,000 officers and NCOs. This would mean that, at any one time, half the personnel in the leaner but fitter armed forces would be volunteers.

What is not clear is how they are going to be paid for, because the Socialists have made it abundantly clear that they do not wish to spend a peseta more on the armed forces than they have to. As a percentage of central government spending, the defence budget has fallen steadily since they came to power. As a percentage of GDP, it rose until 1985 but then began to drop sharply. In other words, the share of the government's income allocated to defence has not kept pace with the country's growing prosperity. Spain's spending on defence in 1994 was budgeted to represent just 1·26 per cent of its GDP – the lowest figure in NATO apart from that of Luxembourg.

That year, half the fleet was being kept in port because of the lack of money for fuel. And some 60 per cent of the army's vehicles were reported to be out of action. The first additional contingent of army volunteers was only paid for by freezing the pay of soldiers already serving. It meant that a private in his first year entered 1993 earning less than a million pesetas ($7,500 or £5,000) a year before tax. As for the conscripts, they were drawing only slightly more than 1,000 pesetas ($7.50 or £5) a month.

CHAPTER 9

A Dwindling Flock: Religion and the Church

In the late sixties the workers at one of the great sherry houses of Jerez mounted what became a prolonged and bitter strike. Among their demands was that they should be given two days off every year for christenings. One of the leaders of the strike later recalled that the head of the firm had asked them why 'a bunch of commies' should need time off to go to church. 'We said that that was different. You might not believe in God, but you had to believe in baptism otherwise your kids would be Moors, wouldn't they?' he said.

Spain, like Pakistan, became a nation in the aftermath of a religious segregation. Christianity came to be considered as essential to Spain's nationhood as Islam was to be to Pakistan's. As the Jerez sherry-worker's remark shows, saying that you are a Christian could, until very recently, be as much a claim to national identity as a profession of religious belief.

And if being a Spaniard meant being a Christian, in Spain being a Christian meant being a Catholic. The *reconquista* had barely ended when the Reformation began, and after centuries of fighting the infidel, Christian Spaniards were in no mood to put up with heretics or dissenters. Spain was the undisputed leader of the Counter-Reformation. A soldier-turned-priest from the Basque country, Ignacio de Loyola, provided the movement with its spiritual shock troops, the Jesuits, and Spanish commanders like Alba, Spínola and the Cardinal Infante Fernando led the military offensive against the Protestant nations of the north.

At home the Inquisition made sure that by 1570 there were virtually no Protestants left in Spain. Abolished in 1813, during the War of Independence, the Inquisition was reconstituted the following year by Fernando VII and was only finally suppressed in the 1830s. Even after that – except under the two Republics – religious freedom was usually more notional than real. Brave souls like George Borrow, author of that exuberantly idiosyncratic classic *The Bible in Spain*, set out to break the stranglehold of Popery but only succeeded in creating the odd prayer group.

Franco, while not actually banning other forms of worship, outlawed their external manifestations. Services could not be advertised in the press or on signboards and since none but the Catholic Church had legal status other denominations could not own property or publish books. The Second Vatican Council's historic declaration on freedom of conscience forced the regime to abandon this policy and in 1966 a law was passed which, while retaining a privileged status for the Catholic Church, freed other creeds from the constraints that had been placed upon them. But it was not until the 1978 constitution took effect that Spaniards secured an unambiguous right to worship as they pleased. Today there are no more than about 60,000 actively practising Spanish Protestants of whom a disproportionate number are in Catalonia.

One result of the virtual absence of Protestantism was that disagreement with the doctrines of Catholicism, which in other parts of Europe was channelled into Lutheranism or Calvinism, tended to take the form of Freemasonry in Spain. Many of the nineteenth-century *pronunciamientos* were the result of Masonic conspiracies.

Persecuted by Franco more than any other group except possibly the Communists, the Masons were effectively obliterated from Spanish life by his dictatorship. Though Freemasonry is nowadays legal, it has made scant impact on the country which has emerged since Franco's death.

Between 1975 and 1986, according to polls taken by the Gallup Institute, the number of Spaniards who said they had a religion other than Catholicism trebled, yet by the end of the period it was still no more than 1·4 per cent. Apart from the Protestants, there are some 15,000 Jews and between 150,000 and 250,000 Moslems. Spain's Jews come from a variety of backgrounds, though more than half have arrived from neighbouring Morocco. Of the Moslems, about 50 per cent are residents of Spain's two North African enclaves of Ceuta and Melilla. Most of the remainder are naturalized Spaniards born in other parts of the world, but perhaps a thousand are native-born converts.

The conversion of Spaniards to Islam is one of the most fascinating developments in the new Spain. It gathered momentum in the early eighties and has been especially pronounced in those parts of the country once ruled by Moslems. There is a community of several hundred converts in the Albaicín, the old Moorish quarter of Granada.

In addition to the established religions and denominations, sects of various kinds are estimated to have from 150,000 to 200,000 followers in Spain. Even so, the total number of non-Catholics in Spain probably comes to less than half a million.

To all intents and purposes, Catholicism in Spain is still not so much *a* religion as *the* religion, and its pre-eminence has long been reflected in the unusually close ties between Church and state.

As the *reconquista* pushed forward the limits of Christian Spain, the Church acquired immense tracts of land, especially in the southern half of the peninsula. No sooner were they confiscated by the *liberal* politician Juan Alvarez Mendizábal in the 1830s than his successors felt they had to make amends. In the pact, or Concordat, drawn up between Madrid and the Vatican in 1851, the government undertook by way of indemnity to pay the clergy's salaries and meet the cost of administering the sacraments. This extraordinary commitment was honoured by every government until 1931, when it was renounced by the authors of the Republican constitution. But two years later, when a conservative government came to power, the subsidy was resumed.

Franco not only continued to pay it, he also provided government money to rebuild churches damaged or destroyed in the civil war and passed a series of measures bringing the law of Spain into line with the teachings of the Church. Divorce, which had been made legal under the Republic, was abolished, the sale (but not, for some reason, the manufacture) of contraceptives was banned and Roman Catholic religious instruction was made compulsory in public as well as private education at every level.

In return, the Vatican granted Franco something that Spanish rulers had been seeking for centuries: effective control over the appointment of bishops. Cooperation between the Church and the regime became even closer after the end of the Second World War when Franco needed to turn a non-Fascist face to the world. Several prominent Catholic laymen were included in the cabinet and one of them, Alberto Martín Artajo, succeeded in negotiating a new Concordat with Rome.

Signed in 1953, the Concordat ended the diplomatic isolation to which Spain had been subjected ever since the Allied victory and Franco was happy to make whatever concessions were necessary to clinch it. The Church was exempted from taxation and offered grants with which to construct churches and other religious buildings. It acquired the right to ask for material it found offensive to be withdrawn from sale, yet its own publications were freed from censorship. Canonical marriage was recognized as the only valid form for Catholics. The Church was given the opportunity to found universities, run radio stations and own newspapers and magazines. The police were forbidden to enter churches except in cases of 'urgent necessity'. The clergy could not be charged with criminal offences except with the permission of their diocesan bishop (in the case of priests) or the Holy See itself (in the case of bishops).

It was the Second Vatican Council which first brought the terms of this cosy relationship into question. The Council, which came down unambiguously in favour of a clear separation between Church and state, invited all those governments which had a say in the appointment of ecclesiastical officials to give it up. But nothing could persuade Franco to surrender what he regarded – correctly – as an immensely powerful instrument of control. Because of it he was able to block the elevation of numerous liberally-minded priests upon whose heads Pope Paul VI wished to place a mitre. Throughout the last years of Franco's life, ministers and officials were flying to and from Rome with suggested revisions of the Concordat. But all attempts to rewrite it foundered on the ageing dictator's point-blank refusal to give up his power over the appointment of bishops.

His death and the disappearance of his dictatorship created a very different political background for relations between Church and state. In its draft form the 1978 constitution did not mention the Catholic Church at all, and it was only after a determined campaign that the bishops succeeded in having a reference to it included. Even so, this reference looks like what it is – an afterthought. Having specifically rejected the idea of an official religion, the constitution went on to say: 'The authorities shall take into account the religious beliefs of Spanish society and maintain the appropriate relations of cooperation with the Catholic Church and the other denominations.' There was no explicit affirmation that the majority of Spaniards were Catholics, nor that the state should take into account – let alone be guided by – the teachings of Catholicism.

In the meantime, preparations had been made for a revision of the Concordat. In 1976, King Juan Carlos had unilaterally renounced the privilege which Franco had enjoyed of being able to name Spain's bishops. In August of that year, the Spanish Foreign Minister, Marcelino Oreja, and the Vatican's Secretary of State, Cardinal Villot, signed an agreement formally restoring to the Church the power to appoint its own leaders in Spain. In December 1979 both sides agreed to a partial revision of the Concordat which appeared to prepare the ground for a financial separation between Church and state. Referring to the state's lengthy atonement for the confiscations of the last century it was agreed that 'the state can neither ignore nor prolong indefinitely juridical obligations acquired in the past'. So, tacitly acknowledging that the Church was incapable of going it alone overnight, the agreement proposed a transitional period of six years divided into two three-year stages. During stage one the government would continue to pay the usual subsidy. But during stage two there would be a new system of finance. Taxpayers would be able to state on their returns whether they wished a small percentage of their taxes to go to the Church and the government would then hand over the resulting sum to the bishops. The press immediately dubbed it the *impuesto religioso* (religious tax), but as it was never conceived of as a separate or additional charge this was a rather inaccurate label. Whatever the individual taxpayer decided would make no difference to the size of his or her tax bill.

And not only that. Under the revised Concordat, the state undertook to ensure that during this second phase of the transition to self-financing the Church would get 'resources of similar quantity' to those it was already receiving. However few or many taxpayers expressed a desire to help the Church, therefore, it would make no difference to what it obtained from the state.

The whole transitional procedure was more a matter of words than substance. If it had a point, it was to accustom people to the idea that, sooner rather than later, the Roman Catholic Church's expenses were going to have to be paid for by ordinary citizens. A point made from time to time is that, because of the state subsidies the Church has for so long been receiving, the faithful in Spain are not used to the idea of having to put more than a token sum into the collection plate.

In fact, the timetable set out in the Concordat has not been adhered to. Stage one lasted, not for three years, but for nine. It was not until 1988 that taxpayers were asked to decide whether they wanted a share of their contribution to be given to the Church or spent on 'objectives of social interest' (i.e. charities). But the share − 0·5239 per cent − was based on an estimate of the percentage of total revenue that would be needed to equal what the Church had received from the state in the year before the new arrangements were introduced. Therefore, only if every single taxpayer opted for the Church would the sum initially allocated to the bishops constitute the 'resources of similar quantity' the state had promised.

In the event, 35 per cent marked their forms in favour of the Church and 12 per cent in favour of the 'objectives of social interest'. The remainder did not put down anything at all, and under the rules drawn up by the government their share also went to the charities. But since the government promptly made the total up to the 14,000 million pesetas the Church could have expected to receive had nothing been changed, the whole exercise was pointless. Very few Spaniards grasp that, however they mark their forms, it will not affect the amount given to the Church. Indeed, it could be argued that the most 'Christian' thing to do would be to opt for the 'objectives of social interest', because that actually increases the amount the state puts aside for charitable purposes.

Every year, though, the same wholly illogical ritual is acted out. The taxpayers fill out their tax forms, and about 40 per cent of them tick the box corresponding to the Church, believing no doubt that it makes a difference. The newspapers publish the numbers, along with tables, graphs and comment from all concerned, just as if it did. But in the meantime, in a tiny clause tacked on to the end of that year's Finance Act, the government will have authorized the payment of a sum which, adjusted for inflation, is pretty much what the Church would have received had Franco still been alive.

Just as the deadline for the implementation of stage one came and went and was disregarded, so the deadline for the transition to stage two came and went and was ignored. A Church which has been formally disestablished thus continues to receive a sizeable amount from government funds under a deal that was meant to have become obsolete in 1986.

Every so often, a report will appear in the press claiming that the government and the Church have agreed to move on to self-financing. But nothing ever happens, and Spain's atheists, its Protestants, Jews and Moslems are still having to pay for the upkeep of a religion they do not share. In order to mitigate this anomaly, the Socialists have agreed that donations received by other religions can, to some extent, be set against tax by the donors. But this is a privilege that the Roman Catholic Church also enjoys.

It is ironic that, rather than shed its obligations to one religion, the new Spain seems to be assuming responsibility for several. It is not at all clear who is principally responsible for this situation.

The Socialists have never done more than whinge, and it may be that they fear losing either Catholic votes or a system which provides them with a useful lever. Once, when Alfonso Guerra took exception to criticism of the Socialists on the COPE radio network, which is controlled by the Church, he hinted that the subsidy might be abolished; almost immediately the offending programme was taken off the air.

Church leaders, for their part, have consistently said they favour self-financing, but in only a few dioceses have they made serious moves towards achieving it. A number of them have sought to justify the present arrangements as compensating the Church for the social work it does.

Though the Church in Spain has recently become much more open about its finances, it is still impossible to get a full picture. The 'budget' it discloses annually is the balance between what it receives and spends at national level: it does not include those amounts which are both accrued and spent in the various dioceses.

However, the evidence which has surfaced at diocesan level suggests that the Church is by no means as dependent on the taxpayer as is conventionally believed. Figures made public by the Barcelona diocese for 1988, and the Madrid diocese for 1989, showed that the government's contribution to their income was 17 and 36 per cent respectively. The rest came from the return on assets, loans and sales, and donations from the faithful.

That said, the outlook for the Church – financially and otherwise – is unquestionably a gloomy one. Spain, like the rest of the developed world, is becoming steadily more secular, in practice if not in theory.

An extensive poll carried out in 1990 for the Fundación Santa María, a body linked to the Marian Fathers, found that 87 per cent of Spaniards claimed to belong to a religion, and of those, 99 per cent said they were Catholics. This was not so very different from the picture that had emerged from surveys a decade earlier.

What had changed were the patterns of observance. The percentage of Spaniards going to church at least once a month had dropped from 53 per cent in 1981 to 43 per cent in 1990. This is still a pretty respectable tally, you might think. But the survey identified two other phenomena.

One was a much closer link than in the past between piety and poverty. Traditionally, church attendance in Spain had followed a complex pattern which was thought to be the result of regional differences in the degree to which the Church was associated with an oppressive local 'establishment'. It tended to be highest in the Basque country and Old Castile and lowest in the south. The 1990 survey, though it still revealed traces of the old pattern, found that attendance was highest in backward and rural Castile-La Mancha and lowest in affluent, urban Catalonia.

The other factor was a strong correlation between observance and age. Some 67 per cent of Spaniards over the age of 65 went to church at least once a month, compared with 22–23 per cent among the under-35s. This bore out evidence from other sources that young Spaniards were not particularly spiritual. One international survey found that fewer than half the young considered themselves religious, compared with much higher figures in countries with a more secular tradition – 67 per cent in Canada, for example.

It would seem that, unless there is a major change in social values, the number of practising Catholics in Spain will drop to around the one in five level. This is what Church leaders mean when they talk about 'galloping secularization'. Even before it began to have an effect on the numbers attending Mass, it had taken its toll on the numbers entering – and leaving – Holy Orders.

Here again, the official figures give an impression that the Spanish Church is in good shape. In 1992 it was reckoned that there were more than 20,000 parish priests, 18,000 monks – both ordained and unordained – and no fewer than 55,000 nuns.* Nevertheless, it is clear that the Church is in the throes of a crisis. In comparison with a decade earlier, the number of monks and nuns had fallen by 12,000 and 24,000 respectively.

The number of parish priests had dropped by fewer than 3,000, but that was largely because of the idiosyncratic age structure of the diocesan clergy. Its main characteristic is an immense bulge in the 60-plus age group, caused by the upsurge in numbers which occurred in the first half of Franco's rule. As age takes its toll of those priests who were ordained during the dictatorship, the number of diocesan clerics will fall rapidly.

Until recently, a low retirement rate among the depleted ranks of those who survived the civil war masked the effects of a fall in ordination, which itself reflected the worldwide slump in vocations that first became apparent in the sixties. In Spain as elsewhere, the phenomenon manifested itself in two ways.

In the first place, there was a decline in the number of young men applying to study for the priesthood. The number of seminarists in Spain, which had reached more than 9,000 in the fifties, fell to 1,500 in the seventies. But there was a slight increase after 1979, and in 1992 the figure was just under 2,000. In some areas, though, the situation was dire. In Catalonia, for example, only 136 priests had

---

*The most extraordinary aspect of Spain's clerical statistics is the number in closed orders – 703 monks and 14,500 nuns, according to figures for 1989. Spain's 918 closed communities represented 60 per cent of the world total.

been ordained in the previous ten years, and the average age of the diocesan priesthood had reached sixty.

Another, more controversial, symptom of the crisis was an increase in the number of priests giving up Holy Orders. During the sixties, more priests are reckoned to have renounced their vows in Spain than in any country except Brazil and Holland. According to the Church's official figures, there are fewer than 4,000 'secularized' priests in Spain, including both former monks and former parish priests. However, COSARESE, a body representing the secularized clergy, maintains that the official statistics fail to take into account those who have abandoned the cloth without being granted a formal secularization.

In 1978, Pope John Paul II decided not to sign any more documents releasing priests from their vows unless they could show that their ordination had been invalid. At the time, one in twelve of those awaiting secularization was a Spaniard. COSARESE's figures suggest that almost 3,000 parish priests, more than 6,000 monks and nearly 10,000 nuns opted to leave Holy Orders in Spain between 1960 and 1990.

The main reason for this wave of secularizations was the Church's policy on celibacy. An unpublished survey in the diocese of Santiago de Compostela, the cradle of traditional Spanish Catholicism, conducted while Franco was still alive, found that almost a quarter of the parish priests there considered chastity an unrealizable virtue. 'What is really serious and worrying,' the authors of the report added, 'is that almost all those priests who judged it unrealizable are consistent in their way of thinking and behave accordingly.' Most of the priests who have left Holy Orders have since married. An organization known as the Movimiento Pro Celibato Opcional (MOCEOP) estimates the number of married former priests in Spain at between 7,500 and 8,000.

Historically, the Spanish clergy has been among the most conservative in the world. The Church that had spearheaded the Counter-Reformation was quite incapable of coming to terms with the new ideas that flooded into Spain during the nineteenth century and took refuge in a forlorn hope that the old order of things could be re-established. The identification of the Church with reaction created by implication a mirror-image alliance between radicalism and anti-clericalism. During the late nineteenth and early twentieth centuries, whenever the right lost its grip on the levers of power there were frenzied outbursts of violence directed against Catholicism and its representatives. Churches were burned or desecrated. On occasion, priests were killed and nuns raped. The civil war provoked the worst atrocities of all – the 4,000 parish priests who died were accompanied to the grave by over 2,000 monks and almost 300 nuns.

The atrocities perpetrated by the Republicans make it a little easier to understand the Church's attitude to the Nationalists. Spanish prelates blessed Franco's troops before they went into battle and were even pictured giving the fascist salute. In a famous broadcast to the beleaguered defenders of the Alcázar in Toledo, Cardinal Isidro Gomá y Tomás – a future Primate of Spain – inveighed against 'the bastard soul of the sons of Moscow and shadowy societies manipulated by semitic internationalism'. On the day of his victory, Franco received from Pope Pius XII a telegram of congratulation which read: 'Lifting up our hearts to the Lord, we rejoice with Your Excellency in the victory, so greatly to be desired, of Catholic Spain.'

Yet within twenty-five years of that telegram, the Spanish Church had changed from being one of Franco's most enthusiastic allies into one of his most vocal critics. This extraordinary about-turn takes some explaining. To an extent it was a reflection of the diminishing support throughout society for Franco's regime. Unlike Spain's army officers, who make great play of being drawn from among the 'people' but are in fact recruited from a quite narrow section of society, the clergy really do come from every stratum and so tend to be more susceptible to the feelings of the nation as a whole. It was partly too a question of morality. The gap between what the regime promised and what it delivered in the way of social justice grew wider every year and was quite soon demonstrably at variance with Christian ideals. In addition, the Spanish Church, like every other Catholic Church, was deeply influenced by the liberal spirit which began to emanate from the Vatican as soon as John XXIII was elected Pope and which took shape in the measures adopted by the Second Vatican Council. But perhaps the main reason for the change was, ironically enough, Franco's own victory.

Just as the Church's political conservatism had helped to forge an alliance between anti-clericalism and radicalism, so the anti-clericalism of the radicals had ensured that the Church remained conservative. The death and exile of so many Freemasons, anarchists and Marxists effectively destroyed anti-clericalism as a force in society and gave the Church a freedom of manoeuvre which had been unthinkable previously. Among other things it encouraged the Church to fish for souls in the traditionally anti-clerical urban working class. In the early fifties, the leaders of the Vatican-inspired lay organization, Acción Católica, set up three new societies, Hermandades Obreras de Acción Católica (HOAC), Juventud Obrera Católica (JOC), and Vanguardias Obreras Juveniles (VOJ) to proselytize among the working classes, particularly the young.

In the event, the urban working classes were to have a much greater effect on the Church than the Church ever had on the urban working classes. The result of the experiment was to raise the social consciousness of, first, the laity and then the clergy more than the religious consciousness of the people they had set out to convert. By the early sixties, a sizeable element within the Church was at odds with the regime. This was the heyday of the *curas rojos* (red priests), who took advantage of the privileges and immunities granted to the Church by Franco to allow strike meetings in the vestry and sit-ins in the nave.

The younger clergy's antipathy to Francoism was further fuelled in some areas by the regime's hostility to regional nationalism. This was especially true of the Basque country, the most devout part of Spain. There, the clergy had always identified closely with demands for the restoration of traditional rights and privileges, although during the nineteenth century this had tended to take the form of support for Carlism. In contrast to what happened in the rest of Spain, the Basque clergy sided with the Republic during the civil war and paid the price for their choice after Franco's victory when sixteen of their number were executed. Understandably, therefore, many Basque priests were sympathetic to the resurgence of militant nationalism.

The revolt within the Church, particularly in the Basque country, reached such proportions that a special priests' prison had to be created at Zamora. At first, the radicalism of the rank-and-file appalled the hierarchy. But towards the end of the sixties, the hierarchy itself began to show signs of dissent. In 1972 the Church got a 'red bishop' to add to its many 'red priests' – Bishop Iniesta, who was appointed to Vallecas, a working-class suburb of Madrid.

The publicity given to the 'red' bishops and priests of the Franco era tended to give the impression that the Church had become more radical than was in fact the case. By the end of the dictatorship it consisted, in Bishop Iniesta's words, of 'a minority right wing, a minority left wing and a majority belonging to the centre'. Cardinal Tarancón, the Archbishop of Madrid, who had been elected President of the Bishops' Conference in 1971, was the embodiment of this ecclesiastical centre. A friend and admirer of Pope Paul VI, he shared the late pontiff's cautious but realistic approach to the modern world. He was, in short, the ideal man to preside over the Spanish Church during the transition. His withdrawal from administrative and pastoral activities in the early eighties caused a discernible shift in the direction of the Church. He was replaced as the head of the Bishops' Conference by the somewhat apolitical figure of the Bishop of Oviedo, Gabino Díaz Merchán, and when in 1983 Tarancón reached the age of seventy-five and was obliged to submit his resignation from the Archbishopric of Madrid, Pope John Paul II replaced him with the Bishop of Santiago de Compostela, Angel Suquía, an admirer and supporter of the reactionary Opus Dei. In 1987, Suquía – by then a cardinal – was elected President of the Bishops' Conference. The Suquía era was to be marked by repeated and corrosive disputes with the Socialist government. In 1990, relations hit perhaps their lowest point when the Church hierarchy attacked a government campaign promoting condoms to prevent the spread of AIDS. Suquía's General Secretary at the Bishops' Conference called it 'disastrous', adding that it was what you would expect from a 'materialistic, agnostic and atheistic political enterprise'. Felipe González returned the compliment by refusing officially even to meet Suquía. The Cardinal once described modern Spanish society as 'sick' and, under his leadership, it seemed the bishops could find nothing positive in the direction it was taking. At one point they even appeared to question the merits of democracy, arguing that the 'dialectic of majorities and the power of the vote' had supplanted ethical criteria.

But in 1993, when Cardinal Suquía resigned, the bishops opted for an abrupt change, handing all three of the top posts in the Conference to men more in line with the ideas of Tarancón. Chief among them was Elías Yanes, the Archbishop of Saragossa, who was chosen to become President. A Canary Islander by birth, he had worked in a Catholic association that was a focus for opposition to Franco, and he had been Tarancón's General Secretary during the transition. On the day of his election, he signalled an entirely new direction when he told a press conference that the Conference 'mustn't be so "anti"'.

Two factors appear to have brought about the change. One was a fear that the Papal Nuncio, Mario Tagliaferri, who had worked hand in glove with Suquía, was beginning seriously to erode the independence of the Spanish Church. The other was growing concern that it might become identified once more with the political right.

The weakening of this link has been one of the most important developments in Spain's recent evolution. Unlike Italy, Spain has never had a Christian Democrat party of any significance. The forces of Christian Democracy had been split into pro- and anti-Francoist factions under the dictatorship and were unable to sink their differences in time for the 1977 elections. Some Christian Democrats stood for the AP, others for the UCD, while a third group who entered the lists as Christian Democrats pure and simple suffered a crushing defeat. The fall of the UCD and the rise of the PP served to concentrate most of them into a single party, but they remain a minority within it.

Similarly, it has been concluded that more than half the country's practising Catholics and a fifth of its daily communicants voted for the Socialists at the 1982 general election. Although the leadership of the PSOE is overwhelmingly agnostic, a study by its Grupo Federal de Estudios Sociológicos in the eighties found that over 45 per cent of members described themselves as believers. Less than 20 per cent of those who had joined during the Franco era were Catholics, but among those who had joined since then, the proportion has been increasing each year until among the most recent entrants it was 50 per cent. Two of the ministers who have served in Felipe González's governments had previously been seminarists and one of his junior ministers was a former priest. Two of the PSOE's regional presidents also wore the cloth at an earlier stage in their lives.

The Church may not have the means with which to intervene directly in politics, but it still has plenty of ways in which to make its presence and its views felt indirectly. Its hand could be clearly discerned in the positions taken by some right-wing politicians during the debates on divorce and abortion. The Bishops' Conference has now sold its newspaper group, which included *Ya*, but it retains a 50 per cent stake in the COPE radio network.* And about a sixth of all Spain's schools are run by religious orders and groups.

Of these, the most controversial is unquestionably Opus Dei, the Work of God. The *Obra* (Work), as it is known in Spain, today claims more than 75,000 members in over eighty countries.

Opus Dei's latest triumph – and latest controversy – came in 1992 with the beatification of its founder, Monsignor Josemaría Escrivá de Balaguer. Escrivá, who died in 1975, cleared the biggest hurdle on the path to sainthood against a background of sustained protest from liberal Catholics. His beatification, the fastest in the history of the Church, was approved despite allegations that he was vain, snobbish, misogynistic, and even – according to a former senior member of Opus – an apologist for the Nazis.

The son of an Aragonese shopkeeper, Escrivá founded Opus Dei in 1928 and in 1939 published his most famous work, a collection of maxims entitled *Camino* (Way).

Like the Jesuits before him, he realized the benefits to be derived from gaining a foothold in the educational world and using it to build up support among the elite. In 1941 José Ibáñez Martín, a friend of one of Escrivá's closest associates, was made Minister of Education. By the time he left the job in 1951, it was reckoned that between 20 and 25 per cent of the chairs at Spain's universities were held by Opus members and sympathizers. The year following Ibáñez Martín's departure also saw the foundation by the Opus of a college near Pamplona, the Estudio General de Navarra. In 1962 it achieved the status of a university and has since been responsible for educating some of Spain's highest achievers. In addition, Opus Dei

---

* It also flirted with the idea of bidding for one of Spain's new commercial television channels, but the idea was eventually rejected.

set up a business school, the IESE, in Barcelona and an administrative college, the ISSA, in San Sebastián. As the young people whose sympathies the Opus had won at university and college moved up in the world, they spread the organization's influence into every area of Spanish life. They became – and remain – powerful in the media and in business.

Parallels have been drawn between Opus Dei and any number of other groups and creeds. Its hierarchical – or at least compartmentalized – structure has inspired comparison with Freemasonry. Its exaltation of work is reminiscent of some of the more po-faced forms of Protestantism. Its induction methods have been compared with those of modern-day cults and sects.

But in one respect, Opus is unique. In so far as its members live in communities and/or are bound by undertakings of poverty, chastity and obedience, they form a religious order. Unlike the majority of monks and nuns, though, Opus Dei's initiates do normal jobs, work normal hours and wear normal clothes.

It is this which has enabled them to attain such influence – and, I suspect, caused them to inspire such misgivings – in secular society. The Jesuits, to take the example of their most implacable enemies, are no doubt capable of exerting immense behind-the-scenes influence. But you are not likely to discover one day that the editor of, say, a financial journal for which you have been writing, or the chairman of an engineering company with which you have been negotiating, is also a member of the Society of Jesus. Nor is it conceivable that the Jesuits, the Dominicans or the Benedictines could have seen, as Opus has, six of their number appointed Spanish Cabinet ministers (five under Franco, and one since).

You do not expect, but you may well find, especially if you live in Spain, that someone you work alongside, or over, or under, does not go home at night to a family, or a partner, or flatmates, but to a community in which there are lengthy periods of silence; that for two hours each day he or she is wearing a *cilicio*, a chain with pointed links turned inwards, on the upper thigh (so that neither it nor the wounds it inflicts can be seen); and that, once a week, your colleague whips his or her buttocks with a *disciplina*, a five-thonged lash, for as long as it takes to say the prayer *Salve Regina*.

Opus Dei's uniqueness has twice been recognized by the Vatican.

In 1947, it became the Roman Catholic Church's first – and, for some time, its only – secular institute. In 1983, it became its first – and remains its only – personal prelature.

Known in full as the Prelature of the Holy Cross and Opus Dei, the organization comprises two groups, one clerical, one lay. The Priestly Society of the Holy Cross is for the priests who make up only about 2 per cent of the membership but wield immense power over it. The lay group, Opus Dei itself, is divided by gender into men's and women's sections, and by vocation or availability into various categories.

At the top are the numeraries. Numeraries are invariably university graduates, and either have a doctorate or are believed to be capable of acquiring one. They are always celibate and mostly live in Opus houses. Whatever they do not need for the sober lives they lead they hand over to the director of the community in which they live. Since the majority have well-paid jobs, this is an important source of income.

Below the numeraries come two classes of inferior academic standing, neither of which live in Opus communities. Associates (once referred to as oblates) are celibate, supernumeraries are not. In addition to its members, Opus recognizes a fourth category of so-called co-operators who can be non-Catholics, or even non-Christians, but who are deemed to have provided the organization with help and support.

In spite of the air of mystery enveloping the organization, it is not difficult to recognize members of Opus. They tend to be unusually fastidious in the way that they talk and dress, and their homes almost always contain somewhere a little model of a donkey, representing the ass upon which Christ entered Jerusalem. Young Opus priests are particularly easy to spot. Unlike their contemporaries, who generally do their best not to look like priests at all, they wear cassocks and dog-collars and, in imitation of Opus Dei's founder, they frequently wear Atkinson's cologne. Somewhat unexpectedly, many of them also have a back-slapping, hail-fellow-well-met, one-of-the-boys air about them and smoke strong Ducados cigarettes.

Theologically, Opus Dei represents a step into the past best illustrated by the movement's attitude to confession. In recent years,

Catholics in many parts of the world have come to regard it as an anachronism. In Spain, some churches, particularly in working-class districts, no longer even have a confessional. Yet Opus Dei has been doing its best to reverse the trend and if you go to the sanctuary run by Opus Dei at Torreciudad, near Barbastro, you will find a crypt packed with confessionals.

Opus's spokesmen vigorously deny that the organization has any view on politics and resent it being described as right-wing. In the sense that Opus Dei was conceived of as a spiritual organization, this is understandable: Opus's conservatism is essentially theological. But it is only to be expected that a traditional approach to religious matters will tend to appeal to those who are to the right of centre politically. No evidence has ever been produced to show that anyone in the leadership of either the PSOE or the United Left is a member of Opus Dei.

That is not to say that the organization's political influence has evaporated. Today's Spain reflects many of the attitudes of the Opus crypto-monks who steered it through its formative years. In *Spain: Dictatorship to Democracy* Raymond Carr and Juan Pablo Fusi described them as 'proponents of rapid − capitalist − growth and of the "neutralization" of politics through prosperity'. It would be difficult to frame a more concise summary of criticism often levelled at González's nominally Socialist administration.

The virtual absence of ideology from Spanish politics is also one of the most evident signs of something commented on in an earlier chapter: a certain moral vacuousness. By that, I do not mean to suggest that today's Spaniards are amoral. When the dividing line between good and bad is clear, they are capable of mounting demonstrations of support or protest that put the rest of Europe to shame. If some young girl disappears into the clutches of a child-molester, for example, you can expect that thousands − and I mean thousands − of people will turn out on to the streets of her home town to support her relatives and demonstrate their outrage. Today's Spaniard usually has his or her heart in the right place.

It is when the choice is difficult, when the moral dilemma is unexpected or unfamiliar, that the gap becomes apparent. How do you reconcile the conflicting demands for higher pay and lower unemployment? To what extent do women have a 'right to choose' over abortion? And what really could be done about Bosnia? It is on these sorts of issues that the quality of debate in Spain can be low, with opinion-formers frequently choosing to take refuge in platitudes and aphorisms.

It is a phenomenon often attributed to the waning influence of the Roman Catholic Church. The theory does not rest on whether the values supplied by the Church were right or wrong, but on the fact that for centuries they were virtually the only ones the Spaniards had. In Britain, France and Germany, and in other societies with more than one religion, there is a tradition of choosing between different moral outlooks which goes back centuries. In Spain, that tradition barely exists. People have had little choice but to take their ethical bearings from the Roman Catholic Church, the only decision open to them being whether to accept or reject what it taught.

The prevalence of instinctively Catholic attitudes is far greater than the Spanish themselves perhaps realize. Castilian is crammed with phrases drawn from Catholic practice and dogma. When, for example, a Spaniard wants to convey the idea that something or somebody is reliable, trustworthy, 'OK' in the widest sense, he or she will say that that person or thing *'va a misa'* ('goes to Mass'). When some terrible thing like multiple sclerosis or nuclear war is mentioned in conversation, in circumstances where an English-speaker might say, 'It doesn't bear thinking about', a Spaniard – even an ostensibly irreligious one – will often say, *'Que Dios nos coja confesados'* ('Let's hope God catches us confessed'). And when the world's first test-tube baby was born, that eminently secular periodical *Cambio 16* headlined its report with the words 'Born without Original Sin'.

Take away the creed which is at the root of those ideas and you – or rather they – are left with little but common sense. Because of the absence of a rival to Catholicism in Spain, the step which might take a British Anglican into Catholicism, or a French Catholic into Humanism, can launch their Spanish counterpart into a sort of ethical void in which he or she has to rely on a largely instinctive sense of what is good and bad.

It can be argued that, in many cases, this will prove to be a lot better than some of the distinctly questionable morality which has been forthcoming from the Spanish Roman Catholic Church over the years. However, the fact that Spaniards find themselves all of a sudden left to their own ethical devices may provide a further explanation for that super-permissive atmosphere which imbues the new Spain.

PART THREE

Coming to Terms with Freedom

CHAPTER 10

Sex: The Lid Comes Off . . . Or Does It?

One of the problems of travelling around Spain is a dire shortage of motorway service areas. Outside Catalonia, nobody seems to have realized the potential for making money out of the captive market which is represented by millions of motorists hurtling up and down a stretch of road they are reluctant to leave. All too often, signs to a *zona de servicios* herald a trip off the motorway to some run-down petrol station with a diner attached where a man in a grimy shirt is to be found frying unrecognizable parts of an unidentifiable animal in what looks like machine oil.

Spain, though, does offer travellers an amenity to be found nowhere else. As you drive across the country, you will every so often see at the side of the road a building whose outlines, or some of them, are picked out in coloured strip lighting. In a sense, these too are *zonas de servicios*, but with a difference. They are roadside brothels.

Inside, the motorist will find a bar crammed with heavily made-up *señoritas* all too willing to join him for a drink and, at the right price, accompany him inside or upstairs or wherever the bedrooms are to be found.

Prostitution has long been widespread throughout southern Europe. The first comprehensive investigation of Spanish sexual attitudes and customs, carried out in the mid-sixties, found that almost two-thirds of the men interviewed had had their earliest experience with a professional. In the last year of the dictatorship, it was estimated that 500,000 women were working as prostitutes in Spain – one in twenty-seven of the adult female population.

At times, one can be tempted into believing that nothing much has changed in the sexual habits of the Spanish since then. But in so far as prostitution is concerned, a very great deal has changed. A study conducted by the Instituto de la Juventud in 1987 found that only 9 per cent of the young men interviewed had been introduced to sex by a prostitute.

What has also become clear is that far fewer Spanish women are selling themselves nowadays. Several town and city councils have quietly undertaken rehabilitation programmes, sometimes offering ex-prostitutes work as local government employees, most commonly as gardeners. Increasingly, Spain's prostitutes are foreigners. A lot come from Latin America, in many cases duped by promises of a new life as a 'dancer' or 'waitress' in Europe.

Another sign of changing mores has been a drop in the space taken up by prostitutes' advertisements in the newspapers. They are still an outstanding example of the live-and-let-live atmosphere of contemporary Spain, nevertheless. The Barcelona paper *La Vanguardia* is the august and stolid journal of the Catalan upper middle classes. During the dictatorship, it was pro-Franco. Nowadays it tends to be identified with the Catalan nationalist government of Jordi Pujol, whose wife is a leading light in the local anti-abortion movement. Yet at the back of *La Vanguardia* you will find column after column of ads like this one from October 1993: 'MARINA will introduce you to sado. and humil., rain, transv. and enemas. 6,000 ptas.'

Of all Spain's cities, Barcelona has long been the most liberated or degenerate, depending on your point of view. It probably has a lot to do with the fact that Barcelona is a port. The *barrio Chino*, the maze of alleyways and tenements depicted by Jean Genet in *Journal du Voleur*, has been a red-light district since the last century★ and although a lot has been done in the last few years to clean it up, the areas to either side of the Ramblas, Barcelona's most picturesque thoroughfare, are still pretty seedy.

Today Barcelona is the Hamburg of southern Europe. You can buy hard porn off the news-stands or watch live sex at the night

---

★In a historic lapse of taste, a board game called *El Chino* was marketed in Spain in the early eighties. Players moved pieces representing pimps, whores and transvestites. Those unlucky enough to catch venereal disease had to be moved to a square marked 'clinic'.

clubs. At the Club Bagdad they used to have an act involving a donkey until the Sociedad Protectora de Animales turned up one day and took it away.

But in this respect, Barcelona differs from the rest of Spain in degree rather than in kind. The years immediately following Franco's death saw a revolution in matters sexual which the Spaniards themselves dubbed the *destape*.* All the big Spanish cities acquired clubs with striptease shows and bars with topless – Spanish – waitresses. Even Burgos, that dour grey bastion of Catholic orthodoxy, got its own sex shop.

The *destape* is over now, but it can often seem as if the Spanish are still locked into an age before AIDS. It is as if they did not feel ready yet to stop marvelling at, and commenting on, and revelling in the sheer fun of sex.

On television it is omnipresent. Spain's pay-TV channel, Canal Plus, puts out hard-core porn in the early hours of the morning once a week, while soft-core porn is a quite frequent offering on the other channels after midnight at weekends.

Not long ago, there was a television advertisement in which the screen was filled with the bosom of a well-endowed girl who then breathed in deeply – so deeply that the buttons of her shirt popped off to reveal an ample cleavage. What were they advertising? Cough lozenges.

At home, getting over a bout of flu recently, I was flicking from channel to channel to find something worth watching. It was late afternoon, so inevitably most of the programmes were for children. On one of them, the children and the presenters were larking around on an elaborate set intended to depict the typical Spanish high street. The artists had meticulously painted in the church, a café, the town hall with its flags, the chemist's, the ironmonger's – and, of course, the local massage parlour.

One of the few people ever to run up against moral censure on Spanish television is Alberto Comesaña, the lead singer of a very popular group called Semen Up. Part of his act is to remove his trousers while singing the band's best-known song which is entitled '*Lo estás haciendo muy bien*' ('You're doing it very well'), and is

---

* *Destapar* is to take the lid off (something).

about oral sex. When he performed it on state-run Televisión Española, it earned him a five-year ban.

The occasional excesses of Spain's sexual revolution are a measure of the intensity of the repression which preceded it. Alone of the countries of southern Europe, Spain was subject to a special, double oppression.

In the same way as the other Catholic countries of the Mediterranean, she has been subject to the doctrines of a religion which, ever since St Paul, has been deeply suspicious of physical enjoyment of any kind. To the monks and nuns in charge of many of Spain's private schools, the penis was the 'diabolic serpent' and the vagina 'Satan's den'. There is of course a direct link between attitudes of this sort and the Spaniards' traditional enthusiasm for the mortification of the flesh. As Monsignor Escrivá, the founder of Opus Dei, wrote: 'If you know that your body is your enemy and the enemy of God's glory, why do you treat it so gently?'

Sex was strictly for the purpose of procreation within wedlock. Pre-marital contact between the sexes was kept to a minimum by the strictures attached to courtship or *noviazgo*. Incredible as it may seem now, the Church had great difficulty in agreeing to any form of physical contact between *novios*. As late as 1959 the Spanish bishops' 'Norms of Christian Decency' stated unequivocally that '*novios* walking along arm-in-arm cannot be accepted'. A Capuchin friar, Quintín de Sariegos, writing in the early sixties, had reconciled himself to the fact that *novias* would not only touch their *novios*, but might even kiss them. But he offered this advice – 'Whenever you kiss a man, remember your last communion and think to yourself, "Could the Sacred Host and the lips of this man come together on my lips without sacrilege?"'

What really distinguished Spain from other Catholic countries such as Italy and Portugal, however, was that for almost forty years the Church was able not merely to advocate but to enforce its ideas with the assistance of a regime that depended upon it for its legitimization.

The Church was involved in official censorship at every level and was particularly responsible for deciding on matters of sexual propriety. As the decree which created Francoist Spain's board of film censors, the Junta Superior de Orientación Cinematográfica, put it:

'on moral questions, the vote of the representative of the Church shall be especially worthy of respect'. The cinema was of particular concern to the Church. Fr Angel Ayala, the founder of the Catholic pressure group ACNP, described it as 'the greatest calamity that has befallen the world since Adam − a greater calamity than the flood, the two World Wars or the atomic bomb'. In spite of its representative's privileged status on the Junta, the Church was apparently unconvinced that the Francoist authorities were sufficiently rigorous in their approach; four years later it set up its own Oficina Nacional Permanente de Vigilancia de Espectáculos whose officials watched the films passed by the Junta after they had been censored and gave them a rating on a scale that went from one ('suitable for children') to four ('gravely dangerous'). Although it had no official standing, the Church's 'moral classification' was invariably printed alongside each film in the listings section of the newspapers.

But not even that was enough to satisfy the more zealous members of the clergy. Sometimes, after one of those 'gravely dangerous' films had slipped through the net, parish priests would take it on themselves to put up a notice in the foyer of the local cinema which said: 'Those who watch today's programme are committing mortal sin.' One bishop, outraged by the authorization of a film to which he objected, went so far as to arrange for groups of pious ladies from Acción Católica to wait at the entrance of the cinema. Whenever someone approached the box office, the leader would cry out: 'Say an Our Father for the soul of this sinner!' and the others would fall to their knees in prayer. It cut down the audiences no end.

Under the Church's guidance, censorship attained extraordinary heights of puritanism. Professional boxing matches were kept out of newsreels on the grounds that they showed naked male torsos. Photographs of the bouts did appear in the press, but with vests painted in by the *retocadores* (retouchers) who were employed by every newspaper and magazine until the fifties. Among their other duties was to reduce the size of women's busts. In later years, producers at state-run Televisión Española had to keep a shawl handy in case a starlet turned up for a show with a dress that was too décolleté. A similar horror of the female mammary glands led

TVE's censors to cut from a Jean-Luc Godard film a glimpse of a magazine advertisement for brassières, and to reject *Moana*, Flaherty's classic documentary about Polynesia, on the grounds that it included too many shots of bare-breasted native women.

In the forties and fifties it could be argued that the moral climate had at least some foundation in the nature of society. Sexual repression may have been severe, but then society was very traditional. During the sixties and seventies, however, the gap between what was considered acceptable by the authorities and what was considered acceptable by the public markedly widened. Official attitudes changed, but not as quickly or as much as those of society at large.

In 1962 the Ministry of Information and Tourism, the department primarily responsible for censorship, was taken away from Gabriel Arias Salgado, the religious bigot who had run the ministry since its inception eleven years earlier, and given to the more pragmatic and secular Manuel Fraga Iribarne. The changeover ushered in a period in which some of the more absurd restrictions were lifted. Even so, it was not until 1964, for example, that the censors allowed a woman in a bikini (Elke Sommer, as it happened) to appear on the cinema screens.

On the other hand, migration from the countryside to the towns, rising prosperity and increased contact with the outside world as a result of tourism and emigration transformed the sexual customs and attitudes of the Spaniards themselves. According to a survey carried out in the last year of Franco's dictatorship for the current affairs magazine *Blanco y Negro*, 42 per cent of Spanish girls had lost their virginity by the age of twenty.

After Franco's death, it was the publishing world which first breached the established taboos. In February 1976 a Spanish magazine called *Flashmen* (sic) carried a photograph of a model in which her bare nipples were plainly visible. Whether by accident or design, it was overlooked by the censor and thereafter *Flashmen* and others of its ilk set about pushing back the frontiers of the acceptable inch by inch and curve by curve. Most of the nude models in the early days were foreign girls, but a previously obscure revue artiste called Susana Estrada won eternal fame by becoming the first Spanish woman in modern times to appear bare-breasted in the pages of a Spanish magazine.

The situation as far as films were concerned was somewhat anomalous, as were so many things at that time. The import of hard-core films for private viewing was banned, but the import of soft-core productions for general release was permitted. For several years therefore there were no soft-core films being made in Spain although hard-core one-reelers were being churned out by the dozen by an outfit called Pubis Films.

Attempts to promote a hard-core movie business were also encouraged by a belief that the administration was about to legalize a new kind of movie house for the showing of explicit sex films. Officials have since said that between 1977 and 1978 the government was deterred by the activities of an Italian group suspected of connections with the Mafia, which was thought to be trying to take control of the Spanish market. Plans for the legalization of porno cinemas were shelved, killing off the fledgling Spanish hard-core film industry. When in 1984 Spain's first 'X' cinemas eventually opened for business, having been licensed by the new Socialist government, it was largely on the basis of US-based productions.

Spain's efforts to break into the soft-core movie business began, and pretty much ended, in 1978. That was the year of *El maravilloso mundo del sexo*, a film so embarrassingly dreadful that the boyfriend of one of the starlets walked out on her half-way through the première.

In other respects 1978 was a turning-point. It was the year that Spain got its first sex shop, *Kitsch*, which was opened in Madrid in February and closed by the authorities five months later. It was also the year that the fashion for topless bathing – which was to change for ever the Spanish attitude to nudity – reached the holiday *costas*. At first, the Guardia Civil did their best to stamp it out – sometimes by charging offenders with not being in possession of their personal documents.* But by the beginning of the following season they had come to realize that it was an impossible task. They began to turn a discreet blind eye and going topless soon became fashionable among Spanish girls as well.

---

*Just as it is an offence for Spaniards to go out without their identity card, the *Documento Nacional de Identidad*, it is also strictly speaking illegal for foreigners to walk around in Spain without their passports.

The years following Franco's death also witnessed important changes in the law that helped to narrow – although not, as we shall see, to close – the gap between what actually happens and what is officially condoned.

The first of these was the legalization of contraceptives. In practice the ban had never been total under Franco. Condoms could always be obtained, albeit with some difficulty, in red-light districts and street markets. The invention of the Pill opened up further possibilities, because – in addition to its purely contraceptive effects – it can be used to treat certain hormonal disorders, such as severe premenstrual tension. The first packets of Schering's Anovial arrived in Spain in June 1964. Thereafter, a small but growing number of doctors was prepared to prescribe the Pill on remedial grounds for women who in fact wanted it for contraceptive purposes. It has only recently emerged that a few stood trial for doing so. By 1975, according to an official report leaked to *Cambio 16*, the Pill was being used by more than half a million women.

Nevertheless, the demand for contraceptives was still vastly greater than the supply. If, by the end of Franco's rule and in spite of official exhortations to the contrary, there were only 2·5 children per family, it was also due to a good deal of self-restraint – *coitus interruptus*, *coitus reservatus* and simple abstinence.

The articles in the Penal Code which made the sale of contraceptives illegal were quietly revoked in 1978. It can be argued that few developments have had as great an impact on the nature of contemporary Spain. As we shall see in succeeding chapters, the increasing availability of effective contraception has had far-reaching effects. It has tilted the balance between the sexes, helped change the structure of family life, and exerted a profound influence on Spain's welfare and education systems.

At first, little was done to ensure that the contraceptives made legally available to Spaniards were used safely and reliably. While the UCD remained in power, there was no sex education in schools and the only family planning centres to be set up were financed, not by the central government, but by local authorities (invariably those run by the left).

All that has changed since the Socialists took office, but the effects of Catholic doctrine and Francoist prohibition can still be seen. They were visible, for example, in the results of a survey carried out for the Instituto Nacional de Estadística, published in 1989. Among married women, almost 85 per cent had tried contraception of some sort, but only 65 per cent had used a reliable method. In fact, the method which had been tried by most married women was withdrawal; following in order were the Pill, the sheath and the rhythm method. Among unmarried women, the condom – not surprisingly in the age of AIDS – was the method which had been most used, followed by the Pill, and withdrawal, which was almost as prevalent as among married women. But the most remarkable finding was that three-quarters of the unmarried women had not used contraception of any sort (though those interviewed included a number who had not had any sexual relations either).

It is important to realize that in some parts of Spain getting hold of contraceptives can still be problematic because of the religious scruples of the local chemists. There are even pharmacies in seemingly secular Barcelona which refuse to sell them. 'In the same way that some people don't do their military service because of conscientious objection, we don't sell condoms,' one dissenter explained to El País.

One would expect that the growing use of contraception would considerably reduce the number of abortions. Among the most remarkable paradoxes of Franco's supposedly Catholic Spain was that it had one of the world's highest pregnancy termination rates. It was never possible to arrive at an exact figure because the abortions were of course illegal, but a report by the High Court prosecutors' department, the Fiscalía del Tribunal Supremo, in 1974 while Franco was still alive put the annual total at 300,000 – equal to about 40 per cent of live births. By the time contraception was legalized, it was generally reckoned that the total was closer to 350,000.

In addition, the seventies saw a huge rise in overseas abortions. The favourite destination was London, which by 1978 was catering for more than 14,000 Spanish women every year. Overall, it would seem that the ratio of abortions to live births was nearly one to two.

The prevalence of abortion contrasted dramatically with the stiff penalties for practitioners. In 1979 the case of eleven Bilbao women charged with carrying out abortions became a *cause célèbre*. In the days leading up to their trial 300 women occupied one of the main court buildings in Madrid and were violently evicted by the police. More than a thousand women, including several well-known actresses, lawyers and politicians, published a document announcing that they had had abortions, and a similar number of men, including other well-known personalities, signed another document declaring that they had helped to arrange abortions. Whether or not it was as a result of this pressure will never be known, but when the case came to court it was thrown out by the judges on the unprecedented grounds that the defendants had acted out of necessity. Their verdict did not, however, put an end to the prosecutions. Shortly afterwards another abortionist was sentenced to twelve years, and a girl who had had an abortion in London was fined.

Nevertheless, the outrage felt among middle-class intellectuals at these sentences tended to distract attention from the fact that a clear majority of the Spanish electorate was opposed to abortion on demand, although polls showed that the level of opposition was much higher among older voters than among younger ones and that in the youngest age groups the 'pros' and 'antis' were more or less evenly balanced. On the other hand, abortion in special cases, such as after a rape or when the foetus was seriously deformed or the mother's life was in danger, commanded more support – that of about two-thirds of the electorate, in fact – and the Socialists in their winning manifesto promised to introduce a bill legalizing abortion in these three circumstances.

It was obviously going to be a political hot potato even so, and the Socialists gave the distinct impression of intending to put off the introduction of a bill for as long as possible. The pressure which forced them to take action came from a most unlikely quarter: the courts. During the first few weeks of the Socialist government, the Provincial Court in Barcelona handed down a succession of judgements in which the judges, while reluctantly passing sentence on defendants who had clearly been involved in abortions, criticized the government for its failure to change the law.

At the end of January 1983 the government decided to bring forward its plans for legislation. Apparently unconvinced of the government's resolve, the Barcelona courts kept up the pressure and in March an attorney acting, not for the defence, but for the prosecution found an even better way of holding the law up to ridicule.

As the law then stood, the only mitigating circumstance which could be taken into account in abortion cases was where the defendant had undergone an abortion 'to hide her dishonour'.* It was such an archaic formulation that it had long since fallen into disuse, but when this particular attorney found himself in the position of having to prosecute a woman who was charged with having an abortion, he argued – doubtless tongue in cheek – that she was just such a case. At all events, the judges accepted his plea and reduced her sentence to one month.

It was clear that unless something was done, every liberally-minded judge in the land would soon be handing out nominal sentences to defendants in abortion cases on the grounds that they had been defending their honour and that this in turn could make Spain look ridiculous internationally. In fact the original case went unnoticed outside Spain, but by the end of the year the Socialists' bill had passed through both chambers of the Cortes. It became law in 1985.

Since then, polls suggest that public approval – or at least tolerance – of abortion has risen to the point at which the pro-abortion lobby is close to being a majority. Indeed, one recent study found that approval outweighed disapproval among those under the age of thirty-four. But despite a lot of talk about changing the law, Spain continues to have the least liberal legislation on abortion of any country in the EU except Ireland. From time to time gynaecologists are prosecuted for overstepping the legal limits, and in 1991 a Málaga doctor, Germán Sácnz de Santa María, was imprisoned for a short period before the government granted him a pardon.

The effect of restrictions imposed by the law can be seen in the statistics. The number of legal abortions in Spain is among the lowest in the EU – 7.6 for every 100 live births in 1988, compared

---

*Defence of one's honour was also a mitigating circumstance in cases involving the murder of an illegitimate child. It applied not only where the child had been murdered by its mother but also in cases in which it had been put to death by her father (with or without the mother's consent).

with 30 in Italy, that other pre-eminently Catholic country whose abortion rate was always reckoned to be on a par with Spain's. In Britain, the rate in the same year was 25.

However, the number of legal abortions carried out in Spain is not the same thing as the number carried out on Spaniards. That year, doctors in Britain alone terminated the pregnancies of more than 3,000 women normally resident in Spain. That would mean that, even without including an estimate for other, less popular destinations like France and Holland, the figure for Spain given above needs to be increased to perhaps 9 per cent.

Then there are the illegal abortions. A report funded by the government's Instituto de la Mujer and submitted to the World Health Organization in 1991 estimated that, of the abortions carried out inside Spain, seven in every ten were performed illegally. So an overall figure, comparable with those for the other Community countries, would seem to put Spain's abortion rate at around 27 per cent of live births, to make it one of the highest in the EU.

It would also suggest that the legalization of contraception has cut the demand for the termination of pregnancy by less than half. Among unmarried Spanish women, it would seem, abortion remains one of the favourite methods of birth control.

Other things being equal, one would also expect the increased availability of contraception to have cut not only the abortion rate but also the number of births outside marriage. In fact the figure has risen, suggesting either more pre-marital sexual activity or a greater willingness to give birth without getting married, or both. As a percentage of all live births, the numbers born outside marriage doubled between 1980 and 1985, from 4 per cent to 8 per cent, but then dropped fractionally over the next five-year period.

Even at its peak though it was an extremely low figure in comparison with those for most other EU nations. In Denmark, for example, it was 36 per cent and in the United Kingdom 25 per cent, though in Italy it was only 6 per cent. This may simply be because the pressure to get married if pregnant is much greater in the southern, 'Catholic' countries. But there is evidence to suggest that, in Spain at least, sexual activity before marriage, though greater than it once was, is not as great as one might imagine.

In the first place, the overall level of sexual activity – that is, inside and outside marriage – is thought to be low, a legacy perhaps of the restrictions, ignorance and puritanism of the Franco years.

A succession of learned inquiries carried out in the latter years of the dictatorship suggested that between 60 and 80 per cent of married Spanish women routinely obtained no pleasure from sexual intercourse. In *Las españolas en secreto: Comportamiento sexual de la mujer en España*, Dr Adolfo Abril and José Antonio Valverde noted that 'no more than 20 per cent of the (female) population is able to use the word "orgasm" properly, another 30 per cent has heard or read the word "at some time" and the rest – half the (female) population – half of all Spanish women – have never heard the word and do not of course know what it means'.

As recently as the mid-1980s, a study by the International Health Foundation aimed at finding out more about the use of contraceptives concluded that there was less love-making in the land of Don Juan than in any other EC country. Sexologists have frequently asserted that the average Spanish married couple make love less frequently than once a week.

A number of factors, moreover, militate against promiscuity among the young in Spain: the fact that, as we shall see later, so many of them live at home; the problems associated with getting abortions; and, to a much more localized extent, the difficulties encountered in buying contraceptives.

In a poll conducted for the Instituto Nacional de la Juventud and published in 1987, 60 per cent of young Spaniards said they had had sex by the age of eighteen. The figure for the number of girls who had lost their virginity by that age was 56 per cent. Now compare that with the findings of the 1975 poll mentioned earlier – that 42 per cent of young Spanish women had lost their virginity by the age of twenty. What you see is a difference, certainly, but something that is a good deal less than a revolution in private morality.

My personal impression – and I think that personal impressions count for as much in this area as pollsters' statistics – is that most young Spaniards still have a strong preference for lengthy, steady relationships, not so very different from the traditional *noviazgo*. Since in the old days it was pretty much unthinkable that either party should back out of an engagement, the parents of the *novios* were sometimes prepared to turn a blind eye to sexual relations. It would be fascinating, though doubtless impossible, to know just how much the level of sex before *noviazgo*, as distinct from sex before marriage, has really altered over the years.

In one area, certainly, attitudes seem hardly to have changed at all, and that is in relation to homosexuality. In line with the tolerant mood of modern-day Spain, overt harassment or discrimination is exceptional. It is widely known that one of Spain's leading politicians is gay, yet so far it seems to have done his career no harm. None the less, it remains acceptable in Spanish society to express views about homosexuality that elsewhere are the preserve of a bigoted minority. As recently as 1987 Isabel Tocino, one of the leaders of the People's Party, was quoted as saying: 'There are attempts to accept, and even excuse it. But fortunately for society as a whole, it continues to be [regarded as] a deviation.' Polls show that the number of Spaniards who admit to being homosexual is suspiciously low. One recent study found that only 2·8 per cent of men and 1·4 per cent of women were prepared to describe themselves as gay. Yet 9 per cent of both sexes acknowledged that they had felt desire for members of their own sex.

Under the dictatorship, the north-eastern coastal town of Sitges was an enclave of tolerance in an otherwise severely repressive society. Franco's contribution to gay rights was to make homosexuality illegal by including it in the 1970 *Ley de Peligrosidad Social* (literally, 'Law of Social Dangerousness'). It was this which led to the founding of a Movimiento Español de Liberación Homosexual. Throughout the late seventies, the Movimiento was responsible for organizing demonstrations on 28 June (International Gay Pride Day). In 1979, however, homosexuality was removed from the terms of the *Ley de Peligrosidad Social* by decree. Gay associations were legalized in 1980 and, as soon as the Socialists came to power, police raids on clubs virtually ceased.

The first lesbian movement to be formed in Spain, the Catalonia-based Grup de Lluita per l'Alliberament de la Dona, did not come into existence until 1979. Even after that, the lesbian movement tended to keep a very low profile indeed. Its first demonstration was staged as recently as 1987 and was prompted by the arrest of two gay women for kissing in public. That year, on 28 June, lesbian activists staged a 'kiss-in' (now an annual event) in the Puerta del Sol, the square which has always been Madrid's rallying-point.

Against this background, it is ironic that Spaniards should seem so fascinated by anything that blurs the distinction between male and female. You have only to glance through the newspaper classified ads to see that transvestite and transsexual prostitution are common. During the years of the *destape*, transvestite cabaret established itself as a popular entertainment. And Spain must be the only country whose principal Saturday-night television variety show – archetypally a programme 'for all the family' – has been regularly presented by a transsexual.

Bibi Andersen, who has appeared in some of Pedro Almodóvar's movies, is nowadays a leading media and social personality in Spain. Her success and acceptance are perhaps evidence that the Spanish feel a need for some sort of antidote to the rigid gender stereotyping which is still so much a part of their culture.

CHAPTER II

Women on the Verge of a Nervous Breakdown

The first feminist demonstration to be held in Spain took place in January 1976. Less than two months had gone by since the death of General Franco. Some 2,000 women, according to the organizers' estimate, lined up behind a banner saying: 'Women! Fight for your liberation'. Their aim was to hand in a petition at the Prime Minister's office, which in those days was at the bottom of the Paseo de la Castellana, in the centre of Madrid.

The route of the march took the demonstrators through the most conservative *barrio*, or district, of the capital. Even today, Calle Goya and the streets leading off its western end form what is often called the *zona nacional*. As the women made their way along the street, as one recalled later, they heard cries of '*Putas!*' ('Whores!') from passers-by. But the reaction of a lot of the men was to stop and applaud as they went past.★

Now, one thing that can be counted on to elicit admiration from Spaniards is a display of courage. And what the men along Calle Goya would have guessed was what the women in the march must already have known – that they were walking straight into a police baton charge. Even so, the anecdote is illustrative of something more than just *macho* values. One of the most striking things about the change in the role of women in Spanish society is that it has prompted surprisingly little controversy or opposition. I do not mean to say that Spanish males have fought shoulder to shoulder with their wives and their sisters, their mothers and their daughters, in the battle for women's rights. That is patently not the case. But

★The details of the march are taken from 'Qué queda del feminismo?' by Ana Alfageme, *El País*, 23 December 1990.

those who have resisted the process have done so mainly in private rather than public, and passively rather than actively.

One reason, I suspect, is that women's liberation, like regional nationalism, became an issue at the same time as Spain was moving from dictatorship to democracy. It thus came to be seen as part of a wider process of liberation which the vast majority of Spaniards understandably regard as beyond criticism. All the same, the lack of fuss is surprising in a country where the repression of women by men has been so extraordinarily severe.

It is no coincidence, perhaps, that the word first coined to describe what English-speaking feminists were to call 'male chauvinism' should have been a Spanish one.

The word *machismo* did not in fact orginate in Spain but in Mexico. Nevertheless, the phenomenon of *machismo* is a product of Mexico's Spanish heritage. Spain, in common with other southern European societies, lived for centuries by a code of moral values at the core of which was a peculiar conception of honour. It was regarded not as a subjective measure of self-esteem, as it was in northern Europe, but as an objective, almost tangible, asset that could be lost not only by one's own actions but also those of others, particularly one's relatives.

A wife could strip her husband of his honour by cuckolding him and a daughter could forfeit her father's honour by losing her virginity before marriage. If the girl were betrothed there was a good chance that the marriage could be held earlier than planned, at which point the loss of honour could be minimized; but if she had had sex without even getting engaged the sanction was horrific, because the only way in which the family could save itself from dishonour was by removing the cause, which in this case was the girl herself. Expelled from home, single mothers were usually unable to find any respectable employment in societies where it was difficult enough for women to acquire a training, let alone a job. As a consequence many drifted into prostitution. In this way, Latin society has divided women into whores and madonnas not just in theory but in practice. For the father of the child, on the other hand, the fact of having had sex before marriage – whatever the circumstances – was as much a distinction as a disgrace.

This was consummately unjust on more grounds than one, since men had less excuse for pre-marital dalliance. Unlike women, they could always resort to prostitutes. But then the reason why frustrated young men were able to afford the services of prostitutes was that they were cheap, and the reason they were cheap was because they were numerous, and *that* was because their numbers were constantly being replenished by cohorts of unmarried mothers who had themselves been unable to withstand the pressures imposed by the taboo on pre-marital sex. Thus the Latin way of sex always had a sort of iniquitous internal logic.

In Spain the discrimination inherent in such a system was given an especially keen edge by the peculiarity of its history – the sustained contact with Islam, a religion which has always held women in low esteem, and the seven centuries of conquest and settlement that were needed to remove Islam from the peninsula and which inculcated among Christians a special respect for masculine virtues.

The division of women into the stereotypes of whore and mother are both deeply embedded in the Castilian language and especially its slang. *Hijo de puta* (son of a whore) is a serious insult, yet *de puta madre* ('whore-motherish') means 'great', 'superb', 'fantastic'. The allegation, in *hijo de puta*, that one's own mother might be a whore is intolerable, but the abstract notion of a woman combining both erotic and maternal qualities is nevertheless thought to be highly appealing.

This whole complex of social and moral values had been sustained and encouraged under Franco's dictatorship. As a way of promoting the growth of a population which had been reduced by civil war, Franco instituted a system of incentives for large families – but the prizes were given to the fathers, not the mothers. Although divorce and contraception were outlawed within a matter of months of the end of the civil war, there was no law to ban brothels until 1956 and even then it was never implemented. At a time when Franco's censors were busy covering boxers' chests and trimming actresses' busts, they were quite content to give their imprimatur to a novel, *Lola*, whose heroine was a prostitute-spy.

It has been said that towards the end of Franco's rule the only European country in which there was a comparable degree of institutionalized discrimination against married women was Turkey, and that on several counts the status of wives in Turkey was actually higher. The assumptions underlying the Spanish civil code were summed up in Article 57: 'The husband must protect his wife and she must obey her husband.' At the crux of their legal relationship was the concept of *permiso marital* (marital permission). Without her husband's agreement, a wife could not embark on any sort of activity outside the home. She could not take a job, start a business or open a bank account. She could not initiate legal proceedings, enter into contracts, or buy and sell goods. She could not even undertake a journey of any length without her husband's approval.

Under the Spanish system, the property owned by a married couple is divided into three categories: that which the husband has brought into the marriage, that which the wife has brought into the marriage and that which they have acquired since (their so-called *bienes gananciales*). But whereas the man did not need his wife's permission before selling, lending or mortgaging the property he had brought into the marriage, she required his for a similar transaction. Not only that, but the wife had no control whatsoever over their *bienes gananciales*, even when she had been partly – or entirely – responsible for earning them. As if that were not enough, the wife did not have proper control over her children either because, unlike the husband, she did not enjoy what was called the *patria potestad* or paternal authority.

Leaving the family home for even a few days constituted the offence of desertion, which meant – among other things – that battered wives could not take refuge in the homes of their friends or relatives without putting themselves on the wrong side of the law. And although adultery by either sex was a crime, punishable by between six months and six years in prison, there were different criteria for men and women. Adultery by a woman was a crime whatever the circumstances, but adultery by a man only constituted an offence if he committed it in the family home, or if he were living with his mistress, or if his adulterous behaviour was public knowledge.

The first significant reform of this system was approved shortly before Franco died. In 1975 Spain abolished *permiso marital* – fifty-six years after Italy and thirty-seven years after France. The laws against adultery were revoked in 1978 and those articles of the civil code which put women at such a disadvantage with regard to their children and the family finances were replaced in 1981.

Since then, women have made up so much ground in Spain that it can seem as if the restrictions on them were lifted, not in the last couple of decades, but in the last century. If the social revolution of the seventies was about sex, the social revolution of the eighties was about gender. It was the decade in which Spanish women flooded into higher education and on to the labour market.

By the start of the academic year 1987–8, there were more female than male students in Spain's universities. In 1981, women had accounted for less than a quarter of the total active population. By 1991, they accounted for a third.

At the time of writing, there are three women in the cabinet. The Vice-President of the Constitutional Court, the head of the state railway network and the mayor of the country's third biggest city, Valencia, are all women. There is a female governor of a gaol that is mainly for male prisoners. Spain's most celebrated young sculptor is a woman. One of its most popular comedy acts, Las Virtudes, is an all-women affair. And of the young bullfighters to have entered the ring in recent years, one of the most promising is Cristina Sánchez, who in 1993 became the first woman (in modern times at least) to kill all six bulls in a *corrida*.*

Almost as striking has been the incorporation of women into Spain's military, and paramilitary, services. The first Civil Guards to wear skirts entered service in 1989, having begun their training a year earlier – at the same time as the military academies opened their doors to women seeking to enter the non-combatant branches of the armed forces as NCOs or officers. It was not until the following year that the government permitted women to apply for admittance to the fighting units – and only then at the insistence of a schoolgirl.

Ana Moreno, from Denia on the east coast, had been inspired by

---

* A ban on women fighting bulls on foot was lifted in the year of Franco's death. It had been in force since 1908. Before that, Spain produced a number of lady bullfighters. The most extraordinary was perhaps Martina García, who fought in her last *corrida* in 1880 – at the age of seventy-six.

one of her teachers, a retired pilot, to dream of becoming one herself. At the age of seventeen, she wrote asking to enter the Military Aviation Academy at San Javier in Murcia; in reply, she had a letter telling her there was no law to say she could. Taking the attitude that there was no law to say that she could not, she appealed to the courts and in 1988 the High Court in Madrid ruled that her case was a violation of the article in the constitution which guarantees equality of the sexes. It took a year for the government to issue a decree to regularize the situation, but in 1989 women were allowed to sit the common entrance examination for Spain's three military academies. Thirty-six did so. None of them passed, though this was hardly surprising since they had only had a few months in which to prepare, compared with several years in the case of the men.

A further change in the regulations in 1992 allowed the recruitment of soldiers, sailors and air force personnel who had not done military service, thereby enabling women to join the ranks.* The first offer of places in the armed services after the amendment elicited some 12,000 applications. The Ministry of Defence was astonished to discover that almost a fifth came from women. By 1993, more than 300 women were serving in the Spanish armed forces, some alongside the Legion in Bosnia.

Qualifications can be made to much of this. Female students in the elite university departments which prepare Spain's engineers and architects are still a rarity. At the same time, the proportion of women in the work-force remains low by the standards of the rest of the developed world.

This is partly because in Spain there is still a considerable reluctance to hire women. When the economy was expanding in the late eighties, unemployment naturally fell. But whereas among men it dropped from a peak of over 20 per cent in 1985 to 12 per cent in 1990, among women it carried on rising until 1988 when it reached almost 28 per cent, and only then began to fall back, much more slowly, to 24 per cent in 1990.

One of the results of this bias against the recruitment of women is that they have tended to carve out niches for themselves within the

---

*The only areas barred to women were the Legion, the Parachute Brigade, submarines and small craft.

labour market. It is reminiscent of the way the Jews turned to certain trades when they were forbidden to bear arms or own land in parts of medieval Europe. An outstanding example is the health sector. Women now account for two-thirds of all health workers in Spain. And it comes as a surprise these days to be served by a male chemist. The same process looks set to take place within the armed forces: three-quarters of the women who had joined by 1993 had made their way into the medical, veterinary or pharmaceutical branches.

Once they have secured a job, Spanish women – or rather Spanish mothers – have the advantage of more extensive nursery-school facilities than exist in many other parts of Europe.* However, they suffer other problems. Union surveys have found that one in every three female employees claims to be the object of sexual harassment by a superior – the highest reported rate in the EU.

Progress in some respects has nevertheless been astonishing. By the early nineties, 14 per cent of the executive posts in the administration and 17 per cent of those in business had been taken by women. Proportionately, Spain had as many female directors and managers as Belgium.

The arrival of vast numbers of women in the labour market is an important reason for contemporary Spain's chronically high rate of unemployment. It is also transforming the Spanish language. Because women had never before occupied certain jobs, the words used to describe those jobs existed only with masculine endings. So the choice has been between inventing new words with feminine endings and using the existing masculine noun with a feminine article. The dilemma is still unresolved, especially since the *Diccionario de la Real Academia Española*, the ultimate authority, continues to list some 300 words like *anticuario* (antique dealer) for which it gives no feminine alternative. So should a woman who sits in the cabinet be *una ministra* or, as the conservative newspaper ABC insists, *una ministro*? Most people refer to Cristina Sánchez as *la torera*, yet she herself prefers to be known as *la torero*. And what do you do about the postal workers? A postman is *un cartero*, but the difficulty with making a postwoman *una cartera* is that the word already exists, and means 'wallet' or 'portfolio'.

---

* See below, p. 264.

For the most part, practice has actually gone further than would seem necessary. Words ending in 'e', which were never gender-specific anyway, have also been changed. Usually, 'the boss' – if a woman – is not *la jefe*, but *la jefa*.

What distinguishes the changes which have taken place in the role of women in Spain from those which have taken place in the role of women elsewhere is that they have occurred with almost no intervention or assistance from an independent feminist movement. The word 'independent' is more significant in this context than it may at first seem.

An authentic and spontaneous women's rights movement did exist back in the 1970s. But its voice tended to be drowned out in the louder and wider debate over how best to build a new, democratic Spain. In a society with little tradition of voluntary association, moreover, it was perhaps inevitable that feminists would prove susceptible to the lure of institutionalization.

The UCD's contribution to the women's cause was well-intentioned. A women's department was set up within the Ministry of Culture whose most memorable initiative was a series of television advertisements aimed at drawing attention to sexism in society. One opened with a handsome (male) executive striding down the street towards a group of women of about his own age. As he drew near, the women looked him up and down and then broke into whistles and catcalls interspersed with suggestive remarks. It was hilarious – though none the less effective for that. The Socialists took a much more thoroughgoing approach. Soon after they came to power, they set up a well-funded Instituto de la Mujer, which attracted many of the activists in the existing feminist movement.

Hijacked – and in some measure, seduced – by officialdom, feminism in Spain exists today more as a belief than a movement. Polls show that no fewer than a third of all Spanish women describe themselves as feminists. Yet demonstrations in support of women's rights, which until the eighties routinely attracted turnouts running into thousands, nowadays draw only a few hundred.

Perhaps because of this, or the southern European emphasis on looking your best, the cause of women's rights in Spain has never been much affected by that singular combination of mannishness and anti-maleness which was characteristic of radical feminism in the English-speaking world. Most Spanish women who think of themselves as feminists would look at you in disbelief if you were to suggest they take off their make-up and put on a boiler-suit to show they were not dressing for male approval. This too may help to explain why the progress of women towards equality in Spain has been so short on acrimony. If there has not been a Spanish Norman Mailer, it could be because there has never been a Spanish Kate Millett.

If anything, there is a tendency, shared by some feminists, to link women's liberation with heterosexual permissiveness. A lot of non-Spaniards would accept there is an overlap. But freeing women from repression by men is not the same as freedom from the repression of sexuality *per se*. And the distinction, I often feel, gets lost in Spain.

Carmen, as portrayed in Carlos Saura's film version, is a promiscuous, predatory troublemaker. Yet when the film came to be shown on television in Spain, the listing in one of the newspapers that day began: 'Carmen, a liberated woman . . .'.

In 1990, the Instituto de la Mujer carried out an extensive investigation into male attitudes. One element of the exercise was to identify different categories by their reaction to certain statements in the questionnaire. For example, the 'household monarch' was someone who agreed with the statement: 'A woman's place is in the home.' One of the statements was: 'For the good of the marriage, it doesn't matter if the woman has the odd fling.' The men who agreed with it were classified as 'feminists'.

Why women's liberation should have become so closely linked to sexual permissiveness in Spain can only be guessed at. My personal theory is that it has a lot to do with the peculiarities of Spain's recent economic and social history. Elsewhere, moves towards sexual equality followed progress towards sexual freedom. That is what happened in Spain too. But the influx of millions of foreign tourists in the sixties allowed Spanish men to indulge in pre-marital relationships without involving Spanish women. The *sueca* (literally 'Swedish woman', but a term which came to be applied to all northern European females) soon figured prominently in Spanish popular legend. One result was that Spanish women were left feeling they had some catching up to do on the men as soon as they had the opportunity.

In a way, Spain has leapt from pre-feminism into post-feminism without having really experienced the feminist upheaval which elsewhere took place in between. Spanish society was never lectured by a Gloria Steinem or a Germaine Greer. As a consequence, profoundly sexist attitudes have survived into an era in which women are acquiring much genuine freedom and equality. This too may be a reason for the lack of anything in Spain approaching a 'battle of the sexes'. However, there are indications that a public debate over gender may now be taking shape – and that it could put an end to the truce which has held so far.

One battle in which Spaniards do not have to engage is over whether a wife should use her own or her husband's name: it has always been customary for married women to retain their surnames. However, Spanish women are still hampered by the rigid division of their numbers into *señoras* and *señoritas*, nor is there an obvious Spanish equivalent of Ms. When one of the women ministers appointed to the Cabinet in 1993 suggested tackling the problem by dropping the word *señorita* she provoked howls of scandalized indignation from male commentators.

The *Diccionario de la Real Academia Española* still contains a host of blatantly discriminatory definitions and distinctions. An *hombre público* is 'one who takes part publicly in public business', for example, whereas a *mujer pública* is a prostitute.

Advertisements that would not get off the drawing-board in Madison Avenue regularly find their way on to the billboards in Spain. An advertisement for quince jelly, which the Spanish eat with sheep's cheese, showed a girl naked from the waist up, cupping a pair of quinces in front of her breasts. The slogan was: 'What the quince-jelly girl is offering you tonight'. Still, it was withdrawn after protests – a sign perhaps that attitudes are changing.

Far and away the most important of the sexist attitudes which have survived in modern Spain are those held by men about their role in the home. For this, women themselves are partly, even largely, to blame. The degree to which boys have traditionally been pampered by their mothers is often difficult for outsiders to credit. One Spanish woman I know says that she discovered that she was a feminist as a child when one of her brothers mentioned he could do with a glass of water. 'You heard him,' her mother said. 'Go and fetch your brother a glass of water.'

Reared in accordance with such a set of values, Spanish men are often feminist in word but not in deed. In the winter of 1976–7 an extensive survey was carried out on the initiative of a multinational advertising agency among young city-dwellers in nine European countries. Asked whether they agreed that 'a woman's place is in the home', only 22 per cent of the young Spaniards said 'yes', compared with 26 per cent in Britain, 30 per cent in Italy and 37 per cent in France. The only countries which returned a lower figure than Spain were the Scandinavian ones. By 1990, the young men who had been interviewed in that survey would mostly have married, and would thus have qualified to take part in a study conducted by the Spanish government's polling institute, the CIS. This found that the number of husbands who helped with work in the home varied from 15 to 20 per cent for everything except preparing breakfast (36 per cent) and home repairs (70 per cent).

Which is where we get to the nub of the issue raised at the start of this chapter. Almost certainly the most important reason why there has been so little conflict over the changing role of Spanish women is that it has so far made relatively little difference to the traditional habits of Spanish men. Women have begun to assume new responsibilities in society, yes. But in addition to, rather than in place of, the ones they already had. To a greater extent than most of their European counterparts, they are trying to fulfil three roles at once – those of wife, mother and wage-earner.

The degree to which they are aware of their predicament was underlined in 1990. The magazine columnist Carmen Rico-Godoy published a novel called *Cómo ser una mujer y no morir en el intento*, a humorous account of the travails of a middle-class Spanish woman with a high-powered job and an unconsciously, but irredeemably, *machista* husband. By Christmas, it had sold 180,000 copies.

The unusually difficult circumstances in which women have been joining the labour market help to explain the outstanding demographic change since the return of democracy: the drop in Spain's fertility rate (the number of children per woman of child-bearing age). UNICEF has called it 'drastic'.

Since 1975, the fertility rate has more than halved. Not long after the Socialists came to power, it sank below 2·1, which is the level demographers reckon is necessary for the regeneration of the population. Ever since then, Spain has been doomed to become an ageing nation – a fact which, as we shall see later, has far-reaching implications for other aspects of Spanish life. By 1990, when Spain's fertility rate stood at 1·36, it was the lowest in the world after that of Italy.

Other factors have undoubtedly played a role: the small number of births outside marriage, the sharp fall in the marriage rate, the increased use of contraception, and also, it has been suggested, a growing preference for material comforts – a nice home, a good car and expensive holidays – rather than a big family. The evidence strongly suggests, however, that the main reason is that Spanish women have been taking up full-time employment without significant changes in the division of domestic work between the sexes. As can be seen in other countries in southern Europe, women who do not wish to give up their jobs and cannot spread the burden of domestic tasks will react by cutting down, or cutting out, their third role – as mothers. By the end of the eighties, the fertility rates in Portugal and Greece had also dropped sharply and were close to that of Spain.

There is nothing to say that fertility rates must go on declining inexorably, though. Quite the reverse. As the conditions affecting women improve, as changing social attitudes and labour legislation provide them with more help at work, in the home and with children, so they recover their freedom of manoeuvre. Sweden today has the highest fertility rate in Europe.

Ironically, it would seem that the longer Spanish men cling to traditional attitudes towards women, the greater the damage they will do to that most traditional of Spanish institutions, the family.

CHAPTER 12

Relative Values

It was the Saturday before Christmas. A typical Madrid winter's day – piercingly cold and bright.

The *gordo* ('fat one'), the world's richest lottery, was being drawn that morning and had just showered 10,000 million pesetas (then worth about $100 million or £55 million) ·on staff at a Madrid department store. It was in the swishest part of town, so assistants who had spent weeks catering to the caprices of Madrid's rich had just been handed a present bigger than any they had sold. In a bar across the street from the store, the ladies from perfumery were toasting their luck with champagne. One of the men sharing a drink with them had bought several shares in the winning ticket and stood to gain 40 million pesetas (about $400,000 or £220,000).

What was he going to do with it? Buy a house and a car and spend the change on a round-the-world cruise?

'No,' he said. 'I come from a big family, you see. There are six of us, so each of my brothers and sisters will get five million, and my in-laws will have to have another five, so that should leave my wife and me with ten million to pay off the mortgage and put something aside for the future.'

'And what does your wife think about it?', I asked.

'Oh, I've phoned her and she's overjoyed,' he replied, wholly missing the point of the question.

Survey after survey has shown that what matters to Spaniards above all else is not an ideal or a belief. It is no longer God or Spain, but the family.

In an earlier chapter, I mentioned a poll which suggested that only 3 per cent of Spaniards were ready to die for love or freedom. No other cause scored higher than 8 per cent – except their immediate family. No fewer than 54 per cent of those interviewed said they were ready to lay down their lives for 'a close relative'. In the survey carried out for the Fundación Santa María, people were asked to choose which of a series of things was important in their lives. Family was chosen by 98 per cent as being either 'very' or 'pretty' important. It was the hands-down winner over work, friends, leisure, religion and politics.

The reliance they place on the family has on occasion been criticized by Spaniards themselves as a product of egocentricity. Nevertheless, it has undoubtedly helped to mitigate the crisis of values in society caused by the transition from dictatorship to democracy and by the declining influence of the Roman Catholic Church. Family values have provided contemporary Spanish society with a much-needed anchor. That said, it is worth asking how long it will hold.

It is all too easy, on a brief visit, to get a distorted view of family life in modern Spain. Typically, holidaymakers go out to a restaurant at lunchtime on a Sunday, see a group of Spaniards of all ages sitting round a table and form the impression that large but close families, all living under the same roof, are still the norm. Sunday lunch is indeed an important way for members of a family to keep in touch. But what you are most likely to see grouped around a restaurant table are the members of several different, though inter-related, nuclear families who are unlikely to see each other again for weeks, or perhaps months. And if grandma and grandpa are there, the statistical probability nowadays is not that they will be going back to a son's or daughter's house, but to their own home or an old people's residence. As with so much in Spain these days, appearances can be deceptive – and, in this area more than any other, one needs to tread warily.

The family is one of the few institutions in Spanish life which seems to have drawn strength from recent developments. The surge in property prices during the eighties, coming on top of high unemployment – and even higher youth unemployment – may well have stanched the tendency, evident in other countries, for children to move out of the parental home once they finish school. Flat-sharing among the young before they get married is still extremely unusual. So is the cohabitation of unmarried partners. In fact, several recent studies have concluded that around 70 per cent of Spaniards aged between 18 and 29, both married and unmarried, live with their parents. In the 30 to 49 age group, the proportion was lower but still considerable: 14 per cent.

But while today's Spaniards are only too keen to have their children stay at home, they are increasingly reluctant to let their parents do so. In that sense, the traditional extended family is fast disappearing. In 1970, 71 per cent of people over the age of sixty-five lived with a member of their wider family. By 1992, that figure had plunged to 23 per cent. Once placed in a home, Spain's elderly would seem to be pretty comprehensively neglected. The people who run the homes say that around 70 per cent of the residents receive only one or two visits a year.

A further, crucial point is that the economic factors which keep Spanish households bigger than they might otherwise be in the short term are the very ones which will ensure they get smaller than they might otherwise be in the long term. Soaring property prices and high unemployment rates may have kept young Spaniards at home, but they have also kept them from marrying. Ever since the beginning of this century, the annual rate of marriages in Spain had fluctuated between about 7 and 8·5 per 1,000 inhabitants. But since the late seventies it has dropped like a stone, and in 1990 it hit 5·5 per thousand. Spaniards, however keen on the idea of the family, were increasingly unable or unwilling to form families of their own. Their country now has the lowest marriage rate in the European Union – an important reason for its unusually low fertility rate. This in turn has produced a low birth rate and ensured that in twenty-five years' time Spanish families will be among the smallest in Europe.

Other qualifications need to be made to the view of family life in Spain that visitors so often take away. The Spanish may show remarkable loyalty and generosity towards their close relatives; but the bonds which unite them are, in many cases, as much of custom and tradition as they are of affection or understanding. A survey carried out by the Instituto de la Juventud in 1984 is particularly illuminating in this respect. It found that 76 per cent of young men and 86 per cent of young women 'rarely' or 'never' talked about their personal problems with their parents.

The statistics also point to a level of violence in Spanish family life which is at least as great as that to be found in other societies. Increased media coverage of women's issues in recent years has brought to light more and more evidence of wife-battering. In 1989, some 17,000 cases were reported to the police.

Cruelty to children is also a good deal more common than is generally believed. The view that the Spanish and other Latin races do not have organizations for the protection of children because they do not need them is simply bunk. They do not have them because for years – for centuries, indeed – it has been more or less taboo to interfere in family affairs. Child abuse exists in Spain just as it exists elsewhere, and as elsewhere it is most often found among the most disadvantaged sectors of society.

Court records suggest ninety children die every year in Spain as a result of parental violence. Experts in the field, though, reckon that the real total is vastly higher. A survey carried out in the main public hospital at Santa Cruz de Tenerife at the beginning of the eighties found that one in every twenty-five of the children brought in to the casualty unit was thought to be a victim of parental aggression. Recent estimates of the total number of deaths per year caused by parental aggression have ranged from 1,000 up to 4,000. The report in which the latter figure occurs, written by a lecturer in paediatrics at the University of the Basque Country, argued that child abuse was the second most frequent cause of violent death in Spain.

Above all, it should be remembered that the strength of the family in much of Latin Europe has only very recently been put to the test. In Spain, as in Italy, the family was kept together by the force and sanction of the law: there was no divorce.

Under Franco's dictatorship, there were two kinds of marriage – civil and canonical. But if only one of the partners was a Catholic* they had to have a canonical marriage. Not the least of the injustices of this system was that Protestants and non-Christians who wanted to marry a Spaniard had no choice but to undergo a Catholic

---

*The law defined as a Catholic anyone who had been baptized in a Catholic church. In 1969 it became possible for baptized Catholics to renounce their faith by notifying the civil and ecclesiastical authorities.

ceremony, often against the dictates of their conscience. The law was changed after Franco's death to allow Catholic – or at least nominally Catholic – partners to have a purely civil marriage. Since then, register office weddings have grown in popularity to a surprising extent. In 1986, they represented 16 per cent of the countrywide total, and in some provinces over 60 per cent.

Since there was no divorce under Franco – the Republican divorce law passed in 1932 had been revoked by the Nationalists six years later while the civil war was still in progress – the only way that a marriage contracted in Spain could be dissolved was by means of an annulment. The circumstances in which a marriage can be annulled in accordance with the laws of the Roman Catholic Church are, on the face of it, highly restrictive. The grounds only extend to such contingencies as one of the partners being physically unable to have intercourse, being under age at the time of the marriage, or not having given his or her genuine consent.

These strictures did not, however, prevent several thousand Spaniards obtaining an annulment during the years before the introduction of divorce. Ordinary members of the public could not help but notice that the people who got the annulments were invariably rich and either famous or influential. Suspicions were increased still further when some of those who had obtained annulments on the grounds of impotence remarried and had children! Perhaps the most extraordinary case was that of the singer Sara Montiel who had not one but two marriages annulled, to become one of the very few Spanish women up to that time to marry three times.

From 1971 annulments became even easier to obtain, provided you had a large amount of money at your disposal. This was because of Pope Paul VI's decision to grant certain dioceses, some of whose ecclesiastical courts had rather more lax standards of evidence than the Spanish ones, power to annul the marriages of expatriates. A number of Spanish ecclesiastical lawyers set up offices in the Puerto Rican quarters of New York, for example, simply for the purpose of accrediting the residence there of Spanish couples seeking to have their marriages dissolved. Dioceses in which the authorities could be counted upon not to look too closely at the grounds for annulment were also found in Haiti, Zaïre, the Central African Republic, Gabon and Cameroon. It is clear, however, that officials employed by the Spanish ecclesiastical courts were also involved in the racket since the annulments granted abroad had still to be ratified in Spain.

Several hundred annulments came from tribunals in the Zaïrean dioceses of Sakania and Lubumbashi, neither of which – as the Vatican subsequently confirmed – had a court authorized to grant annulments. The scandal came to light through the efforts of an ecclesiastical lawyer called Ignacio Careaga, whose persistence caused him to be banned from practising by the legal adviser to the Archbishop of Madrid. The Zaïrean annulments were subsequently declared worthless by the Vatican and a number of well-to-do Spaniards who had paid anything from 800,000 to 2 million pesetas to obtain them in order to remarry found that they had become bigamists overnight.

For those unhappily married Spaniards who lacked the grounds or resources for an annulment the only solution was a legal separation. But the process of obtaining one was a nightmare. In the first place, there was no guarantee of any kind that the courts would grant a separation at the end of it all. The parties and their lawyers had to prove, rather than merely state, that their marriage had fallen apart and the aim of the judge and the court officials (especially the so-called *defensor del vínculo* or 'defender of the link') was to contrive a reconciliation. Secondly, blame had to be apportioned before a case could be settled. Witnesses had to be called, statements had to be taken. More often than not private detectives had to be hired and on occasion even the police were involved, bursting in on couples *in flagrante delicto*. Nor was the question of guilt simply a matter of personal pride. Whichever party was found guilty not only forfeited custody of the children but also the right to alimony.

In normal circumstances it took between two and three years to obtain a separation, but it could take up to eight years. The expense was therefore considerable – in the mid-seventies it cost about 300,000 pesetas. In theory it was possible for couples with low incomes to apply for a separation and have the cost borne by the authorities, but cases of this sort were virtually worthless to the lawyers, and in practice they were postponed indefinitely.

When the dictatorship came to an end there were about a half a million people whose marriages had broken down and who were legally separated, but many more living in misery with partners whom they were unable to leave. Not surprisingly, therefore, some 71 per cent of Spaniards, according to an official survey carried out in 1975, were in favour of divorce.

Its opponents argued that the effect would be to leave thousands of middle-aged women lonely and impoverished as their husbands set off in pursuit of younger wives. But a timely study of the workings of the 1932 Act – Ricardo Lezcano's *El divorcio en la Segunda República* – showed that more than half the petitions during the first twenty-two months that the act was in force were submitted by women. In no fewer than sixteen provinces – of which, interestingly, the vast majority were rural – *all* the petitions came from women.

By the time that the drafting of a divorce bill began in 1977, the question was not whether Spain would have a divorce law, but of what kind. A bill passed through the cabinet without incident in January 1980 and was submitted to parliament later that year.

However, the *proyecto Cavero* (Cavero Bill), as it was called after Iñigo Cavero, the Justice Minister, was considerably less progressive than the mood of the nation. If it had become law, petitions for divorce would have had to be channelled through the old judicial separation procedure with its insistence on a verdict. There was no provision for divorce by mutual consent and the judge was given the power to refuse a divorce if he deemed it to be prejudicial to the interests of one of the partners or to those of the children. The *proyecto Cavero* also suffered from a number of serious technical shortcomings. For example, the partner awarded alimony would have been able to demand it from his or her ex-spouse's heirs – a monstrous injustice whose sole purpose, it seems, was to reduce the government's bill for widows' pensions.

In the summer of 1980 Suárez reshuffled his Cabinet and handed the Justice portfolio to Francisco Fernández-Ordóñez, who had already provided Spain with the foundations of a modern tax system. One of his earliest moves was to withdraw the *proyecto Cavero* from parliament and order the drafting of an entirely new bill. This new bill, inevitably called the *proyecto Ordóñez*, halved the period in which a divorce could be obtained to between one and two years. There was no provision for allotting blame, and in effect if not in name it offered divorce by mutual consent.

The Christian Democrats in the UCD were less than happy with it. The Speaker of Congress, Landelino Lavilla, who was one of the leaders of the Christian Democrat wing of the party, succeeded in postponing any further discussion of the bill in parliament until after the UCD's national conference, which was due to be held in January of the following year, in the hope that by then the Christian Democrats would have regained their ascendancy within the party. During the run-up to the conference, their attitude hardened still further and it was and is generally felt in Spain that the intensification of their campaign against the bill reflected the hostility towards it of the new Pontiff, Pope John Paul II.

The long-awaited UCD conference was pre-empted by Suárez's decision to resign – a decision which was at least in part the result of the pressures to which he had been subjected by the constant warring between Christian and Social Democrats over divorce. The choice of Leopoldo Calvo Sotelo as Suárez's successor and the shock of the abortive coup both helped to shift the UCD to the right, but not far enough for Fernández-Ordóñez to be removed from the Ministry of Justice.

The bill survived its first debate in Congress more or less intact, but then the leadership of the UCD agreed under pressure from the Christian Democrats that it should be amended in the Senate so as to restore the judge's power to refuse divorce in certain circumstances. However, on 22 June 1981, in the final historic and tumultuous debate in Congress, the amendment was removed with the help of the votes of at least thirty UCD deputies who defied the party line. The session broke up in disorder with one Centrist deputy declaring prophetically: 'We may be a coalition but never a party – the models of society which the Christian Democrats and Social Democrats have are just too different.' It was the beginning of the end of the UCD. In less than eighteen months it would be deserted by its founder and decimated by the electorate. The issue which, above all others, sealed its fate was divorce.

So when the dust settled, what sort of divorce law was Spain left with? The answer is, a really quite liberal one. You can get a divorce in Spain by one of two methods – directly or indirectly. In the first case, you have to establish that you have been living apart for at least two years if the separation was mutually agreed, or for at least five years if it was not. In the second case, you have to start by obtaining a legal separation. This can now be done in one of two ways: by citing one of the grounds for legal separation laid down by law, such as adultery, cruelty or desertion, or – provided the marriage has lasted for a year – by simply making a joint approach to the courts. One year after the granting of a legal separation, regardless of how it was obtained, either partner is free to petition for divorce. In other words, whichever path is used, it is possible to get a divorce two years after the break-up of a marriage. And because of that final, dramatic vote in parliament the judges in Spain do not have the power to refuse to grant a divorce as long as the petition fulfils one or other of the conditions laid down by law.

With the new procedure being so straightforward, and with the existence of such a backlog, one could have predicted that the divorce rate would soar. Yet, as so often with Spain, one would have been hopelessly wrong.

By 1990, Spain's divorce rate – with 0·6 divorces per 1,000 inhabitants – was a quarter or less of that in some EU nations. Only in Italy, where the legislation is much more restrictive, was the divorce rate lower. Once more, we seem to be up against good hard evidence of the vigour of the family in southern Europe. But are we?

What went virtually unnoticed – or at least unremarked – while it was being debated was that Spain's divorce law had a gaping loophole. There were no penalties for the non-payment of alimony. It is difficult to see this as anything other than unmitigated *machismo* on the part of those responsible for framing and drafting the bill. Only in 1989 was the gap plugged, non-payment being made punishable by suspended gaol sentences and fines of between 100,000 and 500,000 pesetas. But that still left the problem of getting a court order out of one of the world's slowest judicial systems. And it was not until two years later, in fact, that an ex-husband was actually punished by the courts for failing to pay for the maintenance of his ex-wife and their children, and not until 1994 that one was sent to gaol for the same offence.

According to the association which represents women who are

divorced and separated, 80 per cent of alimony goes unpaid. Divorce lawyers say most cases of non-payment never reach the courts.

This, together with a certain social stigma which attaches to divorcés (and particularly divorcées), explains the popularity of what is sometimes known as *divorcio a la española*. Couples separate rather than divorce because the wife does not believe she will ever get maintenance from her husband and cannot see the point of spending a lot of time and money on formally ending their marriage.

CHAPTER 13

High Stakes

There seems little doubt that the Spanish are among the world's most inveterate gamblers. According to the Spanish association for the blind which, as will be seen, has a keen interest and an important role in this area, Spaniards are the biggest gamblers in Europe and the third biggest in the world after the Americans and the Filipinos.

But gambling is a statistical minefield, and nowhere more so than in Spain where those who compile yearbooks and the like often fail to distinguish between gross spending (i.e. the total gambled) and net spending (i.e. stakes less winnings). The result is that the amount the Spanish lose is often overestimated while the amount they gamble is frequently understated. That said, both figures are considerable.

In 1991, gross spending on all legal forms of gambling was almost three trillion pesetas ($28·5 billion or £16·2 billion).* To make a meaningful international comparison, the biggest but least reliable component, which is an estimate for 'one-armed bandits', is best stripped out. That leaves 1,748 billion pesetas ($16·8 billion or £9·5 billion), which means that, on average, every Spaniard over the age of sixteen staked 56,972 pesetas ($547 or £311) during the course of the year other than by way of slot machines. For the UK, which had an average income some 25 per cent higher that year, the

---

*Some years earlier, it was officially estimated that an additional 500 billion pesetas was being gambled illegally. Bars the length and breadth of the country host games of cards and dominoes. The Basques are inveterate gamblers – they even bet on poetry contests – and in the Canary Islands large sums of money are put up at cock fights.

comparable figure was only £206. The Spanish, in other words, gambled 50 per cent more, even though they earned only three-quarters as much.

In terms of the impact on society, a more significant figure is perhaps the net one, because that is what gamblers actually lose. In 1991, the total for Spain was more than 913 billion pesetas ($8·8 billion or £5 billion). That was a sixth of what Spaniards handed over for food, a third of what they laid out on clothes, and half as much again as they spent on alcohol and tobacco combined. Perhaps the most illuminating comparison, though, was drawn by the *Economist* some years ago. It worked out that the Spanish spent ten times as much on lottery tickets as they did on insurance policies.

All this would seem to have something to tell us about the way the Spanish look at life – two things, I suggest, both of which have a bearing on Spain's prospects in an increasingly competitive world.

The first, more positive than negative, is that the Spanish are born risk-takers. Risk-taking, of course, is at the heart of the quintessentially Spanish activity of bullfighting. But what fewer readers are likely to know is that Spain's most popular indigenous card game, *mus*, also provides for a 'moment of truth' – a defiant, reckless, all-or-nothing fling known as the *órdago*.

Forget gambling for a moment. Just take a drive through any Spanish city. What is it that makes the experience so unnerving? That the Spanish drive fast? No; the Italians drive noticeably faster. That the Spanish drive selfishly? Not at all; compared with the French, they are consideration personified. What distinguishes the Spanish is their readiness – their compulsion, almost – to gamble with their lives and, regrettably, those of others in order to gain a few seconds or metres. Go to any main crossroads in Madrid, stand by the traffic lights, wait for them to turn red, then start counting slowly, and when you get to about 'three' – by which time the first pedestrians will be some way on to the crossing and the first cars will be edging out of the side roads – it is odds on that a car, usually a small car, will come hurtling through. Yet in all the years I have lived in Spain I have never once seen a policeman book a motorist for shooting the lights.

The other point that would seem to transpire from the Spaniards' passion for gambling, this one rather more negative than positive, has to do with their attitude to money and work. Lorca's biographer, Ian Gibson, once came out with the perceptive observation that 'the Spanish work hard, but have no work ethic'. If they feel it necessary, either to make money or keep their jobs, they will put in hours that would astonish trade unionists and company bosses in the rest of Europe. Yet their attitude to what they produce is frequently indifferent and the results slapdash. Except among the Catalans, labour is usually regarded as a necessary evil rather than a source of either pride or satisfaction. Indeed, other Spaniards often take the rise out of the Catalans for the way in which they regard work as something honourable and pleasurable. Outside Catalonia, leisure tends to be seen more as a right than a privilege, and as unquestionably more worthwhile than the means of funding it. For those who live among them, this set of attitudes and values constitutes the Spaniards' most engaging – and frustrating – characteristic. It is the reason why there is so much fun to be had in Spain, but also the explanation for that most ubiquitous of figures in Spanish life, the *chapucero*, or bodger.

It can be argued that the Spaniards' heavy gambling helps to fuel the belief that a fortune can be made *sin dar golpe* (roughly, 'without slogging'). Just as Spanish entrepreneurs have traditionally lived in hope of the *pelotazo* (the 'long ball' or 'big kick'), that single stroke of luck or genius which will bring them a fortune overnight, so the ordinary Spaniard can get by on the hope that one day '*me toca la lotería*' (literally, 'it is my turn to win the lottery').

Before sweeping generalizations are made about the Spanish national character on the basis of their prodigious investment, though, it should be recognized that it is a recent, and possibly transitory, phenomenon. In real terms – that is, discounting the effects of inflation – gross spending on legal gambling has increased fivefold since the end of the dictatorship.

For some, it is symptomatic of the 'get rich quick' mentality which overtook Spain in the eighties (though that argument is undermined by the strong growth in gambling both before and since the Socialists' mini-boom of 1986–90). For others, it is evidence of the country's alleged moral bankruptcy. The Communist leader, Julio Anguita, often makes the gambling mania of the new Spain the centrepiece of his campaign speeches, with the charge that it has been encouraged by successive governments, not just as a way of boosting revenue, but as a substitute for better welfare provision and systematic job-creation. He is not alone in that view. In 1991, anonymous graffiti appeared in several parts of Spain urging '*Más currar y menos cupón*', which roughly translates as 'More elbow grease and fewer lottery tickets'.

A relaxation of the gaming laws was among the first changes to be made in Spain after the return of democracy. Franco had allowed Spaniards to put money on horse-racing (through on-course betting and a restricted form of off-course betting called the *Quiniela Hípica*). He had agreed to a football pool, officially described as the *Apuesta Deportiva* but familiarly known as the *Quiniela Futbolística* or just the *Quiniela*, which was used to finance sporting activities. He also consented to a lottery for the blind, the *Cupón pro-ciegos*. And like every Spanish ruler since the start of the previous century, he raised no objections to the state lottery, the *Lotería Nacional*.

What opened the floodgates to the Spaniards' passion for games of chance was a decision in 1977 to broaden the scope of privately organized gambling. A decree enacted by the then UCD government legalized casinos (which had been outlawed since the dictatorship of General Primo de Rivera), bingo and fruit machines.

As in other countries, the appeal of casino gambling is restricted. According to an Interior Ministry survey published in 1989, only 1 per cent of the population over the age of eighteen had ever been to a casino.

Bingo proved to be a different matter. What had started life in most of the rest of the world as a parlour game for large families and had grown into a compulsive distraction for bored housewives became, in post-Franco Spain, a craze that engulfed people of all types and classes. Hundreds upon hundreds of bingo halls sprang up. Variations in the price of entry and the cost of a card soon established social differences between the various halls. Those at the top of the scale became meeting-places for the rich, the fashionable and the influential. For a foreigner, one of the oddest – and most amusing – experiences to be had in late-seventies Spain was a visit to one of these establishments, where men in immaculately tailored suits and women decked out in jewels could be seen hunched over their cards, solemnly covering up the numbers as they were shouted out by the caller. The gaming went on deep into the night.

Although the running of bingo halls was confined to charitable institutions, irregularities were soon rife. A lot of those who were put in charge were former owners or managers of girlie bars and the like. Within a year of the decree which legalized them, forty-nine bingo halls in the province of Madrid were closed down on the orders of the Civil Governor, but more sprang up to take their place. In 1980, almost half the bingo halls operating in and around the capital had their licences suspended for failing to submit accounts. A few months later, the head of a union representing workers in the gaming industry was quoted as saying that terrorist organizations were among those benefiting from the often extravagant profits generated by bingo; forty-eight hours later, he reported having received a string of death threats.

The wild days of Spanish bingo have since been brought to an end by tighter regulation and surveillance. But there is still scope for improvement: more than one in seven of the inspections carried out in 1991 led to some sort of legal action. Meanwhile, the passage of time has sorted out the dilettantes from the devotees. The Interior Ministry's 1989 survey put the number of habitual bingo-players at just over 2 per cent of the adult population.

A similar process now appears to be overtaking 'one-armed bandits'. The takings from what are known in Spain as *tragaperras* ('peseta-swallowers') rapidly overtook the profits to be had from any other form of gambling. For almost a decade after their legalization, they multiplied like sex-crazed robots until their tiresome bleeping and clicking and their mournfully jolly jingles polluted the air of almost every bar and club in Spain. By 1985, according to an Interior Ministry survey, more than 10 per cent of the population were habitual players. Since then, though, there has been evidence of a sharp drop in the popularity of *tragaperras*. The next government poll, published in 1989, put the number of habitual gamblers at only 3·7 per cent. The law governing these wretched devices was subsequently tightened up, leading to a 16 per cent drop in their numbers. Nevertheless, in 1991 their net 'take' was officially put at 303 billion pesetas ($2·9 billion or £1·7 billion) – a figure which dwarfed the profits from even the mighty *Lotería Nacional*.

Spain's state lottery was the brainchild of one Ciriaco González de Carvajal. A court official in Nueva España, the Spanish colony which included present-day Mexico, he had been struck by the success of the state-run draw that had been held there since the eighteenth century. On his return to Spain, he presented a bill to the Cortes of Cádiz, the parliament set up during the War of Independence, which proposed a similar project in Spain. It was approved with not a single vote against, and the first lottery was held in 1812. The *Lotería Nacional* soon came to be regarded by governments as the only way to get Spaniards to pay taxes.

That may no longer be the case, but in 1991 the state's earnings from its lotteries were enough to pay for the entire legal system. Almost half the money gambled on the *Lotería Nacional* is spent on the first and last draws of the year. The *Niño* ('child') is so called because it is held on the eve of Epiphany, the day on which Spanish children traditionally receive their Christmas presents. The *Gordo* ('fat one'), which takes place just before Christmas, is as good a name as any for what is held to be the world's richest single draw. It has become one of the most important rituals in the Spanish year. The winning numbers are sung out in the style of Gregorian plainchant by children from the San Ildefonso school for the blind, reinforcing the point that chance itself is blind. The whole performance is broadcast nationwide over several hours. Go where you may on 23 December – to shops, offices or cafés – you will be unable to escape this haunting litany of fortune. And for a truly terrifying experience, take a cab ride that day with a driver who has a radio in his taxi and a stake in the draw.

The *gordo*'s gross 'take' in 1991 – 158,864 million pesetas ($1,542 million or £867 million) – represented an average outlay of more than 5,180 pesetas (some $50 or £28) by every adult Spaniard. The net income was enough to cover the entire cost of Spain's diplomatic representation overseas.

The *Lotería Nacional* advertises itself as *la lotería* ('*the* lottery') and until quite recently it was, if not the only lottery, certainly the only state lottery. But in 1985, the government launched the misleadingly named *Lotería Primitiva* ('Original Lottery'), and followed it up with the *Bonoloto* in 1988. Both were attempts to respond to the mounting popularity of the draws made by an organization that has become one of the strangest, and strongest, players on the European business scene.

The Organización Nacional de Ciegos Españoles (ONCE) was created by General Franco's Nationalist government in 1938 to provide employment for the blind, whose numbers had been swollen by the civil war. As a way of financing it, Franco agreed to an idea that had first been tried out during the Second Republic when blind people had banded together to organize local raffles. The new, provincially-based, daily lotteries were exempted from tax (which was the least the authorities could do, since ONCE was relieving the state of what would otherwise have been a considerable financial burden). The blind man or woman, standing on a corner, draped with strips (*tiras*) of lottery tickets and crying '*Iguales para hoy*'* soon became an integral part of Spanish street life. It is a sight which appals many foreign visitors, but one which successive governments – and ONCE itself – have defended on the grounds that the blind in Spain thereby have the opportunity for more regular and normal contact with the rest of society than elsewhere.† The *Cupón pro-ciegos* did what was expected of it and in 1950 ONCE was able to set up a proper welfare system for its members.

It was several years before the spirit of democracy was extended to the organization. But in 1981 a decree was passed which more or less freed it of state interference and enabled ONCE to hold elections the following year for a new ruling body. Control was won by a left-wing alliance whose leader, Antonio Vicente Mosquete, became the organization's first democratically elected Chairman. His arrival marked the start of the first of two revolutions in the way it was run.

Mosquete took over at a time when the organization's income was no longer big enough to finance its burgeoning commitments.

---

* 'Equals for today.' ONCE tickets are divided into equal shares for sale.

† By no means all blind Spaniards sell lottery tickets. Membership of ONCE was originally compulsory. This is no longer the case, but about 90 per cent of the blind – some 40,000 people in all – are members. Of these, about a third are coupon vendors. They form the bulk of a sales force totalling some 21,000. The rest is made up of people who suffer some other form of disability.

What is more, it was in danger of being eroded by the newly legalized casinos, bingo halls and fruit machines. In 1984, he secured permission from the government to launch a single nation-wide lottery in place of the various provincial draws held up until then. So popular was the new lottery that huddles of devotees were soon forming at ONCE points of sale, even before the vendor arrived to start his or her day's work. The tickets usually sold out within a couple of hours, which for the vendors meant less work for the same money. Two years later, Mosquete cut their hours still further by abolishing the Saturday draw and replacing it with a super-draw on Fridays which proved to be even more of a success.

Then in 1987 the ONCE Chairman met a violent and controversial end: he fell down a lift shaft in one of the rare moments when he was without a bodyguard. The police decided it was an accident, but all kinds of sinister rumours circulated about the death of a man whose courage and imagination had given him immense financial power.

The reshuffle that followed brought into the management team, as Director-General, the man who was to mastermind the second of the ONCE revolutions. Blind from birth, Miguel Durán started life in a poor family in Estremadura. He distinguished himself at school, emerging top of his year for the whole country in the Spanish *bachillerato*, and went on to enjoy a glittering career at university. By the time he took over the running of ONCE, its vendors were earning almost double the average national wage. Its senior executives were being driven around in bullet-proof limousines. There again, they had become the administrators of a financial empire with potentially awesome influence.

Roughly half the proceeds from a ONCE draw are returned in the form of prize money. Of the rest, about 50 per cent goes towards operating costs. Most of the remainder had traditionally been spent on ONCE's schools and other institutions, with only a small amount invested to provide future revenue. However, as the overall net profits from the *Cupón* rose under Mosquete's tutelage, marginal economics ensured that the share available for investment soared. But until 1988, virtually all ONCE's rapidly accumulated wealth was in fixed-interest securities. ONCE had become like a millionaire with his money locked up in 'gilts'.

The extrovert Durán's innovation was to change the shape of the organization's bulging investment portfolio. With the consent of two successive chairmen, Durán shifted a growing proportion into equities, which carried a greater risk but promised higher returns. ONCE bought sizeable holdings in some of Spain's biggest banks, in supermarket chains, tourist projects and above all, the media.*

By 1991, ONCE's overall portfolio was worth 70 billion pesetas ($672 million or £382 million), of which 30 billion pesetas ($288 million or £164 million) was invested in shares. Few investment advisers would see this as anything other than a prudent balance of risk for an institution which has immense, continuing – and virtually guaranteed – income. Yet Durán himself chose to justify his policy on other grounds, arguing that the presence of ONCE directors on the boards of many of the companies in which it invested could help create employment for its members and that its presence in the media in particular would help to change public attitudes towards the disabled. Apart from the fact that the independent television channel, TeleCinco – in which ONCE has a 25 per cent stake – now broadcasts the organization's draw every night, there has not so far been much public evidence of these worthy aims being realized.

Durán's change of direction immediately attracted criticism from within the organization with the publication of a 'Document of the Nineteen' – so called because of the number of its signatories. From outside ONCE, attacks have come from several quarters. The business community points out that ONCE, with its tax-free earnings, has an inherent unfair advantage. For as long as its only competition was the state's own tax-exempt lottery and its profits were mostly turned into loans for the state through the purchase of government debt, the issue was academic. That is no longer the case. Every time it takes a large stake in a private company, ONCE effectively transfers part of its preferential status to that company, to the detriment of the firm's rivals.

ONCE has also been accused of wielding its prodigious influence

---

* See below, pp. 314-15 and 320.

on behalf of the Socialists in areas where the government in a free-market economy ought not to have any place. In 1985, the Socialists promulgated a decree to regulate the activities of ONCE that in part reversed the one enacted four years earlier. It put government officials back on to its ruling body and made it answerable to a cabinet minister. So although it is not a government body as such, ONCE is nevertheless reliant on the cabinet's goodwill for its future prosperity. One of its earliest sallies into the world of high finance saw it involved in an attempt to force one of the big banks into a merger favoured by the government. As Durán launched himself into the conquest of a media empire, the press suddenly began to take a more jaundiced view of his activities, dubbing him '*Al Cupón*'.

It soon became apparent, though, that ONCE was a double-edged weapon for the government, for it had shown itself to be rather more successful than the state in holding its share of the overall lottery market. As Spain's eighties boom started to run out of steam, it became clear that the government would soon need every peseta it could get to narrow its budget deficit, and that ONCE's profits had long since passed the point at which they were sufficient for the needs of some 40,000 members.

The last straw was Durán's decision in 1991 to go ahead with the launch of another lottery – the *Cupón-abono* – despite a warning from the Economics and Finance Ministry that it was illegal. The *Cupón-abono* also brought protests from the unions, who claimed it cut the vendors' commissions, and who organized a demonstration in Madrid attended by more than 1,000 vendors at which Durán was burnt in effigy. Against this background, the cabinet ordered the project be scrapped. Its ruling was the first serious setback ONCE had suffered and heralded a more cautious phase in its history, which began in 1993 with Durán's retirement.

CHAPTER 14

A Cult of Excess

Depending on your point of view, coffee-drinking may be considered a pleasure, a necessity, a bad habit or a health risk. In Spain it comes close to being an art form. There are so many ways of imbibing it that it can take some considerable time to explain to a waiter exactly how you want it served.

You can have it *solo* (black), *cortado* (with just a drop of milk) or *con leche* (white). Each of the three varieties can be served with single or double measures of coffee, in either a glass or a cup. The strength can be varied by asking for your coffee to be *corto de café* (short on coffee) or *largo de agua* (long on water), a *solo largo de agua* being known as an *americano*. In the case of *café con leche*, you must decide between a large, medium or small cup or glass, with corresponding amounts of milk added to bring it up to the brim. And with *café cortado*, you have the choice of either hot or cold milk. By my reckoning, that makes for seventy-two basic permutations, though it could be argued that a single *largo de agua* is the same as the corresponding double, *corto de café*.

It does not stop there. There are the various forms of instant coffee – universally known as Nescafé, even if of another brand – and of *café descafeinado* (decaffeinated coffee). Both can be mixed with either milk or water or both. Then there is *café helado*, which is chilled black coffee served with crushed ice and a straw, and not to be confused with *café con hielo* which consists of hot black coffee in a cup served together with a glass full of ice cubes. Finally – I think – there are the alcohol-laced variations. A *carajillo* (a *café solo* with a shot of Spanish brandy) is usually, though not always, partially burnt off before serving and customarily, though not always, served in a glass. There are at least two more elaborate regional varieties of flambéed coffee – Catalan *cremat* and Galician *queimada* – which are prepared with locally-made *aguardiente*, coffee beans, sugar and spice. Add to these at least half-a-dozen imported liquor-enhanced brews – Irish coffee is immensely popular in Spain – and you have almost twenty further ways in which coffee can be ingested.

Ignorant of these subtleties, the newcomer to Spain is most likely to be struck by the sheer strength of the stuff. A lot of visitors to Madrid find they cannot sleep for the first few nights and put it down, quaintly, to the altitude. In fact, they have very likely taken in as much nerve-jangling, sense-awakening caffeine on their first day in Spain as they would normally ingest in a week or more back home.

Most of the coffee served in bars and restaurants comes from Colombia. But simply roasting and grinding one of the world's stronger varieties and serving it in generous measures is not enough to satisfy the Spaniards' requirement for something that enables them to remain alert while getting up early, staying up late and often drinking significant quantities of alcohol in between. The coffee you will normally be served in Spain is known as *torrefacto*, which has been double roasted and finely ground until it is the gastronomic equivalent of Semtex. Every so often, coffee industry representatives will urge their compatriots to switch to something that is easier on the nerves and softer on the palate, but their pleas never seem to make any difference.

The Spaniards' addiction to *torrefacto* is all of a piece with a nation in which there is very little that is bland, gentle or reassuringly soft. So is the way in which they use the word *descafeinado* in a wider, and universally pejorative, sense to mean 'watered-down', 'artificial' or 'bloodless'.

Their seemingly instinctive enthusiasm for whatever is bold, strong and decisive has bedevilled their history, turning it into a succession of abrupt changes in direction. The relatively smooth transition from dictatorship to democracy has often been adduced as evidence that Spain's bloody past has cured the Spanish for good of their propensity for destructive excesses. In so far as politics is concerned, that may well be right. But it is also true that the transition has not prevented – and in some respects may have actively promoted – indulgence in excesses of a different, though scarcely less destructive, kind.

It may have something to do with the generally tolerant upbringing that Spaniards get from their parents – or the utterly shameless pampering they get from their grandparents.* Perhaps it stems from a religion in which one's personal, spiritual profit-and-loss account can be wiped clean by confession and repentance. Or it may just be a hangover from the days when the people of the Mediterranean worshipped gods free of Judaeo-Christian misgivings about pleasure. At all events, the Spanish have a strong streak of self-indulgence that sits oddly with their equally characteristic austerity. A history of Spain could be written around the interaction between these two tendencies and, if it were, the period since Franco's death would unquestionably emerge as one in which self-indulgence was to the fore.

Political, economic and social factors have all doubtless played a part as well. Nearly two decades after the end of Franco's dictatorship, the excesses of the Spanish can often seem reminiscent of those of the archetypal ex-convent schoolgirl, recklessly experimenting with all that was previously forbidden. The country's rapid growth in the late eighties meant that there were more people with the disposable income to indulge their caprices. But more important than any of these factors, I suspect, is the sheer pace of change on all fronts. Other countries have undergone periods of economic, political and social upheaval. But perhaps in no other European country has such sweeping political transformation taken place between two bursts of breakneck economic growth, and against a background of profound change in social values. Spanish society as a whole can often seem to be suffering from shock, and one way in which the individuals in it have tried to mitigate the shock is by resort to drugs, both legal and illegal.

Back in the seventies, Raymond Carr and Juan Pablo Fusi argued that Franco's dictatorship had generated a 'culture of evasion' – a habit of escaping from reality into romantic films, trivial plays,

---

* One way to choke off a braggart is to say, '*Tú no tienes abuela*' ('You don't have a grandmother'). The implication is that he didn't have his praises sung enough when young and is making up for it now.

radio soap operas, football and lotteries. In the years since, that 'culture of evasion' has been replaced by a much more destructive 'culture of addiction'.

It is probably true to say that the Spaniards' overall consumption of the legal drugs, alcohol and tobacco, is the highest of any nation in the European Union. According to *World Drink Trends*, published by the Dutch drinks trade association, the Spanish rank second to the French among the major nations of the world in the consumption of alcohol. Their average annual intake in 1991 was reckoned to be some 12 litres of pure alcohol, compared with 7·6 litres per head in Britain and 7·5 in the United States. Figures from the World Health Organization suggest that as smokers the Spanish rank second in the EU only to the Greeks. In 1989, the number of cigarettes sold per inhabitant over the age of fifteen was 2,560. The equivalent figure for the UK was 2,100.

Other factors may be at work in both cases. Spain is, of course, a wine-producing country where wine-drinking starts at an early age at the family table. The consumption of alcohol can even begin in babyhood: though the custom is dying out as awareness of the hazards spreads, Spanish mothers traditionally dipped their children's dummies in *anis* (aniseed liquor) to stop them crying. Nor is it surprising that smoking should have become widespread, given that so much of the tobacco from America reached Europe through Spain. A Spaniard without a cigar, Richard Ford observed in the last century, 'would resemble a house without a chimney, a steamer without a funnel'.

If, however, for geographical and historical reasons, alcohol and tobacco have for long been cheap, available and socially acceptable, what has boosted sales in recent years has been higher consumption among women, for whom the legal drugs have become symbols of emancipation.

Cigarette consumption has been oscillating at around its historical peak since 1986 – a sign that awareness of the risks is gradually spreading. Nevertheless, the impact of health warnings is blunted by the fact that, for reasons which remain unclear, the incidence of lung cancer among smokers is not as great in Mediterranean countries. One theory is that this is because of the traditional Mediterranean diet with its bias towards fish, fruit, vegetables and olive oil.

If so, the lung cancer rate in Spain is set to rise sharply. Eating habits are changing rapidly; young Spaniards today are reckoned to have the highest cholesterol intake in the EU.

Spanish wine is among the strongest in Europe and spirits in Spain are poured with prodigious liberality. Yet you almost never see people drunk to the point at which their speech is blurred or their movements erratic. Spaniards rarely drink wine without eating something, even if only some *tapas*,* and before or after tackling spirits they will usually take a strong dose of *torrefacto* coffee to offset the effects. Except perhaps in the Basque country, outright drunkenness does not evoke that humorous, conspiratorial tolerance with which it is often treated in northern Europe. Most Spaniards do not need alcohol to help them shed their inhibitions. And in a country where personal dignity counts for so much, the loss of control which accompanies drunkenness is seen as wholly deplorable.

There again, as the foreign boss of a multinational subsidiary once said to me of his employees, 'While none of them is ever drunk, at any one time about half are less than sober.' He was in the computer business and had noticed that the quality of programming dropped as the day advanced. Among manual workers, it is quite usual to start the day with a *carajillo*. Any cafeteria around 11 a.m. will be packed with office workers eating the traditional late-morning breakfast, and plenty of them – male and female alike – will be rounding off their first meal of the day with a beer. Over lunch, most Spaniards will have at least one beer or a glass of wine, often mixed with *Casera* (sweet gassy water). Formal business lunches are traditionally prefaced with a shot of dry sherry and sealed with a *copa*. By 6 or 7 p.m., the cafeterias are once again busy with some of those same office workers taking a quick swig of vermouth, gin or whisky in preparation for knocking-off time and the chance to share in a round of after-work drinks with friends.

This steady intake, made possible by growing affluence, could explain a high – and rapidly rising – level of alcoholism. In 1981,

---

*These were originally titbits served in a saucer or plate set on top of the customer's glass. The word *tapa* means 'lid'.

the estimated number of alcoholics in Spain was 3 million. By 1986, it had risen to 4 million and was forecast to reach 5 million by 1996. But if those estimates are correct, almost one adult Spaniard in eight is currently an alcoholic, and just from personal observation of Spanish society I find that figure difficult to credit.

What is certainly true is that recent years have seen the emergence of a distinctive, and disquieting, pattern of drinking among the young which has none of the traditional safeguards. This is what is known as the 'cult of the *litrona*'. It takes its name from the brown plastic litre bottles of beer which teenagers buy and take away to drink – usually in groups – in the open air. It is a habit which appals most Spaniards over the age of about thirty-five. Sitting amid discarded *litronas*, the youngsters can look like down-and-outs, and many of their elders fear a slide towards the booze-driven vandalism that is so common in northern Europe.

Just before Christmas 1990, on the day that the schools broke up, their fears were given some substance. Reacting to one of those unfathomable common impulses that can move the young, tens of thousands of chanting, singing teenagers converged on the centre of Madrid, swigging from *litronas* and blocking the traffic with their sheer numbers. For the most part, it was a good-natured occasion. But by late afternoon a lot were hopelessly drunk. Fights broke out, some windows were smashed and a few of the youngsters ended the day in jail or hospital. A similar number of British teenagers on the rampage would have left parts of the city temporarily uninhabitable, but it was nevertheless an extraordinary departure from normal Spanish conduct and perhaps a warning for the future.

While beer and spirits have been gaining ground at the expense of wine (which is nowadays regarded as a decidedly unfashionable tipple unless taken with food), there has been a radical change over the past twenty-five years in what the Spanish smoke. Traditionally, as Ford observed, they were cigar-smokers. Right up until the mid-seventies, a good Cuban *puro* could be bought in Spain for a fraction of what it cost in the rest of Europe. Since then, Havanas have risen tenfold in price and the numbers sold have dropped sharply. These days, they are mostly for special occasions, and particularly to be smoked during bullfights.

Since pipe-smoking is rare, tobacco in Spain means cigarettes.*
Recent years have seen traditional black tobacco rapidly ceding
ground to Virginia cigarettes, which are known as *rubios* (blondes).
In 1988, sales of *rubios* overtook those of *negros* for the first time.

Part of the appeal of *rubios* is that for many years they were kept
out by the tobacco monopoly, Tabacalera, and could only be
obtained at exorbitant prices on the black market. But one cannot
help suspecting that the name given to them in Spanish adds to their
allure. Blonde hair continues to exercise an extraordinary fascination
in Spain and one that is vigorously exploited by advertisers.†

Despite the Spaniards' high degree of perilous addiction, their
government remains strikingly unconcerned. The last thing that
Spaniards can complain of is interference from a 'nanny state'.
Alcohol and tobacco cause respectively an estimated 20,000 and
44,000 deaths a year in Spain, yet official campaigns to publicize the
risks are few and far between. And neither the UCD nor the
PSOE has seriously attempted to use taxation as a means of
persuading Spaniards to cut their consumption of either. Despite the
fact that some 60 per cent of traffic accidents in Spain are reckoned
to be directly or indirectly caused by alcohol, the law regarding
breath-testing is a chaotic tangle of ambiguity and contradiction,
with the result that very few motorists are ever convicted of
drinking and driving. Breathalyser tests are voluntary and, at the
time of writing, expected to remain so until 1995. What action
there has been has been directed more towards smoking than
drinking. The government has put warnings on cigarette packets,
banned television and radio advertising of tobacco, and promulgated
a widely ignored, rarely enforced ordinance against smoking on
official premises.

As a drinker and ex-smoker from a country where officialdom
would like to tell you how to tie up your shoelaces, I find the
absence of warnings entirely delightful. But then that is the attitude
of someone who has had the chance to ignore such warnings, and I

---

*Literally so. If you want to ask for cigarettes in a bar or restaurant, you say
'¿Hay tabaco?', not '¿Hay cigarrillos?'

†The cartoonist Forges once drew two yokels watching the 'box', with one
saying to the other that until he got a television he had never realized the majority of
children in Spain were blonde, freckled and blue-eyed.

have to acknowledge that the Spanish government's relaxed approach may not only have allowed thousands of Spanish lives to be cut short, but also helped to create an atmosphere conducive to the spread of yet more perilous drugs.

It is starting to change, but the prevailing belief of Spaniards who regard themselves as minimally liberal has for many years been that what you do with your body is your own business, and yours alone. In 1988, a book was published in France which provided detailed information on available drugs and how they could help to improve physical, intellectual and sexual performance. In France, it caused a scandal. The government described it as an attack on public health and its publisher was put on trial. The following year, the same book was launched in Spain. It carried an enthusiastic introduction by a popular intellectual, and was put on sale with a virtual absence of controversy.

The term 'over-the-counter medicine' takes on a new meaning in Spain. In practice, you can buy virtually anything you want from a chemist without a prescription, just so long as it is not actually lethal, in normal doses, for a fit person. 'Uppers', 'downers' and antibiotics are handed over without a murmur. A few months before the 1992 Olympics, I spent a morning visiting chemists' shops in Barcelona to buy banned steroids for an article in the *Observer*. In none of the establishments I visited was I refused what I wanted, even though all the drugs I asked for were clearly labelled with the equivalent of 'prescription only'.

In so far as narcotics were concerned, the impression throughout the eighties was that 'anything goes'. Spain's Socialist administration, it should not be forgotten, was the first to be recruited almost entirely from the 'generation of '68'. One of its earliest measures, in the year after coming to office, was to legalize the consumption of narcotics both in public and in private.* It was not until 1992 that the government modified its policy and made public, but not private, consumption an offence.

From time to time, in the years before the ban was re-imposed,

---

*So far as hashish was concerned, the reform did no more than reaffirm a previously little-known peculiarity of the law. Even under Franco, the possession of small quantities for personal consumption was not an offence.

one would be sitting in a perfectly respectable restaurant and an equally respectable client would finish lunch or dinner and light up a 'joint' as if it were the most natural thing in the world. In the lavatories of fashionable discothèques, customers would sniff lines of cocaine as unselfconsciously as they would brush their hair or apply their lipstick. In the seedier quarters of the bigger cities, it was not at all unusual to see heroin addicts sitting in doorways injecting themselves.

But while Spain's drug problem was – and to some extent, still is – more visible than those in other countries, is it really more serious? The figures for illicit drugs are inevitably approximate – and not just in Spain. A government survey carried out in 1990 suggested that 4 million Spaniards had tried hashish and almost 1·5 million – about one in twenty of the adult population – smoked it regularly. The results also indicated that around 900,000 had tried cocaine and that 75,000 were addicted to it. In the same year, Spain's Health Minister put the number of heroin addicts at 80,000, though other recent estimates have ranged from 60,000 up to 100,000.*

Of all of these, the only figures which bear any kind of international comparison are the ones relating to heroin addiction. If the Health Minister was right, then there were two addicts per thousand inhabitants in Spain in 1990 – twice the estimated level in Holland, a country that is often cited as having one of the worst drug problems in Europe. In the United States, with an estimated half a million heroin addicts, the equivalent figure was also two per thousand. In the UK in 1990, the number of notified drug addicts – of whom the vast majority were heroin users – was some 17,500. Since the ratio of unnotified to notified addicts is reckoned to be around four or five to one, that implied an overall total of perhaps 75–80,000, or around 1·35 per thousand inhabitants.

This admittedly rough-and-ready calculation suggests that appearances are not deceptive, and that Spain does indeed have a very serious problem – comparable, among the three countries just mentioned, only with that of the US.

---

*The line between heroin and cocaine addicts is no longer as easy to draw as it once was. Fear of AIDS has driven a lot of heroin addicts into cocaine addiction as the lesser of two evils.

A number of specific factors can be adduced to explain why this should be the case. Spain has for some time had one of the youngest populations in the EU. During the late eighties, it also had its fastest-growing economy. Because of its proximity to North Africa and its links with Latin America, Spain has long been an important route into Europe for both hashish and cocaine. It is now reckoned by law enforcement agencies to be the main route for both drugs. None of this, though, explains why such large numbers of young Spaniards took to heroin, which reaches Spain from the Middle and Far East, in the period before its economy started to boom.

Experts in the field say that awareness of the risks, both from AIDS and overdose, seems finally to have turned the tide against heroin. The number of fatalities fell for the first time in 1992. By then, other indicators such as the number of people arrested for trafficking and the amount seized in raids had been dropping for the previous two years. At the same time, though, there were warnings that a huge cocaine problem was taking shape below the surface of society. The move away from heroin and towards cocaine is a Europe-wide phenomenon, like the shift from cannabis and into 'designer drugs' like Ecstasy.

Nevertheless, there are indications that in Spain the rise in cocaine usage has been exceptionally steep. According to one account, based on an internal government report that had been leaked to the press by the heart surgeons' association, the number of Spaniards who had tried cocaine by 1993 had leapt to 4 million, of whom 640,000 were habitual users. That takes a bit of believing. But what is quite clear is that cocaine enjoyed a remarkable degree of social acceptance in Spain during the late eighties and early nineties. Not the least of its attractions for the Spanish, with their fondness for staying up half the night, is that it enables users to go for lengthy periods without sleep.

Against this background, the government's attitude can seem peculiarly complacent. It was not until 1990 that the authorities began offering addicts the alternative of methadone. Campaigns aimed at deterring youngsters from taking to drugs have, for the most part, seemed to pull their punches. As for rehabilitation, the resources invested by the state have been paltry in comparison with the scale of the problem Spain faces. There have never been anything like enough places in rehabilitation centres for the numbers seeking treatment.

Although ministers and officials will, from time to time, assure the public of their concern about the drugs problem, their avowals are nearly always accompanied by an assertion that legal drugs do more damage than illegal ones. There is truth in this, of course. As government spokespeople point out, heroin kills only some 800 people a year, compared with several tens of thousands who die as a result of tobacco and alcohol. But that rather misses the point that heroin addicts tend to die a good deal earlier in their lives than the victims of tobacco and alcohol. And it overlooks two other factors of cardinal importance.

The first is that drug addiction in general, and heroin addiction in particular, have played a huge role in pushing up crime rates in Spain. Since heroin users have not been able to get the drug (or, until recently, a substitute) by declaring their addiction to the authorities, they have routinely taken to either prostitution or crime – usually petty street crime – to finance their habit. In 1990, in evidence to the Interior and Justice Committee of Congress, the then head of the prison service said that 50 per cent of those in gaol had been sentenced or remanded for crimes involving drug dependence.

The other factor is the role of intravenous drug-taking in the spread of AIDS. At the end of 1992, Spain had the highest AIDS rate in the EU. Almost two-thirds of Spain's sufferers were heroin addicts who were believed to have contracted the disease by sharing needles with other drug users. The size of the time-bomb Spain's heroin addicts have placed under the rest of the population remains to be seen. More than 40 per cent of heroin users are thought to be HIV positive. Given the close links between drug addiction and prostitution, and the important role that prostitution plays in sexual relations in Latin society, it is not difficult to understand why 1993 should have seen the start of a steep rise in the percentage of AIDS sufferers who had contracted the disease heterosexually.

The links between criminals and heroin and between heroin and AIDS were evident in figures released by the Justice Ministry in 1990. These indicated that no less than 28 per cent of the prison population was HIV positive. Yet when the government was asked to provide free syringes to prisons, its response was to distribute bleach instead.

CHAPTER 15

Invisible Guardians: Crime and the Police

The first step on the *ruta del bacalao** involved dosing up on a 'designer drug' like Ecstasy or a home-brewed variety like *felicidad* (happiness), which offers a 30-hour trip. The next step was to dance from Saturday into Sunday in Madrid. Then it was off for a wild drive to Valencia, which is 225 miles away, to carry on revelling in the city where *bacalao* was born at the start of the nineties. There, the dancing carried on till late afternoon or early evening, when it was time to return, exhausted but usually at very high speed, along the same busy road.

By the autumn of 1993, the *ruta del bacalao* was sufficiently established among the young of Madrid for nightclubs to have been set up along the way, in the middle of the countryside, solely to cater for those who chose to break their journey for a quick top-up of music, pills, or both. It had been given extensive publicity in one of the national newspapers. A double album of hits from the *ruta del bacalao* was on sale in department stores. And imitations of the route between Madrid and Valencia were taking shape in other parts of the country. The police, in other words, must have known what was going on. Yet it was not until twelve young people were killed in road accidents in a single weekend that action was taken.

The degree of lawlessness which the police – or perhaps more accurately, those who give them their orders – are prepared to tolerate is one of the most striking aspects of contemporary Spanish society. By the standards of other European societies, in fact, the Spanish police are invisible. You can quite easily spend an entire day

* *Bacalao* is an extra-loud, super-rhythmic variety of club music which seems to have evolved from 'techno'.

in either Madrid or Barcelona without seeing a single policeman or policewoman other than those directing the traffic. The contrast with the Franco years, when expressionless, uniformed figures nursing sub-machine-guns formed part of the urban landscape, could scarcely be greater. And that, of course, is part of the explanation.

A lot of the people who run the country or help form public opinion in Spain, people who are now in their forties and fifties, spent their youth in fear of policemen – whether running away from Franco's riot squads or dreading a visit from his secret police, the Brigada de Investigación Social.* A good many others, in the age groups above and below, watched what was happening and developed similar misgivings. As a consequence most of the people who count in today's Spain are deeply reluctant to countenance the more active police presence needed to curb what has gradually become a considerable volume of crime.

The reported rate has more than doubled since the Socialists came to power and nearly quadrupled since the end of the dictatorship. While the UCD was in office, the average yearly increase was about 7 to 8 per cent, but the rate rose after the Socialists took over and in the period to 1989 was almost 12 per cent. However, 1989 marked a peak and the next two years saw slight, though encouraging, falls. Whether fortuitously or not, the turnaround coincided with the arrival at the Interior Ministry of a tough ex-union boss from the Basque country, José Luis Corcuera.

How, though, does the level of crime in Spain compare with that of other countries? Are the Spanish more or less felonious than their neighbours?

International comparisons in this area are notoriously hazardous. This is partly because definitions vary significantly from country to country, but also because it is suspected that there are large differences in the percentage of crime reported. In an effort to get around the second of these problems, the Dutch Justice Ministry devised a survey in which cross-sections of the population in various countries and cities were asked about their experience of crime, regardless of

---

*I have had to use the term 'secret police' because it is the only one in English which conveys the sense of a squad dedicated solely to tracking down dissidents and stamping out opposition, but there was never anything secret about the BIS.

whether they had reported it to the police. The results, published in 1990 and given extensive publicity, suggested that there was more crime in Spain than in Britain, France or Germany. In view of the Spaniards' reservations about the police, it is only to be expected that less crime is reported in Spain than in countries with a longer experience of democracy; even so, the conclusions of the survey are difficult to credit.

It is quite clear that there are now serious problems in Spain's red-light areas and in the working-class suburbs and historic centres of the bigger cities. Indeed, one of the saddest developments in recent years has been the emergence of what are effectively 'no-go areas' in which muggings are commonplace. That said, there are still vast stretches of rural Spain where crime is negligible, and that is not the case in most other European countries.

Moreover, if we make a simple comparison of the total number of crimes reported, the disparity between Spain and the countries mentioned earlier is immense. In 1990, just over a million offences were reported in Spain. In England and Wales in the same year, the figure was more than 4·5 million. Allowing for the difference in the size of their respective populations, this means that the *reported* crime rate in Spain was less than a third of that in England and Wales. So for Spain to have a higher *actual* crime rate, well over two-thirds of offences would have to go unreported.

It is quite clear nevertheless that Spain has undergone an explosion in criminality over the last couple of decades which requires an explanation – especially since the Spanish do not seem to be a particularly delinquent nation. Organized crime, such as the prostitution in Barcelona, has traditionally been in the hands of foreigners – French, Corsican and Latin American racketeers. It is only very recently that Spaniards have been associated with organized gangs involved in the drugs trade and operating from Galicia and Andalucia.

It is never easy to say what makes crime rates rise. In the case of Spain it would have been surprising if the disappearance of the dictatorship and the lifting of so many restrictions within such a short time had not had some effect. But if you look at a graph based on the crime figures, you will see that the line begins its ascent in the year *before* Franco's demise, and this suggests that it had less to do with political factors than with the social and economic pressures that built up during the *años de desarrollo* and which, by coincidence, ended at almost the same time as the dictatorship. One of those pressures was the emergence of a class new to Spain – the disaffected urban young. Sons and daughters of the migrants who arrived in the cities during the fifties and sixties, they tend to measure their wellbeing not by the standards of the impoverished Spanish countryside but by comparison with the glamorous lifestyles they see depicted on television, and fall easy prey to the drug pushers.

One of the difficulties of trying to contain the delinquency that has swept Spain is a multiplicity of law enforcement agencies. The two main forces are the Guardia Civil, which has traditionally patrolled the countryside, the highways and frontiers of Spain, and the Cuerpo Nacional de Policía which is responsible for provincial capitals and other large towns. By 1993, these two forces had strengths of just over 70,000 and 50,000 respectively. In addition, there were more than 35,000 locally recruited municipal policemen and another 7,260 officers in the regional police forces which have been set up in the Basque country and Catalonia.* An international comparison made by the government three years earlier suggested that Spain was, in fact, under-policed – the number of police officers per thousand inhabitants was lower than in Italy, France or Germany. What is more, many Spanish police officers do jobs they would not be required to do in other countries. Much of the work undertaken by the municipal policemen would, in Britain, be done by traffic wardens. And at any one time, almost 10,000 Civil Guards are engaged in the guarding of prisons and the transfer of prisoners.

The Policía Municipal are recruited and administered locally. They are paid for by the town or city council concerned and their job is essentially to uphold the local by-laws. Most of them carry guns (in many cases reluctantly) but they have never really been regarded as a repressive force, even under Franco. In Madrid, attempts have been made from time to time to turn some municipal

---

* Galicia and Valencia also have their own forces, but they are staffed by officers on secondment from the Cuerpo Nacional.

policemen into British-style 'bobbies on the beat'. None has been successful, though this seems to be partly because of a lack of adequate investment. The last time such an experiment was launched, they were not even equipped with walkie-talkies.

The Cuerpo Nacional was formed in 1986 out of two forces which had been created under the dictatorship to keep order in the cities. The Policía Armada and the Cuerpo General were set up in 1941 with the help of advisers from Nazi Germany to replace two forces created in the 1870s – the Cuerpo de Seguridad and the Cuerpo de Vigilancia – which, in the words of the law that abolished them, had become 'imbued with apoliticism'.

The Policía Armada (literally the 'armed police') was perhaps the most hated body of men in Spain during the Franco era. Whether nursing their sub-machine pistols at the entrance to public buildings or cruising the streets in their white shooting-brakes, the *grises* (greys), as they were called after the colour of their uniforms, were the visible symbols of repression. In 1978, in an effort to change their image, the government renamed them the Policía Nacional and kitted them out in khaki and beige.*

In 1989, by which time they formed the uniformed branch of the Cuerpo Nacional they were given another change of uniform, and put into blue. Successive changes of dress have been accompanied by a profound change in outlook and attitude. Between 1979 and 1982 the Policía Nacional was the responsibility of one of those decisive figures of the transition who are virtually unknown outside Spain – Lieutenant-General José Antonio Sáenz de Santa María, a burly moustachioed soldier whose tough professionalism went hand-in-hand with a genuine commitment to democracy. In 1981, when Tejero occupied the Cortes, Sáenz de Santa María sided unhesitatingly with the government and ordered his Policía Nacional to encircle the building. People have not forgotten that. To the average Spaniard today, it is the force which, when the chips were down, took the side of democracy.

Its image improved still further a few months later when the

---

*This led to them being nicknamed *maderos* ('woodies'), the implication being that they were both brown and dense.

close-quarters battle unit of the Policía Nacional, the Grupo Especial de Operaciones (GEO), which had been formed to deal with terrorist sieges and the like, stormed the Banco Central in Barcelona and released more than a hundred hostages unharmed in one of the most spectacular and successful operations of its kind. Men of the same unit later freed the father of the singer Julio Iglesias after he had been kidnapped by criminals.

Trainees for the plainclothes branch of the Cuerpo Nacional, who need to have the qualifications for university entrance, undergo a rigorous three-year course at a special school in Avila. Within the plainclothes branch, there is a sharp division (by no means peculiar to Spain) between the *policías de brigada* who belong to the various specialist squads and branches, most of which are based in Madrid, and the *policías de comisaría* who work in the local stations, traditionally locked in an unceasing and unequal battle against mountains of paperwork. The first are paid more than the second, and whenever the authorities want to show their displeasure with a member of a *brigada* they dispatch him to a *comisaría*.

Not being subject to military discipline, the officers of the Cuerpo are entitled to join a trade union, and in 1983 unions representing the detectives organized a one-day go-slow and a demonstration by some 3,000 officers in front of police headquarters in the Puerta del Sol.

Although often thought of, and even referred to, as a creation of Franco, the Civil Guard actually traces its history back to 1844 when it was set up to combat banditry. Richard Ford, who was living in Spain at the time the force was founded, remarked how efficient it was. But he added, 'They have been quite as much employed . . . for political purposes rather than those of pure police, having been used to keep down the expression of indignant public opinion, and, instead of catching thieves, in upholding those first-rate criminals, foreign and domestic, who are now robbing poor Spain of her gold and liberties.' He was not the last commentator to see in the force an instrument for the oppression of the poor by the rich.

Supporters of the Guardia Civil argue that it has merely stood by authority, whatever its political complexion, and they point out that when the civil war divided Spain into two camps, its members gave their loyalty to whichever faction had come out on top in that part of the country. That is true, although it overlooks the fact that in several areas the Guardia Civil was instrumental in ensuring that the uprising succeeded rather than in defending the legitimately elected authorities. As with the army, the Guardia Civil became ideologically more homogeneous and more reactionary under Franco's influence. But it was always much more popular with the average Spaniard than the Policía Armada. The courtesy and efficiency of the Guardia Civil highway patrols, who not only enforce the traffic laws but also help motorists in distress, enhanced the force's reputation still further.

Yet of all Spain's police forces it was the Guardia Civil which had most difficulty in coming to terms with democracy. As late as 1980 Guardia Civil units received a telex from headquarters – apparently sanctioned at the highest level – stipulating that on all official premises there ought to be, in pride of place, the portrait of 'HM the King and, in a fully visible place, the portrait of Generalísimo Franco'. Tejero's part in the abortive coup was unfortunate in this respect because it provided the most reactionary elements within the service with a hero and martyr.

The reason why the Guardia Civil proved more resistant to change than the police is that it is far closer to the army both sentimentally and organizationally. In spite of its name, the Guardia Civil is and always has been an essentially military body. Its members qualify for military decorations. Those of its officers who do not come up through the ranks are graduates of the Academia General Militar.* Under Franco, moreover, the Guardia Civil was responsible to the Ministry of Defence, whereas the Policía Armada and the Cuerpo General came under the Ministry of the Interior – a division of authority that made it virtually impossible to co-ordinate the policing of the country. During the early years of the transition there was a lot of talk about having to 'civilianize' the Guardia Civil among politicians who did not perhaps fully appreciate how fiercely proud the force was of its military status. A formula was eventually worked out whereby the Guardia Civil was made responsible to the

---

* Both sorts of officer trainees then undergo a course at the Guardia Civil's own training school.

Ministry of Interior in time of peace and to the Ministry of Defence in time of war. But by that time the ultra-right had had a heyday exploiting the force's apprehensions.

In 1983 the Socialist government put the Guardia Civil under the command of General Sáenz de Santa María in the hope that he would be able to bring about the same sort of transformation that he had wrought in the police. Progress has undoubtedly been made since. The Socialists have done their best not to offend the Guardia Civil's corporate sensibilities while at the same time complying with the policy of the European Union, which is in favour of the suppression of paramilitary police forces. The result is a sort of back-door demilitarization. New standing orders which came into force in 1991 reiterated the 'military nature' of the Guardia Civil, yet were actually very different from those for the army.

The Guardia Civil has also had a change of uniform intended to exorcise the ghosts of the past. Their tricorns, however picturesque they may seem to foreigners, inspire nothing but fear in the majority of Spaniards. In the late eighties, they were quietly dropped for all but ceremonial occasions and the guarding of public buildings and foreign embassies.

The Guardia Civil nevertheless remains a problematic corps in more ways than one. Since it is still a military body, attempts to unionize its members are illegal, and the authorities have been caused no end of embarrassment by the activities of a clandestine union, the Sindicato Unificado de la Guardia Civil.

At the same time, numerous Civil Guards have been tried for accepting bribes from smugglers. One of their number was charged with Spain's first racially motivated murder. And it is not uncommon for off-duty Guardias to be had up for wounding, or even murdering, members of the public after using their service pistols to get the better of an argument in a bar.

A wider problem is that the deployment of the Guardia Civil no longer conforms to the realities of modern-day Spain. It has a bigger establishment and is allocated more money than the Cuerpo Nacional, yet it deals with less than a quarter of the law-breaking. Nowadays, much of rural Spain is virtually crime-free. Banditry is a thing of the past and, since the restoration of democracy, there has been no need for a force to keep tabs on everything that happens in the countryside. Already, several hundred posts have been closed down in villages where there has been no trouble for years. The likely future trend is for the Guardia Civil to be less of a rural force and concentrate more on anti-terrorism and other specialist roles. In recent years the government has approved the creation of a close-quarters battle group, a seagoing coastal unit, and an environmental protection service which, among other things, investigates the causes of forest fires, looks into toxic-waste dumping and helps enforce the legislation on protected species and areas.

The way in which the Civil Guard has been deployed until now also casts light on why crime has increased to such an extent in the big cities: fewer than half of Spain's law enforcement agents, in the Cuerpo Nacional, have been trying to cope with four-fifths of the offences. One of the results of their predictably limited success has been to bring to a head the issue of whether to accept greater restrictions on civil liberties in exchange for more effective action against crime.

CHAPTER 16

The Law and Disorder

At the start of the nineties, dissatisfaction with the level of protection offered by the authorities took shape in sporadic outbreaks of vigilantism, especially in the working-class suburbs most afflicted by drug-trafficking. In an attempt to provide the police with more effective powers to deal with narcotics, the government tabled a law, the *Ley de Seguridad Ciudadana*, which would have allowed police to enter private homes without a court order if they had reason to believe that drugs were being – or were about to be – traded. The move provoked an outcry, particularly among Spain's chattering classes. Legal commentators argued that the law contravened the constitution, but the underlying concern was that police would use suspected drug-trafficking as a pretext for bursting into houses for other reasons.

There is a precedent for this in abuses of the anti-terrorist legislation. First introduced in 1977 as an 'emergency' measure, but institutionalized by the Socialists eight years later, Spain's anti-terrorist law allows the security forces to hold suspects for much longer than is normally the case. It has been repeatedly criticized as a licence to torture, and several allegations of police brutality towards terrorist suspects have been upheld by the courts. In 1988, a number of detectives were gaoled for using the anti-terrorist legislation to hold a common criminal, Santiago Corella ('*El Nani*'), while he was tortured to death.

There might have been less disquiet over the *Ley de Seguridad Ciudadana* if the Socialists had had a better record on civil liberties generally; but they have repeatedly appeared to condone police brutality, retaining and even subsequently decorating or promoting officers found guilty of the mistreatment of suspects. Felipe

González's government has never set out the guidelines for phone-tapping. In 1985, officials acknowledged there was a police unit that kept political parties and other groups in public life under surveillance. And apart from the anti-terrorist law, Spain's Socialist governments have been responsible for introducing highly restrictive legislation in other areas, notably an Aliens Act which allows the executive to deport foreigners without having to bring them before a court. The law, though, is an area where the Socialists have an immensely disappointing record – and not just from the civil liberties standpoint. More than a decade after coming to power they had still not provided Spain with the modernized code of criminal laws they promised when first elected.

Not long after taking office, they carried out a partial reform, affecting about a sixth of the articles in the existing code, which dates from the last century. Much of it was concerned with adapting the penal code to the constitution and updating the jurisprudential underpinnings of the system. But it also introduced suspended sentencing, imposed stiff penalties for failure to comply with the food and drink regulations, made pollution of the environment a crime, and created a clear distinction between 'hard' and 'soft' drugs for the purpose of sentencing growers, manufacturers and traffickers. It was also this reform which enshrined the depenalization of drug possession for personal use.

Definitive revisions of Spain's penal code have been repeatedly prepared, only to be withdrawn or shelved. The latest draft surfaced in 1992. It would have introduced probation (a hitherto untried concept in Spain), weekend imprisonment, and a way of adjusting fines to the offender's means. It would also have defined offences and created penalties for the first time in connection with euthanasia, genetic engineering, intellectual property rights, money laundering, pollution of the environment and cruelty to animals. Then Felipe González called the 1993 election and the whole process went back to square one.

Under the rules laid down in the constitution, the administration of Spain's judicial system was entrusted to a twenty-member committee, independent of government, known as the Consejo General del Poder Judicial. But although the relevant passage in the Constitution has never been amended, the Consejo's independence of government is nowadays a thing of the past.

At the outset, eight of its members were elected by parliament and twelve by the legal profession. Then in 1985 the Socialists, claiming that Spain's admittedly conservative legal profession was using its control of the Consejo to block change, ordered that the Cortes be made responsible for electing all twenty members. Since the Socialists at that time had an overall parliamentary majority, the government acquired effective control of the judiciary. It should be noted, however, that the opposition People's Party, which apparently saw in the move an opportunity to boost its influence, agreed to the Socialists' proposals.

The insidious effects of this change can be illustrated by the arrangements for dispensing justice at regional level. Each of Spain's seventeen Autonomous Communities has its own High Court. In each of its *Salas*, or divisions – criminal, civil, etc. – there are three judges. One is chosen by the Consejo and another by the regional parliament. So wherever the regional government is of the same political coloration as the national government (which in 1993 was the case in nine of the seventeen Autonomous Communities), a majority of the judges in each division owe their jobs to the party in power. It is therefore clearly unsatisfactory that their remit should include the judgement of regional parliamentarians on charges of corruption, embezzlement and the like.

The change in the rules for choosing the Consejo may have been tempting as a short-term expedient, but the danger is that the long-term consequences will prove pernicious in a society which has little familiarity with the separation of powers. The view that the judiciary is simply another branch of the executive is deeply ingrained in Spanish thinking. Judges, for example, are habitually referred to as *funcionarios*, which is the same word as that used to describe officials of the executive. Every year, the ministry which handles the government's press and public relations publishes a handbook which deals, among other things, with the workings of Spanish institutions. The section on the judiciary forms part of a chapter entitled 'Politics'.

Nor should one assume that the disappearance of the absolute parliamentary majorities which the Socialists enjoyed till 1993 will free the judiciary from government influence. Since the partners in any future coalition government can be expected to enjoy an overall parliamentary majority, they can also be expected to have a combined majority on the Consejo. The judiciary may be freed of control by a single party, but unless and until the rules are changed it will not be freed of control by the government.

Indeed, because of similar systems of parliamentary designation, the government in Spain not only holds sway over the administration of justice but also exercises an influence over the three bodies to which it is meant to be accountable: the office of Spain's Ombudsman (known as the Defensor del Pueblo), the Tribunal de Cuentas, which audits public-sector accounts, and even the Constitutional Court itself.

The recent record of the first two has given rise to widespread concern. The Defensor del Pueblo decided not to back calls for the *Ley de Seguridad Ciudadana* to be referred to the Constitutional Court, although the Constitutional Court, which had the law referred to it from another source, eventually decided that it was anti-constitutional, as claimed by its detractors. The Tribunal de Cuentas could find nothing worth pursuing in the FILESA case.*

The Constitutional Court consists of twelve members. The government and the Consejo each choose two. The remaining eight are named by parliament. In 1985, the Socialists changed the ground rules so that laws referred to the Constitutional Court did not have to wait for a verdict from the judges before coming into force. Jurisprudentially, the arrangement is questionable – it allows a *fait accompli* to be created by means of legislation which is later shown to be unconstitutional. Nevertheless, even their opponents will acknowledge that in this instance the Socialists were not trying to curb the powers of the judiciary but prevent creeping paralysis of the executive. By referring everything approved by parliament to the Constitutional Court, the opposition was in a position to bring the government's legislative programme to a standstill. Rulings which, in other countries, could be expected in a matter of months can take years to emerge from Spain's Constitutional Court. In only one year since its creation has it managed to pass judgement on more

*See above, pp. 67-8.

than a sixth of the cases put before it. Though it is by no means as overloaded as some others, the Constitutional Court suffers the knock-on effects of a degree of congestion in the Spanish legal system that is not so much chronic as calamitous.

At the end of 1991, the number of cases waiting to be dealt with in the higher courts alone – those with provincial, regional and national catchment areas – was some 297,000. A single division, the *Sala Tercera* of the Supreme Court, had 27,000 cases on its books. As the log-jam has built up, delays have become progressively greater.

In 1983, more than eighty people died in a fire at a Madrid disco. It took ten years for the case to reach trial. In 1982, a dam burst in the east of Spain, damaging or destroying the property of almost 25,000 people. It was not until 1993 that any of the victims received compensation, and then only because of an initiative by the government – the legal proceedings were still meandering their way towards a third trial. In 1981, a mysterious epidemic, blamed on adulterated cooking oil, killed more than 600 people and afflicted another 25,000. Thirteen years later, it was still with the courts. The main hearing had been held in 1989, but the cases against senior government officials accused of negligence were still awaiting trial.

Perhaps the most remarkable case of all was that of Eugenio Peydró Salmerón, who stood trial in 1987 for a property fraud committed in the days when Franco was still alive. By the time his case reached judgement, he was eighty-one years of age. The judges handed down a nine-year gaol sentence, and a week later he died of a heart attack.

The backlog first built up at the end of Franco's dictatorship as a result of the growth in crime, and the mounting complexity and litigiousness of society. The Centrists failed to respond to the growing crisis, and when they left office, spending on justice as a proportion of total government spending was only a tenth of the average in the EEC. The Socialists have repeatedly increased the Justice Ministry's budget by more than the rate of inflation, but the increases have never proved sufficient to cope with the problem.

There is also evidence that successive Socialist ministers have failed to tackle the challenge with the necessary vigour. Reforms described as 'urgent' in the PSOE's 1982 election manifesto were not enacted until 1988. A partial reorganization of the courts which began the following year led to epic confusion, with trials having to be postponed or suspended because there was nowhere for them to be heard. In Madrid, the minister responsible, Enrique Múgica, decided to go ahead with the ceremonial opening of a new courthouse even though it was not yet ready, and was pursued through the unfinished building by court workers chanting 'Múgica. Resign.'

Delay generates corruption, and specifically what Spaniards call the *corrupción de las astillas* – the bribery of court administrators by lawyers in an effort to speed up their clients' cases. It is sufficiently commonplace for the Plaza de Castilla, the site of the courts complex in Madrid, to be known as the Plaza de las Astillas.

Another consequence is simply injustice. People can be kept in gaol for years on remand for crimes it later turns out they did not commit.

The nineteenth-century *Ley de Enjuiciamiento Criminal*, which remained in force throughout Franco's dictatorship, allowed judges to grant bail to anyone not accused of an offence for which the penalty was six years or more in prison. In most cases they did. But in response to concern about the increase in crime and, in particular, the suspicion that criminals caught by the police and bailed by the courts were responsible for much of it, a law was passed in 1980 under which bail was only available to those accused of crimes for which the penalty was six *months* or more. By the time that the UCD left office more than half the inmates of Spain's gaols were still awaiting trial.

The Socialists came to power determined to make bail once again the norm rather than the exception and to ensure that theoretically innocent remand prisoners did not have to spend unduly long periods in gaol. Soon after their victory at the polls, they passed a law which restored the situation provided for by the *Ley de Enjuiciamiento Criminal* and stipulated that no one should remain in custody for longer than three years awaiting trial for serious offences or eighteen months in gaol awaiting trial on minor charges.

The trouble was that, because of the delays in the system, huge numbers of prisoners on remand – guilty and innocent alike – qualified for release on the day that the law came into effect and were promptly let out. The results were catastrophic. During 1983 the number of crimes reported to the police soared by a third. The biggest increase was in armed robberies, which went up by a staggering 60 per cent. Amid the public outcry that ensued, the government hastily raised the detention limits to four years and two years respectively.

But the situation has never gone back to that which existed when the Socialists took power. In the early nineties the ratio of convicted prisoners to remand prisoners was around two to one.

In the meantime, though, another form of injustice had arisen as the average delay between arrest and trial grew longer. Scarcely a month goes by nowadays without a heartbreaking story emerging of some reformed tearaway – a married man or woman with a steady job, a home and family – having to go to gaol for something that he or she did as a teenager.

From the point of view of society as a whole, though, the most noxious result of delay in the legal system is the disrespect it breeds for the law. If you commit a serious crime and are caught, then sooner or later in Spain – and later rather than sooner, as we have just seen – you can expect to pay for it. But if you breach the planning regulations, say, or fail to pay a fine, or a debt, or your rent, or your alimony, there is a very good chance that you will get away with it, because the other party will find it is just not worth his or her while pursuing you. Better to settle out of court, or drop the case altogether.

As the Spanish themselves readily acknowledge, they have a pretty anarchic temperament. Mix in the knowledge that rule-breaking is likely to go unpunished and what you have is a recipe for chaos. Nobody with a grain of sense, in Madrid at least, ever settles a parking fine. The chances of the council managing to pursue you through the courts to the point at which you will be made to pay are so slight that it is far more sensible to throw the ticket in the nearest bin and forget about it. Hence the double- and even triple-parked cars which line every busy street, the cars parked on pavements, on verges, blocking goods entrances and fire hydrants.

Cast your eyes over some of the most naturally beautiful stretches of the Spanish coastline and what do you see? Dozens of weekend and holiday residences that no planning officer would approve unless given something exotic to smoke. You can be sure that few of them were built in accordance with the regulations. But by the time the council has got an injunction, the work is done. And since no one has the heart to order a demolition, especially if the owner wields some influence in the area, the most that is likely to happen is that he or she will have to pay a fine. In the length and breadth of Spain, there are hundreds of thousands of extensions, homes, entire blocks of flats, even housing estates and industrial complexes, which nobody ever agreed should be there.

When Madrid was swept by a craze for *terrazas* (open-air bars), the procedure was always to open for business first and argue with the authorities later. Similarly casual violations surface almost daily in the media. While this chapter was being written, for example, it was reported that a glittering new shopping mall in the capital, authorized to hold fourteen shops, had been found to contain forty-nine.

The clogging-up of the judicial machinery has given new life to a kind of Spaniard who first surfaced in the picaresque novels of the sixteenth and seventeenth centuries. In his contemporary manifestation he is known as a *buscavidas* or *vividor* – an opportunist living, usually in some style, off his wits and one step ahead of his creditors. Some friends of mine have an acquaintance who changes his car every year and is rarely seen driving anything less impressive than a Porsche. He has not owned any of them. He leases them, omits to pay the instalments, then sells them to generate the money for an out-of-court settlement with the leasing company. Each successive leasing agreement is backed by a bank guarantee from the manager of a branch in some out-of-the-way part of the country who is honoured to oblige the sort of customer who turns up out of the blue in a Porsche.

In Spain, the question 'So what are you going to do then – sue me?' has a special, and terrible, ring. The fact that it is so hard to obtain justice generates a lot of entertaining stories, but it is also an important reason for fearing that Spain may not do quite as well in the future as its progress in the eighties might suggest. The difficulty of resolving disputes obstructs business in general by discouraging deals between strangers, and deters – or should at least condition – foreign investment, since the overseas investor cannot help but be a stranger. The story of Spain's mini-boom in the eighties is littered with instances of outsiders who bought into the Spanish market, realized they had been sold a pup, and then found that they had no effective redress through the courts.

What is even more worrying is that from time to time the government itself gives signs of being infected by this same indifference to the rule of law. The circumstances are often trivial, but the underlying implications are not.

Whether rightly or wrongly, the constitution says that governments can only re-allocate responsibilities between ministries by means of an Act of Parliament. Yet ever since 1986, Socialist governments have been doing so by means of a trick – a clause introduced into the Finance Act which allows the Prime Minister to do so by decree. The constitution states that the court procedure 'shall be predominantly oral'. Yet the majority of cases are still dealt with mainly on paper. It provides for trial by jury. Yet none has ever been held. The constitution says that the deputy Prime Minister may take over the functions of the Prime Minister only if the latter is ill, dead or abroad, but in 1991 Felipe González arranged for his deputy, Narcís Serra, to chair a meeting of the Cabinet so that he could go on holiday in Spain.

Despite the delays in the legal system, the rise in the crime rate ensured that in the first decade of Socialist rule the prison population almost doubled, with the number of extra prisoners outstripping the number of new places by more than two to one. By the end of the period, overcrowding was around 30 per cent. Among the distortions that this introduced into the system was a widespread mixing of remand and convicted prisoners. Indeed, in 1992 Spain's remand prisons had more convicted inmates than remand prisoners. An ambitious 130,000 million peseta (£650 million or $1·3 billion) scheme is currently under way which aims not only to do away with overcrowding by 1997, but also to improve conditions throughout the system. It involves the demolition of more than half Spain's existing gaols and their replacement with eighteen new 'macrocentres'.

But what are the conditions like in Spanish gaols? It is not easy to come to an overall conclusion. Contrary to what one might expect, Spaniards themselves tend to be more critical of the system than foreigners. In 1978 a Senate commission submitted a report that gave the impression that the inmates lived little better than animals. Yet only a year before, the International Red Cross had found the facilities 'satisfactory in the majority of cases' and described Yeserias, the Madrid women's prison, as 'a model for the rest of the world'.

There are undoubtedly gaols which leave a good deal to be desired and the prevalence of the AIDS virus among inmates gives an unpleasant edge to the prospect of incarceration. Nevertheless, the overall regime is unexpectedly liberal. Some prisoners are allowed out for periods of between a day and a week, and all inmates are entitled to a two-hour 'intimate' visit once a month. Spain also boasts Europe's only mixed wing – at the Picassent prison in Valencia.

This is very much in line with a national tradition. It is notable that during the last hundred years, when Spain has not exactly been at the forefront of social reform, it has produced two eminent penal reformers – Concepción Arenal and the Republican prisons director, Victoria Kent. And although the measures these two women introduced have now been superseded, their example and inspiration live on. Perhaps one reason for the discrepancy between Spanish and foreign assessments of their prison system is that Spaniards, with their passion for freedom, find the very idea of imprisonment abhorrent and would regard almost any penal system as an outrage.

PART FOUR

Government and the Individual

CHAPTER 17

The State versus Juan Español

'Since Spaniards in general feel an instinctive animosity towards the joining of associations,' wrote Fernando Díaz-Plaja in *El Español y los Siete Pecados Capitales*, 'the state – an organization to which there is no option but to belong – is viewed with suspicion. The state is an abhorrent entity which is regarded, not as the necessary link between the individual and society, but as a conglomeration of interventions trying to regulate the life of Juan Español,* with the sole aim of damaging his interests.'

As some other Spanish authors have pointed out, the nature of the relationship between the Spaniard and the state is deftly expressed in the vocabulary surrounding taxation. A tax in Spanish is an *impuesto*, literally an 'imposition'. A taxpayer is a *contribuyente*, or contributor. The impression created is not that the citizen routinely pays the state for the services he receives from it, but that – faced with a bothersome intrusion in the normal run of things – he every so often, reluctantly but graciously, hands over some cash to make it go away. Until recently, this was not so very far from the truth. However much it may have longed to meddle in his affairs, the Spanish state only had the wherewithal to do so intermittently.

At first glance, weak government would appear to be the last thing Spain suffered from, having been ruled by dictators for most of this century. But although the regimes of Primo de Rivera and Franco may have been strong in the negative sense that they were capable of preventing people from doing this and that, the fact remains that they were weak in the positive sense of being able to encourage them to do things. The police may have been brutal, the

---

*Juan Español is to Spain what John Bull is to England.

bureaucracy obstructive, but the government's capacity to intervene and to regulate, to shape the pattern of society has always been severely limited. The contrast was particularly marked under Franco.

The avowed aim of the Nationalists when they came to power was to impose a New Order that would affect every facet of private as well as public life. In November 1936, a mere four months after the outbreak of the civil war and with battles raging along two fronts, the government issued a decree unconnected with rationing that stipulated the number and content of the courses to be eaten at mealtimes. 'Henceforth,' it solemnly declared, 'both in restaurants and at home the egg dish will consist of a single egg.' All such attempts at social engineering soon ran into the sand and within a few years of Franco's victory they were abandoned. In fact, towards the end of his rule one of the most striking things about Spain was the virtual absence of petty restrictions. You could park three abreast or litter the streets without fear of anyone stopping you.

It is tempting to put the whole thing down to the anarchic Spanish temperament. But there was also a sound practical reason, which was that Franco's ministers were saddled with the same inefficient civil service and the same inadequate financial resources as their predecessors, going back at least until the beginning of the last century. Spanish governments have traditionally been unable or unwilling to reform their bureaucracy or raise enough tax, and they have paid a heavy price for these shortcomings in their inability to influence events.

The problems associated with the bureaucracy go back to the days of the *pronunciamientos*, when changes of government were frequently accompanied by a full-scale reshuffle of the civil service in which the hangers-on loyal to one faction would be replaced by the hangers-on loyal to another. In an effort to protect themselves against politically motivated appointments, dismissals and promotions, groups of specialists within particular ministries – principally lawyers and engineers at first – formed themselves into corps (*cuerpos*), admittance to which was usually conditional on the holding of a particular academic or professional qualification. With time, the *cuerpos* acquired an important say in the hiring and firing of their members and often controlled promotion too. The refusal of successive governments in this century to countenance trade unions in the civil service only consolidated the role of the *cuerpos* as the channel through which civil servants could put their demands to the minister in charge. Inflation and the absence of a pay-review body encouraged the *cuerpos* to drive a coach and horses through the hierarchy of office and scales of pay established by the government.

'Many corps,' Professor Kenneth Medhurst wrote,* 'resolved the financial problems of their members by the simple expedient of abolishing the lower rungs of the career ladder and granting everybody "artificial promotions". The result was, for example, many officials with the rank and pay of departmental heads filling no more than clerical posts . . . But even these devices failed to resolve completely the problem of inadequate pay. The corps therefore used their influence to establish a multitude of sometimes spurious bonus and incentive schemes. Ultimately these were so commonplace that for most officials the basic salary became only a fraction of the net income.' But in spite of all their efforts, the *cuerpos* were unable to ensure that civil service pay kept pace with inflation and during the thirties, long before *pluriempleo* became a feature of Spanish society as a whole, this pernicious practice had taken root in the bureaucracy. The *cuerpos* benefited throughout from the lack of a proper legal framework. Right up until the 1960s the organization of the Spanish civil service rested on a provisional decree issued in 1852 and modified in 1918.

The *cuerpo* system undoubtedly helped to create the idea – and the reality – of a non-political civil service in Spain. But this could have been achieved by other means and the system's disadvantages far outweighed its advantages. The number of officials in a department was frequently a function of the interests of the *cuerpo* rather than the needs of the administration. Promotion was invariably by seniority rather than by merit. Rivalry between *cuerpos* meant there was very little co-ordination between departments and almost no mobility between ministries. This in turn led to duplication of effort.

Under Franco, little serious effort was put into reforming the

*Kenneth M. Medhurst, *Government in Spain* (Oxford: Pergamon, 1973).

civil service. This was partly because of the inherent conservatism of the regime and its leader, particularly where vested interests were concerned. But it also reflected the blurring under Franco of the distinction between the government (i.e. a policy-making body made up of politicians) and the administration (i.e. a policy-executing body made up of officials). Ministers under Franco were often drawn from the ranks of the bureaucracy and were themselves therefore members of a *cuerpo*. A law introduced in 1964 created a new hierarchy and reorganized, but did not abolish, the *cuerpos* while empowering the government to prevent the setting-up of new ones. But the law was never fully put into effect and the overall situation became considerably worse.

Like a huge, untended creeper, Franco's bureaucracy sprouted myriad offshoots. Firstly, there were the *delegaciones provinciales*, each representing a particular ministry in a particular province. Together they made up a huge *administración periférica* which, by the early seventies, employed one in seven of the central government's employees. The *administración periférica* had all the disadvantages of dispersal and few of the advantages of decentralization – its staff, although only intermittently in contact with head office, were first and last servants of the central government so all important decisions, and a lot of unimportant ones, had to be referred back to Madrid. Secondly, there were the quasi-autonomous agencies such as the state holding company INI and a plethora of *Institutos, Comisiones* and *Servicios* set up by different ministries to look after special areas of interest, which became increasingly difficult to control both economically and politically. At the end of the sixties there were 1,600 of them and they accounted for about a third of government spending.

Being the arm of government under a dictatorship, the Francoist civil service was effectively immune from criticism. There was nobody comparable with the Ombudsmen who operate in several European countries, nor – because of laws effectively forbidding pressure groups – could there be a body like Common Cause in the United States, set up to press for better government. Left to their own devices, Spain's bureaucrats did what bureaucrats the world over will do in similar circumstances, which is to make their life as comfortable as possible. A discrepancy, that later became standardized, developed between their notional working hours, which were 8 a.m. to 3 p.m., and their real working hours, which were 9 a.m. to 2 p.m. It also became customary whenever there was only one day between a public holiday and the start or end of a weekend to join them up by means of an extra day off called a *puente*, or bridge.

In Madrid it was – and no doubt still is – theoretically necessary to get official permission to wallpaper a room. Yet to obtain this or any similar permit you had to put in a morning's work. First, there was the queue for the application form. Then the queue to hand it in, only to find that the application was not valid unless presented with two other documents which could only be obtained from other departments which were almost always in a different part of town. Once you succeeded in getting them, and had queued again for your permit, it was time to discover that the permit did not take effect until stamped by the head of the department and that he had gone home for the day. The whole process was made infinitely more difficult by the opening hours of the *ventanillas* (the little grilles from behind which Spanish bureaucrats used to confront the public). Not only did the opening hours vary from department to department, but they were also always as short as possible – some areas of the administration were only open to the public between 11 a.m. and 1 p.m. daily. Anything of genuine importance could take weeks, months or even years. The inefficiency of the bureaucracy has given rise to a phenomenon which, as far as I know, is peculiar to Iberia and Latin America – *gestorías administrativas*. A *gestoría administrativa* is an agency for people who have more money than time. If you want a driving licence, say, you go to the *gestoría* with all the relevant papers and, for a fee, one of its employees will do the form-filling and foot-slogging for you.

To an even greater extent than Franco's ministers, the members of Suárez's and Calvo Sotelo's cabinets were drawn from the bureaucratic elite and although they acknowledged that there was a need for change they were unable to come up with the radical reforms necessary. The civil service which the UCD handed over to González was substantially the same as that which the Centrists had inherited from Franco. According to Javier Moscoso, a former public prosecutor who took over the cabinet portfolio which carries responsibility for the civil service, it contained 290 *cuerpos* and not even his own aides could supply him with a precise figure for the number of people who worked in it. One of the difficulties of arriving at an exact total was that, in addition to the numerous bureaucrats working for the civil service in the morning and for private firms in the afternoon, there were many doing – or being paid for doing – more than one job within the administration itself. An internal survey carried out shortly after the Socialists came to power revealed that there were some senior officials supposedly doing three official jobs and some who had never even been seen in the office where they were meant to be working.

The advent of Moscoso was nothing if not dramatic. Within weeks of his arrival he issued a circular which the press dubbed the *'reforma de los relojes'* ('reform of the clocks') that shortened the Christmas and Easter vacations and ordered civil servants to work the number of hours for which they were paid – forty-eight hours for senior officials and thirty-seven and a half hours for junior officials. The new minister also sent out instructions that the *ventanillas* should be pulled down and that every government department should be open to the public from nine until two, that information desks should be set up to guide people to the right queue, that all the official forms and stamps needed for the processing of a particular document should be available within the same building, and that members of the public should not be called on to locate and produce documents already in the possession of another government department.

Since then, however, the Spanish civil service's legendary capacity for resisting change has begun to reassert itself. The government has had to grant officials an extra six days off every year in lieu of their lost Christmas and Easter holidays and the working week has been trimmed back so that although junior civil servants are still meant to work a $37\frac{1}{2}$ hours week (usually 8 to 3 every day and $2\frac{1}{2}$ hours one afternoon), senior civil servants only have to work 40 hours (from 8 to 3 and then returning for at least $1\frac{1}{2}$ hours later on).*

Moscoso's reforms gave rise to two laws, passed in 1984. One

---

* One of the consequences of the disparity in working hours of junior and senior staff is that during the afternoon, on all but one or two days of the week, some of

forbade civil servants to hold a second job, whether inside or outside the administration, and gave legislative sanction to the new hours. The other was intended to give the government more power over the people who work for it.

The first has succeeded in making *pluriempleo* much rarer, but not in getting the civil service to work to even the modified timetable. Senior officials tend to work more, and junior officials less, than is asked of them. Soon after the new hours were introduced, it became customary to acknowledge a *'media hora de cortesía'* ('half-hour of courtesy') – i.e. to accept that rank-and-file functionaries would arrive up to thirty minutes late. It was not long before the *media hora de cortesía* became an *hora de cortesía*, and then started to be applied at the end as well as the beginning of the working day.

My personal experience is that you can only count on getting hold of ordinary civil servants between 9 a.m. and 2 p.m., except, of course, for the half-hour to an hour they need to eat their breakfast and walk to and from the nearest café. It is often said that the biggest improvements in productivity have come from putting cafeterias on the premises.

As for the second of the two laws, it seems to have been a complete failure. In the words of a study document compiled by the PSOE and published in 1988,* 'The administration cannot freely appoint civil servants to the jobs it needs to fill in line with its priorities. At the same time, it is generally recognized that the disciplinary regime is effectively incapable of bringing about the dismissal of civil servants who fail to do their jobs properly.'

The evidence for this is to be found in a perusal of the figures for the number of public employees. In view of the rise over recent years in the state's revenue, and consequently in its spending, you would expect to find an increase in the number of people required to look after both income and expenditure. That is exactly what you do find. The number of government employees rose from 1·4 million in 1982 to 1·8 million in 1991.

You would also suppose that, as powers were transferred from

---

the busiest and most powerful men and women in Spain are to be found answering their own telephones.

* *Aspectos y problemas de la vida política española. Programa 2000.*

the central government to the regional administrations, the number of officials in the pay of Madrid would fall and that those paid for by the Autonomous Communities would rise. That is indeed the case.

But then you would also imagine that as the process unfolded the numbers of central and regional government workers would be roughly in proportion to the amount of money that each had to spend. And that is a long way from being the case. In 1991, central government employees, who accounted for 49 per cent of the total, were responsible for spending 67 per cent of the money, while regional government employees, 31 per cent of the total, were responsible for spending just 19 per cent. In the nine years since the Socialists came to power, moreover, the number of local government employees had more than doubled.

It was during 1991 that the government implicitly recognized the failure of earlier measures when it agreed to the drawing-up of a 'Plan for the Modernization of the Administration'. Nothing has since been heard of it, and sceptics can be forgiven for believing in it when and if it is seen to have an effect.

Historically, the state's inability to raise revenue was due to Spain's general disarray and poverty and, above all, to the fiscal exemptions which had been granted to various regions during the country's lengthy and difficult unification. Under Franco, however, none of these factors held good. With the single exception of the Navarrese, all Spaniards paid the same taxes and the country became more intensely supervised and more authentically prosperous than ever before. But one of the outstanding characteristics of Franco's regime was that with the exception of the odd working-class fascist all the *Caudillo*'s ministers came from middle-class backgrounds. They held to middle-class values and acted in middle-class interests, and this was never more evident than in their taxation policy – or rather, the absence of one.

Apart from a limited reform in 1940, successive Ministers of Finance left untouched a system that had been in force since the end of the previous century. It was a system which above all favoured the well-to-do. In the first place, the proportion of the government's income raised by indirect taxes, such as the duties on goods and services (which fall equally on all consumers regardless of their wealth or income, was always considerably greater than the share raised by direct taxes, such as income tax (which by their nature fall more heavily on the rich than on the poor). Throughout the sixties the ratio of indirect to direct taxes was about two to one.

Of the indirect taxes, a comparatively high proportion came from charges on necessities like food and clothing and a relatively low share from duties on luxuries. Direct taxes fall into two main categories – those levied on individuals and those levied on companies. As far as personal taxation was concerned, an inordinately large amount derived from the charge on wages (which was usually deducted at source and was therefore difficult to evade) while only a small amount came from the separate 'personal income tax' that was paid by those who received high incomes or incomes from several sources (which was assessed and collected on an individual basis and was much easier to avoid). For those who could, the temptation to dodge taxes was overwhelming. There were very few tax inspectors and evasion was not even a criminal offence. The 'personal income tax' accounted for less than 1·5 per cent of total fiscal revenue. As for corporation tax, the situation was chaotic. Until shortly before the end of Franco's rule, each of the taxes to which a company might be liable was assessed by a different set of inspectors, so none of them could form a clear idea of the company's overall position. Double book-keeping was the norm rather than the exception and evasion became so widespread that for several years the authorities stopped trying to assess firms individually and worked out each firm's liability by the outlandish device of calculating the profits made by a particular industry in a particular region and then dividing the total by the number of firms. This led to a situation in which companies were unable to make even a guess at what their debt to the government might be because their liability depended in large part on the success or failure of their rivals.

Apart from being grotesquely unjust, Franco's tax system ensured that the state remained as poor as ever, because the effect was to exploit that section of the community which had least to give. In 1975, when Franco died, fiscal receipts excluding Social Security contributions amounted to just under 20 per cent of the gross domestic product (GDP). In the other nations of the 'West' – the member countries of the OECD – the average figure was 33 per cent.

The first step towards changing this situation was taken in 1977, a few months after the general election, when the Finance Minister, Francisco Fernández-Ordóñez, steered through the Cortes an elementary tax reform law. It unified the system of income tax so that wage-earners and non-wage-earners were assessed according to the same rules, and for the first time evasion was made an offence. In the meantime, the Finance Ministry installed a battery of computers and recruited some 1,500 inspectors to deal with personal taxation. So that in the future no one would have an excuse for evading their responsibilities, a team of advisers was provided by the government and anyone who had to fill in a return was entitled to call on their services. Among those who did so was the King, who – in keeping with the egalitarian spirit of the new Spain – pays taxes like everyone else. An advertising campaign was launched around the slogan 'Ahora Hacienda somos todos. No nos engañemos.' A literal translation would be: 'Now we are all the Treasury, let's not cheat ourselves', but it lacks the punch of the original.

The combination of carrot and stick worked, up to a point. The number of Spaniards who submitted their returns by 1 August 1978, the deadline for declaring income received during 1977, was much higher than in previous years, even though a number of them turned up on 31 July with blank forms on the principle that if the tax-men wanted the money then they would have to work for it. Of the total number of declarations, about one in ten contained arithmetical errors (the vast majority of which were of course in favour of the taxpayer). More seriously, however, a sizeable number contained flagrant omissions. During the weeks and months that followed, Fernández-Ordóñez put into effect a plan, dubbed Operation Red File, aimed at flushing out the worst defaulters by using the records of other government departments to confirm the ownership of shares, property or whatever else had been left off their returns.

The next step was to increase the number of people who had to fill in tax returns. In 1980, for the first time, anyone who owned or earned more than a certain amount, or who, for example, owned a house worth more than a certain amount or a car of less than a certain age, or who employed more than one servant or had a seat on a board of directors, had to fill in the hated form.

By the time the UCD left power, fiscal receipts as a percentage of GDP had passed the 25 per cent mark, and in 1981 direct taxes overtook indirect ones to make Spain's fiscal system 'progressive' rather than 'regressive' for the first time in the country's history.

It would be nice to think that the *'Ahora Hacienda somos todos'* campaign persuaded Spaniards to pay up gladly for the good of all. Needless to say, it did not. When the Socialists took office, it was apparent that the economy was still awash with undeclared assets, known in Spanish as *dinero negro* (black money).

The struggle to bring it into the light will long be associated with the bespectacled son of a Catalan baker. José Borrell was still in his thirties, though with a doctorate in economics and a professorship of mathematics under his belt, when he was made the number two at the Finance Ministry in 1984. Not a man to suffer fools gladly, he was nicknamed by one of the papers the 'Torquemada of taxation'. This, of course, was precisely the image the government wished to create.

In fact, the Socialists' efforts to cut down on tax-dodging were often ham-fisted and, in at least one instance, counter-productive. The effect of one of their earliest moves – the so-called Boyer decree* – was to drive a lot of the *dinero negro* into property at a time when the sector was still a closed book to the tax authorities.

The key reform of the Socialist years was a law passed in 1985. One of its effects was to provide an ingenious way in which tax-dodgers could launder their 'black money' and at the same time settle their debts with the Treasury. A new kind of treasury note was created which, being made out to 'bearer', could never be traced, once sold. The tax due on it was levied at the time of purchase. For the government, the scheme had the additional advantage that it provided access to a new source of cheap borrowing.

The 1985 act also forced the banks to provide more information about their customers. However, it left a loophole that was soon spotted. Insurance companies, unlike banks and other financial institutions, were not required to collect tax from their customers

* See below, pp. 281–2.

on the interest they earned. Throughout 1986 and 1987, a number of banks advised their customers to transfer money out of their accounts and into single-premium insurance policies run by groups under the banks' control. The wheeze, uncovered by the government in 1989, proved there was still an astonishing quantity of 'black money' in circulation. Some 4,200 billion pesetas – equivalent to £22 billion or $35 billion at the prevailing exchange rate – was eventually estimated to have been spent on single-premium policies. Eighty per cent was thought to be *dinero negro*. What the authorities had discovered was a secret hoard equivalent to 7·5 per cent of that year's Gross National Product (GNP). The affair also showed the degree of social respectability attached to cheating the tax-man in Spain. Some of the country's leading banks had been involved in the operation.

Unravelling the insurance scam represented a major victory for the government. Some of its other initiatives fared less well. The singer Lola Flores, for example, was put on trial for not paying her taxes. Predictably, she turned the courtroom into a stage, melted everyone's heart, and was acquitted.

In 1990, the government appeared to recognize the limits of its ability to clamp down on evasion when it offered an amnesty. Tax-dodgers were given a choice between declaring their *dinero negro* free of the threat of a penalty, or investing it in a new series of special, low-interest government securities. The move brought to light another 1,700 billion pesetas.

Both the trends discernible under the UCD have continued under the Socialists. In 1990, the share of fiscal revenue in GDP reached 34·4 per cent. This was still below the OECD average, which had risen in the meantime to 38·8 per cent. But it meant that over the decade and a half since the end of the dictatorship, the gap between Spain and the rest of the developed world had been cut from 13 per cent to just over 4 per cent.

Notwithstanding the introduction of VAT in 1986, the ratio of direct to indirect taxes has continued to increase, albeit somewhat erratically, since the PSOE took office. In 1982, 43·8 per cent of current revenue came from direct taxes and 37·8 from indirect ones. In 1992, the figures were 48·6 and 39·4 per cent respectively.

The reason for both these developments is that revenue from

personal taxation has gone up by leaps and bounds, just as it did under the UCD. But in neither case was this due to government action as much as to a phenomenon known as 'fiscal drag'. It is particularly prevalent during periods of high inflation and/or rapid growth, and Spain has experienced first the one and then the other. What happens is that, as salaries increase, the people earning them move into successively higher tax brackets with progressively higher tax rates, so that the proportion of the taxpayers' income which the government takes away in tax goes up without the politicians having to lift a finger. In 1987, for instance, revenue from income tax leapt by almost 50 per cent. It was calculated that only a quarter of the increase was attributable to better inspection and collection.

Tax evasion, by those who have the opportunity to practise it, is still rife. According to a study carried out for the Instituto de Estudios Fiscales, half the income earned in Spain is undeclared. It is still common for companies to keep several sets of accounts, and in 1990 the President of the Spanish employers' federation described evasion as an 'entrepreneurial necessity'. As for taxes on the buying and selling of property, it is reckoned that on average the parties to a transaction declare about one-third of the real price when the house or flat is new, and only a fifth or so if it is not.

The government's failure to curb these abuses explains why a disproportionate amount of the tax collected in Spain continues to come from those who do not have the opportunity to fiddle – the country's wage- and salary-earners who have it deducted at source. In 1989, 76 per cent of income tax was still being collected in this way, compared with 83 per cent six years earlier. An OECD report published the same year was highly critical of the Socialists' inability to bring the figure down further. 'The tax burden for those who really do pay tax seems to be much greater in Spain than for the OECD countries as a whole,' it concluded.

If one is to believe the tax returns, employees in Spain are better paid than their bosses. In 1989, with the economy still booming, the country's businessmen admitted to annual average earnings of only a million pesetas, compared with 1·7 million pesetas a year for wage- and salary-earners.

The imbalances in the tax system are not only a powerful source of disenchantment, but also a significant cause of inequality. Remarkable as it may seem, Spanish society has grown more unequal since its nominally Socialist leaders were elected to power.

CHAPTER 18

The Reluctant Providers

For 1992, the research team at the Prime Minister's Office compiled a book which was published in Spanish as *España fin de siglo* and in English translation as *Spain beyond Myths*. Among the conclusions reached by Mr González's advisers was that the Socialist years had been characterized by 'rising average incomes and growing social inequality'.

That does not necessarily mean the rich have become richer while the poor became poorer. Spain as a whole was richer in 1992 than it had been ten years earlier and the evidence suggested that Spaniards of all classes were earning more.

But what the statistics also showed was that the share of gross domestic product which went to employees was almost 5 per cent lower than in 1982. And whereas the economic boom saw the wages of white-collar workers rise by more than 5·25 per cent, the real income of blue-collar workers had risen hardly at all. As for those such as pensioners whose earnings are fixed according to the official minimum wage, they had actually slipped back during the boom years.*

Turning to the distribution of assets rather than income, the Prime Minister's team concluded that developments in the housing market particularly had tilted the balance between the classes much more drastically. 'It is almost certain,' they wrote, 'that the distribution of assets has not only increased inequality, but may also be leading to a dual population in which the rich are becoming rich out of proportion and the poorest are becoming poorer.'

---

*The trend has since changed, though not by much. In 1992, the minimum wage was 3 per cent higher in real terms than in the year the Socialists came to power.

When Felipe González visited Washington in the year after he came to power, the Reagan administration was reported to have concluded, perceptively, that he and his followers were not so much socialists as 'young nationalists'. Mr González's ambition – and it is discernible in almost every speech he makes – is to eliminate what politicians in the early part of this century called *el atraso*, that is to say, 'the lag': the gap which developed between Spain and the rest of Europe in the centuries which followed its Golden Age. From the very beginning, his overriding concern has been to push up Spain's *per capita* GDP to the point at which it reaches the EU average.

The Socialists' welfare policy is best understood in this context. Mr González and his ministers have unquestionably improved social provision. Indeed, by the time of the 1993 election, they were not far from completing the construction of a welfare state. But the task had been carried out without any evident master plan, relish, or pride. Time and again, they have had to be bullied into introducing reforms by threats from the trade unions. They have often seemed bent on testing to the limit the Spanish family's capacity to make good deficiencies in the country's system of social protection. And although investment has frequently been concentrated in those areas where it can be expected to yield electoral dividends, the Socialists make surprisingly little of their generally impressive welfare record on the hustings. PSOE candidates habitually cram the government's achievements in this area into a single paragraph towards the end of their speeches, reserving pride of place for prestige projects like the Madrid-to-Seville high-speed train. It is as if they regarded the creation of a welfare state, not as something they were proud and eager to be associated with, but as a tiresome necessity distracting them from the nobler mission of promoting growth. This is particularly true of unemployment pay, where economic growth and social protection are most obviously in conflict.

For most of the eighties, Spain had the highest rate of unemployment in the European Union – and that despite a boom which created half a million more jobs than had been destroyed in the recession that preceded it. There were various reasons for this. One was that Spain's 'baby boom' lasted longer than in the other countries in the Community, so its 'baby boomers' were still reaching working age during the eighties. Another reason was that a progressively higher proportion of the young people reaching working age did so intending to enter the labour market. This was primarily, indeed almost entirely, because of the change in attitudes among Spanish women described earlier.

To provide every unemployed adult in Spain with an alternative wage would represent a formidable burden – one that successive administrations have done their best to avoid. Indeed, it has become traditional now for Spanish politicians to react to a downturn in the economy or an upturn in the rate of unemployment by swiftly imposing restrictions on either the value of unemployment pay or the number of people entitled to draw it. This in itself is perhaps understandable, except that at no time have they created a 'safety net' benefit comparable to Supplementary Benefit in the UK or Supplemental Security Income in the US for those who have no other means of support. Those who do not qualify for unemployment pay just have to get by as best they can – doing odd jobs here and there, living off friends and relatives and, in extreme cases, taking to the streets to beg.

When Franco died, most of the jobless were eligible for unemployment pay. By 1976, the figure was 62 per cent.* But the reaction of the Centrists to the onset of the recession which Spain suffered in the late seventies and early eighties was to amend the regulations in such a way as to protect the state's coffers. The result was that by 1983 the number of jobless who could claim the dole had dropped to 26 per cent.

The Socialists seemed to have no plans to change the rules, and it was only as part of a deal with the unions that entitlement was extended. The percentage of those covered duly rose, but then fell back again after the government tightened up once more. By 1988, the number of jobless who qualified for the dole had shrunk to 29 per cent.

---

*This and subsequent measures of the proportion of jobless receiving unemployment pay were all arrived at by dividing the number of unemployed entitled to unemployment benefits by the number of people who had signed on at the government employment agency. If the standard measure of unemployment were used in these calculations, the percentages would be much lower.

The government attempted to justify the situation by stressing that an estimated one in three of the unemployed had a job in the 'black' economy. It was also pointed out that in families with members out of work, it was more common than in the rest of the EU for there to be at least one member in work. What this meant, though, was that wages intended for one person were having to be spread between several.

The unions were unimpressed, and greater access to unemployment pay was the main demand behind the 1988 general strike. While never publicly recognizing it had made a U-turn, the government did in fact alter the regulations. The following year a decree was issued which, over the next four years, led to a steady rise in the percentage eligible for the dole (although this was also due in part to a fall in the numbers unemployed). By mid-1993, the figure for those covered by the system reached almost 70 per cent, but then began to fall back again as fresh restrictions imposed by the Socialists in 1992, and again in 1993, started to take effect.

Currently, the situation is that school-leavers in search of their first job are not entitled to any sort of benefit. The assumption – a very Mediterranean one – is that they can live at home, supported by their parents. Depending on how long they have been making contributions, workers are entitled to claim an unemployment benefit (*prestación*) which varies in amount according to the recipient's previous salary, and in duration according to the length of his or her contributions. Entitlement to the *prestación* does not last for ever although in extreme cases it can run for six years. When it runs out some beneficiaries are left without any support at all, but others can fall back on an unemployment grant, or *subsidio*. This is considerably less generous. In 1993 it amounted to 614,565 pesetas (about $5,000 or £3,000) a year, which – in the big cities at least – could scarcely be called a living wage.

Shortly after the 1993 clampdown was announced, the former Economics and Finance Minister, Carlos Solchaga, summed up an attitude which had been amply reflected in the Socialists' treatment of the jobless when he told fellow party members that 'the state is not there to pay for idlers'. However, the state, or rather the government, had for several years been content to turn a blind eye to evidence of fiddling on a remarkable scale in the part of the country from which it derives the support that keeps it in power; for in addition to those claiming the *prestación* or the *subsidio*, over 200,000 Spaniards in the south of the country were receiving hand-outs through a so-called *Regimen Especial Agrario*.*

Back in the seventies, I was at a lunch with the Prime Minister, Adolfo Suárez, when he was asked what it was that made him lose sleep at nights. The army? ETA? The price of oil? Or perhaps the runaway social security budget? Being the smooth operator he is, Suárez began his answer by denying that he ever lost sleep. But he added that, if anything were going to make him do so, it would be Andalusia.

It was a wholly unexpected reply. Nothing had happened in Andalusia that had not happened in the rest of Spain, and the movement in support of autonomy for the region had yet to get up a head of steam. But, as I later came to realize, Suárez – in common with every other Spanish politician of his generation – had been brought up to think of lush, balmy Andalusia, not as Spain's flower garden, but as its powder keg.

Traditionally, much of Andalusia and the smaller but even poorer neighbouring region of Estremadura has consisted of vast estates owned by absentee landlords and worked by huge armies of casual labourers. The potential for social unrest among these day-workers, or *jornaleros*, was evident even before mechanization made most of them superfluous. Migration from Andalusia and Estremadura to elsewhere in Spain, and later to other parts of Europe, in the fifties, sixties and seventies offered a temporary safety-valve. But by the time Suárez came to power it had been closed off, and for some while parts of the south teetered on the edge of destitution. The nub of the problem was a lack of work between harvests – there were villages where, for a month or more each year, people gathered berries to fill their stomachs.

In order to stave off the threat of a peasant revolt, and that is what it came down to, the UCD provided the southerners with a community works programme intended to fill the gaps between

---

*Its beneficiaries are not counted as unemployed, nor as recipients of unemployment pay, so their numbers do not affect the figures given earlier for the percentage of unemployed entitled to unemployment benefits.

harvests. But when the Socialists took office, led by the son of an Andalusian smallholder, they put into effect an altogether more comprehensive, and generous, solution.

Any Andalusian or Estremaduran who could provide evidence that he or she had worked the land for sixty days in a given year would qualify for nine months' *subsidio* to cover the period in which they were out of work. Incredible as it may seem to outsiders, the assumption was – and is – that the land in the south of Spain is incapable of providing farm-workers with more than three months' employment in any one year.

And not only that. Fearing some *jornaleros* would be unable to find even sixty days' work on the land, the Socialists instituted a community works scheme of their own, and decreed that days worked for it could be counted towards the required number. The Plan de Empleo Rural (PER), jointly funded by the central and regional governments, sponsors projects for the improvement of local facilities. It enables ditches to be dug, monuments to be scrubbed, and roads, gutters and pavements to be laid. The projects are recommended to the authorities in Madrid by the village councils. If and when they are approved, it is the local council that is responsible for hiring the labour and buying the materials. However, at no stage is a check made to see that the number of days worked in each village matches the number of days claimed by the villagers.

Unwittingly or not, the Socialists had created a machine for the spread of corruption and patronage. Despite the fact that the number of *jornaleros* was falling, the number of beneficiaries of the government's special dole rose from under 200,000 in 1984 to almost 300,000 in 1990 before dropping back to just over 200,000 two years later. Shortly after the figure peaked, the councillor in charge of agriculture in the Socialist Andalusian government acknowledged that no more than 80–90,000 of the 300,000 drawing the *subsidio* were genuine day-labourers.

It soon emerged that mayors in villages the length and breadth of the PSOE's heartland had been signing vouchers falsely crediting local people with however many days' work on the PER were needed for them to collect the government's hand-out. In some cases, the beneficiaries were genuine *jornaleros* for whom there was just not enough work. But the vast majority were simply country-dwellers who had seized the opportunity to receive a steady, if modest, income for nine months of the year. Since 1991 the majority of beneficiaries have been women, even though women never outnumbered men in the fields.

Most mayors go along with the fraud for fear of what will happen to them otherwise. 'Uncooperative' mayors can expect to be voted out at the next local election. One went into hiding after refusing to oblige. Some, though, are thought to have sold their assistance in return for money or favours. They would not be the only ones. Landowners are known to have signed false papers in return for cash or unpaid work.

The creation of the *subsidio* and the PER has changed Andalusia profoundly. There are village squares that have been re-paved to such a standard that you could imagine you were in rural California instead of one of the poorest regions in Europe. In villages where all the obvious work has been done, councils have been accused of presenting non-existent projects to the government and then diverting the labour and materials to their own ends. More than one mayor is reckoned to have acquired a new swimming-pool or house extension thanks to the PER.

But the changes go beyond even what is visible. The *subsidio* has institutionalized underemployment and, some fear, made Andalusia unreformable. An entire class has grown up which can build on nine months' dole money to create a decent annual income out of the odd bit of work here and there and which has absolutely no incentive to move off the land. At the same time, the mayors – most of them Socialist – have taken over from the landowners as the arbiters of local fortune. Small wonder, then, that the PSOE's vote has gone up in the countryside even though it has gone down in the towns.

In 1993 the number of claimants began to edge up again and at the time of writing was around 240,000. If only a third were not entitled to the *subsidio*, then the state would be being systematically cheated of around 20,000 million pesetas ($160 million or £100 million) a year. It is a considerable amount, although – as some local politicians have stressed – negligible in comparison with what the state loses from tax evasion by Spaniards usually far wealthier than the average Andalusian or Estremaduran country-dweller.

Neither ordinary unemployment benefit, nor the special hand-outs for Andalusia and Estremadura come within the scope of Spain's main welfare system – the Seguridad Social. This was set up in the sixties to replace the various services provided by the *sindicatos*, insurance companies, mutual aid associations and the state-run Instituto Nacional de Previsión, which was founded shortly after the turn of the century. It is not the only welfare system in Spain – there are separate systems for local government, the civil service and the armed forces as well as a Fondo Nacional de Asistencia Social (FONAS) which provides old age pensions for those who do not qualify under any of the other schemes. Nevertheless, the Seguridad Social is certainly the biggest and offers a complete range of welfare provision – cash benefits, health care and social services.

Over the years the share of the Seguridad Social's spending which has been met by the state has grown steadily, while the proportion proffered by employers and employees has declined.

As late as 1976, the state's contribution was a mere 4 per cent. By 1993 it had risen to 31 per cent, a figure comparable with that in other EU states. Under the philosophy evolved by the Socialists, the share which comes from taxes should pay for those elements, like health care, social services and non-contributory cash benefits, to which everyone is entitled, while the employers' and employees' contributions cover only the contributory benefits.

Just under two-thirds of the Seguridad Social's spending goes on cash benefits: family allowances, retirement pensions, and the pensions paid out to widows, orphans and the disabled. Rather less than a third is spent on health and social services. The remainder is accounted for by administrative costs.

By the time the Socialists came to power, the entire system was in crisis. As the recession of the late seventies and early eighties bit deeper, the first thing many companies did in an effort to cut costs was to suspend their social security contributions – something they were able to do then without fear of being penalized.

At the same time, the system had to cope with an upsurge in the demand for cash benefits. This was partly because a lot of people who had lost, first their jobs, and then their entitlement to unemployment pay had succeeded in wangling disability pensions to which they were not entitled. The main reason, though, was that in common with other developed nations Spain's population was getting older, and its social security system was having to pay out more and more in the way of old age pensions.

The problem was particularly acute in Spain's case because it was in this area that cash benefits were most generous. Generous was hardly the word. Old age pensions in Spain vary according to how much the pensioner earned when in work. As a percentage of former earnings, they were the highest in Europe after Sweden's; nor was there any upper limit.

The decline in the number of companies paying money into the system, coupled with the rise in the number of claimants drawing money out of it, had brought about a situation in which officials were talking seriously about the system going bankrupt.

In 1985, however, the government introduced a comprehensive reform which restricted access to disability pensions and imposed much stricter limits on the value of retirement benefits. The effect was to put the funding of the Seguridad Social on an altogether sounder basis.

As a consequence, most of Spain's old age pensioners now have to get by on a distinctly modest income. In 1990, as part of an agreement between the government and the unions negotiated after the general strike, pensions – and not only retirement pensions – were made eligible for automatic revaluation by the amount of the previous year's inflation. Despite this, almost three-quarters of old age pensioners were receiving less than the minimum wage during the early nineties.

In addition to reforming contributory pensions, the Socialists have given Spaniards access to two other forms of protection. In 1987 they took a long-overdue step towards allowing people to make their own arrangements, and relieve the state of part of the burden, when they secured parliamentary approval for a measure to legalize private pension funds. Three years later, another deal between the government and the unions cleared the way for non-contributory pensions to be given by the Seguridad Social on a more comprehensive basis than the hand-outs offered by the FONAS.

It needs to be stressed, though, that these new benefits for people who have not made contributions to the Seguridad Social are, like the FONAS pensions, only available to the old and/or disabled. They are not for those of working age who lack other means of support. In the wake of the 1988 general strike, a number of regional governments began giving those who fell into this category a benefit usually referred to as a *salario social*. Asked why the central government refused to follow their lead, the then Minister for Social Affairs said it was 'not the Socialist way'.

The provision of health care and social services in Spain is uneven. Although it has been reduced under the Socialists, there remains a sizeable disparity between the resources allotted to the two areas. In the 1993 budget, health care accounted for more than nine times as much as social services.

As far as health care is concerned, recent years have brought considerable advances, even though increases in the volume of services and facilities have not always been matched by improvements in their quality. When the Socialists came to power, 86 per cent of the population was entitled to use the health service provided by the Seguridad Social. The Socialists made it their aim to extend coverage to the entire population. It was quite common in the seventies, and still possible in the eighties, for sick or even dying people to be turned away from the state's hospitals because they did not qualify for treatment.

The *Ley General de Sanidad*, passed in 1986, was intended to be the keystone of the system for several decades to come. Unlike earlier health legislation, it was based on the premiss that citizens should be entitled to use the public health service as of right rather than in return for contributions. For the first time, it was referred to as the *Sistema Nacional de Salud* ('National Health System'). As a result of regulations and definitions applied under the *Ley General de Sanidad*, the government achieved its goal of effectively total cover during 1991.* It was one of the outstanding achievements of the Socialist era, yet characteristically the Socialists themselves did little to make the public aware of it.

---

* It should not be imagined that medicine in Spain became 100 per cent public as a result. There is still a large private sector, accounting for about a quarter of the system, many of whose facilities are routinely hired by the state sector.

In fact, Spain – like most other countries with a public health service – offers something rather less than comprehensive free health care. Just over 1 per cent of the population, supposedly with enough money to pay for private treatment, is excluded. The state does not pay for dental treatment other than extractions. In addition, anyone who is not drawing a pension has to pay for 40 per cent of the cost of medication.

The question which was being asked with growing concern in the early nineties was whether, even so, the Socialists might not have overreached themselves; whether, as in some other fields, they might not have moved too far, too fast. The period in the mid-eighties which saw the health service made fully comprehensive also saw hospital waiting-lists triple. Money is at the root of the problem.

Investment has increased, but not enough to cover the additional demands being placed upon state health care. More and more people have become eligible for its services. More and more expensive treatment has become available. Yet as a percentage of GDP, Spain's health spending is lower than that of Portugal or Ireland.

In 1991, Abril Martorell, who had been deputy Prime Minister under the UCD, produced a report commissioned by the government which recommended cost-saving reforms modelled on those introduced by the Conservatives in Britain. But his plans for turning hospitals into companies and giving them the freedom to hire and fire staff brought threats of strike action from health-workers and little has been heard of them since. Unless something is done either to boost income or cut spending, though, the majority of Spaniards will continue to receive the same patchy health care they get at the moment.

A glance at the standard health indicators would suggest that Spain's treatment is, if not the best, then among the best in the world. Life expectancy is the highest in the EU. Infant mortality, which in 1960 was forty-three per thousand, has come down to fewer than nine, and for some years now has been lower than in the United States and all but a few of the EU countries.

The number of doctors per thousand inhabitants is the highest in the world. In fact, Spain is reckoned to have twice as many doctors as it needs. But then that is because far too many young people were allowed to enter the profession in the eighties and is a reflection of the way in which things can rapidly spin out of control in the field of Spanish health care.

Imbalances are rife. Spain has an excess of doctors, but a shortage of dentists. There are so few, in fact, that some French dentists have made considerable sums of money by setting up business in towns close to the Spanish border from which they can offer Spaniards speedier and cheaper attention. There is a similar imbalance between the numbers of doctors and nurses. And the number of hospital beds per thousand inhabitants is the second lowest in the EU.

In general, Spanish medicine is characterized by an extreme emphasis on acute medicine and the use of advanced technology and costly drugs. If you are suffering from a life-threatening disorder, you can expect to receive attention in Spain to rival that of anywhere in the world. You will very likely be sent for full clinical tests at a stage when doctors in other societies would still be making educated guesses. And if an operation is required, it will quite possibly involve the latest in techniques and equipment. But the nursing care will probably be inadequate (because the assumption in Spain is still that you will be cared for by your family). And as for after-care, it is likely to be non-existent. Only in rare cases is there any co-ordination in Spain between health-workers and social workers. State rehabilitation and convalescent facilities hardly exist. A doctor on the Costa Blanca once told me of a stroke patient brought back from hospital by ambulance who was left on the lawn of his home after being unable to produce the key to the door.

The paradigm of the shortcomings of the Spanish health service is the Gregorio Marañón hospital in Madrid. With 2,600 beds, it is said to be the biggest in Europe. Even so, it is too small. It is meant to cater for 800,000 people in south and east Madrid, a catchment area more than three times the maximum permitted by Spain's own law.

The Gregorio Marañón's recent history would be comic at times if it were not so tragic. In November 1988, the roof of the kidney unit caved in, burying a patient. Three months later, some thirty people who had been brought in for treatment were found – and photographed – in the corridors of the casualty department because space could not be found for them in the wards. One was dead. In

October 1989, some of the patients went on hunger strike after reporting that they had found worms and cockroaches in their food. Early the following year, in a single night, two people brought in to casualty died before receiving attention. One had been on the premises for five hours. It was never discovered how long the other had been there. The reaction of the hospital managers was to discipline various of the doctors and nurses who had been on duty, including some who had tried to bring the situation in the casualty department to public attention. As a result, the entire staff went on strike. Joaquín Leguina, head of the Madrid regional government which is responsible for the hospital, once remarked that 'there is an answer to everything in the health service – except the Gregorio Marañón'.

Despite sizeable increases in the amounts of cash available, social services are still the Cinderella branch of Spanish welfare. In 1992, there were only six residential centres for the physically disabled and twenty-five for the mentally disabled.

The biggest challenge over the coming decades, though, will be to cope with the rapidly swelling ranks of Spain's elderly. Between 1981 and 1991, the proportion of over-65s in the population rose from 10 to 14 per cent. By the year 2000, it is expected to be almost 20 per cent.

So far, the Socialists' most innovative response has been to provide the elderly with holidays paid for by the taxpayer. In 1992, there were no fewer than 357,000 places available on the government's scheme. These *Vacaciones de Tercera Edad* are a source of often heated political debate. The Socialists say they have enabled many of the country's old people to see the sea for the first time in their lives, and claim they are neither more nor less than a gesture of appreciation by the new Spain to the old one. For the Socialists' opponents, they are a way of buying votes with taxpayers' money. What is abundantly clear from the massed ranks of wrinkled faces at Socialist rallies is that the 'grey vote' is an important reason why the PSOE stays in power.

In more mundane areas, like the supply of residential care, provision for the elderly is sketchy. Government and independent figures for the number of places in old people's homes vary considerably. But there appear to be somewhat more than 100,000, of which 20 to 40 per cent are in the public sector and 60 to 80 per cent in the private sector.

At all events, there are clearly not enough. With proportionately only half as many places available in Spain as in the rest of the EU, waiting-lists extend for up to three years. The disparity in the quality of residential care in Spain is immense.* Contrary to what one might expect, the homes run by local, regional and central government tend to be much better than the privately managed ones. Because of the shortage of places, the authorities have been willing to turn a blind eye to conditions that are a lot less than satisfactory. A judge who saw one home in Barcelona which had previously been vetted and passed by the Catalan administration's inspectors was so appalled by conditions there that he closed it down and had the owner sent to prison. His attention had been drawn to the home by a Barcelona-based volunteer organization, the Coordinadora de Usuarios de Sanidad, which first became concerned about the plight of the elderly in the winter of 1988–9, when a strike by the deliverers of butane gas left thousands without heating. The CUS has since used the butane deliverers as an intelligence-gathering service to provide it with information on elderly people in need.

In 1992, the government launched a Plan Gerontológico which aims to increase the number of residential places for the over-65s from twenty-five to thirty-five per thousand. But even this would leave Spain some way behind the rest of the EU, and the government is hoping it can bridge the gap by providing more extensive help in the home.

As the political clout of the elderly increases along with their numbers, it may well be that future governments will come under irresistible pressure to increase both the facilities and benefits offered to them. At the 1993 election, the over-65s already made up 18 per cent of the electorate – and almost all of them turned out to vote.

---

*One of the best residences for the elderly is said to be La Meca in Pamplona, which is financed by the sale of tickets for the bullfights during the San Fermín festival.

CHAPTER 19

Education: All Change in the Schools

One of the fondest memories I have of the early years of Spain's restored democracy is of the dank night I found myself in a bare, whitewashed storeroom in the shadow of the flyover that channels the traffic from Bilbao into Rekaldeberri. Rekaldeberri is one of the satellite towns which sprang up during the industrial revolution that transformed the Basque country at the end of the last century. Before the civil war, it was known as 'Lenin's Nook' and until much later, when the flyover was built, gangs of youths roamed the borders of the area mugging anyone entering or leaving.

I had gone there to report on a meeting held to discuss the future of the 'People's University of Rekaldeberri'. 'University' was a more-than-somewhat grandiloquent title for what in essence was a scheme for twice-weekly night classes financed by a rag-and-bone operation – every week students toured the neighbourhood collecting jumble, which they then sold off. But it was nevertheless a brave attempt to bring some learning into a community which sorely lacked it and obviously felt the need for it.

I subsequently heard that the experiment collapsed a few years later. But it had not been in vain. Some of the councillors elected when the left took control of many of the towns and cities in the local elections of 1979 had heard about the Rekaldeberri project and decided to imitate it. The first municipally sponsored People's University was set up in San Sebastián de los Reyes near Madrid the following year. Unlike Rekaldeberri, where the curriculum mirrored that of a conventional seat of learning, the new generation of People's Universities tend to concentrate on imparting the basic knowledge, starting with reading and writing, that many working-class Spaniards have never had the chance to acquire.

Quite a lot of the students are housewives whose children have gone on to university and who fear they will no longer have anything in common with them, for there is nothing which separates the generations in Spain as pitilessly as their differing levels of education. The divisions are most starkly evident in the figures for illiteracy. A survey published by the Education Ministry in 1993 put the overall rate at 3·5 per cent – just over a million people, of whom the overwhelming majority were among the over-45s.

The level of illiteracy in Spain has been falling dramatically, year by year, as a progressively larger proportion of the population consists of those who had a chance to benefit from the advances made by successive governments. Spain, indeed, has been recognized by the OECD as having undergone the most spectacular educational transformation among member countries in recent years.

When prosperity came to Spain during the *años de desarrollo*, education received the largest share of the new-found wealth. Between 1962 and 1976, the share of the budget given to education more than doubled, whereas the proportion spent on health and social services rose by just over half and the share allocated to housing actually fell. Since the return of democracy, public spending on education has more than doubled again in real terms.

But then the amount of money spent on education by politicians is simply a reflection of the priority which Spaniards of all classes attach to it.

Under the Second Republic, working-class aspirations to learning took shape in travelling libraries and in the *ateneos libertarios* and *casas del pueblo* which were the anarchist and Socialist equivalents respectively of the *casinos* set up by the middle and upper classes so that members could read the newspapers and discuss the affairs of the day.

More recently, they have been reflected in the rising numbers taking advantage of government-sponsored and funded adult education initiatives. During the first half of the eighties, the number of adults receiving basic education from the government-run Servicio de Educación Permanente de Adultos rose by almost 50 per cent. By 1985–6, it had almost 150,000 students and more than 3,000 teachers. Advanced studies can be pursued through the Universidad Nacional de Educación de Distancia, which provides correspondence courses and broadcasts radio lectures. In 1988–9, its total enrolment had grown to almost 75,000.

One can only hazard a guess at the reasons for the Spaniards' respect for learning. Certainly, it goes hand-in-hand with a traditional disdain for manual labour. But perhaps too it is another result of Spain's leap from a pre-industrial to a post-industrial environment. All too often in those parts of Europe which had a lengthy experience of industrialization, 'working-class values' have come to be synonymous with pride in a lack of education and culture.

Such an attitude is wholly lacking in Spain. *Educación* and *cultura*, and the words derived from them, have universally positive connotations in daily speech. *Culto* has come to mean 'educated' and *educado* 'well-mannered'. The opposites – *inculto* and *maleducado* – are really quite serious insults in Spain and if you ever happen to be in a working-class bar when an argument breaks out, it is odds on that sooner or later you will hear someone tell his adversary that '*Tu no tienes cultura ni educación*' ('You're uncouth and bad-mannered').

A figure who has loomed large in modern British writing, the working-class father denouncing his son for having 'betrayed his class' by going to university, has no equivalent in Spain. A poll carried out for *El País* in 1989 showed that 81 per cent of Spaniards with children of school age wanted them to go on to university. The variation from end to end of the social scale was not that great: 88 per cent at the top and 74 per cent at the bottom. But even more significantly, for the first time since the end of the dictatorship more than half of those who wanted their children to go to university thought they would. It is eloquent testimony to the success of the reforms which have transformed the schools system, and are still doing so.

Just under a third of all Spanish schoolchildren are educated at privately-run schools. Slightly less than half are owned by religious orders. The rest are operated for profit by secular proprietors.

By and large, the religious orders offer an excellent education. The Colegio del Pilar, run by the Marian Fathers in the fashionable Madrid *barrio*, or district, of Salamanca is the closest Spain has to an Eton or Harrow. It has given post-Franco Spain at least half-a-dozen Cabinet ministers, two directors-general of the state broadcasting corporation RTVE, a chairman of the Consejo General del Poder Judicial, and numerous leading figures in the arts, sciences and finance. The leader of the opposition, José María Aznar, was a *pilarista*. So was the first editor of *El País*, Juan Luis Cebrián, and the latest editor of *ABC*, Luis María Ansón. The Colegio de las Madres Irlandesas, also in Madrid, is perhaps Spain's most socially prestigious girls' school. The Queen Mother attended a boarding-school in Seville, since closed, which was run by the 'Irish Mothers'.

There are also a number of first-rate secular institutions. Among them are the Colegio Base in the wealthy Madrid suburb of La Moraleja, the capital's two SEK schools (run by a company with colleges in several Latin American capitals, as well as in Dublin and Miami), and those that teach in a language other than Spanish, such as the Liceo Francés, the Colegio Americano and the Colegio Británico. But a lot of other secular private schools are shoestring efforts, run from a large apartment with poor facilities, and as often as not staffed by the Head's relatives.

The state schools are more homogeneous in the standard of education they offer, and on that count rank about midway between the two extremes among privately operated secular schools. But they came into existence to provide education for those whose parents could not afford to pay fees, and although, as will be seen, privately managed does not necessarily mean privately funded any longer, the state schools suffer a certain class stigma.

The modern Spanish schools system was built on the 1970 *Ley General de Educación*, often referred to as the *Ley Villar Palasí* after the then Education Minister, a multilingual lawyer and academic, José Luis Villar Palasí. The 1970 Act made it compulsory for children to attend school from the ages of six to fourteen. This compulsory education, known as Educación General Básica (EGB), was meant to be available free.

It was divided into three 'cycles'. Although Villar Palasí's law provided for the introduction of continuous assessment, this aspect of it has never been fully implemented. Pupils still have to sit exams at the end of each 'cycle' and those who fail have to stay in the same class for another year, unless they can pass a further exam in the autumn – a practice which has given rise to the profitable business undertaken by many private schools of giving one- or two-month 'recovery courses' during the summer. Pupils who fulfil the requirements for all three 'cycles' before the age of sixteen qualify for the diploma of a *graduado escolar*.

It is impossible to draw exact parallels with other countries because standards vary, but the fact remains that for many years Spain had one of the highest failure rates at the end of EGB among countries with a comparable education system.

Under the UCD, the high failure rate was regarded with considerable anxiety and in 1981, after three years' work by a team of psychologists, teachers, academics and Ministry officials, the government introduced its *Programas Renovados*, a revised curriculum for the EGB, which – in addition to updating the system by, for example, introducing the study of the constitution – set out a list of things that every teacher was supposed to teach and every pupil was expected to learn. The *Programas Renovados*, however, were criticized by educationalists for perpetuating the very emphasis on teaching – and learning – by rote, which they claimed was one reason for the high failure rate. The Socialists have taken an altogether more relaxed view of the situation, going as far as to abolish homework for all six- to fourteen-year-olds. The failure rate is now one in five, compared with one in three when they came to power.

The improvement, though, may also have something to do with the better pay of public sector teachers. A criticism of the 1970 law was that it extended compulsory schooling on the cheap. By entrusting several years of what in other countries would be regarded as secondary-school education to primary-school teachers, it saved the government the cost of large numbers of more highly qualified – and highly paid – masters and mistresses.

In 1978, the public sector teachers brought the state schools to a halt for sixteen days in pursuit of higher pay and ten years later closed them down for twenty days in a strike which caused the downfall of the Education Minister, José María Maravall. His successor, Javier Solana, signed a deal the same year that conceded what the teachers had long been seeking: parity with other government officials of comparable standing. Even so, the teachers' basic pay was modest. After the rise, that of an EGB master or mistress was 1,803,338 pesetas (just over $15,000 or £9,000) per annum.

Only those pupils who become *graduados escolares* can go on to study for the *Bachillerato Unificado Polivalente* (BUP), which takes three years. If they succeed in passing the *bachillerato*, they are entitled to take a further one-year course, the *Curso de Orientación Universitaria*, intended to prepare them for university entrance.

Those who fail to become *graduados escolares* and those who get the diploma but do not want to do the academically orientated BUP can go on to vocational training – *Formación Professional* (FP) – instead. The idea of FP is to provide Spain with its hairdressers, secretaries, mechanics, electricians and the like. It is divided into two two-year phases. The first is about one-third general, one-third scientific, and a third vocational. Pupils who stay the course qualify as *técnicos auxiliares* and become eligible for the second phase, which can be either a general two-year course or a practical three-year course. Those who finish it are entitled to call themselves *técnicos especialistas*.

Perhaps the oddest aspect of the 1970 Act was that it made basic schooling compulsory at a time when there were still not enough places to go round. During the *años de desarrollo* the government had initiated a crash programme of school construction, but it had not yet caught up with the demand for new places created by the movement of population from the countryside to the towns, by increased prosperity (and expectations), and by the 'baby boom' which, from the late forties onwards, affected not just Spain but the whole of Europe. As late as 1977 when the UCD took power there was a sizeable gap between the number of children between the ages of six and fourteen and the number of places for them, so that the beginning of each school year saw harrowing scenes as children and parents were turned away from schools that had either not been completed or had reached saturation point.

The problem for the UCD was that at that time some 40 per cent of the places were being provided by fee-paying private schools. This was a far larger percentage than was required by those families who actually wanted to pay for their children's education. A lot of parents who had to pay would rather have sent their children to state schools. The authorities could claim that there were now enough – or almost enough – places to go round. But the places on offer were not, as Villar Palasí's law required, freely available. In Madrid, for example, there were considerably more places than children, but no less than 60 per cent of them had to be paid for.

The Centrists' answer to the problem was to enlarge on a solution that had already been tried out by their Francoist predecessors, which was to give money to the private schools to enable them to provide their services free. In the years immediately preceding the Socialists' arrival in government the increase in that part of the education budget devoted to private schooling was eight times the increase for the system as a whole. By the time the Centrists left office, only a handful of EGB schools were not receiving state aid.★

The Socialists inherited a situation in which the government was paying the piper, but was unable to call the tune. It was meeting the costs of the private schools, yet it could not, for example, insist that they give preference to local children. Because of the unplanned way in which schools were built and pupils enrolled, children often had to travel long distances to get to school when there were schools in the vicinity filled with children from other parts of the city. When the Socialists came to power there were children in Madrid, where the situation was particularly dire, who were spending five hours a day travelling from one side of the city to the other on buses which the government provided specifically for this purpose – 2,000 of them in the capital alone.

The *Ley Orgánica del Derecho a la Educación,* or LODE as it is known, which was passed in 1984, made a government subsidy conditional on the private school in question accepting the same criteria for admission as those laid down for state schools. It stipulated that every school should have a governing body, called the Consejo Escolar, with the power to hire and fire the Head and his staff. The Consejos are made up of the Head, three representatives named by the proprietor, four teachers, four parents, two pupils and one member of the school's non-teaching staff. The LODE

★ Since then, state funding has been accepted by almost the entire private sector. Some 90 per cent of secular 'private' schools and 98 per cent of religious 'private' schools, including El Pilar, but not Las Madres Irlandesas, are now run with taxpayers' money. Those few which have refused government subsidies and still charge fees constitute a genuine elite.

also decreed that teachers' salaries were to be paid directly by the government, rather than – as before – paid from the government subsidy at the proprietor's discretion.

Not surprisingly, the LODE was regarded by many middle-class parents as a threat to the educational exclusivity of which their children had seemed assured. With the backing of the Church, they set out to block it. No single piece of legislation laid before parliament during the Socialists' first term of office caused as much controversy as the LODE. Demonstrations brought hundreds of thousands of parents on to the streets. More than half the government's total allocation of parliamentary time was taken up debating the numerous amendments to the bill tabled by the opposition, and it was not until after an unsuccessful appeal to the Constitutional Court that it finally came into effect. The government's determination to see it on to the statute book more or less intact was a measure of its conviction that only a radical measure of the kind represented by the LODE could open the way for a more egalitarian, and perhaps more secular, Spain.

The LODE transformed the relationship between the state and the schools, but it did not pretend to tackle shortcomings in the structure of the system which have become increasingly apparent with the years.

It has been clear for some time that certain pupils are failing at an early stage in their schooling to assimilate enough basic skills and knowledge to enable them to get by as the subject-matter becomes more demanding. Paradoxically, this is a reflection of the ample provision of nursery schooling in Spain. The late sixties and early seventies saw an upsurge of enthusiasm for nursery education with first the private and then the public sector racing to fulfil the demand. Today more than 90 per cent of Spanish children go to school for at least one year before they start their EGB. For some parents, nursery education represents an opportunity to give their children a better start in life than they themselves have had. But for others it is simply a cheap and socially acceptable way of getting the children off their hands during the day – a lot of so-called nursery schools in Spain are more nurseries than schools. Even so, it is obvious that those who have had some sort of education, however rudimentary, have a head start over those who have had none.

Although the EGB curriculum did not envisage that every child would have been to nursery school, a lot of teachers now work on that assumption. The effect is to create a disadvantaged minority right at the start. Since almost 40 per cent of the places at nursery schools are still fee-paying, it tends to be composed of children from poor backgrounds. These children, known as *los de la cartilla* (those of the primer) because they are still learning the alphabet when the others have moved on to more advanced exercises, often never catch up and for some time there has been a feeling within Spain that nursery schooling, now that it is all but universal, should – like basic education – be free for everyone who wants it.

A more obvious inconsistency is that the system created by the 1970 law does not make education compulsory up to sixteen, the age at which it becomes legal to start work. In fact, as any tourist can see from the number of children serving in bars and restaurants in Spain, a lot who fail to become *graduados escolares* leave school at fourteen and take a job of sorts.

One of the reasons why they do is because of the shortcomings of *Formación Profesional*. Inevitably, in a country where manual labour is so thoroughly despised, it has always had an 'image problem'. Only a quarter of those who get their EGB diploma opt to do FP afterwards.

The real problem area is the first phase. A lot of students drop out. The failure rate among the rest is high, and even those who do qualify as *técnicos auxiliares*, but do not move on to become *técnicos especialistas*, find their certificate is pretty much worthless in the job market.

In 1987, the Socialists unveiled their first draft of a law that would give Spain's schools their biggest shake-up since the *Ley Villar Palasí*. Among those who helped shape the new plan was Thorsten Hussen, the father of Sweden's educational reforms. After much consultation and controversy, the *Ley de Ordenación General del Sistema Educativo* – known, thankfully, by its initials as the LOGSE – was approved by parliament in 1990.

During the intervening three years, the bill's fiercest opponents were the Roman Catholic bishops, who saw it – not without reason – as another attempt to loosen their grip on the hearts and minds of the young. Under Franco, religion was compulsory and could only be taught by teachers approved by the local bishop. But in the later years of the dictatorship, in keeping with the increasingly liberal mood of both the nation and the Church, many of the classes ceased to offer instruction in the catechism of Roman Catholicism and became generalized discussions of religious culture.

In 1979, the Church's right to vet religious teachers was endorsed by the agreements signed between the Vatican and the state. But, in deference to freedom of conscience, the two sides agreed that pupils should have the right to take another subject if they wished. In fact, very few do. Only about 10 per cent of EGB students and 20 to 30 per cent of those doing BUP or FP opt for the classes in ethics which were devised as an alternative. One reason is said to be that it is easier to pass in religion than in ethics. Catholicism, moreover, is not only an important aspect of Spanish culture but also, for many Spaniards, still a badge of respectability. A lot of parents fear that if they ask for their children to attend ethics rather than religion, they will be branded as atheists.

At all events, and to the dismay of liberal Catholics, the creation of an alternative had the paradoxical effect of making religious teaching more proselytizing than it was before the 1979 agreement. The Catholic hierarchy, which became progressively more conservative under Cardinal Suquía, argued that since the ethics course offered an alternative moral education, those who opted for religion were implicitly requesting straightforward instruction in the tenets of Catholicism.

Ironically, what incensed the bishops about the LOGSE was that it did away with the classes in ethics. As it comes into force, there will be no alternative to religion. It is intended that pupils who do not take it as a subject will study by themselves during the period allotted to it on the timetable. But the Church fears that the real alternative will be the playground or home. It suspects a lot of principals will put the once-a-week religion class at the end of the timetable, and that only the most devout parents will insist that their children stay on at school for the extra hour on Fridays. The bishops, though, have not succeeded in mobilizing the degree of parental resistance which accompanied the passage of the LODE, and the government has held firm to its original intention.

The first changes brought about by the LOGSE were made to the schools system at the beginning of the 1991–2 school year, but such is the scale of the exercise that its introduction will not be completed till the start of the next century.

Under the terms of the new law, all nursery care and education from birth to the age of six will become the responsibility of the authorities, allowing them to insist on minimum standards for the premises, the teachers and so on. Pre-school education will not be obligatory but, as far as 4- to 6-year-olds are concerned, the LOGSE commits the government to provide schooling free of charge to all who want it. Only those who opt to pay fees will do so.

EGB – renamed *Educación Primaria* – is to end at the age of twelve, leading into *Educación Secundaria*, which will be compulsory to the age of sixteen. After that, pupils will be able to choose between leaving school altogether, doing a one- or two-year further professional training course, or going on to do a *bachillerato* to the age of eighteen. Pupils who take the *bachillerato* but do not move on to university will, in addition, have the opportunity to do an advanced professional training course before they look for a job.

Apart from changing the structure of the schools system, the LOGSE introduces several new elements into the curriculum. Language teaching (English is rapidly displacing French) will start at the age of eight. For older pupils, there will be a number of new subjects, including peace studies, environmental conservation and sexual equality, intended to undermine traditional attitudes. The new curriculum also aims to reverse the Spaniards' traditional aversion to manual labour with courses including design, technical drawing, and management and production techniques.

The number of pupils per class will be limited to 25 in primary schools, 30 in secondary schools and 35 in the *bachillerato* colleges. By comparison, as recently as 1986 the number of students per BUP class was 42. Since then, though, demography has been on the side of the authorities for the first time in Spain's modern history.

As in the rest of Europe, Spain's birth rate ceased its giddy ascent in the early sixties. But whereas elsewhere in Europe the birth rate then dropped, in Spain, where contraception was illegal, it stayed much the same right up until the year before Franco's death. There then followed a slow decline until 1977. Thereafter, with contraception readily available and the recession taking its toll of jobs and income, the fall accelerated to the point where Spain's birth rate was dropping faster than any in Europe.

A demographic 'lump' was thus working its way through the schools system throughout the eighties. The number of pupils doing EGB peaked in 1984–5 and since 1986–7 the combined total for BUP, FP and COU has also been declining. Implementation of the pupil–teacher ratios laid down by the LOGSE will be made a relatively easy task by the further slackening of demographic pressure on Spain's schools system.

No such respite is yet in sight for its overstretched universities. It is not just that they are still struggling to cope with the repercussions of Spain's protracted 'baby boom'. The improvement in school teaching is likely to mean that a progressively higher percentage of students will be able to pass the university entrance exams, while a rise in both the number and value of grants is already enabling more of them to take up the places for which they are qualified.

The improvement of the university grants system is unquestionably among the Socialists' most significant contributions to a more egalitarian society. By the start of the 1992–3 academic year, they had more than tripled the number of grants since coming to power. Almost one in five of the student population was receiving a grant and, on average, it was worth 125 per cent more in real terms than in 1982–3. Even so, the proportion of students who work their way through college remains high. At the University of Barcelona, it was recently one in two.

The growth of the university system during the *años de desarrollo* was even more rapid than that of the schools system. In the sixties, total enrolment tripled to over 200,000 and the government initially had every intention that it should go on growing at the same rate. Villar Palasí's Act entitled anyone who passed the *bachillerato* to a place at college. Four years later, with the economy facing a recession and the full implications of this undertaking becoming clear, another law was passed reintroducing university entrance exams.

But the numbers kept on growing, and have risen vertiginously since the PSOE came to power. By the end of the 1991–2 academic year, Spain had some 1·2 million university students. Despite this, the number of campuses was quite small. There were only forty-one universities in Spain, including the Universidad Nacional de Educación de Distancia, so the average student population was high. Madrid's Complutense, which was founded in 1499 and counts Cervantes among its alumni, had an enrolment of some 130,000 – the highest in Europe after Rome.

The oldest of Spain's universities is Salamanca, which was founded in 1218. About half have been created since 1970, eight of them since the PSOE came to power. One is a truly pioneering effort – the Universidad Carlos III, whose campus is a converted army barracks in the industrialized, proletarian south of Madrid.

In 1991, in a further effort to ease the log-jam in the system, the Socialists issued a decree setting out the ground rules for a new generation of private universities. The existing ones were all run by the Church – three by the Jesuits and one by Opus Dei. Together they accounted for only 3 per cent of the student population.

All the new foundations are likely to be secular initiatives. The first to open its doors was the Ramón Llull University in Barcelona. At least three others were expected to be inaugurated in Madrid during the nineties. It will be some years, though, before they can absorb more than a fraction of the demand for higher education. None of the proposed new universities envisages an enrolment of over 20,000. Some of the new projects, moreover, are based on existing *colegios universitarios*. These are privately owned and run institutions which give courses in the university disciplines but whose students take their exams at, and their degrees from, a public university to which their *colegio universitario* is attached.

On paper, Spain's university attendance rate of around 30 per cent is higher than that of Britain and several other EU states. But the figure is a little misleading.

For a start, fewer than 750,000 of Spain's undergraduates were doing what, in Britain at least, would be considered university subjects. Spanish universities offer two sorts of courses: their *facultades, colegios* and *escuelas técnicas superiores* impart the traditional university disciplines, but there are also the *escuelas universitarias* which train nurses, teachers, physiotherapists and the like, who in many other countries would pursue their studies elsewhere.

It is also relevant that the attendance rate is measured as a percentage of the population between the ages of 20 and 24. This would seem logical. The courses given by *facultades, colegios* and *escuelas técnicas superiores* are mostly designed to last for between four and six years and those offered by the *escuelas universitarias* are usually meant to run for three. In fact, though, a lot of the students who make up the total have stayed on for longer than the notional length of their courses. Spanish universities, like Spanish schools, are forgiving. A student who fails to make the grade does not just have to leave without a degree. He or she can carry on trying for as long as it takes to reach the necessary standard. This is a very sensitive area, in which the statistics are either incomplete or outdated. But according to Education Ministry figures for the 1984–5 academic year, only 44 per cent of *facultad* students, and just 29 per cent of those in the *escuelas técnicas superiores*, finished their degrees on time. In the *escuelas universitarias*, the figure was even lower – just 19 per cent. At the Politécnica de Cataluña, one of the few universities which has made comprehensive statistics available, the average time taken to complete a degree was recently 8·65 years for five-year courses and 6·09 years for three-year ones. Quite a number of Spanish students are thus in their thirties when they graduate. At the time of writing, there is a legendary character known as *El Gordo* ('the Fat One') haunting the Sociology faculty at the Universidad Complutense in Madrid. He is said to have been there so long that none of the other students knows when he matriculated.

The high rate of 'repetition' is among the arguments used by those who believe the increase in numbers has ceased to be of benefit to the country. Under Franco, the universities were kept firmly under the thumb of the government, which could remove lecturers and professors whose political outlook it disliked. The 1983 *Ley de Reforma Universitaria* gave the universities their autonomy in matters of internal organization. But it left the government to decide how many students they should take in every year.

Several academics have claimed that the universities are being used by the administration as a way of disguising unemployment. Gustavo Villapalos, the Rector of the Complutense, is on record as saying they should be 'for training elites, and not the masses'.

The quality of the university education currently imparted and the degree to which it varies from campus to campus is extraordinarily difficult to judge. The only clue in recent years came from the French newspaper *Libération*, which got some 600 academics from all over Europe to rate the continent's universities subject by subject. Only one Spanish faculty – the Politécnica de Barcelona's architecture school – gained a place in the top five in any discipline. Among arts colleges, the Escuela de Bellas Artes in Barcelona was ranked fourth and among business schools, Opus Dei's IESE, also in Barcelona, was ranked fifth.

No authoritative comparative ranking has ever been drawn up within Spain because, as some university teachers have openly admitted, none of them dares to court the wrath of the rest of the academic community. By and large, the Church's foundations offer better facilities, just as the new private colleges are expected to do. But most of the internationally renowned lecturers and professors are concentrated in the bigger public universities, notably Madrid's Complutense and Barcelona's Central. A few of the regional universities, such as Granada, also enjoy an excellent reputation. But there are clearly enormous disparities from faculty to faculty which have never been dragged into the open – until now.

Hitherto, prospective students have not been able to 'shop around'. By government decree they have been steered towards the university closest to home. In future a school-leaver from, say, Valencia will be able to apply to the university with the best reputation in his or her chosen subject, rather than be forced to study it in or near Valencia. The idea is to introduce some competition in the hope that it will raise standards.

CHAPTER 20

Housing: Through the Roof

Horcher is one of Spain's finest restaurants. It occupies the ground floor of an impressive building on Calle Alfonso XII, which runs down the more fashionable side of the Retiro park in Madrid. To find similar premises in London or New York, you would need to look along Park Lane or Park Avenue. At the start of the nineties, Horcher's owners were reported to be paying a monthly rent of 2,000 pesetas ($20 or £11). A lot of the well-connected and well-heeled families in the spacious flats upstairs were thought to be paying even less.

To enter the world of Spanish housing is to take a step through Alice's looking-glass. Almost nothing is what it seems – and what it is is often scarcely credible.

Yet the step is well worth taking. For there is nothing which offers quite as many clues to why Spain is the way it is as the way in which Spaniards are housed. It explains why some people with modest incomes seem to have money to burn, while others you would expect to be rich appear to be watching every peseta. It is one of the keys to the country's prudent transition from dictatorship to democracy and the reason why there will probably never again be a revolution in Spain. It exerts an influence on matters as diverse as sexual behaviour and artistic creativity.

The importance of housing in Spanish life does not have to be traced back very far. It is essentially a result of the migration from the countryside to the towns during the fifties and sixties and the way in which the authorities opted to cope with it.

It has been calculated that one in seven of the population moved on a permanent basis from one part of the country to another during those years, and a lot set off without any guarantee of accommodation at the other end.

The government, whose experience of housing was limited to a relatively modest programme of reconstruction after the civil war, only became involved with the greatest reluctance. It was not until 1957 in fact that Spain acquired a separate Housing Ministry and from the beginning it was clear that the new ministry would not have the resources to build and manage a massive stock of state-owned rented accommodation like the 'council houses' in Britain. In any case, the aim of the technocrats who dominated government thinking from 1957 onwards was to create an economically advanced but politically conservative society in Spain and one of the keys to this was to encourage property ownership. There is nothing like having to meet monthly mortgage payments for deterring people from going on strike and, in a broader sense, property ownership gives people a stake in the prosperity and stability of the society in which they live.

All but a very small proportion of the millions of houses and flats built during the *años de desarrollo* were thus offered for sale rather than rent.

The scheme devised by the Francoist authorities to cope with the hordes of Spaniards who had made themselves homeless by the early sixties was the Plan Nacional de Vivienda (National Housing Plan). Its aim was to ensure the construction, between 1961 and 1976, of four million new dwellings.

It must be stressed that not all of this accommodation was to be provided at the behest of the state. It was expected that much of it (about half, as it turned out) would be supplied by the private sector on its own terms.

The rest was accounted for by subsidized housing – Vivienda de Protección Oficial (VPO). But VPO was not 'state housing' in the sense that the term is understood in much of the rest of Europe. Only a fraction was bought by the state and then let to the occupants at a subsidized rent. The rest was bought by the occupants, and what the state subsidized was merely the rate of interest at which the cost of the property was repaid. The buyers had to meet the real cost of land and construction, but in order to do so they were given access to loans at concessionary interest rates with the state paying the difference between the rate charged to the owner and the rate charged by the financial institution providing the loan.

There were – and are – two kinds of subsidized homes under the Spanish system. In the case of VPO de Promoción Pública, the state, in the form of local authorities or the central government's own housing development corporation, the Instituto para la Promoción Pública de la Vivienda, buys the land and hires the builder. With VPO de Promoción Privada, the work is done by a commercial developer.

In both cases, the buyers have to get together a deposit. And despite improvements in the financing of property purchases in recent years, the minimum down payment in Spain is usually still a fifth of the total value. The interest rates charged to the buyers of publicly developed state-subsidized housing have always been fairly low, but the rates for privately developed state-subsidized property have never been more than a few per cent below the market rate. What is more, the period in which the loan has to be repaid is longer for VPO de Promoción Privada than for VPO de Promoción Pública. Yet the amount of VPO housing brought on to the market by private developers has always been much greater than the amount sponsored by public bodies.

The target of four million dwellings set by the Plan Nacional de Vivienda was more than fulfilled. Acre by acre, the shantytowns gave way to the stark multi-storey blocks which can be seen standing amid the wasteland on the outskirts of most Spanish cities. There are often no leisure facilities in the immediate vicinity and the apartments themselves are usually cramped and noisy. But they are a lot better than a leaky shack. To pay for them it was often necessary to take in lodgers from among the ranks of those who had not yet been able to find or afford a place of their own. Francesc Candels, a Catalan author who wrote a bestselling book about Barcelona's immigrants, *Els Altres Catalans*, estimated that by the mid-sixties one fifth of all the working-class families in the city were living in someone else's apartment. If it was simply a matter of a man on his own sleeping in the spare room or, in the case of one-bedroomed apartments, in the sitting-room, it worked reasonably well. It also worked, although to a diminishing extent, with two, three or even four men on their own (and it was by no means uncommon during this period for a family with two or three children to be sharing a two-bedroomed flat in a tower block with several lodgers). It was when the men got together enough money to bring their families that the system usually broke down. Left alone all day, often with children to look after, the wives would sooner or later start rowing and then the husbands would get sucked into their disputes. But as more blocks went up, even the horrors of lodging became less commonplace.

Because the scale of internal migration turned out to be even greater than expected, the fulfilment of the Plan did not solve the problem of homelessness altogether. After it had run its course, there were still some million and a half families without a home of their own. Some still lived in shantytowns but most were living as lodgers, often with relatives – '*con la suegra*' ('with the mother-in-law'), as the saying went.

The real failing of the Plan Nacional de Vivienda, though, was not that it failed to ensure enough housing, but that the housing subsidized by the government went to the wrong people. The problem was – and still is – that, because they rely on property developers to supply most of the housing they sponsor, the authorities have only a limited say in the type of accommodation produced. And since there are bigger profits to be made from expensive accommodation than from cheap accommodation, there has always been a tendency for the property developers to go as far up-market as the guidelines will allow. A senior official at the Housing Ministry during the Arias government is on record as saying that between 65 and 70 per cent of all VPO housing went to middle- and upper-class families. By contrast, many of the high-rise blocks thrown up to accommodate the shantytown immigrants were put there by private enterprise without any kind of subsidy and the apartments in them were sold off on the open market at commercial rates.

While arranging for the bulk of newly-built homes to be made available for purchase rather than rental, Franco's ministers perpetuated a ludicrous arrangement which encouraged the owners of existing surplus properties to keep them off the market rather than rent them out.

Back in 1936, with his government still operating from its wartime headquarters in Burgos, Franco had ordered rents throughout Spain to be frozen in what was probably an attempt to secure for his regime a bit of cheap popularity. Tenants acquired the right to insist that their contracts be renewed with the rent unchanged. And not only that: they could leave their leases, with their rights to automatic renewal, to any relative who happened to be living with them when they died. In the case of an elderly partner, this was admirably humanitarian. But it became manifestly unfair to the landlord or landlady when applied to the tenant's sons, daughters, nephews and nieces. A law introduced in 1964 retained the tenant's entitlement to the automatic renewal of his or her lease, but gave the owner the right to raise the rent by the rate of inflation. Not surprisingly, the owners of surplus property became loath to let it out and the stock of housing available for rental shrank with each passing year.

The effect of Franco's housing policies was to make Spain into a nation of owner-occupiers, sharing all the cautious inclinations that go with the possession of property. Before 1960, more than half the population lived in rented accommodation. By 1970, the figure was down to 30 per cent and in 1990 it was less than 12 per cent – the lowest percentage for any country in the EU. In Britain that year, the figure was 37 per cent; in France, 38 per cent, and in Germany, 58 per cent.

If the old dictator and his ministers envisaged that a high rate of owner-occupancy would reduce social conflict, they were right. Strikes may have become more frequent, but they are rarely protracted. If, however, they thought it might foil the demise of dictatorship and the advent of democracy, they were wrong, for the prevalence of home-ownership helped to dilute that strain of communitarian extremism in Spanish politics which in the past had provoked a violent response from the forces of reaction. This in turn may help to explain why democratic administrations have been loath to do more than tamper with the arrangements that Franco bequeathed.

For several years, the aim was to find a way of ensuring that VPO accommodation was made available to those for whom it was intended. The earliest attempt to do so had been made under the dictatorship.

A limit was put on the selling price of state-subsidized homes, but the maximum was so high that it was virtually meaningless. The next step was to limit the size of VPO apartments to ninety square metres, but there again that was well above the prevailing European average. The obvious thing to do would have been to introduce a means test. But in a society where there were no reliable tax returns and almost everybody was doing more than one job, this was not practicable.

It was only after Fernández-Ordóñez's tax reforms that the UCD was able to make low income a criterion for access to VPO accommodation. In its Three-Year Plan (1981–3), publicly developed VPO housing was restricted to those right at the bottom of the social pile. The Socialists, in their Four-Year Plan (1984–7), extended means testing to privately developed VPO accommodation. Anyone could apply, but the rate of interest charged to buyers varied according to their income.

The Socialists also introduced a number of other well-intentioned innovations. A larger share of publicly developed VPO was offered for rental. Financial adjustments were made so that buyers of privately developed VPO did not have to find such large down-payments, or pay such high interest in the early years.

But by the time their first plan ended, the Socialists' housing policy bore only the most oblique relation to reality, for it had been overtaken by the most spectacular property boom in Spain's history. Prices began to lift in 1984, the very first year of their Four-Year Plan. Then they climbed. Then they soared. And, finally, they went into orbit. By 1991, it was reckoned that the cost of a house or flat in one of the big cities had risen fivefold in the previous seven years.

Yet interest rates – and therefore mortgage rates – had remained high throughout. In 1990, when they were around 14 to 15 per cent, a consumers' group, the Federación de Usuarios Consumidores Independientes, calculated that to own a cheap flat in a big Spanish city, a family needed to be earning 4,800,000 a year ($48,000 or £26,000) – ten times the minimum wage.

The property boom of the late eighties transformed Spanish society every bit as much as the educational reforms of the early seventies. Those who had enough money to buy a house or flat in addition to their principal residence enhanced their families' fortunes as handsomely as many a sixteenth-century adventurer returning from the Indies. But just as the gold and silver of the Americas enriched a few in the short term and impoverished so many in the long term, so too the property boom of the late eighties did considerable damage to the fabric of Spanish society. Because of its differential impact, the rise in prices widened the gaps separating one class from another, and reduced mobility between them.

It can be argued that the Socialists were not responsible for the boom; in so far as its origins are concerned, that is true. What happened was that the end of the long recession that had begun in the mid-seventies freed savings and encouraged borrowing, thereby increasing the potential demand for housing. But although the end of the recession was what the government had been striving for ever since coming to power, its implications for the property market appear never to have been thought through.

Nor, it seems, was much attention given to the knock-on effects of the Socialists' campaign to tighten up on tax dodging. Investing in property was soon seen as an ideal way to launder *dinero negro*. It offered not only spectacular capital growth, but also impressive tax efficiency. Under the peculiar arrangements governing property transactions in Spain, the value of a house or flat for tax purposes could be whatever the buyer, with the seller's consent, chose to make it. Overnight, 20 million pesetas of real money could be transformed into 5 million pesetas for the tax records, and while remaining as 5 million on the tax records would have grown, between 1984 and 1991, to 100 million.

The upward spiral in prices was given additional momentum by two other factors. One was a fiscal regime which encouraged property speculation. Until 1989, taxpayers were allowed to set against tax the cost of purchasing an unlimited number of properties, provided the amount they claimed as an allowance did not come to more than 30 per cent of their total liability. The second factor was land hoarding. By keeping land approved for building off the market while the boom lasted, landowners could assure themselves of a fat profit towards the end. Between 1984 and 1988, according to the Centro de Política de Suelo y Valoraciones de la UPC, the price of land rose by 434 per cent in Barcelona and 360 per cent in Madrid. What made the speculation in Spain so scandalous was that public bodies were as guilty of it as private companies and individuals. Land expropriated for housing was often rationed to developers as a way of improving local authority finances.

Despite this, it was several years before an order for the compulsory purchase of land for development ran into serious resistance. When it did, it provoked one of the whackiest episodes in Spain's recent history. In 1990, the Madrid council served notices to quit on the occupants of a collection of humble single-storey dwellings at Cerro Belmonte in the generally prosperous north of the city. The owners of the houses had mostly built them with their own hands when they arrived on the outskirts of the capital in the fifties. The council offered them a choice between either making improvements to the area that were beyond their means or taking as compensation a pittance and a flat in one of the most crime-infested areas of Madrid.

Spurred on by a young lawyer, Esther Castellanos, whose father owned a plot of land in the area, the inhabitants of Cerro Belmonte embarked on a succession of increasingly bizarre publicity stunts culminating in an appeal to the Cuban leader, Fidel Castro. It happened that, at the time, he was locked in a tense and bitter international dispute over Spain's refusal to hand over a group of Cuban dissidents who had taken refuge in the Spanish Embassy in Havana. In a speech at the height of the crisis, and to the intense embarrassment of the Spanish government, the Cuban leader cited the goings-on at Cerro Belmonte as evidence of the evils of capitalism. He then invited twenty-four of Cerro Belmonte's residents on a free trip to Cuba. The Cerro Belmontese subsequently began making arrangements to declare themselves independent. Barricades were thrown up around the neighbourhood. And it was only after a flag had been designed and a constitution drafted that the Madrid council was finally embarrassed into making them a fairer offer.

It had been quite clear from an early stage that the property boom required a carefully thought out response from the government if the most vulnerable sectors of society were to be shielded from its effects. The housing finance system devised by Franco's 'technocrats' was quite unsuited to dealing with a boom of this sort.

For a start, it placed the emphasis on purchase rather than rental. And poorer families soon found that, even if they were government-subsidized, the rise in prices which began in 1984 made it impossible for them to save up the deposit or make the payments that were needed for them to buy a home of their own.

The existing system also made the volume of subsidized housing on the market largely dependent on the initiative of the private developers whose role it was to arrange for VPO de Promoción Privada. It had already been seen that when the economy was sluggish, they were only too happy to accept work from the government, but that when the economy was booming, most were far too busy on juicier commercial projects to be interested in meeting the needs of the state. The pattern was repeated as soon as the economic upswing gathered momentum in the mid-eighties. In 1987, the number of starts made on state-subsidized, commercially developed properties dropped by almost a fifth.

A comprehensive response would have involved switching the emphasis to VPO de Promoción Pública and making the accommodation available for rental rather than purchase. But a lot of the responsibility for housing was in the process of being transferred from the central to the regional governments, and when the Socialists' Four-Year Plan came to an end, it was simply not replaced. Instead, the government contented itself with making a yearly announcement of the progressively smaller amounts of money it intended to spend on subsidized housing.

The results can be seen in the figures. Between 1987 and 1990, the total number of properties reaching the market averaged around 250,000 – more than under either the UCD's Three-Year or the Socialists' Four-Year Plan. But that was purely because of the call for property developed on a commercial basis, particularly for speculative purposes. The increase in the number of starts made on unsubsidized properties, modest at first, rose by 50 per cent in 1987 and carried on growing for the next two years.

By contrast, the decline in the subsidized sector was dramatic. By 1990, VPO de Promoción Privada starts had dropped by more than two-thirds. VPO de Promoción Pública starts had fallen by almost four-fifths. An ostensibly Socialist government was thus providing about an eighth as much housing for working-class families as the supposedly more conservative UCD administration had done.

Even in 1987, Spain's state housing aid as a percentage of its GDP had been the lowest in the European Community – 0·9 per cent, compared with 3·4 per cent in Britain, 2 per cent in France and 1·5 per cent in Germany. But between 1987 and 1989, government investment in VPO fell by more than three-quarters.

But then even if the government had made more subsidized housing available, working-class families would not have been able to afford it. In 1990, the research department of the communist-led trade union federation, Comisiones Obreras, calculated – on the basis of the terms laid down by the government – that in one of the big cities a family who wanted to take one of the bigger state-developed, government-subsidized flats put on the market that year would have had to find between 75,000 and 90,000 pesetas ($750–900 or £410–492) a month to pay for it. At that time, according to the government's own figures, the average net monthly pay of a Spanish worker was 118,000 pesetas ($1,180 or £645).

In the meantime, the cost of renting had risen at almost the same rate as the cost of buying. This was partly because of a 'spill-over' effect. But it was also, ironically, a result of the one measure taken by the Socialists to palliate the effects of the boom. In 1985, the Economics and Finance Minister, Miguel Boyer, had issued a decree intended to encourage owners to rent out their property; but as so often happens in Spain, things were made to swing from one extreme to another.

The so-called *decreto Boyer* did not attempt to curb the rights of tenants in flats and houses occupied under existing leases. Instead, it allowed new agreements to be signed which granted the owners complete freedom to fix a new rent whenever the lease ran out and to evict tenants who refused to pay it. In a lot of other countries, such an arrangement would normally lead to a reasonable deal. Both sides would have something to lose if the contract were terminated. The tenant would have to pay removal costs, but the owner would have to pay an agent a fee to find a new occupant. In Spain, however, it is the lessee, not the lessor, who has to compensate the agent (normally with one month's rent). So property-owners took to insisting on one-year contracts, knowing that as soon as they expired they could count on the tenant accepting any increase less than one-twelfth of the existing rent plus estimated removal costs. The result was that rents on properties subject to the *decreto Boyer* all rose at well over the rate of inflation.

The advantages bestowed on property-owners by the decree should have ensured that most of the houses and flats bought for speculative purposes during the boom were let out to provide their owners with a regular income as well as capital growth. But because of the difficulties of getting redress through the courts in Spain, a lot were not. Fearing that it would be more trouble than it was worth to evict non-payers, many owners have preferred to let their properties stand empty. In fact, the number of dwellings brought on to the market under the terms of the *decreto Boyer* has been far outstripped by the number withdrawn.

By the early nineties, Spain's property market had become a study in absurdity. The disparity between 'new' and 'old' rents was risible. The Asociación de Propietarios de Viviendas de Renta Congelada (Association of Owners of Properties with Frozen Rents) reckoned that in 1990 60 per cent of Spanish tenants – some 830,000 families – were paying monthly rents of below 3,000 pesetas ($30 or £16), and of those, more than 190,000 were paying below 300 pesetas, which was less than the cost of a newspaper, a coffee and a pastry for breakfast. Yet for those new to the property market, the monthly outlay needed to secure even the meanest flat was around 80,000 pesetas ($800 or £437).

Because of the effects of the drift from the countryside to the towns, one of the EU's poorest countries not only had the Community's highest level of owner-occupancy, but also its highest level of second-home ownership. Many of those who had migrated during the fifties and sixties never sold the houses they left behind, and by the early nineties, many owners who had paid off their mortgages were in a position to do them up. The traffic jams which build up around Spain's major cities on Friday and Sunday evenings bear witness to the fact. In addition, many relatively well-to-do Spaniards had used the tax breaks which remained in force until 1989 to take advantage of the property boom and buy a house or a flat they did not need to occupy. The 1991 housing census found that, for every 100 first homes, there were more than 22 second homes. Almost a quarter of all Spanish families, in other words, either had a 'place in the country' or owned a property for the purposes of investment.

Yet while a large proportion of the population had two or more homes, many had none. A study by the state-run Banco Hipotecario in 1990 put the number of people who wanted a home but could not get one at around 700,000. There were still plenty of shacks around the main conurbations. But their numbers were halved during the Socialists' first decade in power, and by 1993 the countrywide total was officially put at just over 12,000. The vast majority of those living in shantytowns were either gypsies or immigrants. However, there was a less dramatic, but more widespread, problem hidden from sight by the strength of Spanish family ties. A growing number of young people were unable to move away from home because they could not afford separate accommodation. For all but a minority of young Spaniards – those with rich parents or lucrative jobs – even flat-sharing was out of the question. It is hardly surprising that Spain was the EU nation with the highest number of occupants per dwelling.

One consequence can be seen in the number of discarded contraceptives littering any park, alleyway or patch of waste ground in a Spanish city. The fact that so many Spanish young people live with their parents has made their sexual relations more evident, but it has almost certainly acted as a brake on promiscuity. It may also provide the key to the lack of anything resembling a youth culture in Spain. For while the young people of this 'young nation' depend on their parents for board and lodging, their inclination to challenge the ideas of their elders, their propensity to experiment and innovate, will inevitably be circumscribed.

Finally, the property boom of the late eighties put the cost of a house or flat beyond the means of an entire generation of young people whose parents had failed to benefit from it. It is, I suspect, a key reason for the noticeably more mercenary outlook of the young women and the evidently more crestfallen air of the young men who came to maturity as it was taking place. For this is still a society accustomed to the idea of the man as provider and the woman as provided for.

The plight of would-be couples – and of those who had married but were living with one or other set of parents – is made all the more dramatic by evidence that vast numbers of homes, bought for their speculative value, are standing vacant. Excluding weekend and holiday homes, official estimates suggest there are around 2·5 million unoccupied properties in Spain, of which more than 200,000 are in the Madrid area. Inevitably, the late eighties saw a growth in squatting by communes calling themselves *Okupas*.*

Yet it was not until they began to sound out voters ahead of the 1991 local elections that the politicians seem to have realized that housing had become a major issue of concern. The Socialists eventually responded by offering to bring on to the market over a period of four years some 460,000 new homes at reduced interest rates.

But the debate over how to deal with the problem caused a bitter division between government ministers and party officials, from which the PSOE has never fully recovered. The Economics and Finance Minister, Carlos Solchaga, rejected the pledge as impractical and was swiftly and publicly defied by the man who had launched the proposal, the PSOE's organizational boss, Txiki Benegas. Within days, Mr Benegas's most candid thoughts about the diminutive Mr Solchaga, whom he described as 'the dwarf', had been heard by millions on the private radio network, SER. A tape of conversations Mr Benegas had held on his car telephone was delivered anonymously to the network which, after verifying their authenticity, decided to broadcast them. Most embarrassingly, from the Socialists' point of view, Mr Benegas was heard to identify the Prime Minister, Felipe González, as the real obstacle to a more progressive government policy.

The PSOE's initiative nevertheless helped to stir up a debate, for the first time in many years, about the reasons for Spain's housing problems. As was speedily pointed out in the media, the real problem was not the rate of interest but the fact that the rise in prices had put the cost of a house beyond the means of all but the most well-off. A housing expert writing in *Diario 16* calculated that the PSOE's proposals would enable a first-time buyer earning the

---

* *Okupa*, in the singular, derives from *occupar* (occupy). The use of a 'k' to replace 'cc' or 'c' before 'a', 'o' and 'u' has of late become a cipher for rebellious sentiment. It was one of the orthographic innovations employed by the founder of Basque nationalism, Sabino Arana, to differentiate Basque from Spanish, and for recent generations it has come to symbolize Basque rejectionism. Not without reason, the inhabitants of Vallecas – a drug-plagued, crime-infested, working-class suburb of Madrid – feel they have been let down by the Spanish state as much as any Basque. They make the point in wall daubings by spelling Vallecas 'Vallekas'.

average wage for a Spaniard under the age of thirty-five to buy a flat in only one of Spain's fifty-two provincial capitals. Others made a point later acknowledged as correct by the cabinet minister responsible for housing: that even if the Socialists' offer were taken up in full, it would only satisfy a third of the accumulated and forecast demand over the four-year period envisaged.

PART FIVE

Society Reflected

CHAPTER 21

The Press: More Influence than Readers

Every so often, a statistic will crop up which serves as a reminder that the reality of Spain is very different from the impression a visitor might gain on a swift trip to sophisticated Madrid or Barcelona. In the mid-eighties the government published a survey according to which more than half of all Spaniards had never read a newspaper.

Never. Ever.

In 1992, Spain's national and regional dailies, including those which are devoted exclusively to either business or sports, sold an average of slightly less than 3·9 million copies. To put it another way, only one in ten of all Spaniards was a regular newspaper-buyer, compared with 40 per cent of Britons, 35 per cent of Germans and 15 per cent of French. The Spanish figure, in fact, was lower than for any other EU country except Portugal.

Nevertheless, 1992 was the first year in which it reached the 10 per cent mark which UNESCO uses as one of its yardsticks of a developed nation. Spain may have ceased to be economically under-developed in the early sixties but, according to the definition used by the United Nations at least, it was not until the early nineties that it ceased to be culturally underdeveloped.

It needs to be stressed that the number of people who buy a newspaper is not the same as the number of people who read one, and that in Spain readership per copy is reckoned to be higher than in many other countries. A report published in 1990 by the media buying group, Carat International, calculated that the proportion of the adult population which read a newspaper was in fact 30 per cent. But that still compared with 85 per cent in Britain, 82 per cent in what used to be West Germany and 51 per cent in France.

To a large extent, of course, newspaper-reading is a reflection of economic progress. It is no coincidence that Spain is poorer than any of the other countries just mentioned. Some 3·5 per cent of Spaniards are absolutely illiterate and a great deal more are thought to be functionally illiterate. Almost a third never finished basic schooling, although the proportion is falling rapidly as the results of successive educational reforms take effect. As more and more Spaniards have reached newspaper-buying age able and keen to read, the sales of the daily press have grown steadily. The nationwide circulation figure for 1992 was 28 per cent higher than five years earlier.

But the correlation between progress and newspaper sales is not consistent. The British, for example, are certainly not as well-off, and arguably not as well educated, as the French; yet they buy twice as many papers.

Various theories can be put forward to explain these and other similar discrepancies. In the first place, it is noticeable that newspaper-reading diminishes the closer one gets to the Mediterranean. And that the closer one gets to the Mediterranean, the more oral is the nature of the culture. Newspaper purchasers are almost as scarce in Italy as they are in Spain – less than 12 per cent of the population in 1992.

Another possible explanation is that international differences in newspaper sales have something to do with the relative incidence in each country of a popular press. A comparison between Spain and Britain is particularly interesting in this respect since Britain has such a highly developed popular newspaper market whereas Spain has none. If you compare the number of copies sold by Britain's national 'quality' newspapers with the number of copies sold of *all* the newspapers published in Madrid and Barcelona, the figures as a proportion of the population are identical – 3·8 per 100 inhabitants in 1992. It would seem to bear out what is observable in any Spanish bar or on any Spanish street: that the sort of people who read a 'serious' daily in Britain also read a 'serious' daily in Spain, but that the kind of people who read a tabloid in Britain read nothing at all in Spain, and for the simple reason that there is nothing designed to meet their needs.

In Spain most of the big dailies have a tabloid format, and several, like *El Periódico*, *Diario 16* and *El Mundo*, use the design techniques of popular journalism – eye-catching layouts and jazzy graphics. But even *El Periódico*, which makes a more conscious appeal to working-class readers than the others, is not a popular newspaper in the sense that the term is understood in Britain, Germany or the United States. It gives extensive coverage to 'serious' political and economic news and although it carries stories about, for instance, the private lives of celebrities, it will rarely lead the paper with them. In fact it is precisely the sort of non-sensationalist 'popular' paper that middle-class critics elsewhere would like to see replace working-class tabloids such as the *New York Daily News*, the *Sun* and *Bild Zeitung*.

Two attempts have so far been made to establish a comparable product in Spain. The first was *Diario Libre*, which was launched in 1978 and whose demise a few months later is perhaps best explained by one of its more memorable headlines, '*Maricas en el Ministerio de Cultura*' ('Poofters in the Arts Ministry') – not exactly an issue of burning concern in the ground-down workers' suburbs around Spain's big cities.

The second was an altogether more serious effort. *Claro*, backed by a fifty-fifty joint venture between Germany's Axel Springer group, which publishes *Bild*, and Spain's Editorial Española, which owns the conservative daily *ABC*, hit the newsstands in 1991. Its editor and some of his senior staff had spent weeks at *Bild* before the launch, being introduced to the techniques that have made it Europe's best-selling daily newspaper. What they produced was essentially a *Bild* tailored for the Spanish market – more scandalized than scandalous, and using a layout technique once described as 'typographical terrorism'. It was launched with a cover price thirty pesetas below that of the rest of the national daily press, an initial print-run of 600,000, and a pledge of enough money to keep it on the market for up to three years. In the event, it took just three months for its backers to realize that *Claro* was never going to work. When they pulled the plug on it, newsstand surveys by rivals estimated that its sales had fallen to just 22,000 copies a day.

Why, then, is Spain seemingly incapable of sustaining a popular press? One explanation points to the comparable absence of popular newspapers in most of the rest of southern Europe. Perhaps there is something unique to Latin societies which makes them inimical to popular journalism, though it is not immediately apparent what this might be. Another theory is that Spain's well-established gossip magazines and sports newspapers already cover the stories on which a popular press would depend. There again, a newspaper like the *Daily Mirror* is not exactly brim-full of stories about celebrities and socialites, nor does it devote proportionately any more space to sport than many a 'heavyweight'.

A more convincing argument, in my opinion, is that southern European journalists, unlike their northern European counterparts, have been unable – or unwilling – to come up with a product capable of luring working-class readers. According to this view, newspaper-reading remains a middle-class habit in Spain because newspaper journalism in Spain has become a middle-class profession. What is quite clear is that Spanish journalists do not choose to write for their readers in the language of everyday speech, nor do they seem bothered about translating for them the technical terms in which stories are relayed to them from their sources. Most of Spain's journalists enter the profession as university graduates, fresh out of the journalism schools that were originally set up under Franco as a way of bringing a traditionally troublesome profession within the framework of his corporatist state. Graduation from a 'Faculty of Information Science' became a precondition for registration as a journalist. An incidental effect was that it restricted the profession to the children of those relatively well-to-do families who were the only ones who could afford to send their children to university.

As the Socialists' policy of grants takes effect and more and more working-class graduates issue from the universities, so more and more working-class youngsters will find their way into journalism. But for as long as university remains the accepted path into the profession, most will continue to bring with them an intellectual's interpretation of its nature and purpose. They will continue as at present to regard themselves as members of the intelligentsia, whose mission is to write for other members of the intelligentsia in the sort of terminology both parties understand.

As things stand, Spain's major general-interest dailies fall into three clearly defined categories: those which have remained in business since the Franco era, those which were founded in reaction to it, and a single product of the late-eighties boom.

There are three survivors from Franco's time – *La Vanguardia*, *ABC*, and *Ya*, though only the first two have managed to achieve a secure foothold in the market. It is notable that neither was a creation of the dictatorship.

La Vanguardia was founded in Barcelona in 1881 and became the voice of Catalonia's upper middle class, many of whose members supported Franco's regime after the civil war. But its dependence, for advertising as well as circulation, on the nationalist middle- and lower-middle classes was brought home to it by a curious episode in 1960. *La Vanguardia*'s then editor, outraged at hearing a sermon being delivered in Catalan, interrupted the service and harangued the priest. A boycott organized by Catalan nationalists threatened to put the paper out of business and cost the editor his job.

After his departure, and within the bounds imposed by censorship, *La Vanguardia* gradually acquired a reputation for sound, objective reporting, especially of international news. By the time that democracy returned, it was Spain's biggest-selling newspaper. The lifting of censorship has permitted the rigorous standards once applied only to foreign coverage to spread to other parts of the paper and a redesign has put colour on the front page without costing *La Vanguardia* that air of Olympian detachment which is its hallmark.

Yet it has never managed to break out of Catalonia to become the truly national paper it deserves to be. That, more than anything else, explains why its professional stature has not brought it higher sales. Its circulation of just over 200,000 in 1992 was much the same as when Franco died. *La Vanguardia* lost its place as Spain's best-selling newspaper to *El País* at the start of the eighties and, within what might be called the quality conservative market, it was overtaken by *ABC* in 1985. The *La Vanguardia* group's commercial growth has come through diversification into, first, radio, and later, television.

ABC, which publishes separate editions in Madrid and Seville, was founded in 1905 and had established a distinguished reputation for worldwide coverage long before the civil war. It was allowed to continue publishing after Franco's victory because its monarchist proprietors, the Luca de Tena family, favoured the Nationalists during the conflict.

Ever since the return of democracy it has been a loyal supporter of the People's Party (formerly Alliance). But its approach has little in common with the moderate conservatism which José María Aznar would like his party to be seen as representing. It has stubbornly refused to give up the wrap-around cover with prominently displayed photographs which was a quirk of the Francoist press. And, unlike La Vanguardia, it can hardly be said to have made a virtue of detachment. Indeed, the bias of its selection and presentation sometimes verges on the hysterical. It is a policy that has nevertheless brought ABC handsome dividends, especially since the Socialists' accession to power in 1982. Circulation has grown steadily and in 1992 stood at more than 300,000.

Ya is quite simply the basket case of the Spanish press. It was launched in 1939 to be the mouthpiece of the Spanish Church and by the time the dictatorship ended it was selling more than 140,000 copies a day. Although the paper carried a daily religious affairs section, its ecclesiastical content was not particularly onerous, so its subsequent demise cannot be attributed solely to the waning power of the Church.

For several years, it was a rather livelier product than either of the other two Francoist survivors. But it did not make itself into a blue-chip journalistic product like La Vanguardia, nor did it have the attraction of a contentious editorial line like that of ABC. Rarely did Ya come up with a scoop. By 1989, when the Church sold its shares to the owners of the Basque newspaper El Correo-Español-El Pueblo Vasco, Ya's circulation had shrunk to a mere 63,000. An attempt was made by its new owners to relaunch it as a Madrid-only tabloid, but they were unable to stop the rot, and at the time of writing it is being kept alive solely by the efforts of a workers' cooperative.

Ahead of both ABC and La Vanguardia, at the top of the quality newspapers' sales table is El País. First launched in 1976, it is the journalistic expression par excellence of the post-Franco years and the Socialists' subsequent rise to power. Its parent company, PRISA, had been set up with a broadly based shareholding in which almost every leading personality with an interest in the consolidation of democracy had a stake. The first editor of *El País*, Juan Luis Cebrián, who was only thirty-one when he was appointed, was given generous resources that enabled him to take his pick of Spain's most able young journalists. From day one, his newspaper was required reading for anyone seriously interested in the nation's affairs.

Its clean, clear modern format stood out on the newsstands, proclaiming that this was a newspaper which intended to highlight what was noteworthy rather than obscure it. During the UCD's years in power, *El País*'s reporters 'broke' several important stories, but perhaps an even greater contribution was made by its leader-writers who, day in, day out, explained patiently and clearly how this, that and the other was done in a democracy. It was an invaluable contribution in a country whose voters – and leaders – could be forgiven then for failing to grasp such concepts as collective responsibility, ministerial accountability and where to draw the line between a permanent administration made up of officials and a transitory government made up of politicians.

Since the Socialists' accession, *El País*, which has been broadly supportive of successive González administrations, has had to cope with a more difficult role. Newspapers which back the government of the day are always thought to be at a disadvantage. But in 1992 *El País*, which is published in both Madrid and Barcelona, had an average daily circulation of some 407,000, and in only one year in its history, 1990, had it known a fall in sales.

The paper's accumulated successes have enabled PRISA, headed by Jesús de Polanco, to become Spain's most influential media group. It owns stakes in the financial daily, *Cinco Días*; the radio chain, SER, and the Canal Plus TV channel. In 1990, PRISA took a 12·5 per cent holding in Britain's *Independent*, which has since been upped to more than 18 per cent.

The other two dailies to be born of the transition were both founded on the back of the profits to be made at that time from magazine publishing. *Diario 16* was created as a counterpart to *Cambio 16*. *El Periódico* was founded by the Zeta group, owners of *Interviú*. The history of the two newspapers has a lot to say about regional sensibilities, for it would seem that a product launched from Madrid is acceptable in other parts of the country, whereas one projected from Catalonia is not.

El Periódico was initially set up in Barcelona as a national news-paper, but failed to sell outside its region of origin and swiftly retrenched. With sales of 181,000 in 1992, ranking fourth among Spain's general newspapers, it was very much a product designed for the Catalan market, as its full title – *El Periódico de Catalunya* – suggested. It tends to favour the Socialists, though not without occasional critical sideswipes.

Diario 16 was also a troublesome infant. It was conceived as Madrid's first 24-hour-day journal; that idea, though, did not work and it went on to become first an evening, then a morning, paper. By 1978 its circulation had slumped to less than 50,000 and was showing only the most vapid signs of recovery when 28-year-old Pedro J. Ramírez was appointed editor in 1980. During his first year in the job, sales rose by more than 60 per cent and carried on growing for as long as he remained in charge. By 1989, with a daily circulation of 145,000, it ranked fifth among Spain's newspapers in terms of sales.

Diario 16's revival under Ramírez also to some extent defied the newspaper trade's conventional wisdom that support for the govern-ment of the day is bad for sales. *Diario 16* was broadly supportive of the Centrists while they were in power. After the UCD's collapse it threw its weight behind the Socialists, although it became a strident opponent as its editor's disenchantment with González and his policies grew.

The years immediately following the end of the dictatorship also saw the re-creation of a vernacular daily press in Spain with the launching of the Catalan-language *Avui* and two papers written partly in Basque – *Deia*, which is the organ of the non-violent Basque Nationalist Party, and *Egin*, which has become a mouthpiece for the Basque terrorist group ETA. All three papers have survived, though none has a circulation of more than 50,000.

A major obstacle facing the papers set up in the early years of Spain's restored democracy was that they had to compete for both circulation and advertising with a chain of newspapers whose losses were automatically met by the state.

In 1936 Franco had decreed the expropriation of all those news-papers which belonged to parties, unions or individuals favourable to the Republic. Four years later, the papers concerned were handed over to the Movimiento. The state's interest in the written media was later boosted still further by the creation of a Madrid evening newspaper, *Pueblo*. Right up until the seventies, the majority of these newspapers paid their way. *Pueblo* was at one time the daily with the largest sales in the country. But in the last years of Franco's life their circulations plummeted and from the point of view of the new, democratic government, the state-owned newspapers were as much an economic liability as a political embarrassment. Enfeebled as they were, the state-owned newspapers were none the less capable of draining enough circulation from the privately owned press to distort the operation of a free market.

In 1979, the government closed six of the biggest loss-makers in the state chain. The following year it got rid of two more. But that still left another twenty-eight (excluding *Pueblo*), which, towards the end of the UCD's period in office, were costing the treasury a cool 2,876 million pesetas a year. One, *Suroeste,* had a circulation of only 1,645 in spite of being published in a city the size of Seville. In 1981 the Cortes approved a UCD bill to auction them off with the proviso that cooperatives formed by the employees would be allowed to bid. The bill was opposed by the Socialists on the grounds that the newspapers concerned had effectively been stolen from their rightful owners and that to privatize them would be to endorse an injustice. But by the time that they themselves came to power, they had little option but to carry out the spirit, if not the letter, of the UCD's policy. The new government immediately closed a further six papers and put all the rest – with the exception of *Pueblo* – up for sale in the early months of 1984.

The biggest-selling title to go under the hammer was the sports paper, *Marca*, which has since overtaken *As* to become the leader in this intensely competitive but highly profitable sector of the market. In 1992, *Marca* and *As* ranked third and eighth respectively among Spain's dailies. The combined daily circulation of the sporting press, aimed mainly at soccer fans, was well over half a million.

Only one of the state's newspapers was acquired by an employees' cooperative. More often than not they went to local businessmen, not a few of whom had close links with the Socialist Party. But only a handful had to be shut down and those printers and journalists who were deprived of jobs as a result of the auction were offered posts in the civil service. As for *Pueblo*, it too was closed a short while later, in spite of protests from the Socialist trade union UGT, which had wanted to convert it into a modern trade-union newspaper.

The disposal of the state's press empire cleared the way for a further round of new initiatives when the Spanish economy began to perk up in the mid-eighties. Appropriately, the earliest signs of a renewed interest in the written media came in the form of additions to Spain's daily financial press.

Until then, its only representative was *Cinco Días*, founded in 1978 and nowadays jointly owned by, among others, the PRISA group, *Expansion* of France and the Dow Jones-*Wall Street Journal* group in the United States. In 1986 it was joined by *Expansión*, in which the *Financial Times* subsequently took a 35 per cent interest. Three years later, a third financial daily, *Gaceta de los Negocios*, was launched by the Zeta group. The result is a severely overcrowded market. *Expansión* has for some years now been the market leader, yet its audited circulation for 1992 fell short of 35,000.

The outstanding, indeed the sole, survivor among the non-specialist dailies founded in the late eighties has been *El Mundo*.* The story behind its creation is quite as interesting as its subsequent evolution. In March 1989, the Chairman of *Diario 16*, Juan Tomás de Salas, sacked its editor, Pedro J. Ramírez. Ramírez maintained he was dismissed for refusing to tone down the paper's investigations into the GAL.† De Salas insisted it was because he felt *Diario 16* was becoming too sensationalist.

At all events, it was a decision that was to cost the *16* group dear. First, de Salas's brother Alfonso, a senior executive of the group, threw his weight behind Ramírez's plans to set up a new daily and took on the chairmanship of the company created to launch and manage it. Then Ramírez set about stripping his old newspaper of much of its brightest talent. Among those who joined him were Spain's most original columnist, Francisco Umbral; one of its most

---

* *El Independiente*, which had earlier put a toe in the water as a weekly, went over to daily publication in 1989, only to collapse two years later. *El Sol* lasted from 1990 until 1992.

† See above, pp. 62-3.

popular cartoonists, 'Forges'; the head of the GAL investigation, Melchor Miralles, and several experienced roving correspondents, notably Alfonso Rojo who in 1991 attracted worldwide attention as the only non-Arab press reporter to stay in Iraq throughout the Gulf War. Ramírez also signed an agreement with the *Guardian*, one of *El Mundo*'s founding shareholders, which allowed his paper to reprint material from the British daily.

Within eight months, *El Mundo* was on the newsstands sporting a layout that was to win it more prizes at the following year's US Society of Newspaper Design awards than had ever been given to a European paper. Its relentless criticism of the Socialist government has gained it a solid following among the well-educated, disenchanted urban young – precisely that section of the population which holds most attraction for advertisers. With the help of a big cash injection from the Italian publishers of *Corriere della Sera*, who took a 45 per cent stake, *El Mundo* overhauled *Diario 16* for the first time in 1992 and by the middle of the following year, with an audited circulation of well over 200,000, it was on its way to becoming Spain's third national newspaper after *El País* and *ABC*.

Meanwhile, *Diario 16*'s progress has been steadily downhill ever since Ramírez's departure. In early 1994, Juan Tomás de Salas quit the board of a paper which by then was laden with debt and repeatedly afflicted by labour disputes. Few people in the Spanish newspaper industry could be found who were prepared to bet on its survival.

Already, though, Spain is a country in which the daily press offers readers a remarkably, not to say alarmingly, narrow choice. In the twenties and thirties, Madrid and Barcelona – each a third of their present size – supported eighteen and sixteen newspapers respectively. By 1994, the comparable figures were five and three.

No one visiting Spain for the first time can fail to be impressed by the newsstands in the big cities – particularly the ones on the Gran Vía in Madrid and the Ramblas in Barcelona. Shut up at night to form mysterious steel boxes on the pavements, they open out in the morning like variegated tropical blooms. Every available space on the walls, the counter and on the opened-out doors is taken up with the vividly coloured covers of every conceivable kind of magazine. Usually there are so many on sale that the owner of the stall has to set out trestles at the front and sides to accommodate them. There are news magazines and general and special interest magazines, including a good many published in the States and elsewhere in Europe. There are humorous magazines, educational magazines, 'adult' magazines (for gays and lesbians as well as for heterosexuals), literary and scientific reviews, partworks, comics for children and comics for adults.

The newsstands are a tribute not only to the Spaniards' genius for display, but to the resilience of the Spanish magazine trade. Spaniards' enthusiasm for periodicals serves as a corrective to the view, based on a glance at the newspaper circulations alone, that Spaniards are not keen readers.

In Spain, the habit of subscribing to a newspaper or magazine has never taken root. The press is sold almost entirely from newsstands. Magazines suffer more from this than newspapers, because reader loyalty – and this is not just a Spanish phenomenon – tends to be weaker towards weeklies than dailies. The result is that the sales of individual Spanish magazines vary wildly from week to week, depending on the attraction each successive edition holds for the idle browser. Competition is fiercer than in any other section of the media. The lengths to which Spain's magazine journalists will go to secure an exclusive sometimes border on the piratical, and particularly 'hot' photographs can fetch upwards of 10 million pesetas.

As in most countries, the magazine business inhabits the gaps left by the newspaper industry. None of the Spanish newspapers, for example, has an equivalent of the social diaries or gossip columns you find in the British and American papers. But then Spain has a plethora of highly profitable glossy magazines devoted to the lives and loves of the famous.

The pioneer was ¡Hola!, an extraordinary enterprise which remains firmly in the hands of the Sánchez Junco family which founded it in 1944. Each week's edition is made up in Eduardo Sánchez Junco's front room with the help of his mother, his wife, and his niece. ¡Hola! is the journalistic embodiment of that 'culture of evasion' identified by Carr and Fusi and mentioned in an earlier chapter. It had seemed to be a product suited only to a particular time and place. But not so. A magazine which helped its readers to escape from the rigours and the colourlessness of Francoist Spain has, against all predictions, shown itself to have immense appeal in the Britain of the late eighties and early nineties.

In 1988, an English-language edition, *Hello!*, was launched with the same outdated design and cravenly respectful approach to the rich and famous. Within four years it had won a weekly circulation of almost half a million and given the English language a new word – 'helloization'.

¡Hola! has been joined over the years by others like *Pronto*, Spain's best-selling magazine, *Diez Minutos*, *Lecturas*, and *Semana*. These magazines – generically known as the *Prensa de Corazón* ('Press of the Heart') – occupy five of the top ten places in the magazine sales table and sell more than two and a half million copies a week.

Sensing another gap in newspaper coverage, the magazines did their best to satisfy the clamour for uninhibited reporting of current affairs during the latter years of the dictatorship and the early years of the monarchy when newspapers were unwilling or unable to do so.

The first opposition current affairs magazine was the quaintly titled *Cuadernos para el Diálogo* ('Notebooks for the Dialogue') founded by a group of Christian Democrats back in 1963. But *Cuadernos* was above all an intellectual publication with a penchant for the results of sociological investigations. The first real news magazine was *Cambio 16*, which hit the newsstands in 1972. Similar to *Time* or *Newsweek*, it rapidly achieved a high standard of professionalism and was followed into the market by a host of similar weeklies. By 1977 there were fifteen of them, selling a total of 2 million copies a week. But as *El País* and the other new newspapers began to assert themselves they started to wilt. *Cuadernos* was one of the first to go. Others followed in rapid succession. Today *Cambio 16* is the only survivor of those giddy days, although it has since had to face competition from *Tiempo*, a mildly sensationalist offering from the Zeta group, the conservative *Epoca*, and the liberal *Tribuna*.

Cambio 16 was a product of the rather serious, impassioned atmosphere that prevailed in the years leading up to Franco's death. But the magazine which captured and reflected the more liberated spirit of the years that followed is *Interviú*. Founded in Barcelona soon after the end of the dictatorship, *Interviú* set out to provide its readers with two things they had been denied under Franco – uninhibited coverage of politics and pictures of naked women. It did so in a way that proved particularly appealing to the Spanish market. Instead of wrapping its reports in code and metaphor in the way that had been customary until then, *Interviú* went straight to the politicians themselves, asked them blunt, provocative questions and printed the answers word for word. Rather than rely on the professional, usually foreign, models who were beginning to make their appearance in other magazines, *Interviú* approached Spanish actresses and singers with the beguiling proposition that by shedding their clothes they would be putting their democratic credentials beyond question. The message projected to the reader was – and is – that sexual and political liberation are one and the same thing. To anyone who did not live in Spain during the late seventies it is a peculiar concoction, and for the non-Spaniard it is made even more peculiar by the regular inclusion of full-colour photo-features on surgical operations, killings and accidents, often made up of pictures considered too explicit for use in the daily press.

When it hit its peak in 1978, *Interviú* was selling almost three-quarters of a million copies a week. The cash it generated formed the basis on which its proprietor, Antonio Asensio, has since been able to build up his empire, the Zeta group, in which Rupert Murdoch's News International took a 25 per cent stake in 1989. *Interviú* itself, though, lost circulation steadily throughout the eighties, and by 1992 the weekly average was barely 200,000.

Tacky though it often is, *Interviú* has helped to fashion a specifically Spanish style of journalism which has evolved in the years since the end of the dictatorship. Perhaps surprisingly in a country that has borrowed much from the other side of the Pyrenees, it has little in common with the elliptical French approach to reporting in which articles frequently start with a question. In their news stories at least, Spaniards favour the Anglo-Saxon method of beginning with a summary which is then expanded.

The singularity of Spain's journalism is to be found in a high degree of personalization which faithfully reflects the Spanish fascination with individuals and a relative indifference to depersonalized institutions and associations. The proportion of space occupied by signed opinion columns must be the highest in the world and there is a quite extraordinary degree of concentration on the precise words spoken by news-makers. Interviews are invariably left in their raw 'question and answer' form and if a report is not headlined with a 'quote' it as often as not starts with one. Yet I have rarely, if ever, heard anyone in Spain complain of having been misquoted, or quoted out of context.

There have, none the less, been plenty of complaints about the Spanish press as its power has grown in recent years; for there are perhaps no other journalists in Europe whose influence is so disproportionate to their readership.

As will be seen in the next chapter, Spaniards are avid consumers of the other media but, in contrast to what happens in many other countries, the agenda followed by radio and television news is largely set by what appears in the press, and not vice versa. Only one Spaniard in twenty may have read a particular exclusive in a morning newspaper, but it is a fair bet that by evening he or she will have heard or seen it summarized elsewhere.

Moreover, Spain – like the United States – has a system of government that permits only limited parliamentary control of the administration. Spanish journalists, like their US counterparts, thus have an inherently more important role to play in bringing the government to book. In Spain, the importance of the press was boosted by the arrival in office of a government which, for more than a decade from 1982 until 1993, did not need the approval of even a part of the opposition for its legislative programme. An instinctive sense among editors of their natural role in such a situation may explain more effectively than personal beliefs or prejudices the remarkable degree of opposition to the Socialists which has developed among Spain's newspapers and news magazines.

By itself, this would have been enough to earn written journalists the hostility of the government. But it was also the press in the form of a newspaper, *Diario 16*, which brought to light the GAL case, and the press in the form of a magazine, *Epoca*, which broke the Juan Guerra scandal. ★ As the second of these two controversies reached its height early in 1990, González and his ministers began to

★ See above, pp. 66–7

talk openly of subjecting the press to increased control. In the context, it understandably produced an outraged response from journalists.

But you do not have to be a politician with skeletons in the cupboard to believe that a re-ordering of the rules governing the press is needed. Indeed, the issue had been raised a year earlier in the press itself when a succession of controversies involving magazine journalists focused attention on the right to privacy.

On the one hand, many of the laws to which they are subject are outdated or unjust. It is against the law to defame institutions, such as the government, as well as people, both living and dead. And the truth of an allegation is immaterial in deciding whether a journalist has committed the offence of attacking someone's – or something's – honour.

Just as seriously, though, particularly in view of the commitment to introduce trial by jury, there is no law to prevent defendants from being judged by public opinion before they are brought to court. Almost every day in the Spanish press you can see headlines stating unequivocally that the police have arrested the murderer of so-and-so or the thief of such-and-such. Reports frequently quote anonymous police sources as identifying by name terrorist suspects who have not even been arrested, let alone tried.

Up till now, the law has given the press this freedom on the assumption that the professional judges charged with deciding innocence or guilt could not be influenced by what they read in the press. The same cannot be said with such confidence of a jury.

A further issue that will need to be tackled if Spain's democracy is to flourish is that of relations between the press and the state. Almost two decades after the end of Franco's dictatorship, the government is still Spain's biggest media proprietor.

The disposal of the state's newspaper holdings did not put an end to its presence in the written media. The country's biggest news agency, EFE, from which the press takes much of its raw material, is still run by the government. Executives who defy the line set down by the ruling party are swiftly removed. And at times the government uses EFE in ways more appropriate to a dictatorship. One of the most internationally significant, and controversial, decisions Felipe González has taken since coming to office was to write to George Bush during the Gulf War calling for an end to the bombing of Iraqi cities. His letter was not announced at a press conference, nor distributed to news-rooms. An account of it, which may or may not have been correct, was leaked through EFE at the government's bidding. In such circumstances, foreign correspondents reporting from Spain have no option but to source their stories to the 'official news agency'. It makes it sound as if Spain were still a totalitarian state.

In addition to EFE, the government exercises direct control over vast swathes of both radio and television. But although its media interests have grown under the Socialists, the government's overall influence has probably diminished. And nothing has done more to shrink it than the advent of commercial television.

CHAPTER 22

Change 'on the Air'

The Spanish state's television monopoly ended on Christmas Day, 1989. At one o'clock in the afternoon an announcer, Miguel Angel Nieto, said: 'Antena 3 Television, Spain's first privately-owned television channel, has been born.' In the control box, the station's Director-General was so overcome by emotion that there were tears in his eyes as he tried to make a speech to the guests who had come to see the network launched. Characteristically, Spanish commercial television* had been got on the air at breakneck speed – Antena 3 had learnt it had been awarded a franchise just four months earlier to the day.

Although it had to be pulled out of them like a tooth, the Socialists' decision to allow competition on television is likely to be seen with hindsight as one of their most valuable contributions to the consolidation of democracy, comparable with their taming of the army. That may seem a ridiculous contention in view of the often trivial output with which the commercial channels have since waged a ratings war on the state-owned network. But you only need to look at the size of Spain's TV audience to see that it is not.

Surprisingly perhaps, the Spanish are a nation of TV addicts. The viewing figures for Europe as a whole reveal a situation that is precisely the opposite of what you would expect. By and large the people who watch television least are those with a reputation for being withdrawn and who live in the colder northern countries, whereas the people who watch television most are those who live in

---

* This is a less than satisfactory description of the privately-owned channels, since the publicly-owned ones also take advertising. But it is the most usual phrase in English and makes the point that the new channels have to make a profit.

the warmer southern nations and have a reputation for being gregarious. There is an exception to this general rule. Britain, a northerly country with a proverbially reserved population, has the highest viewing figures of all, but this may be because of the exceptionally high quality of British television's output. Leaving aside the British, the people who spend most time glued to their TV sets are the Spanish, followed by the Portuguese and the Italians – a pattern consistent with the view that media preferences are influenced by the prevalence of an 'oral' culture in the Mediterranean.

Almost every home in Spain has a television set – even those which lack other, more useful, amenities. I have not been able to find out if it is still true, but in the early eighties in Andalusia, which is the hottest region in Europe, more homes had television sets than had refrigerators. In 1989, according to a study by the research department of state-owned TV, the proportion of the population over the age of fourteen that watched television on a normal day was 85 per cent in summer and 87 per cent in winter. The average length of time Spaniards spent watching TV was almost three and a half hours a day – and only fifteen minutes less in summer than in winter. Whether 'watching' TV is actually the correct phrase is open to question. Spaniards will often leave the television on while they are doing other things. I suspect that the amount of undivided attention they give to TV is nothing like as high as the viewing figures suggest.

That said, research also shows that around 70 per cent of Spaniards form their political views on the basis of what they see on television. It is therefore no exaggeration to say that whoever controls what they call *la caja tonta* (the silly box) is in a position to control the mood and outlook of the nation. Though he could not have foreseen the extent of the Spaniards' addiction to television, Franco decided that the medium was too powerful to be left in any other hands but his own.

Televisión Española (TVE) was set up as a state monopoly in 1956. As with every sort of creative activity under the dictatorship, the programmes it transmitted were subject to censorship. But TVE was subject to a unique double filter. First, the programming plans were scrutinized by 'advisory commissions' made up of judges, priests, officers in the armed forces and the like. Then the finished product, whether made in Spain or bought from abroad, underwent what was euphemistically described as 'content evaluation'. As a result, things that were permitted in films and on stage were not allowed on to the small screen.

In 1980 *El País* got hold of the reports of one of Franco's censors, a Dominican monk called Antonio Sánchez Vázquez. These are the cuts he ordered in Billy Wilder's *The Lost Weekend*:

1. Kiss at the point of farewell.
2. When he steals the woman's handbag, eliminate the shots in which she and her companion behave with excessive affection (two or three times). At least, temper these shots.
3. Kiss and conversation while holding one another. Temper the kiss.
4. After the nurse says good-night ... one of the patients suffers *delirium tremens*. Allow it to start, cut quickly to when the doctors come in and he makes off with the doctor's coat.

But Fr Antonio was not just concerned with sex and violence. After seeing a French comedy film, he wrote that: 'Although the intention may be humorous, the Gestapo and their chief in Paris are held up to ridicule in their behaviour and references to the Führer.' Indeed, he seems to have had a remarkably sensitive set of political antennae for a priest. Mindful of Spain's position as a colonial power, he cut from a film called *Jaguar* a phrase about how the English exploited the Africans. Soon afterwards, relations with Britain entered one of their periodic crises over Gibraltar and the records show that Fr Antonio sent in another report suggesting that the phrase be re-inserted. Perhaps his most memorable remark, though, accompanied a recommendation not to show a film called *The Morals of Mrs Pulska*. '"Strong" subject,' he wrote. 'Criticism of hypocrisy. I warn you this will cause a rumpus.'

The censors did not disappear with the ending of the dictatorship. Fr Antonio was one of four on the staff of TVE as late as 1980, although by that time their job was not so much to cut material as to find ways of toning it down – substituting 'dung' for 'shit' in subtitles, for instance.

More importantly, the advent of democracy did not free TVE from government interference with the political content of its programmes. In this respect it was particularly unfortunate that the first Prime Minister of a democratic Spain should have been a man who had held high office under Franco in RTVE, the state corporation which controls both state-run radio and television. Suárez had been controller of the first television channel and subsequently the corporation's Director-General. He was thus thoroughly imbued with the Francoist notion of television as an arm of government.

It was only at the insistence of the Socialists and Communists that the 1977 Moncloa Pacts included a commitment to set up a governing body, responsible for guaranteeing RTVE's objectivity, scrutinizing its finances and – most important of all – drawing up a charter. Even then, the composition of this *Consejo Rector*, as it was called, was heavily weighted in favour of the ruling party. The charter which it drew up for RTVE, and which came into effect in 1980, created a new governing body called the *Consejo de Administración*, made up of members elected by the Cortes. Its membership tends therefore to reflect the composition of parliament, which in turn is weighted in favour of the government. So far the *Consejo de Administración* has proved itself to be a pretty toothless watchdog. Although the charter says that the Director-General cannot be replaced except for manifest incompetence, the UCD managed to get through three of them in its last two years in office.

The arrival of the Socialists did not bring about any obvious change in attitude. Soon afterwards an edition of the current affairs programme *La Clave*, which was to have featured a rebel Socialist councillor, was abruptly cancelled. In the campaign leading up to the NATO referendum, the 'box' was overtly manipulated to bring the electorate around to the Socialists' new-found point of view.

Since then, the use of television for the promotion of the government has become progressively more subtle. During the 1989 general election campaign, the last to be held before the advent of the commercial channels, *Diario 16* put the stop-watch on TVE's newscasts. It found that the bulletins' special campaign reports had been pretty balanced, with each party receiving air time more or less in proportion to its share of the vote. But the rest of the news was another matter. A total of an hour and forty-three minutes had been spent on coverage of the government and the PSOE, as opposed to just four minutes given to the country's main opposition party, the PP. *Diario 16*'s figures highlighted the most frequent cause of bias: that TVE does not routinely 'balance' coverage of government initiatives with comment from the opposition.

Neither has it given more than a passing nod to successive controversies affecting the government. In February 1990, the Socialists were finally forced to give a public account of the Juan Guerra affair at a special debate in the Cortes. Defying a petition signed by the editors of all its bulletins, TVE refused to televise the debate 'live'. The head of news and current affairs said the scandal, which had been at the centre of public attention for months, 'was only of interest to a specialized audience'. After a government reshuffle the following year, this is how TVE's lunchtime news described the new Cabinet: 'a government notable for its members' high level of experience and preparedness to tackle the challenges facing Spain in the future'.

TVE's usefulness to the Socialists and their predecessors in office may explain why successive governments were prepared to turn a blind eye to evidence of wholesale abuse in its management – at least, for as long as it made a profit.

The earliest allegations came soon after the end of the dictatorship. In 1977 a group of workers set up an 'anti-corruption committee' and the following year *Cambio 16* published a lengthy report exposing some of the worst abuses – inflated salaries, people drawing two salaries for doing (or pretending to do) jobs in both radio and television, members of staff being paid on a freelance rate for work they did in RTVE's time, and so on. 'There are those who earn, literally, twice as much as the King,' remarked the authors of the report, who among other things unearthed the case of a gentleman who, while living and working in Brazil where he was the representative of a Spanish company, was earning 65,000 pesetas a week for 'co-ordinating' a programme which, as the magazine commented, he probably never even saw.

It was partly no doubt because of all this extravagance and graft that RTVE had to ask the government for a subsidy in 1976. The whole of the next year was spent in a state of acute financial crisis. It was clear that unless something was done to sort out the corporation's finances, RTVE would soon get into the habit of taking ever larger hand-outs from the state. In 1978 Suárez sent in the government's auditors to find out where the money was going. Unfortunately for the government the report they produced found its way to *El País*, which found enough material in it to fill seven articles.

Written with a wry sense of humour, the auditors' report revealed a degree of inefficiency and dishonesty that at times beggars belief. For a start, there were no proper accounts. 'There is an abundance, even an excess, of accounting data,' the authors of the report remarked, 'but one cannot speak of a genuine system of accounting. It is impossible to draw up a balance or calculate the income and outgoings . . .'

After nine months of investigation, the government's accountants confessed that they were unable to say for certain how many people worked for RTVE or how much property and equipment it owned. There were employees with job descriptions that meant nothing and others who were called one thing but did another – 'In RTVE, there are production assistants presenting programmes, reporters who direct, directors who present, commissionaires who film and even radio announcers who'll do their job in front of the cameras if they're paid a bonus, with which anything becomes possible.'

Huge numbers of books and records and large amounts of clothing and film were found to be missing. In fact, theft was so widespread that there was a special euphemism for stolen goods at RTVE. They were called *depósitos personales* (personal stores). Theft apart, the auditors noted that there seemed to be genuine confusion in people's minds over where to draw the line between what belonged to the corporation and what belonged to individuals. 'There are cases of directors and producers who regard their programmes as private property and, in extreme cases, flatly refuse to return them.' This could explain why so little archive material is shown on Spanish television. The government investigation also discovered that it was customary for performers to hang on to the clothes in which they appeared and that this had given rise to a tax dodge whereby artistes received a share – sometimes a large share – of their payment in clothing. 'To look at some contracts,' the authors of the report remarked, 'you'd think that RTVE hired its performers naked and then proceeded to dress them.'

More than a decade later, *Diario 16* got hold of a draft report on RTVE by the Tribunal de Cuentas, the body responsible for auditing the public sector, which covered the period since the Socialists had been in power. RTVE still did not have a reliable inventory and different departments within the corporation were operating on different estimates of the number of people who worked for it. 'Investment plans, work programmes and budgets have turned out to be mere formal documents, lacking any kind of follow-up,' said the draft. One programme, with an initial budget of 11 million pesetas, had actually cost 150 million. In some cases, advances had been given for films that had already been made.

Not surprisingly, given this degree of maladministration, there were widespread fears both in RTVE and the government that Televisión Española would have difficulty competing with the new independent stations. One of the ways in which RTVE reacted was by moving to give both its channels a fair chance in the coming battle. TVE-2, which had been launched in 1965 as a 'minority interests' channel, was given a broader role and more resources to enhance its appeal. Re-christened 'La 2', its average daily audience by 1989 was 34 per cent of the adult population. In the same year, TVE-1's 'reach' was 78 per cent.

The overhaul of TVE-2 was not the only development in the run-up to the launch of commercial television which could be seen as prejudicial to the private channels' eventual success. There was, for example, the odd saga of Spain's first satellite channel, Canal 10, which began transmissions from London in January 1988. Despite government denials, the opposition became convinced that Canal 10 had been dreamt up by the government as a 'spoiling exercise'. The first Socialist Director-General of RTVE, José María Calviño, was an adviser to the project – and, some believed, its mastermind. Canal 10 did not succeed in scooping the advertising market ahead of the conventional private channels. But when it abruptly disappeared after less than seven months, it left behind quite a number of Spaniards who, having made a down-payment of 15,000 pesetas ($130 or £72) to watch its programmes, were less than thrilled with their first experience of commercial television.

In the meantime, the government had been busy increasing the number of publicly-owned stations in the regions, thereby increasing the competition that the privately-owned channels would have to face. The original idea behind regional television had been to offer a vernacular service in those regions where people spoke a language other than Castilian. The autonomy statutes of these regions stipulated that the stations created to provide this service would be run by the regional administrations in much the same way that RTVE was run by central government. Regional television thus became a means of giving additional powers to the governments of those areas with a solid claim to a separate identity, and the issue of whether it should be exclusively vernacular soon became blurred.

The first two channels were launched with a cavalier disregard for the law which is characteristic of many recent developments in the broadcast media. The Basque government's television service, Euskal Telebista (ETB), began transmissions on New Year's Eve, 1983, several days before the entry into effect of legislation authorizing the regions to apply for franchises. It now operates two channels – ETB-1, which broadcasts in Basque, and ETB-2, which transmits in Castilian. The Catalan government, which felt obliged to take up the gauntlet thrown down by the Basques, inaugurated TV-3 a few days later. Galicia subsequently got a channel of its own, as did Valencia, where a substantial minority of the population speaks a dialect of Catalan. In 1988, Catalonia acquired a second Catalan-language channel, Canal 33. Its launch was yet another act of defiance; unlike that of the Basque country, Catalonia's statute of autonomy did not entitle the area to more than one channel. Canal 33's earliest broadcasts were actually jammed by Madrid until the row with Catalonia's home-rule government was patched up.

Plans for additional regional services, in areas without a separate linguistic identity, had been shelved in 1984, but as the date for the launching of commercial television drew nearer they were taken down and dusted off. To no one's great surprise, both the regions which got channels of their own during 1989 were run by Socialist administrations.

Canal Sur was launched in Andalusia, with its first Director-General declaring that: 'We shall have an output for the majority of Andalusians, but you have to remember the majority of Andalusians vote for the PSOE.' The new service soon gained a more-than-respectable audience, though at no small cost. Within three months of its going on the air, Canal Sur had spent almost 50 per cent more than its budget for the entire year. Telemadrid, or TM-3, proved to be a surprise of another sort. Responsible to a regional government headed by a maverick Socialist, Joaquín Leguina, it became in his reported, and no doubt half-joking, words, 'the enemy within'. Its bulletins have not noticeably held back on news disagreeable to the government or the PSOE.

The three independent television franchises – awarded by the Cabinet – eventually went to Antena 3, Tele 5 and Canal Plus.★ The Antena 3 consortium was led by the radio network of the same name, which in turn had been created by La Vanguardia. Between them, Antena 3 Radio and La Vanguardia held a quarter of the stock. ABC's owners also took a small stake. Tele 5's major shareholders, each with a 25 per cent holding, were the Italian media tycoon, Silvio Berlusconi; the Barcelona publishing house, Anaya, and Spain's financially muscular association for the blind, ONCE. Canal Plus was called after the privately-owned French channel of that name which took a 25 per cent stake in it. Its leading Spanish shareholder was the El País-based media group, PRISA.

It was assumed from the start that each of the privately-owned television channels would have an identifiable political bias, like that of the privately-owned radio networks in Spain.† Antena 3 could be expected to be critical of the Socialists; Canal Plus could be relied on to support them. The third channel, Tele 5, had made it clear in its prospectus that it did not intend giving much air time to news and current affairs, aiming instead to build up a mass audience with games shows, variety programmes and popular films. Indeed, it could be argued that the scales were weighted against the government

★ The losing consortiums were Univisión Canal Uno, in which the Zeta group and Rupert Murdoch's News International each had a 25 per cent stake, and Canal C, promoted by a group of Catalan entrepreneurs. A prospectus submitted by the *16* group was ruled to have been presented too late.

† This is the case in much of continental Europe. Within Europe, the idea that the broadcast media do not have the same right as the written media to follow an editorial 'line' is a mainly British concept, inherited from the BBC's first Chairman, Lord Reith.

because, unlike Antena 3 which also considered but rejected the idea, Canal Plus opted to become a pay channel, thus restricting its potential audience.

It is against this background that a boardroom *putsch* at Tele 5, only days before it went on the air in early 1990, should be viewed. Berlusconi's representatives joined forces with those of ONCE to remove the channel's Chairman, who had come from Anaya. He was replaced by ONCE's Director-General, Miguel Durán. It was the first time a blind person had ever been given day-to-day control of a television station. Anaya's directors had fallen out with Berlusconi over the extent to which the new channel should depend on the Italian magnate's Spanish production and advertising subsidiaries. But a lot of commentators, bearing in mind that ONCE is subject to a government ministry, saw in the row a manoeuvre by the PSOE to redress the balance of commercial television's coverage.

If there was any truth in that theory, though, there is no sign yet that the supposed aim is being achieved. Antena 3 has, as expected, pursued an anti-Socialist line, even though its ownership has changed since it was launched. In 1992, the owner of *La Vanguardia* resigned the chairmanship in favour of Antonio Asensio, head of the Zeta magazine group. His departure signalled a prolonged shake-up in the financial structure of the company which allowed in the Asensio–Murdoch alliance that had failed to win a franchise in the competition three years earlier. By the time the restructuring was over, almost three-quarters of the shares were owned by companies controlled by either Asensio, Murdoch or the then Chairman of Banesto, Mario Conde. Antena 3's evening bulletins – presented by a former *ABC* correspondent, José María Carrascal – have continued to be highly opinionated and consistently hostile to the government. But Tele 5, which also mixes commentary with the news in the form of injects from 'columnists', is quite prepared to countenance attacks on government policy. And Canal Plus, which has a more conventional news format, seems so far to have aimed for a lack of bias.

As was only to be expected, the independent channels have significantly eroded TVE's monopoly of both the viewing audience and the advertising market. At the end of 1993, TVE-1 still topped the ratings with a share of more than 28 per cent. But Antena 3 was breathing down its neck with almost 27 per cent, and Tele 5 had built up a following of some 19 per cent. As early as 1991, RTVE had revealed that for the first time in almost a decade it was in the red. The biggest single contributory factor to its 20,000 million peseta ($192 million or £109 million) loss was an 8,500 million peseta ($82 million or £47 million) drop in advertising revenue. The shortfall was covered from reserves, but made it inevitable that the corporation would be subjected to a draconian overhaul of the kind that has been taking place ever since. Despite cuts, though, RTVE's losses had risen by 1993 to 127,000 million pesetas ($900 million or £600 million).

Both sides in the battle for viewers and advertisers claim that they are at an unfair disadvantage. The commercial stations, who have taken their case to the EU Commission, argue that the two state channels should be paid for out of public funds and ought not to be tapping the private sector by means of advertising sales. RTVE, meanwhile, complains that it has had to meet a series of extra costs from which its competitors are freed. TVE has to subsidize the state-owned radio network, Radio Nacional de España (which no longer takes advertising), fund the corporation's external broadcasting services and the national Radio and Television Institute, and make good the losses of RTVE's orchestra and choir. In 1994, for the first time, the government was to provide RTVE with a subsidy intended to meet these additional costs.

The regional television stations, which had around 15 per cent of the audience, at the end of 1993 had also suffered from the introduction of commercial television and were starting to become onerous burdens on their respective autonomous governments. TeleMadrid, which claimed to be the least subsidized, nevertheless received some 7,500 million pesetas ($54 million or £36 million) in 1993 – and still made a loss.

Canal Plus, which had said it needed some 500–600,000 subscribers to break even, ended the year with more than 750,000, and may be set to become the most profitable venture of them all. Certainly, there were doubts about whether Antena 3 could keep its ratings lead over Tele 5 without the generous funding that had been made available by Mario Conde before he was removed from the chairmanship of Banesto on the orders of the Bank of Spain in late 1993.

One of the first weapons to be brandished in the ratings war between the various channels was, perhaps inevitably, sex. It was first brought into play by Tele 5 in the summer of 1990 when it launched a thrice-weekly, late-night quiz programme-cum-striptease show which had been bought from an Italian channel. In its dubbed version it went by the title of *¡Uf! ¡Que Calor!* which freely translated means 'Phew! What a Scorcher!'. TVE hit back with a professional striptease routine to round off its chat-and-variety show, *Un Día es un Día.** It later showed a series of made-for-TV films based on erotic classics such as *Roxanne* and resumed the transmission of X-rated films such as *Emmanuelle*, which had been a feature of its programming in the first years of the Socialist administration. Meanwhile, and with a minimum of publicity, Canal Plus began showing pornographic movies – 'hard' not 'soft' porn – once a week in the early hours.

Sex, though, soon lost its impact, and the ratings war has since been waged mainly with imported Latin American soap operas, known as *culebrones* (serpents),† and locally-produced variety shows and situation comedies. What has given Antena 3 the advantage over Tele 5, in fact, has been its success in developing in-house sitcoms like the hugely successful *Farmacia de Guardia*, which centres on the comings and goings at a local chemist's.

Fierce competition has long been a feature of Spanish radio, which has a place in Spanish affections that is very possibly unique. You will sometimes hear Spaniards say with pride that they have the 'best radio in Europe' – and they may well be right. Spaniards are natural broadcasters. They tend to be fluent speakers as well as brilliant improvisers, and the radio professionals among them seem to realize that the medium is at its best when it is spontaneous, flexible and just a little unstructured. Radio, unlike television, moreover has a solid record of achievement in the service of democracy.

---

* TVE took *Un Día es un Día* from the Catalan channel, TV3. The last edition broadcast by TV3 won the programme widespread notoriety: it ended with the presenter persuading the entire audience to take off their clothes in front of the cameras.

†Because they go on and on.

Most adult Spaniards' first experience of uncensored news was gained by listening to the SER network's late-night current affairs programme, *Hora 25*, during the transition to democracy. As radio was freed from the constraints imposed on it under the dictatorship, numbers of listeners shot up from around 7 million at the time of Franco's death to some 16 million by the late seventies.

But it was the broadcasters' performance during the abortive coup attempt in 1981 that really made the difference. The radio correspondents in the Cortes press gallery stayed on the air until the moment that Tejero ordered his men to loose off their fusillade. Throughout the night that followed their colleagues elsewhere, in studios and outside-broadcast vehicles, succeeded in conveying urgency and concern without seeming to panic. Spain's most famous radio sports journalist, José María García, climbed on to a car outside the parliament building and kept up a running commentary from there.

A lot of Spaniards felt that the broadcasters had 'held their hand' during that anguished night, and they have not forgotten it. Listeners still number more than 16 million. Well over half the adult population listens to the radio every day, making it proportionately the highest audience in Europe.

Competition for the big morning audiences* is a contest without respite between the networked magazine programmes, whose presenters are national celebrities. For some years now, it has been a duel between Cadena SER's Iñaki Gabilondo, who rose to fame as the anchorman of *Hora 25*, and Onda Cero's Luis del Olmo, who has been broadcasting since he was a teenager.† Their peak audiences are well in excess of a million. The queen of the afternoon is Encarna Sánchez, who draws almost a half a million listeners to Cadena COPE, while the czar of the night is still José María García – 'Supergarcía' – whose programme, also on Cadena COPE, is tuned in to by more than a million sports fans.

---

*It is a reflection on the Spaniards' weird timetable that listenership does not reach its peak until after 11 a.m., and that the total audience between midnight and 1 a.m. is higher than between 7 and 8 a.m.

†His father was the stationmaster of a small town in Galicia at which the trains to and from Madrid had to make a lengthy stop. Armed with a tape recorder, he would scour the first-class carriages in search of celebrities, who in the circumstances found it difficult to refuse him an interview.

In Spain, it is customary for radio stars to pay the salaries and expenses of their entire back-up team, and that fact has to be borne in mind when assessing their earnings. Nevertheless, their earnings are astronomic. When Onda Cero signed up Del Olmo in 1991, it was reported that he had been promised an annual payment of 600 million pesetas ($5·8 million or £3·3 million) *plus* a percentage of his programme's advertising revenue.

Until the civil war, the only stations in Spain were private ones. But in 1937 Franco created a state network, Radio Nacional de España (RNE). During the course of his rule he also allowed pressure groups within the regime such as the Movimiento, the *sindicatos* and the Church to set up networks of their own. By 1964 there were some 450 stations all competing for space on the AM frequencies. The government succeeded in getting the number down to fewer than 200 by the mid-seventies. But this was still far higher than envisaged by the 1975 Geneva Conference which allotted only three medium-wave networks to each country. Spain was unable to meet the requirements of the Geneva Conference, but in 1978 it did manage to cut the number of medium-wave networks to four: RNE; Radio Cadena Española (RCE), which was made up of stations formerly owned by the Movimiento and the *sindicatos*; Cadena de Ondas Populares Españolas (COPE), owned by the Church, and finally, the largest of the commercial networks, SER. Stations not belonging to one of these four networks were either closed or transferred to FM.

In 1988, RNE absorbed RCE. It now runs two AM channels – Radio 1, which is primarily for general interest and current affairs programmes, and Radio 5, a sports and entertainment service with local opt-outs.

All the main AM networks also have a major presence on FM. Two of RNE's channels are broadcast on VHF – Radio 2, which carries classical music, and Radio 3, which broadcasts pop and rock.* SER's pop- and rock-orientated 40 Principales, has the highest audience of any channel in Spain.

FM began to grow in importance in the late seventies. Between

---

*Radio 4, which was aimed at regional audiences, was closed down as a cost-saving measure in the early nineties.

1979 and 1981, the government issued more than 300 new licences. Many went to entrepreneurs sympathetic to the then Centrist administration and formed the basis for several new chains, notably Antena 3, whose programming is similar to that of a conventional AM channel. Two other networks which emerged from this period were Cadena Rato and Cadena Ibérica. A number of leading radio personalities were lured away from the medium wave – there is virtually no long-wave broadcasting in Spain – and they in turn persuaded more listeners to tune in to VHF. Today, far more people listen to FM than to AM.

The Spaniards' enthusiasm for radio and their disregard for the law has also led to the setting-up of several hundred unlicensed stations, some 500 of which are run by town councils.* In 1989, despite the fact that Spain already had more radio outlets in proportion to the size of its population than any other country in Europe, the Socialist government launched a further round of some 250 FM franchise concessions. A lot went to Socialist town councils, some of which were already running 'pirate' stations. As happened under the UCD, many of the licences went to businessmen and others close to the ruling party. ONCE acquired a number of franchises either directly or through companies it controls. It subsequently bought sixty-three stations from Cadena Rato and, as a result of other acquisitions, its new network – dubbed Onda Cero – now has a chain of some 160 stations.

Even leaving aside ONCE's holdings, the state and its various dependent bodies now control a media empire of unusual, and unhealthy, proportions. For, while expanding the private sector, the Socialist government has simultaneously been promoting the public sector to the extent that it is probably larger today than when Franco died. It comprises an international news agency, eleven television channels and numerous radio stations. Yet as the evidence mounts on all sides that Spaniards prefer a commercially produced output, so the debts of the public sector are growing at a frightening rate.

---

*In 1988, EFE – the state-owned news agency – signed a contract to provide more than a hundred illegal stations with a regular service of bulletins prepared at its head office in Madrid.

In 1991 – long before the full impact of commercial television had been felt – a senior executive of Canal Plus, whose backers are scarcely hostile to the Socialists, calculated that the losses of the state's media empire that year would be 100,000 million pesetas ($960 million or £545 million). The same amount of money would have enabled the government to triple university grants or build a medium-sized power station.

CHAPTER 23

Art and the Possible: the Politics of Culture

It is not often that an exhibition of seventeenth-century paintings poses a threat to public order. But it has happened in Spain.

In 1990, the Prado put on the most comprehensive exhibition ever of works by Velázquez. The response from the public was astonishing. More than half a million people visited it.

On the day before the show was due to close, the director of the Prado ill-advisedly promised that the doors would stay open for as long as there were people still arriving. The Spanish having a tendency to leave things to the last minute, people were only too happy to take him at his word. Despite heavy rain, several hundred turned up at the gallery after dinner on the last day, only to find the doors had been shut at 9 p.m. They quickly formed an angry mob, pushing at the doors and hammering on them with their sodden umbrellas.

To prevent further disorder, staff hastily reopened the gallery. But the queues just carried on growing till they again stretched right round the building. When the doors were again closed at 10.30 p.m., this time for good, there followed what the next day's papers described as '*incidentes*' between irate members of the public and the Civil Guards guarding the gallery. At midnight, *El País* recorded, some forty people were still gathered at the doors of the Prado, chanting 'We want to come in'.

When the erstwhile Marxists who run Spain talk – one might think pretentiously – about *la demanda cultural*, they are actually referring to something that is a palpable, and occasionally awkward, reality.

In the Spanish view of things, culture, like education, is axiomatically good. Elsewhere in Europe, that belief has been dented by the events of this century, and in particular by the role the arts played in Hitler's Germany. Spain did not take part in the Second World

War, so Spaniards are neither as interested in, nor as familiar with, the awkward questions Nazism raises. Their intellectuals have never wrestled with the conundrum of how the gas-ovens came to be stoked by workers humming Wagner.

Spain also differs from the other big nations in Europe in that most of the country did not experience an industrial revolution. One of the effects of industrialization is to bolster a sense of working-class identity by promoting the formation of trade unions and the spread of collective bargaining. In Spain, that process was largely restricted to Catalonia, Asturias and parts of the Basque country, and even in those areas it was put smartly into reverse when Franco took power, outlawed the unions and imposed a Fascist notion of wage-bargaining. The Spain which eventually came out from under his shadow was one almost wholly devoid of working-class consciousness. It is particularly true of the millions who fled the countryside in the fifties and sixties. They may not be ashamed of being, or having been, poor. But the idea that poverty could in any way be a source of pride, or that wealth might be a source of shame, would strike them as just plain silly. And just as there is no real questioning of 'bourgeois values', nor is there any real objection to 'bourgeois culture'. You rarely if ever hear working-class Spaniards talk disparagingly about, say, Cervantes in the way that their British or American equivalents will often refer to Shakespeare. What happens in practice is that most choose to watch Tele 5 rather than go to the theatre, but what rejection exists is passive rather than active, silent rather than vocal.

The need for 'culture' is something to which everyone, but everyone, in Spanish society pays lip-service. Talk to the mayor of any God-forsaken little *pueblo* and he will invariably round off his list of the village's grievances and deficiencies by saying, '. . . y hay un terrible déficit cultural'. As if he were talking about a shortage of drinkable water. Or telegraph poles.

Against this background, it is easier to understand why Spanish politicians at all levels regard it as being in their own best interests to see that 'cultural demand' is met with an adequate 'cultural supply'. What, in the same Gradgrindian vein, is sometimes called the 'cultural infrastructure' has undergone vast improvements in the years since Franco's death.

323

The single biggest problem by the time Franco died was one of geographical imbalance. Spain's cultural resources were concentrated almost exclusively in Madrid and Barcelona. The rest of the country was largely neglected. Andalusia, for example, has much the same population as Switzerland. It is a region with a rich cultural tradition and a huge cultural appetite. Yet as late as 1982 it had not a single functioning theatre or orchestra.

The shortage of facilities in the provinces has been tackled in two ways. In line with the provisions of the constitution, much of the responsibility for administering the arts has been handed, with the necessary funds, to the regional governments. In addition, recent years have seen the central government paying greater attention to local needs.

The arts are generally reckoned to have benefited from the transfer to the new Autonomous Communities of power over arts policy. Even so, the move has been accompanied by a fair amount of controversy. One accusation has been that of narrow-mindedness by regional administrations: that, in deciding the allocation of funds, they judge projects less on their intrinsic cultural merits than on how much they will further the cause of that area's regional, or 'national', culture.

The new Basque administration, for example, was criticized for earmarking a quarter of its arts funds for the creation of Basque-speaking media. 'We can get by without Basque song, music or theatre for ten years,' a senior official retorted, 'but if we spend ten years without speaking Basque and without offering a real solution to the problem of our language, it'll be lost.'

As the transfer of responsibilities and funds went ahead, the budget of the Arts Ministry in Madrid shrank steadily. By 1992, it was some two-thirds less in real terms than it had been a decade earlier. The central government nevertheless continues to be involved in a number of important projects, set in motion by the Socialists, which aim to improve facilities in the regions. One is for the restoration of some fifty provincial theatres, most of them put out of business during the dictatorship by a combination of government indifference and competition from radio, TV and cinema. Another scheme is for the building of seventeen new concert halls. The most important to have opened so far is the Teatro de la

Maestranza in Seville, which can also be used for operatic productions.*

Several new music festivals have sprung up, notably the Alicante Festival of Contemporary Music and the Cuenca Festival of Religious Music. Recent years have also seen the emergence, or revival, of a plethora of local orchestras. There could be no more striking evidence of Spain's progress than that two of her traditionally most backward regions, Murcia and Estremadura, both areas once associated with back-breaking labour, parched landscapes and dreadful poverty, now have their own youth orchestras.

A number of regions have also acquired public art galleries for the first time. The outstanding success has been the Instituto Valenciano de Arte Moderno (IVAM) which first made news in the eighties, notching up an international success with its acquisition of a collection of works by the early twentieth-century sculptor, Julio González.

Despite all this, a study carried out for the Catalan *Generalitat* found that between 1983 and 1987, half the money invested by the Arts Ministry was still being spent on Madrid. There again, Madrid, being the capital, is also the venue or headquarters for most of Spain's national cultural institutions. Over the last decade or so quite a lot of money has had to be spent on bringing them up to scratch, or in some cases bringing them into existence.

Spain is frequently credited with possessing the richest theatrical tradition in the world after England. Yet the country which produced Lope de Vega, Tirso de Molina, Guillén de Castro, Calderón, Benavente and Guimerá did not have a repertory company dedicated solely to staging the classics until 1985 when the Compañía Nacional de Teatro Clásico came into being under the direction of the actor and producer Adolfo Marsillach, who has been running it for much of the time since. Marsillach has been the target of a lot of criticism. The main accusation levelled at him is that he trivializes classics in an effort to draw the crowds.

*Whether it will be is another matter. Twelve months after a showy opening in 1992, there was still no sign of a proper season being arranged. The paralysis was widely blamed on lack of co-ordination between the national (Socialist) and local (PP) authorities involved in establishing and running it. If that is the case, then it is a sorry example of the pitfalls of decentralization.

In so far as contemporary drama is concerned, the role of the state is directed towards ensuring that a modicum of quality work is staged. There are two ways in which it does this. The first is by subsidizing commercial theatres which undertake to stage 'serious' works. The second is through the *Centro Dramático Nacional*, which was set up in 1978. The CDN, which is based at the Teatro María Guerrero in Madrid, is not a repertory company like, say, the National Theatre in Britain. It is a production centre headed by a director which vets original scripts and ideas for revivals and then puts on a season of quality productions, contracting different actors for each of them. The María Guerrero is used for staging mainstream plays, while experimental works are put on at another theatre run by the state, the Sala Olimpia. Shortly after coming to power, the Socialists took the adventurous step of appointing a thirty-year-old Catalan producer, Lluis Pasqual, to become director of the CDN. His work there was widely acclaimed. In 1989, he left to take up an offer from Jack Lang to become director of the Paris-based Théâtre de l'Europe. But by that time, publicly-funded drama in Spain had been put on a solid basis.

It was just as well that the authorities – and not only the central government, but also the regional and municipal authorities – stepped in when they did, because the eighties witnessed the beginnings of a virtual collapse in the private sector. As in many countries, the vast majority of private theatres are in the capital; in 1984, Madrid – a city of only 4 million people – had thirty-nine theatres. Its stage life was comparable with that of London or Paris and much livelier than, say, Rome's. Nine years later, the number of theatres had dropped to twenty-two. The difference between the two figures was accounted for almost entirely by the closure of commercial venues.

By the middle of 1993 there were only thirteen left, of which one was given over exclusively to musicals. Several Madrid theatres had been turned into cinemas showing pornographic films. One became a discothèque; another a fast-food restaurant. The owner of the Teatro Benavente sold out after being unable to find an impresario willing to put on a work by the Nobel Prize-winning playwright from whom the theatre took its name. The principal reason for the slump was a loss of enthusiasm for the theatre, the possible causes of which are discussed in the next chapter. Another factor, though, was the leap in Madrid property prices: the profits to be gained from selling out to developers dwarfed the income to be made from staging plays. Without the role played by government, it is very likely that drama in Spain would have entered a fatal downward spiral in the eighties. Nevertheless, under the Socialists the greatest attention has been paid to other art forms – to music and, above all, to painting and sculpture.

For years, Spaniards' attitude to modern art had been much the same blend of majority hostility and minority enthusiasm that is to be found in other Western nations. But at some point in the early eighties it underwent a profound change. It is difficult to say exactly when that change took place, but it is possible to pinpoint the moment when it began to manifest itself – February 1983, when the second government-sponsored International Festival of Contemporary Art, held in Madrid under the title of *Arco-83*, was almost overwhelmed by the number of people who packed in to see it. When I visited Madrid a year later, I was struck by an atmosphere that I had never encountered before – that of a city gripped by art fever. Everywhere I went, in cafés, bars and restaurants, there were posters advertising exhibitions and on all sides friends and acquaintances had a story to tell of how they had to queue for hours to get into this or that exhibition. As the Professor of History of Art at the Universidad Complutense, Antonio Bonet Correa, wrote at about that time:

All of a sudden, the Spaniards – who for years knew nothing of the art world and were deprived of contemporary international art – have woken up to discover a new terrain. The habit of going to exhibitions in order to know about modern art has entered into the customs of those professional people who would wish to be considered as cultured.

According to an Arts Ministry survey carried out in 1985, 20 per cent of all Spaniards over the age of fourteen go to a public or commercial art gallery at least once a fortnight. One can only guess at the reasons for this remarkable level of interest. History shows that painting is an art form for which the Spanish have shown a special genius and it may simply be that it is the one to which they have an innate attraction. To some extent, art in Spain benefited from the worldwide surge of interest in painting and sculpture during the eighties, much of it inspired by the financial rather than the cultural possibilities fine art offers. In this respect, though, the subsequent development of the *Arco* series of exhibitions is illuminating. Sales, according to the gallery managers taking part, peaked in 1990. Two years later, the whole future of the enterprise was being questioned. In 1992, for the first time and at the request of gallery-owners, the organizers did not release a figure for total sales. Yet the number of visitors, at 176,000, was higher than ever. In other words, more and more Spaniards were coming to look, even though they no longer had the money to buy.

The degree of interest shown by the public in art, and particularly contemporary art, helps to explain the government's strenuous (if not always successful) efforts to give Madrid a museum that bears comparison with the Pompidou Centre or the Tate.

Shortly after seven o'clock on the morning of Sunday, 26 July 1992, the most famous painting of the twentieth century, packed in a container weighing more than a tonne and a half, was attached by chains to the jib of a crane and eased into the sunlight of a Madrid summer morning. Amid roaring controversy, Picasso's *Guernica* was on the move for the second time in eleven years. In 1981, it had travelled all the way from New York's Museum of Modern Art in compliance with its creator's wish that it be given to the Spanish people once democracy was restored. Now, against the wishes of many of Picasso's surviving relatives, it was being moved again – from an annexe of the Prado to the new Reina Sofía Art Centre less than a mile away.

Some critics feared the already flawed canvas would suffer further damage. Others believed the move ran counter to the artist's stated intention, which was to have his masterwork hung in the Prado and thereby open a bridgehead for contemporary art in a collection which otherwise comes to a halt in the last century. For the government, though, getting *Guernica* moved to the Reina Sofía was essential to the scheme of things they had devised. This was that the Prado proper should be retained for Old Masters; its annexe, the Casón de Buen Retiro, should be kept for nineteenth-century works, while the Reina Sofía was given over to modern art. It was also a way of providing the controversial and beleaguered new gallery with a centrepiece for its permanent collection that would bring in the visitors and finally justify the immense sums of money which had been spent on it.

The Reina Sofía had been conceived as a replacement for the Museo Español de Arte Contemporáneo which, in a move that reflected Francoist reservations about twentieth-century art, had been opened on the fringes of Madrid in 1969. Work began in 1981 on converting an eighteenth-century hospital near the end of the wide avenue on which the Prado stands. But when it was opened in 1986 – many felt precipitately, to win votes at the general election of that year – the building did not even have proper air-conditioning. Works by the American artist Cy Twombly were put on display and started to warp. A new round of work was begun three years later, and in 1990 the museum was closed down for seven months for refurbishment which eventually cost over 50 per cent more than initially budgeted. By the time it was re-opened, the Reina Sofía had acquired – among many other additions – three controversial glass towers on the outside of the building to accommodate lifts. Even then, the director predicted, work on the converted hospital would need to continue for another twenty or thirty years.

It still lacked a permanent collection, and as its curators' plans for one began to leak out, the Reina Sofía found itself plunged into yet more controversy. The director was accused of attempting the impossible in trying to assemble a collection that explained the development of twentieth-century Spanish art. The painter Antonio López, the 'star' of Victor Erice's film *El sol del membrillo* (*The Quince Tree Sun*), complained bitterly that it did not do justice to Spain's figurative artists. Nevertheless, plans for the inauguration of a permanent collection went ahead after *Guernica* was delivered, and although some believe the IVAM in Valencia is a more coherent museum, the mere presence of Picasso's masterpiece puts the Reina Sofía in the very first rank of modern art galleries worldwide. During 1993 the Reina Sofía enjoyed a much-needed respite from controversy as the focus of attention switched to another eighteenth-century building at the opposite end of the Paseo del Prado.

The Villahermosa Palace is now home to most of what was widely regarded as the world's finest private art collection after that of the British Royal Family. By the mid-eighties, Baron Heinrich von Thyssen, the Dutch-born steel tycoon, had expanded the art collection he had inherited from his father to the point where it included some 1,500 paintings and sculptures of note. Faced with the impossibility of displaying them adequately at his home in Lugano, he began casting around for a new home for his treasures and set off a sort of international competition for the privilege of providing one. The Prince of Wales was even said to have flown to the Baron's Swiss home in an attempt to talk him into handing over his collection to Britain. The Baron's Spanish wife, Carmen 'Tita' Cervera — an ex-Miss Spain and former wife of the screen Tarzan, Lex Barker — proved more persuasive. In 1988 he chose Spain instead, undertaking to loan some 800 of the best works for an initial period of nine and a half years.

It was agreed that the bulk of the collection should be housed in the Villahermosa Palace, and that the remainder should go to the medieval Pedralbes monastery in Barcelona. Both buildings were specially refurbished for the purpose. The deal was made permanent in 1993, with the Spanish government effectively buying the collection for 44,000 million pesetas ($315 million or £210 million). Six years earlier, a panel of Spanish experts had concluded that that part of the collection which had come to Spain was worth almost seven times as much. Art prices had, it is true, dropped in the meantime; but by any reckoning the deal was a bargain for the Spanish administration.

Quite apart from its cultural value to the Spanish people, the acquisition of the Thyssen collection, together with the creation of the Reina Sofía centre, gave Madrid a new dimension as a tourist destination. It can be argued convincingly now that the triangle formed by the Villahermosa Palace, the Reina Sofía centre and the Prado houses one of the greatest, and densest, accumulation of fine art anywhere in the world.* Despite the fact that the money for the Baron's treasure trove was handed over at a time of deep economic gloom, surprisingly few reservations were expressed

---

* The Thyssen collection has not, however, proved to be as much of a tourist attraction as originally forecast. Initial projections put the number of visitors per year at around a million. But halfway through the first twelve months, the director of the museum was quoted as saying that an 'optimistic assessment' would be 700,000 visitors.

about the deal. That is not to say that everyone was delighted, though. Across the road at the Prado, officials had long been fearing the purchase of Baron Thyssen's collection.

The Prado's problem is a perverse one for a museum: it has too many good things. In 1992, it owned 19,056 works. Only 1,781 of them were permanently on view. The rest form what are known as the *Prado oculto* (the hidden Prado) and the *Prado disperso* (the scattered Prado). The first is made up of works confined to the store-rooms beneath the gallery. The second comprises the paintings, sculptures and drawings the Prado loans out to government buildings. Among works the general public never, or rarely, gets to see are some by El Greco, Velázquez and Murillo. Between them the *Prado oculto* and the *Prado disperso* make up a collection that could well be as valuable as Baron Thyssen's, yet the acquisition of the latter has made their eventual display much more problematic.

By putting the Thyssen collection in the Villahermosa Palace, the authorities deprived the Prado of a building that had previously been used for temporary exhibitions of some of the treasures in its basement. Having spent such a vast sum on it, moreover, the government is unlikely in the near future to be able to find the money needed to solve the Prado's problem.

A controversial proposed extension to the building which it was hoped could be funded partly from private sources, was unveiled in 1992. However, it could only provide an additional 15 per cent of permanent display space. A definitive solution probably depends on the government making available one of the large, but currently occupied, buildings in the vicinity. These include the Army Museum, and the Agriculture and Health Ministries, all of which would need extensive work before they were ready to house paintings.

Spanish art may enjoy a worldwide reputation, but the same could not really be said of its music. An important reason for its traditional backwardness has been a straightforward lack of funds. Concerts, operas and ballets require large premises, sizeable numbers of performers and a lot of costly equipment. Yet the Spanish monarchy and aristocracy were always reluctant to patronize music, and in this respect Franco was a typically Spanish ruler. The amount of money allocated to music while he was in power was pitiful. As the conductor Jesús López Cobos once remarked, being born a conductor in Spain was a bit like being born a bullfighter in Finland. By the time Franco died, Spain had no classical ballet; there were only two state-aided orchestras, the Orquesta Nacional de España and the Orquesta Sinfónica de RTVE, while the capital had no proper opera-house or concert-hall.

The Teatro Real, opposite the Royal Palace, had begun its eventful life as an opera-house in 1850 – thirty-three years after it was ordered to be built. In the 1920s it was closed by fire. During the civil war it was blown up after someone hit on the idea of using it as a magazine. It was not reopened until 1966, and then solely for concerts and recitals.

Madrid's only other musical forum was the Teatro de la Zarzuela, which opened two years after the Teatro Real. As its name suggests, it had been intended for the staging of Spanish home-grown light opera, or *zarzuela*;* but of necessity it came to be used for what little opera and ballet was staged in Madrid, as well as for operetta.

The logical first step in any rearrangement was to erect a purpose-built concert-hall. The Teatro Real could then be closed down for the changes needed to turn it back into an opera-house. In 1984 work began at a site in the eastern part of the city, and four years later Spain's first-ever Auditorio Nacional was ready for its ceremonial inauguration. Its acoustics have since won lavish praise from visiting conductors.

The Teatro Real was meant to be ready in 1992. but repeated setbacks forced the deadline to be put back to 1995. That left the Barcelona Liceo, or Liceu as it is called in Catalan, as the only building in Spain built solely for, and devoted exclusively to, opera. In 1994, it burnt down. A fire started by a welder's torch reduced the nineteenth-century structure to a pile of smouldering rubble. At the time of writing, it is hoped to rebuild the Liceo on the site it

---

* *Zarzuela* is so called because it was originally staged, in the early seventeenth century, at the palace of that name outside Madrid. The present Palacio de la Zarzuela, where King Juan Carlos and his family now live, stands on the same site. The word *zarzuela* means 'little bramble'.

occupied on the Ramblas. For the moment, though, Spain – uniquely among the bigger European nations – is without an opera-house in the full sense of the term.

Until after Franco's death the only ballet companies in Spain were devoted exclusively to *ballet español*, a fusion of flamenco, classical and modern influences. There were schools of conventional Western dance, most notably the one run by María de Avila in Saragossa. But after graduating, promising young dancers who wanted to pursue a career on stage had to go abroad.

In 1978 the Arts Ministry set up a Ballet Nacional de España consisting of two companies – one for *ballet español* and the other for classical ballet, each directed by a leading dancer in the field. Antonio Gades was recruited to head the first and Victor Ullate, the principal male dancer in Maurice Béjart's Twentieth-Century Ballet, returned at the height of his career to direct the second. His original idea was to reunite the many talented dancers who, like himself, had been forced to work abroad. But it soon became apparent that most of them had other commitments and Ullate was left to do the best he could with the youngsters emerging from the schools, in particular the state-funded school which was set up at the same time as the Ballet Nacional and run by his wife, Carmen Rocha. Given these inauspicious beginnings, it is to his immense credit that within the space of a mere five years Ullate managed to form a national ballet company worthy of the name. In 1983 the incoming Socialist government – apparently concerned that the two supposedly na-tional companies were becoming the fiefdoms of their respective directors – sacked Ullate together with Antonio Gades's successor, Antonio Ruiz, and put María de Avila, Ullate's old tutor, in charge of both companies. It was an unseemly and unjust reward for the man who had single-handedly resurrected Spanish classical ballet. Ullate's parting words were: 'I shall go away saddened because I do not understand a great deal of what has happened. Or rather, I do understand, but it seems impossible.'

Subsequent developments have been ironic. María de Avila's directorship of the combined company was surprisingly undistin-guished. In 1986 she left following a bizarre scandal in which three of the male classical dancers were expelled for turning up at an official reception in Germany dressed in women's clothes. On her departure, the BNE was again split. The Spanish ballet kept the title of Ballet Nacional de España and acquired a new director – José Antonio Ruiz, who dances as simply 'José Antonio'.

After a year of indecision and uncertainty, the classical ballet company was put under the temporary stewardship of a Russian dancer, Maya Plisetskaya. Then, three years later, it was once more entrusted to a returning 'exile', the choreographer and former dancer in the Nederlands Dans Theater, Nacho Duato. In the meantime, though, it was a company formed by Victor Ullate, using young dancers from the original school and *corps de ballet*, which had emerged as the main hope for the future. In 1992, his heroic efforts on behalf of classical ballet in Spain were recognized when the newly-opened Teatro de Madrid was offered to his company as a permanent home.

As for *ballet español*, it seems to be entering its own phase of uncertainty and indecision. By 1992, when José Antonio stood down, the Spanish troupe had burned its way through three of the leading exponents of the art in just fourteen years of existence. With José Antonio gone, the authorities could find no better solution than to appoint, for a one-year period, a triumvirate of former dancers.

As far as orchestral music is concerned, the key break with the past was the return of López Cobos, who took over control of the Orquesta Nacional de España in 1983. Like France and Italy, Spain is not a country with a great orchestral tradition. Perhaps it has something to do with Latin society, which values spontaneity more than discipline and rewards individual rather than collective achievement. At all events, the conservatories of southern Europe are designed to turn out soloists rather than rank-and-file players. A former member of the ONE once said that the problem with tuning up in a Spanish orchestra is that 'everyone has his or her own conception of *la*'. López Cobos, who had spent much of his career conducting German and British orchestras, set his sights on inculcating what he calls 'musical discipline'. In 1988, however, he resigned the conductorship of the ONE in somewhat perplexing circumstances. A newspaper article had anonymously quoted members of the orchestra as criticizing him for, among other things, taking on too much work outside Spain. 'There does not exist the minimum of harmony necessary for the continuance of my work,' stormed López Cobos before disappearing abroad the following year. He has a reputation – not exactly unique among conductors – for being temperamental and authoritarian. Nevertheless, there appears to have been more to his departure than mere over-sensitivity to criticism. In particular, he was known to have been dismayed by the government's approach to musical education.

The early eighties saw the creation of a national youth orchestra, the Joven Orquesta Nacional de España. Since then, there have been increases in the number and the value of grants and prizes for the young. But there is still a crying need to reform the conservatories.

That said, Spanish music can ill afford the tempestuous resignations and arbitrary dismissals that have characterized recent years. Spain is still a long, long way behind much of the rest of Europe in music. Nor, in the years to come, can it be expected that people like Ullate, Gades and López Cobos will be prepared to break off promising international careers just to *hacer patria*.* If Spanish music is to catch up, then all concerned will have to go back to putting national interest above the personal and political. For the moment, though, music in Spain is at least moving forward. The same cannot be said of the cinema, which in Spain has grown accustomed to the idea that it is – and should be – a substantial business.

Franco's rule turned one of the raciest countries in the world into one of the most tedious. Films offered Spaniards some of the glamour and excitement that was missing from their lives. At one time, Spain had more cinema seats per thousand of the population than any country in the world except the United States.

That alone made Spain a gold-mine for foreign distributors. But in addition, foreign language films had to be dubbed. Dubbing was

---

*Literally, 'make fatherland': an ironic, mock-Francoist phrase used to refer to the career sacrifices – some imagined, many real – that younger Spaniards were prepared to make in the late seventies and early eighties in order to help build a new Spain.

made compulsory in 1941 so as to give the censors total control over the content of imported films.

Dubbing, especially in a society with a high rate of illiteracy, makes films vastly more accessible, and thus vastly more profitable, than subtitling. Without protection, it is almost certain that the introduction of compulsory dubbing would have put Spain's own film industry out of business. But Franco liked Spanish films – he even wrote the screenplay for one, called *Raza (Race)* – and he saw that they offered a way of propagating the regime's ideas. In 1955 the Spanish government was so firm in its insistence on protectionist measures that the American Motion Picture Export Association called a boycott which lasted three years. But in the end it was the MPEA which had to capitulate. It reluctantly accepted a stipulation that the number of foreign films distributed in Spain must not be more than four times the number of Spanish ones. It also agreed to a tax on the takings of dubbed films, the proceeds of which went into financing Spanish productions. By the end of the dictatorship, domestically directed and produced works accounted for almost 30 per cent of box-office receipts – a healthy figure by any standard.

In 1977, however, a decree which virtually abolished censorship in the cinema and replaced it with a classification system also did away with the four-to-one distribution rule and replaced it with a much stricter condition that one day had to be allotted for the showing of Spanish films for every two days of foreign films. This so-called *cuota de pantalla*, or screen quota, was intended to strengthen the industry, but it was enacted at a time when – for a variety of reasons including the chaotic state of the financial arrangements for domestic film production – Spain's film-makers were unable to rise to the challenge. The cinema owners and managers, who had to dredge up films from the Franco era to meet the demands of the decree, appealed to the courts and in 1979 the Supreme Court abolished the screen quota altogether.

The Supreme Court's decision brought the industry face to face with disaster. It was only saved by a law passed the following year which, while re-introducing the screen quota, fixed it at the more reasonable ratio of three days of foreign films to one day of Spanish. It also set up a complex system whereby the number of dubbing permits granted to a distribution company was dependent on the success of the Spanish films financed by that firm, the aim being to make it impossible for foreign distributors to get foreign movies into Spain by financing the production of low-cost, low-quality Spanish films.

When the Socialists swept to power in 1982, one of their boldest moves was the appointment of Pilar Miró to be the official in charge of the movie business. Miró, a rising young director, had spent more than a year in the period before Tejero's coup battling with the authorities to get permission for the showing of a film of hers, *El crimen de Cuenca*, which had upset the military. For better or worse – her supporters and detractors are still arguing over which – Miró was to make a huge impact on the Spanish film industry.

Within a year of taking over, she had given Spain one of the most liberal film censorship laws in Europe. As a consequence, though hard-porn films cannot be shown to under-18s, all the other ratings are simply for guidance. Miró also arbitrated the first-ever agreement between the movie business and state-run Televisión Española. Under the deal, TVE undertook to show a certain minimum percentage of Spanish films, agreed to new re-transmission fees, and underwrote a framework for joint projects.

But the law with which Pilar Miró was most closely identified – to the point that it came to be known simply as the *ley Miró* – was a decree that came into force at the start of 1984. This added to the existing protectionist measures a quite extraordinarily generous system of subsidies. Producers could get from the authorities as much as half the estimated cost of their films in advance. The hand-out was repayable, but out of a series of further subsidies partly intended to compensate for the alleged fiddling of box-office returns. Producers in Spain had long claimed that the figures cinema owners declared to the authorities were around 20 per cent below the real take. Under the terms of the *ley Miró*, all Spanish-made films qualified for a grant equivalent to 15 per cent of gross receipts. But a further 25 per cent was available if they were judged to be of 'special quality', and 25 per cent more was provided for high-cost enterprises. The government only stopped doling out the cash when the subsidies came to more than the cost of the film. But even then, the excess was set aside for the producer's next project. As an

337

official of the European Commission drily commented: 'If I were a Spaniard, I'd resign from my job and go and make films.'

One of the effects of the Miró decree was to tip the balance of advantage towards art-house movies and away from the silly, vulgar, but popular, sex comedies which had been the bread-and-butter of the industry since the early seventies. Another outcome was inflated production budgets.

The years in which the *ley Miró* was in force saw the rise to fame of Pedro Almodóvar, the most acclaimed creative talent to emerge from Spain in recent years. They saw the production of Spain's most expensive film, Carlos Saura's not particularly successful *El Dorado*. But – crucial to any argument over its pros and cons – they also saw the number of films made in Spain drop by more than half.

By 1988, when Jorge Semprún★ took over as Arts Minister, Spain's cinema industry had never been held in such high esteem. Almodóvar's *Mujeres al borde de un ataque de nervios* (*Women on the Verge of a Nervous Breakdown*) was playing to packed houses around the world. Yet the number of films made in Spain that year was just fifty-four (compared with 118 six years earlier when the Socialists took office). In the background, EU officials were warning Madrid that the *ley Miró* appeared to contravene Community law.

In 1989, it was replaced by a *ley Semprún*. The level of financial support for the industry was maintained, but less of it was channelled towards producers. The 15 per cent subsidy based on box-office takings was kept, but a limit was set on the advance.

The change of tack was accompanied by an unholy row. Several producers predicted it would kill the industry altogether. Miró's successor,† Fernando Méndez Leite, stormed out in protest at the new proposals. Semprún accused him of having given precedence to

---

★ Semprún, who held the job until 1991, was among the most remarkable characters ever to sit at a Spanish cabinet table. An ex-member of the wartime French resistance, he survived Buchenwald to become the leader of the Communist underground resistance in Madrid under Franco. Expelled from the PCE for advocating many of the ideas which subsequently formed the basis of 'Eurocommunism', Semprún turned to full-time writing. He is the author of novels written in both French and Spanish, and co-scripted the Oscar-winning movie 'Z'.

† Miró had left in 1986 to become Director-General of RTVE.

friends in the handing-out of subsidies, and Méndez Leite responded with a suggestion that the minister see a psychiatrist.

Subsequent developments gave the prophets of doom the balance of the argument. In 1990, only forty-two films were made in Spain, including co-productions – the lowest figure since 1952. In the same year, TVE refused to go on subsidizing Spanish films, and the industry was left to face the approaching recession in pretty bad shape.

Since then, the authorities have renewed their efforts to strengthen the industry, but they have done so by reinforcing its protectionist armour. In 1992, the *cuota de pantalla* was re-cast in such a way as to conform with EU legislation. For every three days of non-EU (i.e. mainly American) movies, cinema managers had to project one day of EU material. A year later, in an attempt to beat GATT restrictions that were never finally agreed, another decree was introduced which, while tailoring the screen quota in accordance with the size of the town in which the movie house was located, introduced stiff penalties for cinema owners who breached it and tightened the conditions for granting dubbing licences. The result was a one-day strike by the exhibitors, who accused the government of trying to force the public to watch films it did not want to see. The previous year, EU films had accounted for 22 per cent of the box-office 'take' and Spanish films for just 9 per cent.

It was not the first time that the Socialists had been accused of cultural elitism. Their readiness to invest lavishly in collections of fine art, and in the building of concert-halls and opera-houses, has laid them open to similar criticism.

With regard to classical music, there is certainly more than a grain of truth in this. The huge amounts of money spent on it could be more easily justified if a determined effort were made to extend the appeal of serious music. Yet a decade after the Socialists came to power it remained almost impossible for members of the public to get tickets for a concert in Madrid unless they had the considerable means – or influence – necessary to acquire a season ticket. The lobby of the Auditorio Nacional immediately before a concert is a sea of fur coats, diamond collars and expensively-cut suits.

But that is not the whole story. The Socialists can claim with justification to have tackled, where their predecessors ignored, what was perhaps the single biggest gap in Spain's 'cultural infrastructure'. In 1982, Spain had 1,436 general public libraries with just 8 books for every 100 inhabitants – a lower figure than that for Morocco. Some 90 per cent of the population had never set foot inside a library. By 1990, the number of general public libraries had risen to 2,940 and there were more than 50 books per 100 inhabitants. This was still the lowest figure among EU member states, and well below the UNESCO-recommended level of 2–3 books per person, but a considerable improvement nevertheless.

Impressive progress has also been made in bringing the arts closer to the people in some of the Socialist-run regions. An outstanding example is the Community of Madrid, whose administration funds a system of itinerant exhibitions as well as a network of theatres in the suburbs and villages surrounding the capital. Móstoles is a typical working-class dormitory town on the southern outskirts of Madrid; on the day that this is being written, its inhabitants could visit an exhibition of engravings or, if they preferred, watch the Cuban National Ballet.

CHAPTER 24

A Journey without Maps

The scars left by the civil war healed at different rates according to where they were inflicted. The economy regained its pre-war level in 1954. Politics returned to its normal course in 1977. But the arts have never recovered, and looking around the somewhat frivolous, materialistic Spain of today one may be forgiven for wondering if they ever can.

In 1936 Spain was what you might call a creative superpower. She had given the world three of its greatest contemporary painters – Picasso, Dalí and Miró. She could lay claim to one of the finest established composers – Manuel de Falla – and to several of the more promising younger ones like the Catalan, Roberto Gerhardt, and the Valencian, Joaquín Rodrigo. Her fledgling film industry had already managed to produce a director of the calibre of Buñuel. In literature, the leading figures of the celebrated 'Generation of '98' – the philosophers Unamuno and Ortega y Gasset, the novelist Pío Baroja, the playwrights Benavente and Valle-Inclán, and the poets Machado and Jiménez – were all still alive, able to advise and influence younger writers. But more importantly, a further generation, the 'Generation of '27', was just reaching maturity. Outside Spain, the best-known of the writers who belonged to it is Federico García Lorca. But there were many others considered by Spaniards to be of equal stature – poets like Rafael Alberti, Vicente Aleixandre and Luis Cernuda, whose achievements were finally recognized by the award of the 1977 Nobel Prize for Literature to Aleixandre.

The vast majority of Spain's artists and intellectuals took the side of the Republic against the Nationalists. Some, like Lorca, were killed. Of those who survived, most fled into exile. Once the fiercest period of retribution was over, they faced a grim choice.

Returning home offered an opportunity to re-establish contact with the cultural traditions of their homeland, but it also meant handing the regime a propaganda victory and resigning themselves to a lifetime of censorship. Staying abroad meant losing touch with their roots but it did guarantee them their creative integrity. Miró returned, but the majority opted to remain in exile. Seen as a set of individual personal decisions it was understandable. Seen as a development in the nation's cultural history it was catastrophic. Most of what the exiles wrote, painted, sculpted and filmed went completely unnoticed within Spain until the sixties, when Fraga at the Ministry of Information and Tourism eased the restrictions on imported works. But by then, much of it was ten, fifteen, even twenty years old and of little or no use as a stimulus or inspiration.

The intellectuals' opposition to Franco meant that throughout his dictatorship he and his supporters harboured a deep suspicion of all things intellectual. Culture *per se* became dangerous. 'At home, we didn't even listen to the radio,' the Catalan folk-rock singer Pau Riba later recalled. 'Books were simply bound objects that you didn't touch.' What makes his reminiscence all the more remarkable is that Pau Riba did not come from a family of shopkeepers or factory-workers, but from a line of eminent literary figures – his grandfather, for example, was the poet and philologist, Carles Riba.

The artists and intellectuals born in the twenties, thirties and forties had to make their way as best they could without guides or maps. In retrospect what is surprising about Franco's Spain is not that there was so little good music, art and literature, but that there was so much. Probably the best-known creative work of the Franco era was Rodrigo's popular classic, the *Concierto de Aranjuez*. But the same period also saw the emergence of a number of outstanding painters like Tàpies, Saura, Gordillo and Millares and at least one internationally renowned sculptor in Eduardo Chillida. Alternately duping and defying the censors, playwrights like Antonio Buero Vallejo and film-makers like Luis García Berlanga, Juan Bardem and Carlos Saura managed to create works of depth and integrity. The printed word became a medium of protest – a way of recording the shallowness and hypocrisy of Franco's Spain. The pioneers were the poet Damaso Alonso and the novelists Camilo José Cela and

Miguel Delibes, who began to make an impact in the late forties. Then came an entire generation of writers committed to 'social realism', of which perhaps the most talented representative was Juan Goytisolo.

But by no stretch of the imagination could Franco's Spain have been described as a major force in world culture. Indeed, it was probably incapable of becoming one while only a very small proportion of the state's resources was devoted to cultural activities. The lack of encouragement and opportunity prompted many creative young Spaniards to seek their fortune elsewhere. López Cobos, who became general director of the Berlin Opera, and Josep María Flotats, star of the Comédie-Française, are just two examples of the cultural 'brain drain' of the Franco era.

The period immediately following Franco's death was one of tremendous disorientation and introspection. The regime which had provided so many creative Spaniards with a target on which to unleash their energies had been whisked away overnight. While the regime's supporters were complaining that 'Con Franco vivíamos mejor' ('We lived better with Franco'), the novelist Manuel Vázquez Montalbán spoke for many of his fellow intellectuals when he remarked that 'Contra Franco vivíamos mejor' ('We lived better against Franco'). At the same time, there were new freedoms to exploit and influences to absorb. Sex was no longer taboo and the temptation to describe or depict it proved irresistible to all but the most ascetic. Then there were the exiles who returned to Spain in considerable numbers and whose work, it was felt, had to be published or exhibited and then assessed before any further steps were taken. As for the public, a lot of Spaniards found that they were too worried about the fate of democracy to be over-concerned with the fate of the arts.

This rather abnormal period ended in the early eighties. To some extent, it was simply that people had grown tired of sexploitation and had begun to decide what of the exiles' experience and output was worth re-incorporating. But it also had something to do with Tejero's abortive coup which, while it may have fulfilled people's worst fears, also dispelled them – like the cloudburst which comes at the end of a thundery day.

The most obvious sign of a new mood was to be found in the

phenomenon known as the *movida madrileña*. *Movida* is not an easy word to translate. Perhaps the nearest approximation in English is 'scene'. The *movida madrileña*, 'the Madrid scene', came into being at a time when Spain's newly-liberated young were getting into the habit of *salir de copas* – going out to drink until the early hours, usually from Friday into Saturday or Saturday into Sunday. By the late seventies, even the smallest provincial capital had its *movida*, its network of bars and discos that stayed open till dawn at the weekends. But Madrid's was not only the most extensive but also the most exciting, and gradually the term *movida madrileña* came to be used as a description of the people who inhabited it. There are parallels between the *movida madrileña* of the 1980s and 'swinging London' in the 1960s. Both were phenomena that arose among the young. Both reflected or channelled a certain amount of artistic creativity. But to a greater extent than with 'swinging London', the *movida madrileña*'s centre of gravity was to be found in the nightspots of the city from which it took its name, particularly the now-defunct Rock-Ola Club. Those who were at the centre of the *movida madrileña* trace its origins back to 1977, the year in which Spain became a democracy again. It was not until about 1982, however, that non-initiates became aware of its existence or that the people identified with it began to exercise an influence on the rest of society.

Foremost among them was the son of a petrol-station attendant born in 1949 in the parched and backward Don Quixote country of La Mancha. Recalling his childhood, Pedro Almodóvar once remarked, 'I felt as if I'd fallen from another planet.' In 1969, he moved to the capital and set about making Super-8 underground movies while earning a living at the national telephone monopoly, Telefónica. His first full-length film, *Pepi, Luci, Bom y otras chicas del montón*, was released in 1980. The movies which followed, filled with candy-bright colours and packed with improbable events and personalities, are quintessentially a product of the frenetic mood that took hold of Spain in the eighties. What made them so popular outside the country was perhaps that they were so utterly at variance with the earnest, blood-stained tragedies people had come to expect of Spanish directors. Almodóvar's films served to turn two of his actors, Carmen Maura and Antonio Banderas, into international stars. *Mujeres al borde de un ataque de nervios*, in which both appeared, was the highest-grossing foreign film in the United States in 1989.

Apart from the work of Pedro Almodóvar, though, the creative fruits of the *movida madrileña* have been modest. Among those once associated with it are one of Spain's leading fashion designers, Agatha Ruiz de la Prada, and a handful of rock and pop musicians. Overall, it is difficult to argue with the verdict of José Luis Gallero, the author of a book on the *movida* called *Sólo se vive una vez* (*You only live once*). 'What has endured,' he wrote, 'is the *salir de copas* habit' – and that had caught on even before Franco's death.*

What Spain offers today is a perfectly creditable artistic output. But few would claim it measures up to the admittedly extraordinary standards set in the 1930s. And whether it is any better or worse than what came out of Franco's Spain is debatable. It would be mis-guided in these post-modernist times to expect there to be a Spanish school of anything, though what is discernible is a recurrent tendency to go 'over the top'. A number of Spain's contemporary creative talents, Almodóvar among them, have been captivated by melodrama and kitsch; entranced by the outlandish and the outrageous. It is a fascination which has deep roots in Spain's cultural history: Spanish baroque, Gaudí's modernism, Dalí's surrealism, and the *tremendismo* to be found in the work of novelists like Cela have all involved taking a good idea one step – or many more – beyond what good taste might deem to be prudent. Done consciously and skilfully by an Almodóvar, it can produce wonderful results. Done unconsciously or unskilfully, it can lead to resounding and embarrassing failure.

In conventional terms, Spain's most internationally fêted film director is not in fact Pedro Almodóvar, but José Luis Garci, who in 1983 became the only Spanish movie-maker ever to win an Oscar –

---

* Recent efforts by the authorities to limit the *movida* in various provincial cities have met with spirited resistance. In 1991, several hundred people chanting 'Let's have some fun,' and 'If you're not prepared to go home at three, defend your liberty,' rampaged through the streets of Cáceres in protest at a by-law imposing a closing time of 3 a.m. Dustbins were overturned, shop-fronts smashed and telephone booths wrecked by youths armed with rocks and staves and wearing balaclava helmets. The riot ended only after police fired rubber bullets at the protesters as they tried to storm the provincial Civil Governor's offices.

for best foreign film. The story of Garci and his Oscar is a peculiar one.

He was – and is – regarded in Spain as a competent but not outstanding director and his film, *Volver a empezar*, had been a box-office flop in his native country. Spaniards found the subject-matter – a romance between a returning exile and his childhood sweetheart – too sentimental for their taste. No doubt its popularity with the Hollywood jury owed something to its strongly American flavour – the principal character had spent much of his life in the United States and the theme tune was Cole Porter's 'Begin the Beguine'. Even so, it is hard to explain how a director judged that year to have made the best film in the world outside the US should be regarded with such indifference in his own country not only before, but after, the award of the movie industry's supreme accolade. Garci has made various films since. None has won him much favour in Spain with either the critics or the public.

Of the directors who had established a reputation by the time the dictatorship ended, three have enjoyed recurrent success since. Berlanga and Saura have both, coincidentally, distinguished themselves with trilogies: Berlanga's a political satire woven around the declining fortunes of a family of eccentric aristocrats; Saura's a projection of southern and gypsy folklore through the medium of choreographed flamenco. Victor Erice, meanwhile, continues to beguile art-house buffs the world over with occasional exquisitely structured offerings.

Within Spain, the most respected directors of the generation to emerge soon after Franco's death include Manuel Gutiérrez Aragón, Fernando Trueba, and Mario Camus, whose 1984 film, *Los santos inocentes*, held the distinction for several years of being Spain's biggest box-office success. Of the latest crop of film-makers, the one who has made the biggest impact is Juan José Bigas Luna, whose outrageous *Jamon, Jamon* enjoyed considerable international success in 1992.

Antonio Buero Vallejo remains Spain's most acclaimed mainstream playwright, though he has been joined in the front rank by two authors who also had solid reputations before Franco's death: Antonio Gala and Francisco Nieva. The eighties have revealed a good deal of additional talent. One of several accomplished younger playwrights is José Sanchís Sinisterra, whose *Ay, Carmela* was made into a highly successful movie by Carlos Saura. In so far as avant-garde theatre is concerned, the name that stands out is that of the Catalan company, Fura dels Baus. A wider public was given a glimpse of their visually arresting, often disturbing work during the opening ceremony of the Barcelona Olympics.

Experimentation has not been much to the fore in Spanish literature of late. The single, and remarkable, exception is the work of Julian Ríos. In the early seventies Ríos – with the encouragement of the Mexican writer Octavio Paz – began a work which, in the words of one critic, aims 'to integrate the whole of universal literature, destroy and construct the literary language of its time and take up the most audacious and scandalous position in the vanguard in order to move ahead of it . . .'. Quite some task for an author who had published hardly anything before he embarked on it. Ríos intends that the as yet unnamed series will consist of five volumes plus an appendix. The first of them, *Larva*, which took him ten years to write, was published in 1984. It was an account of an orgy written primarily in Castilian that hopped at intervals into a variety of other languages, including Bengali. The notes which appear on the left-hand pages are a commentary on the text, which appears opposite. As with Sterne, the writing is interspersed with diagrams. While his fellow-writers are impressed by Ríos's dedication and ambition, many of them have deep misgivings about what he has so far produced. As one of them put it: 'What is the point of doing what Joyce did, only sixty years later and in Castilian?'

Nevertheless, it can be argued as evidence of a need for innovation in 1989 that, when the Nobel Prize for Literature was once more awarded to a Spaniard, the recipient was an author whose best work was already forty years behind him. The difference between the circumstances surrounding Camilo José Cela's Nobel Prize and that of the retiring, invalid Aleixandre's could scarcely have been greater. Cela, who has a genius for self-publicity, had long since turned himself into a leading social and media personality. For most Spaniards, he was the crotchety old gent with the young *compañera* who did the adverts on telly for the CAMPSA petrol chain's guide to hotels and restaurants. When it was announced that he had been awarded the Nobel Prize, the country reacted as if the Spanish soccer team had just won the World Cup. The day before the award ceremony, newspapers devoted two-page spreads to diagrams illustrating the seating arrangements. Albeit in a different way, the response to Camilo José Cela's Nobel Prize illustrated as well as any Almodóvar movie the spirit which inspires post-Franco Spain, for rarely if at all was reference made in Spain to a fact worried at endlessly in foreign reports and commentaries – that immediately after the civil war Cela had been a censor of his fellow-writers' work.

Significantly perhaps, a reluctance to recall – let alone judge – the past is the chief distinguishing characteristic of what has come to be known as the *nueva narrativa española*. The term, which was first coined for a series launched by Ediciones Libertarias in 1985, has since come to be applied to the output of around 150 Spanish novelists, most of them in their thirties or forties. Among the most successful are Almudena Grandes, Javier Marías, Juan José Millas, and Antonio Muñoz Molina.

Their subject-matter is, for the most part, rigorously contemporary. But not always. Some have dabbled in historical fiction and fantasy. Indeed, doubts have been expressed as to whether the *nueva narrativa española* is in fact a literary movement or just a promotional slogan, for the phrase was coined at a time when the whole relationship between writers, publishers and the reading public in Spain was being revolutionized.

Publishing in Spain had long been an important industry, but that was mainly because so many people around the world spoke Spanish. Spaniards themselves read very little. What is more, a lot of what was read in Spain was from abroad; this was particularly true of the sixties and seventies, the heyday of Latin American prose. Typically, Spain's novelists were intellectuals writing for a tiny audience – a few thousand at most.

The earliest attempts to provide more popular writing came in the form of crime novels. The first *novela policiaca* to be written by a Spaniard was Mario Lacruz's *El inocente*, published back in the fifties. But the genre did not acquire any real impetus until it was embraced by Manuel Vázquez Montalbán who created the now internationally popular private detective, Pepe Carvalho. Two other highly praised Spanish thriller-writers who have emerged in recent years are Eduardo Mendoza and Juan Madrid.

What happened in the mid-eighties, though, was a sea change in the status of the general novel. As with so many developments in contemporary Spain, it seemed to happen overnight. In 1986, to be precise, it became apparent that Spanish novelists were consistently making it into their own country's best-seller list. With hindsight, it can be seen that they did so on the strength of subject-matter that had direct relevance to the lives of a new readership – middle-class Spaniards, products of the 1970 Education Act, who did not think it odd to read a book on the beach or the terrace.

For the first time in Spain, authors started to be treated as celebrities. The profits to be gained from novel-writing soared. Established authors like the late Juan Benet, accustomed to minute sales, suddenly found themselves allotted print runs of 25,000 or more. Every month seemed to bring a new and more lucrative literary award. The playwright Antonio Gala decided to try his hand at novel-writing. His first, *El manuscrito carmesí*, won the 1990 Planeta prize and earned him an initial print run of 200,000.

At the same time, publishers were discovering a sizeable market for humorous writing. The pioneering enterprise was a collection launched by Ediciones Temas de Hoy under the 'El Papagayo' label.★

The other important development in recent years has been the growth in the reputation of vernacular literature. In 1990, the cause of Basque-language culture was given a major boost when Spain's highest official award for the novel, the Premio Nacional de Narrativa, was given to a work originally published in Basque, Bernardo Atxaga's *Obabakoak*.

Poetry in Spain, as in many countries these days, is a minority enthusiasm. There again, recent years have not produced a movement able to engage the interest of a wider audience. The most important poets to emerge in the latter part of Franco's rule were

★ One of the El Papagayo titles was *Cómo ser una mujer y no morir en el intento* by Carmen Rico Godoy, referred to in Chapter 12.

the so-called *novísimos*, whose work was characterized by an adventurous admixture of antiquated and vernacular language, an interest in symbolism and a fascination with the media culture.

Unrepentant social realists regarded them as decadent, reactionary *señoritos*,* but the *novísimos* saw themselves as successors to the Generation of '27 and seem to have been regarded as such by the older poets – or at least by Aleixandre, who wrote a prologue to one of their earliest anthologies. The *novísimos* were – and are – poets of considerable stature. Pere Gimferrer's *Arde el mar*, published in 1966, Guillermo Carnero's *El Sueño de Escipión* (1973), Antonio Collinas's *Sepulcro en Tarquinia* (1976) and Luis Antonio de Villena's *Hymnica* (1979) are regarded throughout the Hispanic world as major works. So far, no one group nor single voice has emerged to replace them, even though there has been talk of *postnovísimos* (the title of a collection published in 1986). Valuable work may be being published but, for the moment at least, poetry in Spain seems to lack a clear direction.

Among the painters and sculptors who have risen to prominence in the last decade or so, two names stand out – at least on the basis of the international recognition accorded to them. One is Miquel Barceló. Born on Mallorca, he has led a singularly peripatetic professional existence, producing his highly textured, often glittering canvases from studios in Lisbon, Naples, Tunis and Marrakesh, as well as from permanent bases in Paris and on his native island. The Barcelona-born sculptress Susana Solano is the other major figure to emerge in the last few years. Her stern, bleak, iron and steel constructions began to win her a solid worldwide reputation in the late eighties, a time of considerable accomplishment in Spanish sculpture generally.

If the late eighties were a turning-point for Spain's sculptors, then the early nineties offered a golden opportunity to its architects. With the world's attention fixed on the venues for Expo and the Olympics, they had a unique chance to shine. Probably the Spanish

---

* Although strictly speaking no more nor less than the masculine equivalent of *señorita, señorito* has acquired a distinctively pejorative connotation. It is used to denote a rich, idle young man – a playboy or a dilettante.

architect best known outside his country is still Ricardo Bofill, one of whose neo-classical buildings formed part of the main complex of Olympic venues. Currently, though, the most fashionable name is that of another Catalan, Oriol Bohigas, who was the guiding spirit behind Barcelona's urban renewal programme and the chief architect of the Olympic village. Though he first studied architecture, the Valencian-born but Zurich-based Santiago Calatrava has since made his name as an engineer. One of his elegant bridges was the gateway to Expo. His graceful communications tower, set – controversially – beside the Olympic stadium, was perhaps the structure most readily identified with the 1992 Games.

The Barcelona Olympics, or rather the opening and closing ceremonies, also gave the Spanish a chance to point out to the rest of the world that their country is the source of a quite remarkable array of operatic talent. Plácido Domingo, Monserrat Caballé, José Carreras, Teresa Berganza and Alfredo Kraus all come from Spain. Yet, because of developments described in the last chapter, Spanish opera in the sense of the number and quality of the performances staged in Spain is still relatively unimportant. So Spanish singers, to an even greater extent than is normal in this quintessentially cosmopolitan art form, have no choice but to spend the bulk of their working lives outside their country of origin.

A similar disparity between talent and opportunity is apparent in the field of dance. Trinidad Sevillano was lured to Britain in the mid-eighties to become the prima ballerina of the London Festival Ballet. By the end of the decade, there were Spanish soloists in the companies of several other European capitals – Ana Laguna at the Cullberg Ballet in Stockholm, Arantxa Argüelles in Berlin and José Carlos Martínez in Paris.

A number of Spain's most distinguished conductors, including Jesús López Cobos and Rafael Frühbeck de Burgos, are based outside their native country. The same is true of Spain's finest instrumental musician, the harpist Marisa Robles, who lives in London.

For centuries now, music has been the Cinderella of the Spanish arts. In the sixteenth century the quality of the music composed in Spain was comparable with that of almost any other European nation. But the Counter-Reformation isolated Spain from the

Protestant north of Europe just as Germany was taking over from Italy as the leading musical influence within Europe. The works of Bach, Handel, Haydn and Mozart reached Spain as but faint echoes. In the last century Spain was again open to foreign influence and through the achievements of, first, Albéniz, then Granados and, finally, Falla it was beginning to recover its reputation when the civil war broke out and it was once again shut off from the rest of the continent.

It is all the more extraordinary therefore that a number of fine composers like Luis de Pablo, Cristóbal Halffter, Carmelo Bernaola and Juan Hidalgo should have risen to prominence during the Franco era. They now offer a core of solid achievement to inspire and encourage younger composers.

Popular music in Spain offers some pretty dramatic contrasts. Essentially, the softer and more melodic the sound, the more Spaniards seem to excel. Julio Iglesias's 'Begin the Beguine', released in 1981, was the first single recorded (though not titled) in a language other than English to sell more than a million copies worldwide and Iglesias himself is now unquestionably an international rather than just a Spanish, or Hispanic, star. Yet his success was no fluke, he was simply the best of the numerous talented ballad-singers of his generation emerging in Spain.

It is in the field of pop and rock that Spain lags. During nearly two decades of association with the country, I doubt if I have heard more than a half-a-dozen numbers I would want to listen to again, and hundreds – no, thousands – I would pay good money not to. The lyrics are often good, but the music is invariably unoriginal.

Hardly any Spanish groups have made an impact abroad. One which succeeded was Los Bravos back in the sixties (with a song called 'Black is Black'). More recently, Mecano, a slick trio from Madrid, has had some success in France, and Duncan Dhu from the Basque country has made modest headway in Britain. But there again, Mecano and Duncan Dhu are at the softest end of pop. No one illustrates the peculiarities of Spanish popular music better than Luz Casal, who featured on the sound track of the Almodóvar film *Tacones Lejanos* (*High Heels*). She has a bewitching, hauntingly stark, voice. Her ballads, if they were sung in English, could I am sure be worldwide hits. Her rock-cum-pop is simply dreadful.

In this latter respect, Spain is no different from most other countries in continental Europe, although it is interesting that the northern nations – and especially Germany – are more capable of producing authentic rock than the southern ones. Once again, it probably has a lot to do with the nature of Latin society. Rock is the product of a youth culture which is in turn the result of a rejection of established social values. In societies where family ties are still strong, it is impossible to create such a youth culture. The problem with Spanish rock musicians – even the most talented of them – is that they look and sound like (and indeed are) nice kids with well-scrubbed faces who would not recognize a generation gap if they fell into one. But then rock is also a product of urban rather than rural society and of the working class rather than the middle class. City life in Spain nowadays requires at least some of the toughness and slickness that is needed to get by in, say, Detroit or Liverpool and the economic progress of the sixties and eighties has given the Spanish working class a prosperity and influence that they never had before. All this has to some extent served to narrow the gap between Spain and the Anglo-Saxon countries.

There may nevertheless prove to be an unbridgeable distance created by differences in language. Spanish is an intensely melodious tongue to which the abrupt rhythms of rock and pop can be adapted only with difficulty. It is noticeable that some of the best music to have been produced in the nineties has been written for a new generation of singers performing and recording in Catalan, a language characterized by a profusion of short, sharp sounds.

However, there is an important exception to the general rule that the rock music produced in Spain is merely an inferior imitation of the songs turned out in Britain and the United States a few years earlier, and that is the fusion of rock with flamenco. Back in the seventies, several young Andalusian musicians were fired by the idea of blending rock and flamenco. Two groups – Triana and Veneno – were formed and although both have since disappeared, the idea they implanted has grown. Today the principal exponents of the genre in Spain are Ketama and Pata Negra. But the most successful flamenco-pop group is not Spanish at all. The Gypsy Kings come from France. Their repertoire consists of variations on rumba, just one of the many styles that make up the flamenco canon.

True flamenco offers Spaniards much the same as it offers tourists

353

– a dash of the unusual in an increasingly drab world. The songs are exotic, the dances are dramatic and flamenco history is dotted with performers sporting gloriously improbable names like 'The Child of the Combs', 'Frasco, the Coloured One' and 'Mad Matthew'. But the flamenco tradition also offers one of those links with the world of a younger mankind in which Spain is so rich, for it is capable of generating that feeling of ecstasy whose inculcation is thought to have been the object of all early music. A flamenco singer ought not to perform until he or she has drifted into something approaching a trance – a state of suppressed emotion in which the need for expression gradually becomes so strong that it can no longer be contained. This ecstatic element in flamenco is splendidly captured in José María Caballero Bonald's description of a gathering at a wayside inn in the midst of the undulating Andalusian countryside:

> The night draws on. Already daylight has begun to show over the trees. At the inn, there is a group of seven or eight people. They are drinking wine parsimoniously, calmly. The guitarist is tuning his instrument. All of a sudden, the notes coincide with the beginning of a song and someone utters the preliminary wails. The singer clears his throat and searches for the beat. Everyone maintains a respectful, religious silence. At length, the lyrics emerge. Hands begin to clap miraculously in time with the guitar. The singer, gazing into infinity, moves his face and contorts his body in response to the difficulties of the song and raises his hand in a gesture of majesty.

Though its origins are obscure, it is thought that flamenco began in the late eighteenth century among the gypsies of the provinces of Seville and Cádiz. What is indisputable is that gypsy music has remained at the core of the flamenco tradition even though a number of southern Spanish songs such as the fandango, which is of Moorish origin, have been absorbed into the repertory. In the same way, many non-gypsies have become masters of the art as *cantaores* (singers), *bailaores* (dancers) and *tocaores* ('players' – i.e. guitarists). The vast majority of flamenco songs are true folk songs – devised by some now forgotten villager and modified by endless repetition until they gell into the form which is considered most attractive. All attempts to transcribe the music have proved abortive, so the flamenco tradition is reliant entirely on word of mouth, instruction and example. But it also means that there is great scope for individual interpretation.

The songs, or *coplas*, vary between three and six lines in length, but because each word is drawn out by wails and ululations they take several minutes to sing. The language is always very simple and direct. There are about forty different types of song. Some are intended for specific occasions, such as weddings. Of the remainder, the exuberant ones which can be danced to and which the tourist is most likely to come across comprise only a relatively small proportion. Most are agonized laments for the death of a loved one, particularly a mother (a figure who is even more important among the gypsies than among their Latin neighbours), or for the loss of freedom (for the Spanish gypsies have spent more than their fair share of time in the country's gaols), for the transience of life's pleasures and the persistence of its miseries. As the flamenco critic and researcher Ricardo Molina wrote, flamenco is 'the response of a people repressed for centuries', and this may explain why it became so popular among the non-gypsy peasants of Andalusia in the nineteenth century as they too fell victim to another kind of oppression when their commons were enclosed and they were left as landless labourers.

The spread of flamenco in this century has been uneven. Twice it has seemed to be on the point of going into a permanent decline and twice its fortunes have been revived by organized competitions – those of Granada in 1922 and of Córdoba in 1955. These inspired a succession of smaller contests that rekindled interest and unearthed talent. The second revival was less dramatic than the first but proved to be more enduring. It was largely due to the work of just one man, the *cantaor* Antonio Mairena, who died in 1983. Flamenco loses its impetus when it loses its integrity. Mairena insisted on singing an unadorned, undiluted repertoire. He was also tireless in promoting festivals of authentic flamenco. The spread of the purified idiom that Mairena and his disciples rediscovered, or rather reinforced, was helped by social, economic and even political factors. The recovery of 'genuine' flamenco came at just the moment when hundreds of thousands of Andalusians were preparing to pack their bags and start a new life in Madrid or the industrial cities of the north. Their migration to other parts of Spain gave flamenco a following in every region of the country except perhaps the north-west and the Balearic and Canary Islands.

In the late seventies and early eighties, flamenco derived a further benefit from the growth of a sense of Andalusian identity – a process which fed off the granting of a generous measure of autonomy to the area. Andalusia's regional government, the Junta, was soon putting money into a month-long flamenco competition, the Bienal, held every two years in Seville. Smaller festivals, dedicated to the preservation – or recovery – of the style characteristic of each locality, sprang up in scores of towns and villages across Andalusia.

The period immediately following Spain's transition to democracy was also the heyday of two outstanding exponents of the flamenco art – the guitarist Paco de Lucía and the singer Camarón de la Isla.

As has been noted, flamenco is an art form that was inspired by, and dwells on, hardship and oppression. Though it has rarely, if ever, been used to express political attitudes, it is not surprising that it should have thrived in the earnest atmosphere which prevailed in Spain during the early years of its democracy. By the same token, its bleak sincerity was quite unsuited to the materialistic and hedonistic mood which characterized Spain after the end of its post-Franco recession in the mid-eighties. Ever since then, in fact, flamenco – 'pure' flamenco as distinct from the bastardized wailings and gyratings to be seen on the television variety shows – has been in retreat.

Surprisingly, in view of the number of Andalusians occupying serious positions in the administration, the central government has failed to offer any support; quite the reverse, in fact. In 1988, the Arts Ministry withdrew a subsidy which had allowed an annual festival, known as the *Cumbre* (Summit), to be staged. I may be wrong, but I sometimes think I can detect in official publications just a trace of embarrassment that something as unrefined as flamenco should have survived into the 'European' Spain of six-lane highways and satellite television receivers. It is an attitude one might expect would also apply, and to an even greater extent, to that other indigenous Spanish art form, the bullfight.

CHAPTER 25

The Taming of 'the Bulls'

The village of Valdemorillo lies just beyond the commuter belt rapidly enveloping Madrid. It has a medieval church with a tower topped by a straggly stork's nest, and a post-modernist shopping centre made of, or at least faced with, the same local granite that went into Philip II's grim monastery-palace of El Escorial a few miles away. Valdemorillo's main claim to fame is that each year it hosts Spain's first bullfight festival – in February, when a wickedly chill breeze is still rippling off the nearby Guadarrama mountains. Few but true *aficionados* would consider sitting for two hours in the uncomfortable makeshift ring in which the *corridas* are held. But on the day I visited it during the 1993 *fiesta* it was very nearly full, and the friend I went along with assured me it had been even more packed a few days earlier.

It is enough to make the bullfight's many critics, inside and outside Spain, despair: in defiance of every expectation and prediction, bullfighting in the enlightened Spain of today is more popular and fashionable than it has been since the sixties.

It needs to be stressed that the *fiesta nacional*, as the taurine lobby likes to call it, has – and always has had – a limited following. In recent years, around 2 million tickets are reckoned to have been sold annually for the thousand or so first- and second-class bullfights held in a season. That compares with over 10 million tickets to first- and second-division football matches.

Surprisingly few opinion polls have been carried out on the subject of 'the bulls'. I know of only five with any claim to reliability conducted within the last twenty years. What all of them point to, though, is that about half the population shows no interest or enthusiasm. Indeed, there is firm evidence to suggest that the

Spanish as a whole are more 'anti' than 'pro'. The only poll to ask people whether they actually liked bullfighting was published by the magazine *Tiempo* in 1985. The 'No' response exceeded the 'Yes' by 51 per cent to 35 per cent, with the remainder indifferent. However, since then the balance may have shifted in favour of bullfighting. In 1987, critics and others closely associated with the bullring claimed to notice a sudden upsurge in popular interest and support. A survey commissioned by *El País* and published in July that year bore them out. Asked about their degree of enthusiasm for bullfighting, fully 46 per cent of those interviewed replied 'none'. But the big surprise was among those who admitted to some degree of engagement. All the earlier polls, including one carried out the previous year, had indicated that true *aficionados* were greatly outnumbered by those who took only a passing interest. On this occasion, though, 38 per cent claimed to be 'very' enthusiastic.

Further evidence of a revival is provided by a look back at the annual number of *corridas*. A sharp rise began in the late fifties and continued throughout the following decade. Higher disposable incomes and increased leisure both seem to have contributed to the boom, as did the emergence of an outstandingly controversial *torero** in the person of Manuel Benítez, *El Cordobés*. But these were also the years in which large numbers of fights were being staged primarily for the tourists who were flooding into Spain, and that meant the upward curve was much steeper than it would otherwise have been. The number of *corridas* peaked in 1971 at 682 and then began to fall rapidly to below 400 ten years later. Ever since then, with the exception of a dip in 1985–6, the annual total has been gradually increasing. In 1992 it was 646. That was still some way short of the record set twenty years earlier, but it nevertheless meant that twice as many *corridas* were being fought as in the days when Hemingway first wrote about them.

---

* A *torero* is a bullfighter. A *torero* may be a *picador*, responsible for lancing the bull from on horseback during the first stage of the fight, a *banderillero*, responsible for placing the darts in the second stage of the fight, or a *matador* (literally 'killer'), the senior member of the team who puts the bull to death in the third and final stage. He may even be a *rejoneador*, a mounted *matador*. But he is never, in Spanish at least, a 'toreador'.

This in itself could be explained, in the same way as the sixties boom, by increased prosperity. From the mid-eighties onwards, Spaniards found themselves with more money to spend on entertainment of all kinds, 'the bulls' included. What is more difficult to account for is the change in attitude towards bullfighting which became apparent at roughly the same time. All of a sudden, Madrid's month-long San Isidro festival became a social occasion of the first magnitude. Show-business personalities were spotted among the crowd, along with avant-garde designers and the owners of fashionable discos. PR companies began buying season tickets so as to be able to offer clients a ringside seat. At the same time, *matadores* began to be viewed for the first time as socially acceptable celebrities. Traditionally they had been admired and even fêted, but regarded as unsuitable for more than occasional admittance to polite society. Several of the latest crop, though – men like Roberto Domínguez and the Portuguese *torero*, Victor Mendes – were a far cry from the low-life personalities who had traditionally inhabited the bullring and its environs. They were young men from well-to-do backgrounds, with cultured tastes and a good education.

None of this squares with what was once the common wisdom: that as soon as Spain became more prosperous, more democratic, and more closely involved with the rest of Europe, the Spaniards' support for this bloody ritual would melt away. For one thing, it was argued, no one but a hungry and desperate peasant would have sufficient incentive to get into a ring with such a dangerous animal, let alone try to use its aggression to create art.*

One theory is that the popularity of bullfighting in recent years is attributable to precisely those forces which it had been thought would bring about its disappearance – that it is a reaction to the breakneck pace of modernization, an unconscious attempt to cling to symbols of identity at a time when the country's leaders are urging the Spanish into an increasingly homogeneous Europe.

*In Spain at least, bullfighting has been considered an art ever since the revolution effected by the *matador* Juan Belmonte in the early years of this century. The journalists who report *corridas* are known as critics and they come under *jefe de sección de cultura* (i.e. the arts editor). For the moment, bullfighting is the responsibility of the Interior Ministry, but there is a feeling among *aficionados* that it should be dealt with by the Arts Ministry.

What is demonstrably the case is that democracy has so far done much more good than harm to the cause of bullfighting. It was not long before Spain's local politicians worked out that one way to improve their chances of re-election was to invest ratepayers' money in making a success of the town or village *fiesta*. Since, in most parts of the country, bullfights are traditional at festival time, one of the easiest ways to do this is to increase the quantity, or more rarely the quality, of the *corridas*. At a national level, democracy has brought to power a Socialist administration which is unquestionably one of the most pro-taurine ever to have governed Spain. A number of the PSOE's leading members – like the Prime Minister himself – are from bullfighting's heartland of Andalusia.

For several years after coming to power, he and his ministers nevertheless seemed content with a policy of benign neglect. But the appointment of José Luis Corcuera as Interior Minister in 1988 handed responsibility for 'the bulls' to a lifelong *aficionado*. The degree of his complicity with the aims of the bullfighting lobby was apparent in an interview he gave to an Andalusian paper two years later. Reforms, he said, needed to be carried out 'with speed, but without making too much noise, because it would not be a good idea if the echoes were to reach those inside and outside Spain who are openly against the *fiesta*'. He has since provided it with an entirely new legal framework. Corcuera's 1991 *Ley de Espectáculos Taurinos* was, remarkably, the first law ever to be enacted by a Spanish parliament to deal exclusively with bullfighting. It defined it as a 'cultural tradition', thereby strengthening the hand of those who seek to identify bullfighting with patriotism. It provided much-needed statutory backing for penalties imposed by the authorities for infringements of the rules. And it paved the way for the introduction of an updated rule-book, or *reglamento*, to replace the one which had been in force since 1962. The new *reglamento* took effect soon after the start of the 1992 season, and at once set off a raging controversy.

Perhaps the most remarkable thing about it, in view of mounting pressure from outside for the abolition of bullfighting, was that its authors should not have seen fit to include more than a nod in the direction of animal rights. The conditions in which bulls are transported were improved. But reports at the time suggested that this was to make sure they reached the ring in a satisfactory condition rather than to save them from unnecessary suffering. The first stage of the *corrida*, in which the bull is lanced by mounted *picadores*, was modified – but not with any evident intention of reducing the cruelty involved.

This has long been the most hotly debated phase of the fight. One reason is that, whatever changes are made, they lead either to more punishment for the bull or to greater risk for the horses. In the old days, when the *picador* had a more or less ordinary and unprotected mount, it was the norm for horses to be gored, and to be stumbling over their own entrails by the time they left the ring. Half-a-dozen or more were usually killed every afternoon. To reduce the amount of gore, it was decided in 1928 to equip the horses with a mattress-like covering known as a *peto*. At first, it was quite light and covered only the belly and flanks. But it soon grew in size and weight to the point at which it was impeding the horse's mobility. In the meantime, and in order to make things easier and safer for themselves, the *picadores* gradually ensured that their mounts became progressively heavier and stronger, to the point at which they were using virtual – if not actual – carthorses. Sitting atop these equine tanks, the *picadores* were in a position to mete out severe punishment to the bull, while the *matadores*, who were just as keen to limit the risks they were going to have to run in the second and third stages of the fight, often encouraged them to do so.

Corcuera's *reglamento* tried to redress the balance. It made the lance-head smaller, set a maximum weight for the *peto* of 30 kilos, banned carthorses and reduced the top weight for a *picador's* mount from 900 to 650 kilos. The first *corrida* held under the new rules took place in Seville on May Day, 1992, and there was keen interest to see what effect the new rules would have. The first bull, after lifting one of the *picador's* horses into the air and dropping its rider on to the sand, ended the opening phase only slightly weaker than when it began. As the *banderillero* Manolo Montoliú raised his arms over the bull's head to thrust the darts into his back, the bull drove his horns through his chest, splitting his heart and killing him almost instantly. The *picadores* and *banderilleros* blamed the new regulations and immediately called a strike which, if it had been allowed to continue, would have forced the cancellation of that year's San Isidro festival a few weeks later. It was only called off after a climb-down by the government. Corcuera stuck by the upper weight limit, but allowed the ban on carthorses to be interpreted in such a way as to allow back into the ring the *percherones* (Breton horses, often interbred with Spanish or English strains) which had been used before.

A further ostensible aim of the new *reglamento*, as of the *Ley de Espectáculos Taurinos*, was to tackle what is unquestionably the biggest single abuse in modern bullfighting: the shaving of the bulls' horns. To a bull, horns are what claws are to a cat. But they are more than that. To extend the analogy, they are his 'whiskers' and his 'tail' too – they help him judge distance and maintain balance. Shaving involves trimming the horns so as to put him at a disadvantage in the ring. It is done with a hacksaw, and finished off with a file or even, it is said, with a blow-torch. So skilled have its practitioners become that the signs of shaving can usually only be detected under a microscope. Nowadays, the animal is invariably tranquillized before being shaved, and unless the 'barber' accidentally cuts into the nerve which runs through the horn, a 'shave' is as painless for a bull as a manicure is for a human. However, the doping, confinement, and tampering with the bull are all immensely traumatic, and he often emerges psychologically beaten. At all events his horns are more sensitive, as well as shorter and blunter, and he may well have been given a false sense of balance.

The problem is that shaving has come to be in the interests of almost everyone involved in the business – except, of course, the fans who pay to see the equivalent of a rigged fight. The *matador* gets an opponent which is less likely to kill or maim him (gorings are less common, and less severe, with a blunted horn). And the more a *matador* fights, the more his manager, or *apoderado*, earns. As for the *empresario*, who runs the ring, stages the fight and actually buys the bulls, it is nowadays highly likely that he will himself be the manager of one or more of the *matadores* on any given afternoon. The bull ranchers, or *ganaderos*, may not be the instigators of the fraud, but they can be put under intense pressure by their customers, the manager-promoters, to let their bulls be tampered with.

Shaving has been going on since at least the forties. Today it has become so widespread and accepted that when the breeders last revised the statutes of their association, they dropped the clause whereby members were liable to expulsion if found guilty of allowing their bulls to be shaved. Not that they ever were found guilty. It could never be proved that they had consented to the shaving, and in any case the rules did not have proper statutory backing. The 1991 law, which specified penalties of up to 25 million pesetas ($240,000 or £140,000), provided that backing. It also seemed to offer a way round the jurisprudential problem that someone – in this case, the breeder – is held responsible for something that he or she did not do or incite others to do, and cannot be proved even to have known about. Under the new rules, a rancher can overrule the objections of the veterinarians at the pre-*corrida* inspection and insist that a suspect bull be fought, provided he accepts full responsibility if – in the post-*corrida* analysis – the horns are shown to have been shaved. However, horns are rarely sent for analysis in the conditions stipulated, and fines under the new arrangements have so far been few and far between.

Shaving, though, is only one symptom of a broader phenomenon – the taming of the Iberian fighting bull. The historic decline can be traced back at least as far as the civil war. So many fighting bulls were slaughtered either for meat or vengeance during the conflict that breeders were unable, during the years immediately after the war, to provide enough bulls of the right age and quality. The *reglamento* stipulates that *matadores* should only fight four-year-olds. But during the forties, skinny three-year-olds became the norm. Though the stock was later to recover, the improvement came at a time when the *empresarios* were gaining ascendancy within the world of bullfighting, often becoming managers to 'strings' or 'stables' of *toreros*, each subject to an exclusive contract with the promoter-manager. In a process which paralleled the spread of shaving, the *empresarios* began to exert pressure on the *ganaderos* to supply them with bulls which looked impressive, but which lacked the *casta* ('breeding', 'spirit') to present any serious challenge to the bullfighters whose salaries they were now paying. In an earlier age, when rearing bulls was simply a pastime of the aristocracy, the *ganaderos* might have been able to resist, but it had become an increasingly commercial activity and since, at that time, more bulls were being bred than was necessary, the *ganaderos* were in no position to put up a fight. The post-war bulls, although small and young, had at least been fiery. Those of the sixties became progressively more docile and by the seventies some were actually falling over in the ring before the fight had run its normal course. Although that is less common nowadays, predictable, 'collaborative' bulls have become the accepted norm.

One of the few ranchers to have bucked the trend is Victorino Martín. The outstanding breeder of recent years, he is not an aristocratic landowner but a self-made man – a former butcher's assistant from Galapagar, between Madrid and the Guadarrama mountains. His spirited *Victorinos* can cost a promoter up to 2 million pesetas. In 1989, though, a shadow was cast over Martín's career when he too was accused by the veterinary inspectors of allowing the horns of his bulls to be tampered with. Martín vigorously denied the charge, and for two years refused to let his animals be fought in Spain.

The prevalence of relatively manageable bulls with shaved horns offers an alternative explanation of why bullfighting has confounded predictions of its demise. According to this argument, today's bullfighters are not being dissuaded by the risks involved because the risks are not as great as those faced by their predecessors.

Among the *matadores* of recent years, the dominant figure has been Juan Antonio Ruiz, who fights under the name of *Espartaco*. For a *matador*, the standard measure of success is the so-called *escalafón* – an annual table which ranks *matadores* according to the number of *corridas* fought, and thus the number of contracts secured. In 1991, *Espartaco* topped the *escalafón* for the eighth time, and for the seventh year in succession – the first *matador* ever to do so.* Bullfighting is far more sensitive to changing social circumstances than is generally realized outside Spain. And just as *El Cordobés* reflected to perfection the rebellious sixties, so *Espartaco* is precisely the kind of bullfighter one would expect to have emerged from the eighties. Handsome in a clean-cut, bright-eyed, lantern-jawed way; diligent, skilful, consistent, yet rarely inspiring, he was – and is – the

---

*Domingo Ortega headed the *escalafón* seven times between 1931 and 1940. José Gómez (*Gallito*) did so six times consecutively in the years 1913 to 1918.

very model of a 'yuppy' *torero*. Although immensely popular at local festivals, it was not until 1988 that *Espartaco* managed to triumph in the major rings.

Over the years, *Espartaco* has had various challengers. *Joselito* made a big impression in 1986. *Manili* triumphed twice in the 1988 San Isidro before being injured later that season. Roberto Domínguez seemed a promising challenger throughout the next couple of years. But the bullfight fraternity had to wait until 1991 for a *torero* capable of combining artistic purity, technical skill and a willingness to take risks that can seem to border on the suicidal. The bullfighter in question is not a Spaniard, but a Colombian, César Rincón, who burst out of obscurity and was carried shoulder-high from the Las Ventas ring in Madrid four times in a season, a feat never previously achieved. Though he has never quite hit the same heights since then, his performances are rarely less than impressive and there are many who believe that Rincón could evolve into one of bullfighting's few acknowledged maestros.

His emergence came after a period of growing emphasis on purity of style. *Joselito* is one of several *matadores* currently fighting who use passes that had long fallen into disuse. One reason for this has been the spread of schools for aspiring bullfighters, usually backed by public funds. The most celebrated is in Madrid and dates from the early seventies when it was founded by an unemployed *novillero* (junior bullfighter), Enrique Martín Arranz. There have rarely been as many promising *novilleros* emerging as in the last few seasons, most of them dedicated to preserving technical soundness and sophistication.

It is difficult to imagine Spain without 'the bulls'. Bullfighting has inspired some excellent writing as well as some brilliant art. Everyday speech is crammed with expressions which would become meaningless without it. We have all heard of *la hora de la verdad*, if only in its English version of 'the moment of truth'. But there are hundreds of others, some of which I suspect have no equivalent in any other language. *Dar largas*, for example, derives from the term for one of the most spectacular manoeuvres in bullfighting, the *larga cambiada*. The *matador* kneels in front of the gate through which the bull charges into the ring, then sends him careering harmlessly out of the way with a wide sweep of his cape. In its metaphorical sense, *dar largas* provides Spaniards with a single, immensely expressive phrase to describe the way in which people get out of a difficult situation by talking at length about something quite different.

Nor should it be forgotten that bullfighting – art, spectacle, or whatever – is unquestionably a business. It has been asserted that it has a turnover, at all levels, of some 90,000 million pesetas ($900 million or £500 million) and affords employment (by no means all of it full-time) to around 170,000 people. Both figures seem to me to be far too high, but the presence of bullfighting in Spanish society is nevertheless considerable, and a lot of people have a keen interest in its survival.

That said, bullfighting is today facing unprecedented pressures outside and inside Spain. Large numbers of people in other European countries have always been opposed to the *corrida*; but they have never been able to exert such direct and effective pressure as became possible in 1986, when Spain joined the EC. In 1990, a German member of the European Parliament tried to pass a motion that would have banned the *picadores'* role in the bullfight. And although his resolution was kicked into touch by Spanish MEPs, it is clear it is only a matter of time before a further attempt is launched.

Spain itself has long had an anti-bullfighting lobby. Torquemada was against it. So was Isabel the Catholic. In the eighteenth century, Felipe V and Carlos III both banned the nobility from taking part. But in the last few years something has happened which had never happened before: parts of Spain in which support for the *corrida* is weak have announced a ban on 'the bulls'.

The first was declared in 1990 in the Catalan resort of Tossa de Mar. The next year, the regional assembly of the Canary Islands voted for prohibition. The move was ridiculed by *aficionados* who pointed out that the last big bullring in the Canaries, at Santa Cruz de Tenerife, had closed in 1986. The vote, they said, was a blatant attempt to curry favour with foreign tour-operators and distract their attention from the fact that the very legislation which outlawed bullfighting legalized cockfighting, a pastime which has a much stronger tradition on the Islands.

That, though, missed the point that a precedent had been set, and that there are several other Spanish regions – Catalonia and Galicia, for instance – whose bullfighting traditions are almost as feeble as those of the Canary Islands.

The prospect of bullfighting withering away in Catalonia is by no means remote. The regional government, the *Generalitat*, has already banned mobile rings. One of Barcelona's two *plazas de toros*, Las Arenas, is no longer used for bullfights. And, in 1989, the *Generalitat* published a survey according to which only 8 per cent of the population in Catalonia was in favour of bullfighting. The same poll suggested that 53 per cent wanted it banned. *Aficionados* quite correctly criticized the poll for having a statistically invalid sample; but perhaps the most significant point was that the *Generalitat* should none the less have seen fit to release it.

In Catalonia, and to a lesser extent the Canary Islands, anti-taurine attitudes draw strength from anti-centralist sentiment – bullfighting is seen as something for the amusement of uncouth mesetarians and hot-blooded southerners. If other peripheral regions were to follow the lead given by the Canary Islands, it would severely undermine a key argument of the bullfighting lobby: that the *corrida* is a *fiesta nacional*, quintessential to Spanishness.

Other things being equal, this would still leave bullfighting impregnable in its Castilian and Andalusian heartlands. But in 1992, something happened (and went almost unnoticed) which suggested that other things may not in fact be equal. Tres Cantos is a new town built to the north of Madrid, within sight of several bull ranches. It is an impressive, if soulless, place which has attracted quite a number of firms operating in the new, 'clean' industries, as well as hundreds of thousands of the new sort of suburbanite Spaniards who work in them. In 1992, the town council decided to drop *corridas* from the annual festivities in view of the lack of spectators at the previous year's bullfights and 'the anti-taurine character of the majority of the population'.

PART SIX

A Fissile State

CHAPTER 26

Centrifugal Forces

You may have noticed that in addition to or instead of an inter-national car registration plate bearing the letter E (for España), Spanish cars often have a plate or sticker with, for example, the letter G on a white background with a blue band across it, or C on a red-and-yellow striped background. Each represents one or other of the regions of Spain. G stands for Galicia and C for Catalonia, and there are others bearing the initial letters and regional colours of each of the other areas. They are not officially recognized by anyone, least of all the Spanish authorities, but that has not stopped them selling like hot cakes ever since the return of democracy.

Nothing could better illustrate the division of loyalties felt by so many Spaniards. More than most people in Europe, Spaniards tend to put loyalty to their region on a par with, or even ahead of, loyalty to their country. Regional sentiment bedevilled attempts to build a strong unitary state in Spain during the sixteenth and nineteenth centuries. And it is separatism in the shape of ETA and its supporters which now poses one of the greatest challenges to today's Spain.

To some extent, the strength of regional feeling in Spain is simply a manifestation of the Mediterranean tendency to subjective-ness. Southern Europeans, far more than northern Europeans, will tend to favour whoever is closest to them, physically or socially, regardless of their merits. This is why face-to-face contact is so vitally important in business dealings and why corruption in the form of favouritism towards friends and relatives is so common. The same, I think, applies to places. Traditionally, a Spaniard's greatest affection has always been reserved for his or her native town or district, which the Spaniards themselves, in a telling phrase, often refer to as their *patria chica*, or 'little fatherland'. Next comes their region and, last of all, the state. A number of other factors – geographical, historical and cultural – have combined to divide Spaniards from each other and to produce in many of them the conviction that the region comes first and the state comes second – and, in extreme cases, nowhere at all.

By European standards at least, Spain is a big country. If you leave out Russia, the only country in Europe bigger than Spain is France. It is very nearly half as large again as Germany and, at slightly less than 200,000 square miles or rather more than 500,000 square kilometres, it is almost twice the size of Italy and four times the size of England. Yet throughout its history, Spain's population has been modest. As a result, it was – and is – a country of widely spaced communities. Since earliest times their isolation from one another has been made more acute by a dearth of navigable rivers and, because of the poverty which was Spain's lot, road and rail links developed only very slowly. For example, it was not until 1974, when the *puente aereo* – the air shuttle between Madrid and Barcelona – was opened, that one could travel between the country's two largest cities with ease. Right up until the late seventies, when a lengthy stretch of motorway was built, the journey by car took about nine hours of solid driving.

The *meseta* which one might think would have drawn the country closer together has, if anything, had the reverse effect. Apart from being a formidable obstacle to communication between the peoples of the periphery, it is itself riven by a succession of mountain ranges – 'those East–West ramparts,' as Laurie Lee called them, 'which go ranging across Spain and divide its people into separate races'.

Spain's geography may not have exactly favoured unity, but it did not make it unthinkable. France is almost as varied and marginally bigger, yet the French today are a remarkably homogeneous people. What ensured that Spain would remain so divided was the course of its history.

Like much of the territory bordering the Mediterranean, the Iberian peninsula was visited by Phoenicians, settled by Greeks and finally conquered and occupied by the Romans. When Rome's power declined, the peninsula – in common with most of the rest of

Europe – was invaded by tribesmen from the north and east of the continent. At the start of the fifth century, three German peoples – the Alans, Vandals and Sueves – crossed the Pyrenees. The Alans were all but wiped out when the Visigoths, a Christian people loosely allied with Rome and who had carved out a kingdom for themselves with its capital at Toulouse, raided the peninsula in a short-lived attempt to return it to the Empire. The Vandals moved on to North Africa. This left only the Sueves, and by the middle of the fifth century they were on the point of taking over the entire peninsula when it was once again invaded by the Visigoths. This time, the Visigoths came to stay. Soon after their invasion of the peninsula they lost most of the territory they controlled on the other side of the Pyrenees and from then on their kingdom became a predominantly Iberian enterprise.

The task of bringing the entire peninsula under Visigothic rule took more than a century. Successive monarchs had to contend not only with the Sueves, who had retreated into the north-west, but also with an army of Byzantines, who – in return for helping a Visigothic pretender on to the throne – helped themselves to a large chunk of territory in the south-east. The Sueves were finally overcome in 585 and the last bit of the Byzantine colony was annexed in 624. The Visigothic monarchs continued to be plagued by uprisings among the native population, and in particular by the Basques; but there again, so had the Romans. If anything, Visigothic Iberia was rather more united than the other realms that were emerging in Europe after the collapse of the Roman Empire. Both the Visigoths and the majority of their subjects practised Christianity and spoke a form of Latin. Moreover, in the middle of the seventh century the Visigothic monarchy imposed upon the entire country a code of laws applicable to all.

Doubtless, Visigothic rule would not have lasted for ever, but there is no reason why – barring a bolt from the blue such as the one that ended it – it could not have survived for a few centuries longer. And when it did fall, it is quite possible that the peninsula might have survived to this day as a single political entity in the way that France has. At the very least, the Visigoths would have been able to bequeath to their successors a land which was in the process of evolving a common language and way of life, so that if – like Germany and Italy – Iberia had then disintegrated into a plethora of tiny states, a strong sense of national identity could have survived.

But Iberia was not to follow the same path as the other great geopolitical entities of Europe. Her fate was being decided 3,000 miles away on the shore of the Red Sea, where a man who believed himself to be God's messenger was preaching the doctrine of Holy War. Mohammed's followers burst out of Arabia after his death in 632 and by the end of the seventh century their descendants had conquered the whole of North Africa. The first Moslem incursion into Iberia was in 710, when a small reconnaissance force landed at the southernmost point of the peninsula. The following year a former slave, a Berber by the name of Tariq ibn-Ziyad, led an army of about 7,000 ashore at a point close to the huge rock which dominates the entrance to the Mediterranean (the Moslems named the rock Jabal Tariq, or Tariq's Mount, and eventually clumsy Christian tongues changed it to Gibraltar). It took no more than two years for Tariq's small force to subdue the whole of what is now Spain and Portugal. But after crossing the Pyrenees and penetrating the very heart of France, where they were defeated by the Franks, the Moslems withdrew into the southern three-quarters of the peninsula. Most of the indigenous inhabitants fell under the rule of the Moslems, but some of them fled across the Pyrenees or took refuge in the line of hills and mountains that stretches along the top of the peninsula from Galicia to Catalonia.

The Moslem invasion shattered the tentative unity that had been achieved by the Visigoths. When the Christians began to fight back, they did so not in unison but grouped into tiny statelets that soon acquired distinct traditions. The first was formed by Visigothic noblemen who had retreated to the mountains of Asturias. Supported intermittently by some of the Basques, the Kings of Asturias expanded westwards into Galicia and southwards until, in the tenth century, they were able to establish their capital on the *meseta* at León. This Asturo-Leónese kingdom was responsible for giving birth to two counties in the strict sense of the word – Castile and Portugal – which subsequently grew into kingdoms themselves.

Another miniature state was set up by the Basques in Navarre, while further to the east – but still within the foothills of the Pyrenees – a number of little counties were created of which Aragón, soon boasting its own monarchy, emerged as the most powerful. Finally, on the Mediterranean coast, an army composed largely of the descendants of men and women who had fled across the Pyrenees fought its way back into Catalonia, where another network of counties then emerged.

The arrival of the Moslems also put paid to any hope of a single language. Cut off from one another in the mountainous north and brought into much closer contact with the languages of the pre-Roman peoples who lived there than would otherwise have been the case, the descendants of the Latin-speaking refugees who had fled from Tariq's conquering army evolved no fewer than five separate new languages – Galician, Bable (the language of Asturias), Castilian, Aragonese and Catalan. In the south, the Christians living under Moslem rule developed yet another tongue – Mozarabic. With the exception of Mozarabic, all these languages have survived to the present day, although Bable and Aragonese are nowadays spoken by only a tiny number of people in remote rural areas. Together with Basque and such curious linguistic relics as Aranés (a variety of Gascon Provençal which is spoken in the Aran Valley of northern Catalonia), they constitute a rich heritage – and a source of persistent friction. Today almost a quarter of Spain's inhabitants speak a vernacular language in addition to, or instead of, the official language of the state.

It is noticeable that all but one of the early Christian states started life in the mountains, and mountain regions – Switzerland is a prime example – tend to favour the development of representative systems of government at an early stage in their history. The indigenous inhabitants of the mountains of northern and north-western Iberia were no exception. When they moved south in alliance with descendants of the refugees from the Moslem invasion, they took with them their institutions and customs, albeit in a progressively diluted form. In the north-east, the political and social system was much closer to the feudal model developing elsewhere in Europe, but even certain sections of Catalan society were able to win from their rulers political freedoms in exchange for their financial or military contributions. For most of the Middle Ages, therefore, the inhabitants of the Iberian peninsula enjoyed far greater individual freedom and carried far greater individual responsibility than their contemporaries in other parts of Europe. As a consequence, Spaniards tend to look back at the medieval period when the regional states were at the height of their power not as a time of disunity so much as one of freedom and equality.

The *reconquista* was neither continuous nor co-ordinated. The petty Christian states spent quite as much time fighting each other as they did fighting the Moslems. Outstanding monarchs tried and occasionally succeeded in uniting two or more states either by treaty or conquest, but time and again they were persuaded by factional interests to re-divide their territories in their wills. In fact, the process whereby the various kingdoms came to form a single state lasted far longer even than the *reconquista*. In 1137 the County of Barcelona – which by then had absorbed most of the other Catalan mini-states – was joined by marriage to the Kingdom of Aragón. Together the Catalans and the Aragonese went on to conquer Valencia and the Balearic Islands during the thirteenth century. Castile, which was in the process of recovering a large chunk of Andalusia, and León, which by then took in Asturias, Galicia and Estremadura, eventually came together in 1230, having united and divided twice in the preceding hundred years. The conquest and settlement of Murcia at the end of the thirteenth century was a joint venture by the Crown of Castile (the name given to the state formed by the unification of Castile and León) and the Crown of Aragón (the state formed by the federation of Aragón and Catalonia). The Navarrese meanwhile, whose most outstanding sovereign, Sancho III, had come closer than any of Spain's medieval rulers to uniting the Christian domains, had for several centuries been looking northwards. At its point of greatest expansion Navarre took in a large stretch of what is now France, and its rulers became entwined by marriage with several French royal and noble families to the extent that it came within a hair's breadth of being incorporated into France.

The members of the royal families of the three other kingdoms – Portugal, Castile and Aragón – had so often inter-married that it became inevitable that sooner or later two of these states would be united by inheritance. In the event it was later rather than sooner; it was only in 1474, when the ineffectual Enrique IV of Castile died without leaving a son, that the opportunity arose. The two claimants to his throne were Isabel, his half-sister, and Juana, the woman he claimed was his daughter but who was alleged by opponents to be the illegitimate offspring of an affair between Enrique's wife and a courtier. The nub of the matter was that Juana was married to Afonso V of Portugal while Isabel was the wife of Fernando, heir to the throne of Aragón. Whichever of these two won the throne would determine whether the peninsula was to be dominated by an alliance between Castile and Portugal or one between Castile and Aragón. It took a war to settle the issue. But by 1479 – the year in which Fernando succeeded to the throne of Aragón – Isabel's forces had overcome Juana's. Technically, Castile and Aragón remained separate. Under the agreement worked out between Fernando and Isabel each was to reign as sole monarch in his or her own country while ranking as no more than a consort in the realm of the other. But in practice Isabel concerned herself with the domestic affairs of both countries, while her husband looked after their foreign affairs.

One of Isabel and Fernando's most celebrated joint ventures was the ten-year campaign which culminated in the surrender in 1492 of the Kingdom of Granada – the last Moslem stronghold on the peninsula. The fall of Granada marked the end of the *reconquista*. It had lasted for almost 800 years and it had had a profound effect on the characters of both the Spanish and the Portuguese, although – as more than one historian has pointed out – the fact that Portugal was fully reconquered more than 200 years before Spain meant that it left a much greater impression on the latter than on the former. The legacy of almost eight centuries of conquest and colonization can, I believe, be seen in many aspects of Spanish life, such as an almost casual acceptance of violence and bloodshed, and in the two most contradictory aspects of the Spanish character – their immense respect for firm leadership and their uncompromising faith in their own judgement and ability. It also, I suspect, gave rise to a trait which is characteristic of other frontier societies, like those of North America and South Africa – an inordinate love for the land that has been captured and settled.

The gradual spread of the Christian peoples through the peninsula had cleared the way for a corresponding expansion of the Romance languages that had begun life in the highlands of the north. Some prospered more than others. In the west, Galician had given birth to Portuguese. In the east, Catalan had spread to the Balearic Islands and to much of Valencia. But it was Castilian which had become pre-eminent – to the point that it would come to be known in most of the rest of the world as 'Spanish'. Spaniards who speak one of the other languages tend to believe that Castilian gained its ascendancy by dint of force – by conquest in medieval times and by repression and coercion more recently. This is only partly true. An equally important reason for its expansion has been that it is a superbly efficient means of communication which, whenever it has come into contact with another language, has tended to be adopted solely on its merits. In the centre of the country, it had made inroads into the Kingdoms of León to the west and Aragón to the east, displacing Bable and Aragonese respectively long before Castile had acquired any political clout in either area. Its linguistic excellence also won it a foothold in the Basque country centuries before anyone tried to force the Basques to abandon their native tongue. It was undeniably force of arms which allowed it to spread through Andalusia. But it is significant that when Castilian clashed head-on with Catalan in Murcia, following a campaign in which the Castilians and the Catalans both took part, it was Castilian – sprinkled here and there with Catalan words and phrases – which emerged as the language of the region.

Events following Isabel's death in 1504 underlined the shakiness of the alliance between Castile and Aragón. For one thing, she had added a codicil to her will barring the Aragonese and their confederates, the Catalans and the Valencians, from trading with the New World discovered by Columbus in the same year that the Christian Spaniards conquered Granada. Isabel's only son and Fernando's posthumous son had both died before the death of Isabel herself, so the Crown of Castile passed to her daughter, another Juana, who, being mentally incapable of ruling, had to have a regent. Since Fernando had remarried and had gone to live in Italy, the task fell to Juana's husband. It was only his sudden death in 1506 that caused Fernando to become involved once more, as regent, in the affairs of

Castile. In this capacity he was responsible for the incorporation of the third of the medieval peninsular kingdoms when, in 1512, he masterminded the annexation of most of Navarre.

Fernando died two years later. Although it was Isabel who had consciously aspired to the unification of the peninsula, it was he who had done most to bring it about. Appropriately, he left his own kingdom, Aragón, to his daughter Juana's son Carlos. Rather than follow in his father's and grandfather's footsteps by becoming regent in Castile, Carlos insisted on being made king.

His accession in 1516 is traditionally regarded as marking the unification of Spain. But that is only true with hindsight. The goal had always been – and remained – the reunification of the whole of Iberia, and that was not achieved until 1580 when Carlos's son, Felipe II, annexed Portugal after its king had died on a madcap expedition to North Africa, leaving behind him no obvious heir. What then happened was that the process of unification suffered a reverse – as it had many times in the past. This time it was not the result of a will but a war. In 1640 the Catalans and the Portuguese, both of whom had been chafing at Castile's insensitive centralism, rebelled against Madrid. The Catalans were finally beaten into submission in 1659, but the Portuguese survived as a separate nation ruled by a new dynasty until in 1665 they confirmed their independence by defeating the Spaniards at the Battle of Montes Claros.

Spain and Portugal were never again to reunite, although the dream of reunification through a loose confederation of the traditional regions was to persist until this century. That the six states which emerged in the north of the peninsula should have evolved into two nations – one of them made up of five of those states and the other consisting of the remaining one – was a matter of the purest chance. Had a battle here or there gone the other way, had this or that son not died in infancy, had this or that mother not perished in childbirth, the division might have been altogether different. Contrary to what the more rabid of Spain's centralists claim, there is absolutely nothing 'sacred' about the unity of Spain, because there was nothing pre-ordained about its shape.

The Habsburg and Bourbon monarchs who ruled Spain from the

beginning of the sixteenth until the end of the eighteenth centuries were aware that their realms were circumstantial conglomerations of states that had once been independent. It did not mean, however, that they were happy with the situation in which they found themselves; several regions enjoyed political faculties and economic privileges that seriously limited the power of the central government and made the construction of a modern state virtually impossible.

The choice of Madrid as a capital was a response to this dilemma. Until the middle of the sixteenth century, the Spanish court had moved from place to place. But in 1561 Felipe II decided that the machinery of government ought to have a permanent home. In an effort not to boost the power and status of any one region, he hit on the idea of putting his court in the geographical centre of the peninsula. Madrid is almost totally devoid of natural advantages. It does not have a harbour. It does not stand by the shores of a lake or at the meeting-place of two rivers. The reason why human beings settled there is because of an escarpment which offers commanding views across the surrounding plain. Throughout the Middle Ages the military importance of that escarpment made Madrid a valuable prize for Moors and Christians alike. But with the end of the *reconquista*, Madrid would almost certainly have withered into insignificance had it not been for Felipe's initiative. Like Bonn and Brasilia, Madrid is an 'artificial' rather than an 'organic' city and it has therefore never had much of a hold over the country's affections.

The change of dynasty from Habsburg to Bourbon was marked by a lengthy and bloody war – the so-called War of the Spanish Succession, lasting from 1702 until 1713, in which the traditional regions of Spain were again split into two opposing camps, each of which supported a rival claimant. It also marked a shift in the Crown's approach to its more restive subjects. Whereas the Habsburg Felipe IV had refrained from taking reprisals against the Catalans after they rebelled in 1640, the Bourbon Felipe V who emerged as the victor from the War of Succession punished the Catalans, Aragonese and Valencians who had supported his opponent by annulling their laws and institutions and thus creating within the Catalan-speaking part of Spain an undercurrent of discontent that has persisted to this day.

The Spaniards' reaction to the occupation of their country by the French in 1808 underlined something which foreigners, and indeed many Spaniards, find difficult to understand: that for most Spaniards patriotism and a form of regionalism or nationalism that borders on separatism are not mutually exclusive. In what came to be known as the War of Independence, Galicians, Basques, Castilians, Aragonese, Catalans and Andalusians turned on the interloper with a ferocity which proved that, however distinct they might feel themselves to be from one another, they felt a good deal more different from foreigners. Yet they did so in a characteristically independent way. The vacuum left by the overthrow of the monarchy was filled, not by a provisional central government set up in opposition to the administration installed by the French, but by a plethora of local *juntas* (committees), most of which ran their own tiny armies.

France's short-lived occupation introduced the relatively small Spanish middle class to a number of ideas about government that were then regarded as progressive. As was mentioned earlier, one of these was that the monarch ought to be subject to a constitution. Another was that a modern state ought to be uniform. It could not tolerate feudal rights and privileges. The result was that the cause of centralism in nineteenth-century Spain was taken up by the bourgeois proponents of a constitution – the *liberales* – while the defence of traditional local laws was left to the supporters of absolutism, who were mostly to be found among the most reactionary sections of the aristocracy and the peasantry. Unhappily for Spain, a dispute over the succession enabled these two opposing groups to identify themselves with rival claimants to the throne. Twice during the last century the ultra-reactionary Carlist pretenders waged unsuccessful but highly disruptive wars against a monarchy which, although not progressive by instinct, was forced to turn for support to the *liberales*. The Carlist cause appealed above all to the pious, reactionary and fervently independent Basque peasantry, and when Carlism was finally defeated in the 1870s the central government penalized the Basques – including a large section of the community which had stayed loyal to the central government – by abolishing their traditional rights and privileges.

As Spain entered the final quarter of the nineteenth century, the central government had succeeded in alienating precisely those regions – Catalonia and the Basque country – where conditions existed, or were about to develop, that would foster the growth of modern nationalism. In the first place, the Basques and Catalans had a language and a culture of their own (this factor alone was sufficient to stimulate the growth of a modest nationalist movement in Galicia). Secondly, these two parts of Spain were the first to become industrialized and were therefore the earliest to nurture a substantial middle class of the kind which, in many parts of the world, has been eager to support nationalist aspirations. Among the Basque and Catalan middle classes, a sentimental hankering after traditional values mingled with a feeling of superiority with regard to the hated Castilians. This feeling stemmed largely from the quite reasonable belief that Madrid was incapable of understanding the problems of advanced industrial societies such as theirs. But it was also in part the result of an instinctive desire to dissociate themselves from Spain's decline, the scale of which was to be made embarrassingly obvious by Spain's defeat at the hands of the United States in 1898.

Unfortunately for Madrid, both the Basques and Catalans live hard by the two main routes into France and in each case there are people who speak the same language as they do on the other side of the border. Rebel Spanish Basques and Catalans have never found it difficult to find refuge or supplies, especially since it has often proved convenient for Paris to turn a blind eye to the activities of the Basques and Catalans under French rule as a means of distracting the Spanish government and exhausting its resources.

The defeat of Carlism put paid to any chance that regional aspirations might be fulfilled by the accession of an absolute monarch. From then on, the best hopes of the Basques and Catalans lay with the overthrow of the *liberal* monarchy by opponents at the other end of the political spectrum. Spanish radicals had already developed an affection for federalism which came to the fore when they ruled the country for less than a year during the First Republic (1873–4). When the monarchy was once again overthrown in 1931, the pressure for home rule was immense. The Catalans were granted a Statute of Autonomy in 1932 and the Basques and the Galicians were on the verge of gaining a limited form of home rule when civil war broke out again in 1936.

Although General Franco and his allies described themselves as Nationalists, what they meant was that they were Spanish nationalists – wholly opposed to the regional nationalism which they regarded as one of the principal reasons for the turmoil that had bedevilled the Second Republic. During the early years, not only was it forbidden to teach the vernacular languages but serious efforts were made to stop people from speaking them. They could not be used on official premises or at official functions. Stickers were even put up in telephone booths telling callers that they had to conduct their conversations in Castilian or – to use the parlance of the regime – 'speak Christian'. A ban on the publication of books in vernacular languages did not last long, but a similar prohibition on their use in the press, and on radio and television, remained in force until Franco's dying day.

Indeed, such was the intransigence of Franco's centralism that it succeeded in creating nationalist regionalist groups in areas such as Estremadura and Murcia where no one had previously questioned their Spanishness. Ironically, although not perhaps surprisingly, it was regional nationalism in its most radical and violent form which ensured that Franco's style of government would not survive him when, in 1972, his Prime Minister and chosen successor, Admiral Carrero Blanco, was blown to pieces by terrorists drawn from among the most fiercely independent minority of all – the Basques.

CHAPTER 27

The Basques

The most obvious difference between the Basques and their neighbours in France and Spain is their extraordinary language which the Basques themselves call *euskera* or *euskara*, depending on which dialect they speak. Although over the years it has absorbed individual words from both French and Spanish, the basic vocabulary and structure of the language bears absolutely no resemblance to either. One sixteenth-century Sicilian author was convinced that the Basques' strange tongue enabled them to communicate with the monsters of the deep.

A phrase taken at random from a text-book, 'The table is laid – you can bring in the food', when translated into Basque is *'Mahaia gertu dago. Ekar dezakezue bazkaria.'* The syntax is no less exotic. The definite article 'the' is not a separate word but a suffix. Nouns used with numerals remain in the singular. Auxiliary verbs vary according to the number of objects as well as the number of subjects, and what we would call prepositions are in Basque suffixes and prefixes, which alter according to whether the word to which they are attached represents something animate or inanimate. The author of the first Basque grammar could perhaps be forgiven for entitling his work *The Impossible Overcome*.

It seems always to have been assumed that Basque was a language of great antiquity. In the Middle Ages, when it was believed that the various languages of the world were the product of God's intervention at the Tower of Babel, a number of scholars argued that it was the language which Noah's grandson, Tubal, was said to have taken to Iberia and that in ancient times Basque must have been spoken throughout the peninsula. Long after the biblical explanation of the origin of languages had been called into question elsewhere in Europe this theory was stoutly defended within the Basque country itself, largely because of the immense authority there of the Church. Some Basque authors went as far as to claim that theirs had been the original language of Europe, or even the world. There is no doubt that Basque was once spoken over a much larger area than it is today – an area which almost certainly included the entire Pyrenees, since it is known to have been spoken in parts of Aragón and Catalonia during the Middle Ages. But it is unlikely to have been the language of all Iberia, much less that of Europe or the world.

Modern scholarship has, however, shown that it is an extremely old language. The touchstone of modern philology was the discovery towards the end of the eighteenth century that many European and Asian languages – subsequently given the name Indo-European – came from a common source. Throughout the nineteenth century, Basque resisted all attempts to find it a place in the Indo-European family and philologists have eventually had to reconcile themselves to the conclusion that Basque predates the migrations from the East which brought the Indo-European languages into Europe some 3,000 years ago. But there is also evidence that it may be much older even than that. It has been suggested, for example, that words like *aitzkor* (axe) and *aitzur* (hoe) derive from *aitz* (stone) and date from the time when tools were made of stone.

Recent research has concentrated on trying to find a link between Basque and other pre-Indo-European languages, such as those still spoken in the Caucasus and among the Berbers of North Africa. A method invented by the American linguist Morris Swadesh compares a hundred-word passage in one language with a hundred-word passage in another language to discover the percentage of similar words. Up to 5 per cent is regarded as no more than coincidence. But it has been found that there is a 7 per cent overlap between Basque and two of the three Caucasian languages, Georgian and Circassian, and a 10 per cent overlap between Basque and certain Berber languages, which suggests that there could well be a distant link.

While linguists have been puzzling over the singularity of the Basques' language, doctors and scientists have been discovering that they have other, less evident, peculiarities. To understand these, one has to make a brief detour into the world of serology, the study of blood.

On occasions, when the blood of two individuals is brought into contact, it coagulates. This is because the blood of at least one of them contains what is called an antigen. There are two types of antigen – A and B. Some people have both and their blood is classified as A/B. Other people's blood contains only one antigen and is classified as either A or B. But there is also a third type, O, which contains no antigens at all. There are two reasons why all this is of importance to anthropologists. Firstly, antigens are hereditary – no one can have either A or B in their bloodstream unless at least one of their parents had it in his or hers. Secondly, the proportion of each blood type in the population varies significantly from place to place. As one moves across Europe from east to west, for example, the percentage of A increases while the percentage of B decreases. The Basques conform to this pattern, but to an exaggerated degree. The percentage of A is higher and the proportion of B lower than one would expect even for a people perched on the Atlantic coast.

In 1939 an American researcher opened up new fields for exploration when he discovered a substance in the blood of the Macacacus Rhesus monkey which was also found to be present in the blood of some humans. According to whether or not their blood contained the new substance, people could thereafter be divided into Rhesus positive (Rh +) and Rhesus negative (Rh −). In Europe the percentage of Rhesus negatives is higher than in other parts of the world and for the most part varies from 12 to 16 per cent. The relevance of this to the Basques was discovered, not by researchers in the Basque country, but by an ordinary general practitioner working thousands of miles away in Argentina who was concerned with an entirely different problem – eritroblastosis. This is an often fatal illness which affects newborn children whose blood is incompatible with that of their mothers. In most cases, the problem arises because the mother is Rh − while her child is Rh + , having inherited the substance from its father. The general practitioner, Dr Miguel Angel Etcheverry, noticed that an unusually high proportion of these unfortunate mothers were, like him, of Basque descent. To test his suspicion, he took samples from 128 Argentinians who had four Basque grandparents and discovered that fully one third of them were Rh −. After his findings were published in 1945, a series of studies in the Spanish Basque country all produced figures in excess of 30 per cent, and one, carried out in the French Basque country, put the proportion of the population who did not have the Rhesus substance in their blood at 42 per cent − the highest figure recorded anywhere in the world. As far as blood grouping was concerned, therefore, the Basques were emerging as exceptionally 'European' (by virtue of their Rhesus count) and very 'Westerly' (by virtue of their antigen pattern).

Throughout history, the Basques had been thought of by their neighbours as being bigger and stronger. A great deal of measuring and weighing by anthropologists, especially during the early part of this century, proved this to be the case. The Basques were found to be, on average, two to three centimetres taller than the average in France and Spain and, although they tended to be more muscular, their limbs − and in particular their hands and feet − were inclined to be quite delicate. The anthropologists also established that the typical Basque had a distinctive 'hare's head', broad at the top and narrow at the bottom, and that he or she was likely to have a high forehead, a straight nose and a distinctive bulge over the temples.

By themselves, these findings proved nothing. But when they were put alongside the archaeological discoveries of that period, they became very interesting indeed. Shortly after the First World War, two Basque researchers, Telesforo de Aranzadi and José Miguel de Barandiarán, had begun excavating a number of dolmens dating from around 2000 BC, the time of the Indo-European invasions. On the basis of the bones they found in them it was suggested that the people who had lived in the Basque country at that time had the same physical characteristics as the Basques of today. Even more interestingly, and controversially, a skull found in the mid-thirties by the two men in a cave near Itziar in Guipúzcoa dating from the late Stone Age − about 10,000 BC − was held to have several typically Basque traits, suggesting that the Basques of today might be the direct descendants of Cro-Magnon man.

A good deal of doubt has since been cast on the significance of these finds, but the absence from Basque folklore of any sort of migration legend, when combined with the linguistic and serological evidence, would seem to suggest that the Basques have lived where they are now to be found since the Stone Age. Secure in a homeland of steep-sided hills and valleys much of which was covered in dense forest, they seem to have had only the most limited contact with the peoples who entered Europe two millennia before Christ and who brought with them their Indo-European languages and their distinctive blood group distribution, characterized by a high proportion of B and Rh +. Thereafter, isolated from those around them by language as well as geography, the Basques began to inculcate that resistance to outside influence — and especially outside rule — which is the hallmark of their history.

The Basques enter written records with the arrival of the Romans. The Latin authors noted that there were four tribes in what is now the Spanish Basque country — the Vascones, the Vardulos, the Caristios and the Autrigones. Interestingly, each of the areas in which a particular Basque dialect is spoken today coincides roughly with an area occupied by one of these tribes. Navarrese is, or was, spoken in the area once inhabited by the Vascones. Guipúzcoan corresponds to that of the Vardulos, Biscayan to that of the Caristios, and the part of the Basque country outside Navarre in which Basque has long since ceased to be spoken was once the land of the Autrigones.

In the seventeenth century, the theory was put forward that the Vascones were the only genuine Basques and that they imposed their culture on the other tribes in the period following the Roman occupation of Iberia. The theory gained wide acceptance and Biscay, Guipúzcoa and Alava came to be known as the *provincias Vascongadas* (Vasconized provinces). The theory has since been discredited, but you will still see the phrase used in old-fashioned newspapers like *ABC*.

One of the most enduring myths about the Basques is that they were never subject to Roman rule. Spaniards will earnestly assure you even now that the reason why the Basques are so fiercely independent is that they were never given a taste of Roman discipline. It is true that the Romans had to contend with persistent rebellions in the Basque country, but their grip on the area was firm enough to enable them to build roads and settlements there and even run the odd iron mine. Basque soothsayers were renowned throughout the Empire.

The collapse of Roman rule marked the last time that all Basques were subject to the same administration, although that is not to say that the Basques on both sides of the Pyrenees had formed a single administrative entity either before or during Roman rule. After the legions departed, it was left to the Romans' 'barbarian' successors to try to impose their will on the area – the Franks strove to control an area roughly corresponding to the modern French Basque country and the northern part of Navarre, while the Visigoths attempted to govern what is now Guipúzcoa, Biscay and Alava. Neither succeeded fully.

At the beginning of the seventh century the Franks set up a dependent Duchy of Vasconia, which at one stage stretched from the Garonne to the Ebro. It was shaken by a succession of violent revolts until, in 788, a Frankish army returning from an unsuccessful campaign against the Moslems was ambushed by Basques in the valley of Roncesvalles. The ensuing battle was immortalized in the *Chanson de Roland*, although its author depicted the attackers as Moors, not Basques. Soon after Roncesvalles, the Basques in the south of the Duchy declared themselves independent. The state they founded, which at first controlled no more than a small area around Pamplona, was destined to become the Kingdom of Navarre. It subsequently expanded to take in much of the French Basque country and a large area, non-Basque in speech and custom, to the south of Pamplona.

The Visigoths, meanwhile, were forced to wage repeated wars against the Basques of Alava, Biscay and Guipúzcoa, but never seem to have actually ruled all of them except for brief spells. The Visigothic nobles who founded the Kingdom of Asturias inherited the Visigoths' claim to the western Basque country. But they and their successors, the kings of Castile and León, had to contend not only with the Basques' stubborn refusal to be ruled, but also with the rival ambitions of the new Kingdom of Navarre. Next to nothing is known about the provinces of Alava, Biscay and Guipúzcoa during this period, but it was clearly a pretty wild place. It was the last area of southern and western Europe to be converted to Christianity, probably in the ninth or tenth centuries. Local legends suggest that pockets of paganism survived for quite a long time afterwards, and as late as the twelfth century nominally Christian Basques were harrying pilgrims on their way to the shrine of St James at Compostela. It was also the last region of Europe to acquire towns – the last to be civilized in the strict sense of the word. The earliest inland settlements in Guipúzcoa were not founded until the second half of the thirteenth century and those in Biscay were not established until the latter half of the fourteenth.

Treaties were drawn up solemnly allotting this or that province, or the entire area, to either Castile or Navarre, but to all intents and purposes power was held locally. The Alavese were ruled by nobles, but Biscay and Guipúzcoa retained a kind of primitive democracy in which the heads of all the families in a valley either elected or formed a council that sent representatives to a provincial assembly. The provincial assembly decided who should be responsible for taking decisions about the affairs of the province when the assembly was not in session. At different times, this power was delegated to councils of notables or to elected or hereditary lords (there was an aristocracy in both provinces, but its power seems to have been more economic and social than political).

Although the Basque country was a poor area, serfdom disappeared there more swiftly and completely than elsewhere in Spain, and by the end of the Middle Ages the liberties enjoyed by ordinary Basques would have been the envy of their counterparts elsewhere in Europe – they could bear arms, they were free to hunt and fish and they were entitled within their native district to make use of what were usually extensive common woodlands and pastures.

The Kings of Castile acquired sovereignty over the western Basques only very slowly and gradually. The Guipúzcoan notables in the thirteenth century and the Alavese aristocracy in the fourteenth century both voted to offer the Castilian Crown the overlordship of their respective provinces, while the lordship of Biscay passed to Castile by inheritance in 1379. Navarre, on the other hand, remained fully independent until 1512 when Fernando, the King of Aragón and Regent of Castile, who was at that time waging a war against the French, demanded that the Navarrese allow his troops free passage through their realm. The Navarrese refused and Fernando invaded and annexed their kingdom. In 1530 the newly united Kingdom of Spain relinquished the bulk of what had been Navarrese territory on the other side of the Pyrenees and the Spanish Basque country took on more or less its present shape.

Although nominally integrated into the Spanish state, the Basques held back a good deal of power from the central government. In Guipúzcoa and Biscay they retained intact their system of local administration. The Guipúzcoan assembly could veto laws submitted by the Spanish sovereign with the words 'we obey but do not comply' and the Biscayan elders insisted that as soon as a monarch succeeded to the throne, he or she or a representative had to go to the province and swear to uphold its laws beneath the tree in Guernica where their assembly met. The Navarrese for their part enjoyed the privilege of being ruled by a viceroy – the only one outside the Americas – and were allowed to retain their own local legislature, executive and judiciary. They also had the right to mint their own money – as late as the nineteenth century the Navarrese were striking coins depicting King Fernando VII of Spain as King Fernando III of Navarre. These political rights, together with a number of valuable economic and social privileges such as immunity from Spanish customs duties and exemption from military service outside their native province, were embodied in codes of traditional law known as *fueros*.

Nationalists tend inevitably to emphasize the extent of the Basques' independence under the Castilian Crown, but remain silent about their close links with the Castilian people. Yet one of the reasons why the Basques enjoyed such a privileged status was precisely because they had been associated for so long and so intimately with the Castilians, even if it had always been on their own terms. Basques helped the Castilians to establish their earliest settlements on the *meseta* and subsequently played a prominent role in many of the decisive battles of the Castilian *reconquista*. Under the Habsburgs, the Basque country provided Spain with some of its finest administrators, two of its greatest explorers – Pedro de Ursua and Lope de Aguirre, whose doomed search for Eldorado provided the inspiration for Werner Herzog's film *Aguirre, Wrath of God* – and two of its most celebrated religious figures, St Ignacio de Loyola and St Francisco Xavier.

Another distinguished Basque from Spain's Golden Age was Sebastián Elcano, who took command of the first expedition to circumnavigate the globe after its commander, Magellan, had been killed in the Philippines. The Basques had for centuries had close links with the sea. They seem to have learnt deep-sea fishing from the Normans and, until the eighteenth century, they were also renowned whalers. Some of their terminology was picked up by the whalers of the Azores, who passed it on to the seamen from Massachusetts who used the Azores as a supply base in the last century. The word for a sperm whale, cachalot, is ultimately of Basque origin. But although the fishing villages of the Guipúzcoan and Biscayan coast have always played a large part in the life and lore of the region, its soul lies inland where, between the end of the *reconquista* and the start of the Carlist Wars, there evolved a highly idiosyncratic society, the last traces of which can still be detected in the Basque country of today.

Its outstanding characteristic is the relatively low proportion of the population concentrated in villages and the correspondingly high proportion scattered over the countryside in homesteads. This pattern is thought to have developed in the stable and prosperous sixteenth century, at the same time as the characteristic Basque farmhouse – called *caserío* in Spanish and *baserri* in Basque – began to take shape. The earliest *caseríos* consisted of a ground floor containing accommodation for both humans and animals and a top floor where grain was stored. In later designs the people slept upstairs, but the cooking and eating continued to take place downstairs next to the stables. With their steep roofs, the *caseríos* look very like Alpine chalets. Most of them are held on tenure (although the number of owner-occupiers has been increasing since the fifties) and they almost always stand on the land which their occupants farm. The farms are small (about six hectares on average) and invariably include a wide variety of crops and livestock. They are as a result extremely uneconomic. Traditionally, the *caseríos* housed a larger social grouping than the nuclear family – a couple, their children, an unmarried brother or sister, the parents of either the husband or wife and one or two servants, all living under the same roof.

The status of Basque women has always been relatively high and it could well be that this is a last distant echo of the matriarchies which are thought to have existed throughout northern Spain in prehistoric times. The rural Basque country is also one of the few areas in Europe where there has never been more than a minimal division of family wealth. In much of the region this was achieved by transferring the *caserío*, the land attached to it and the family's entire wealth to the first-born (in some parts, regardless of whether the eldest child was male or female). Elsewhere, the parents chose whichever child appeared most capable.

Like many historically poor peoples, the Basques are renowned for the excellence of their cuisine and for eating to excess whenever they have the opportunity. The traditional Basque drinks are beer, cider and an acid 'green' wine called *txacolí*, but in recent times they have had increasing access to the excellent wines of the Rioja. Drunkenness does not incur quite the same fierce social disapproval that it does in the more southerly parts of Spain.

Another distinctive trait of traditional Basque society is the important role accorded to sport. The Basques have invented numerous games. The most famous is *pelota*, a game not unlike squash, which dates back at least to the sixteenth century when it was played by between eight and ten players wearing gloves and when, long before the development of professional sport in the rest of the world, there were semi-professional *pelota* players touring the Basque country giving demonstration matches. Since then, it has undergone numerous changes and several variants have evolved. The name of one of them, *Jai-Alai*, is sometimes used to describe the sport as a whole. The arm basket or *txistera* which is used in one form of the game – and which allows players to throw the ball at the wall at extraordinary speeds – is not as traditional as is sometimes assumed. It only made its appearance in the middle of the last century. Some of the other sports which still thrive in the Basque country are caber-tossing, wood-cutting, stone-lifting, tug-of-war, and one (*sokatira*) in which oxen are made to drag huge lumps of stone over short distances – often across town squares. There also used to be games similar to golf (*perratxe*) and cricket (*anikote*), but they have died out. Not surprisingly in view of where they live, the Basques are celebrated hill-walkers and rock-climbers, and their mountaineering clubs have traditionally been a breeding-ground for radical nationalist sentiment.

Perhaps because of the importance attached to sport, gambling has always played a big part in Basque life. It is not unusual to see a blackboard in a Basque bar smothered with wagers struck between the customers. Even the folk culture of the area has a competitive edge, exemplified by the *bertsolariak* or poetry competitions – in which the participants improvise in accordance with a given metre, each taking his cue from his rival's poem. But then the way in which most of the arts are expressed or practised in the Basque country is quite different from in the rest of Spain. Basque art is unusually symmetrical, for example. The music has none of the sinuousness of flamenco and it employs several instruments unique to the region. One is the *txistu*, a kind of flute with two finger-holes at the top and one at the bottom which is played one-handed, allowing the musician to beat a drum with his other hand. Then there is the *trikitrixa*, a small accordion, and the *alboca*, which is made from a bull's horn and sounds like the bagpipes. The songs are unusual within Spain in that each note corresponds to a syllable, and the dances, which include equivalents of the Greek glass dance and the Scottish sword dance, are more athletic than sensual, the object being to prove one's agility rather than one's grace.

To an even greater extent than the rest of Spain, this isolated, innocent society was quite unprepared for the new ideas that were to enter the country during the nineteenth century – and in particular the Napoleonic concept of a centralized state whose citizens should all be subject to the same laws. The Basques soon learnt to equate this new way of thinking with antipathy to the *fueros*. They were first abolished by Napoleon himself after the invasion of Spain, and then by the *liberales* when they seized power for a brief period in the 1820s. On each occasion they were re-established by the reactionary Fernando VII and so it was natural that when his brother, Don Carlos, raised the standard of absolutism, the Basques should be tempted to rally round it. But Don Carlos's fanatical Catholicism, which so appealed to the rural peasantry, appalled the urban bourgeoisie and throughout the Carlist Wars the bulk of the middle class in towns like Bilbao sided with Madrid against Carlism.

As a way of punishing the Basques for supporting the Carlist rebellion, the *fueros* of Biscay and Guipúzcoa were again revoked in

1841 following the First Carlist War, only to be restored subsequently. But at the end of the Second Carlist War in 1876 the government decreed the abolition of the *fueros* of Guipúzcoa, Biscay and Alava – but not those of Navarre – in a move that was never to be rescinded. All that remained of the Basques' traditional privileges in the three western provinces was a special tax-collection system called the *concierto económico*. But the problem with using the abolition of the *fueros* as a punishment was that it affected all Basques and not just those who had supported Carlism. In fact, the class whose economic prospects were most severely affected was the urban lower middle class, who had tended to support the central government. Within a few years of the abolition of the *fueros*, moreover, the Basque country was to embark upon a period of rapid industrialization in which this newly-disaffected lower middle class was to play a key role.

The origins of the industrialization of the region are to be found in its ample supplies of iron and timber and the abundance of fast-running streams and rivers. The period of fastest growth was between 1877 and 1902 when the industrialization was largely confined to Biscay. It was not until the end of the period that industry began to seep into Guipúzcoa. Although there were and are several large factories in the area, the outstanding characteristic of Basque industrialization has been a multitude of small workshops both inside and outside the cities. Whereas the upper-middle-class owners of the factories, together with the owners of the big banking and insurance concerns which grew up alongside them, tended to align themselves with the Spanish economic oligarchy, often acquiring titles of nobility in the process, the lower-middle-class bosses of the workshops came to regard industrialization as a process from which they had gained less than they had lost. It did not make them particularly rich, yet it caused an influx of hundreds of thousands of workers from other parts of Spain – *maketos*, they called them – who threatened the survival of Basque society in its traditional form.

The man who systematized their fears and resentments into the political ideology which we know as Basque nationalism was one Sabino de Arana Goiri. Born in 1865, Arana was the son of a Carlist whose political sympathies had earned him a period of exile in

France. Arana first entered the ideological battlefield at the age of thirty, appropriately enough with an article on the spelling in Basque of the word 'Basque'. His earliest writings were all about philology and etymology. In fact, one of his less fortunate legacies was to distort and complicate written Basque in an attempt to cleanse it of what he considered to be Hispanicisms. In his efforts to avoid any taint of centralism, he also invented a series of Basque christian names to replace Spanish ones, so that Luis, for example, became Koldobika. His most useful contribution was to provide the Basques with a word for the land they inhabited. There had always been a word for the Basque-speaking region – *Euskalerría* – but it had the disadvantage of excluding all those areas populated by Basques where Castilian had taken hold. Arana filled the gap with a neologism, *Euskería*. He later changed his mind and opted for *Euskadi* (often spelt *Euzkadi*), which means 'collection of Basques', and this is the word which has been used by Basque nationalists ever since to describe the nation they hope to create.

It was not until 1892 that Arana published his first full-length political work. As a political theorist, he was profoundly reactionary. He wanted to return the Basque country to a state of pre-industrial innocence in which society would be guided by the dictates of religion and the choice between socialism and capitalism would be irrelevant. At the core of his doctrine was an undisguised hatred for the immigrants – 'They came up here bringing with them their bullfights, their flamenco songs and dances, their "refined" language so abundant in blasphemous and filthy expressions, their fighting knives and so many, so many splendid means of "civilization",' he once wrote in bitterly ironic vein. What Arana sought was a kind of apartheid. In his writings he inveighed against 'mixed' marriages, and in the community centres or *batzokis* which he founded to spread the nationalist faith it was forbidden to play Spanish music or discuss Spanish politics. The rules of the first *batzokis* demonstrate the depth and intensity of Arana's racism – members were divided into three categories according to the number of their Basque grandparents and only those whose four grandparents had Basque surnames were entitled to hold executive office.

Arana's involvement in practical politics lasted from 1893, when he made a formal declaration of his ideals at a dinner given by a group of friends (the so-called Oath of Larrazábal), until his death in 1903. This period saw the launching of a nationalist newspaper and the birth of the Basque Nationalist Party (PNV) in 1894. At first, Arana and his supporters were ignored by Madrid but by 1895 the authorities were sufficiently concerned by their activities to gaol Arana for a few months. Four years later, the administration initiated a serious clampdown on regional nationalists of all kinds and Arana decided to change tack, with the result that during the latter years of his life his public demands were for autonomy rather than independence. He thus left an ambiguous legacy, but one which has enabled separatists and autonomists alike to find a home within the PNV.

For Basque nationalists, *Euskadi* consists of the French Basque country, which is traditionally (but not officially) divided into the three districts of Soule (Zuberoa), Labourd (Laburdi) and Basse-Navarre (Benavarra), and the four Spanish provinces which have a Basque population – Alava, Guipúzcoa, Biscay and Navarre. Nobody in Spain questions the 'Basqueness' of the first three provinces. Paradoxically, since Navarre was the only state ever to be created by the Basques, it is the province which has become the subject of controversy. This is partly because Navarre has always contained a large number of non-Basques, but it is also partly due to the failure of nationalism to strike roots there – at least until recently. The Navarrese, as we have seen, did not lose their *fuero* at the same time as the other provinces, so they already enjoyed a considerable measure of autonomy. Moreover, Navarre – in common with Alava – was a predominantly agricultural region, lacking the sort of industrial middle class which provided the PNV with much of its support in the two coastal provinces.

When in 1932 the Republican government asked the town councils of the Basque country to decide whether they wanted their respective provinces to form part of a self-governing *Euskadi*, the Navarrese chose to stay out. Alava also opted out shortly afterwards. The 1936 uprising widened the gulf between these two inland provinces on the one hand and Guipúzcoa and Biscay on the other. Given the deeply reactionary outlook of the Basque peasantry and the quasi-fascist ideology of the middle-class nationalists, there can be little doubt that – other things being equal – a majority of all four provinces would have come out in support of Franco's rebellion. Indeed that is what did happen in both Alava and Navarre. But by opting for autonomy Guipúzcoa and Biscay had thrown in their lot with the legally constituted government of Spain. They remained loyal to the Republic and the Republic returned the favour by granting them a provisional statute of home rule after the outbreak of the civil war in October 1936.

Guipúzcoa and Biscay were to pay dearly for their choice both during and after the war. Perhaps the most horrific single act committed by either side during the conflict was the systematic pulverization in April 1937 of Guernica – a town which, as has been seen, had a special place in the affections of the Biscayans in particular and the Basques in general. As soon as Guipúzcoa and Biscay had been subdued, moreover, Franco passed a special 'punitive decree', abolishing not only their provisional statute of home rule, but also the *conciertos económicos* of the two provinces – the last vestiges of the *fueros* that had been abolished sixty years earlier. Alava, on the other hand, was allowed to retain its *concierto económico* and Navarre was allowed to keep its *fuero* with all that that entailed. During the thirty-six years that Franco ruled Spain, Navarre remained an outstanding exception – an island of autonomy within a sea of uniformity, boasting its own legislature and government.

Having been publicly singled out for punishment, it is not surprising that Guipúzcoa and Biscay should be the only provinces of Spain in which there was sustained and violent opposition to the regime. The letters ETA – standing for *Euskadi Ta Askatasuna* (Euskadi and Freedom) first appeared during 1960, daubed on the walls of towns in the two coastal provinces. The movement which lay behind them had coalesced during the late fifties around a clandestine publication called *Ekin* (Action) set up by university students. In 1961 ETA carried out its first terrorist operation when some of its members tried to derail a train taking Francoist veterans to a rally in San Sebastián. The police response was savage. A hundred or so people were arrested. Many were tortured and some were charged, tried and sentenced to up to twenty years in gaol. But the leaders of ETA escaped to France. Thus began a cycle of terrorism and repression which has continued to this day.

The history of ETA is of a succession of internal conflicts. In

1966 the movement split into two groups, ETA-Zarra (Old ETA) and ETA-Berri (Young ETA). The latter forsook violence and eventually became the Movimiento Comunista de España. In 1970 ETA-Zarra divided into ETA 5th Assembly and ETA 6th Assembly. ETA 6th Assembly also gave up the armed struggle and re-named itself the Liga Comunista Revolucionaria. Then in the mid-seventies there was yet another parting of the ways when ETA 5th Assembly gave birth to ETA-Military and ETA-Politico-military. Finally in 1981 ETA-Politico-military was fatally weakened when it split into ETA-pm (7th Assembly), whose members dissolved their organization the following year, and ETA-pm (8th Assembly). Ever since then, ETA has consisted of ETA-military, plus the rejectionist rump of ETA-pm. The disputes which prompted these splits are too arcane and complicated to explain in detail here, but each time the more violent, less intellectual group has survived intact.

Although ETA was founded by university students and professional people, the active end of the organization rapidly came to be dominated by Basques from the *caseríos*. This was particularly true of the *Milis*. The region which provided them with more *gudaris* (soldiers) than any other was the Goierri, a Basque-speaking redoubt in Guipúzcoa and an area of strange contrasts between industry and agriculture where it is not unusual to see a *caserío* and a small factory or workshop side by side. The rise of ETA thus saw the reincorporation into the nationalist struggle of the peasant farmers who fought for Carlism. For all its revolutionary rhetoric, ETA – like the IRA – has always had a strong streak of conventional Roman Catholic morality and from time to time it has mounted campaigns against what it regards as decadent activities – threatening to murder drug pushers, for example, or planting bombs in bars and discos or in cinemas showing sex films.

The spread of violent, radical nationalism in the Basque country coincided with an altogether more peaceful process of cultural reaffirmation, particularly in so far as the language was concerned. Basque had been ceding terrain to Castilian – literally as well as metaphorically – for centuries, not because of repressive measures ordered from Madrid but because Castilian, being the dominant language of the peninsula, was more useful to those who had to maintain contacts with the outside world. It thus became the language of the upper and middle classes and of those such as the Alavese who were not cut off from their neighbours by mountains. But that is not to say that the repression of Basque when it was ordered by Franco was ineffective. Indeed, it was far more savage and enduring than anything put into effect in either Catalonia or Galicia and caused a good deal of linguistic self-censorship among the Basques themselves. Basque not only disappeared from the media, it virtually vanished from the streets as well. I have a friend from San Sebastián who is as Basque as it is possible to be, but who speaks not a word of her mother tongue because her parents, who were both Basque speakers, forbade her to speak it.

The late fifties, however, saw the start of a renaissance. It was then that the first *ikastolas* were founded. An *ikastola* is a primary school at which the lessons are given in Basque. In the early years many of them were run from private homes and while Franco was still alive they never had access to public funds. But although the authorities viewed the *ikastolas* with immense suspicion, going as far as to get the police to obtain lists of their staff and backers, they never had an argument for banning a movement which, however subversive, was undeniably helping to supplement the lack of state schooling which was characteristic of the entire Spanish education system at that time. Subsequently, many thousands of adult Basques embarked on the arduous task of learning their mother tongue, among them Carlos Garaikoetxea, who was to go on to become the first President of the Basque country's home-rule government.

Teachers reckon that it takes between 300 and 500 hours of study for a Castilian speaker to get to the point where he or she can chat easily. For several years, moreover, the revival of the language was hindered by the existence of no fewer than six – arguably seven – dialects (four in Spain and two or three in France). But in 1968 the Academy of the Basque Language completed the task of codifying a standard literary Basque called *euskera batua*. In 1990, a government survey found that more than a quarter of the population in the Spanish Basque country said they could speak *euskera* well.

Soon after the Socialists came to power in 1982, one of ETA's leaders was asked by *Le Monde* whether in view of the immense political changes that had taken place in Spain they might consider altering their policies. 'Even if it were to convert itself into a model of democracy,' he replied, 'it won't change things as far as we are concerned. We are not, nor have we been, nor shall we ever be Spaniards.' That may be true of him and his fellow gunmen, but – for better or worse – it is no longer true of the population of the Basque country as a whole. Almost a century of economic growth interrupted only by the civil war saw Biscay and Guipúzcoa, which were the poorest provinces in Spain in 1877, climb to first and third places respectively on the table of income *per capita* in 1973. Throughout that period, non-Basques in search of work flowed into the Basque country in an almost uninterrupted stream. The sixties saw the process of industrialization extended with even greater rapidity, first to Alava, and then to Navarre. By 1970 a higher proportion of the population of Alava was employed in industry than in any other province in Spain. All the other Basque provinces – including Navarre – were in the top ten.

In Navarre the new businesses mainly recruited their work-forces within the province, but in Alava they took them from outside, increasing the population by almost 50 per cent in ten years. By the end of the sixties, 30 per cent of the inhabitants of the Basque country had been born outside it. Today less than half the population are Basque in the sense that both their parents were born there, and even that proportion includes many whose grandparents came from other parts of Spain. The distinctive way of life of the Basque countryside is meanwhile fast disappearing. Some young people live in *caseríos* and work in factories or offices, but the majority go and live in the cities when they marry, returning only at weekends.

In spite of the viciously hostile reception their forebears received, the 'immigrants' have integrated well. One reason for this is that more than half came from León and Old Castile, which were not as wretchedly poor as some of the southern regions, and they tended to originate from within the rural lower middle class. By and large, they were better educated and more skilled than the typical migrant to Catalonia and although, for obvious reasons, fewer migrants learn Basque than learn Catalan, the rate of intermarriage between 'natives' and 'immigrants' has always been higher in the Basque country than in the Catalan provinces. A lot of the more recent migrants arrived to take up jobs as technicians, officials and foremen, so that nowadays there is very little difference between the average earnings of Basques and those from outside. A second reason for the relatively harmonious relations between 'natives' and 'immigrants' is that both were equally affected by repression under the dictatorship. Of the eleven 'states of exception' declared by Franco, four were nationwide. But of the remaining seven, no fewer than six applied to Guipúzcoa or Biscay or both. It has been estimated that by the early seventies a quarter of the entire Guardia Civil was stationed in the Basque country. Tear-gas does not discriminate between natives and immigrants. Nor did the police when they stopped people in the street, often submitting them to humiliating searches. A Bilbao or San Sebastián car number-plate was often enough to get you pulled off the road half-a-dozen times between the Basque country and Madrid.

That, of course, was exactly what ETA and its followers wanted. Immigration had made it increasingly difficult to justify separatism on racial grounds alone, but repression suffered by all sections of the community enabled the separatist left which supported ETA to argue with some credibility that the Basque country was subject to a unique double oppression by both capitalism and centralism. According to the view put forward by these revolutionary nationalists, or *abertzales* (patriots), economic and social liberation could only be attained through national independence.

By the time Franco died, many of the inhabitants of the Basque country, whatever their ethnic origins, felt deeply alienated from other Spaniards. Among children, it showed up in a survey carried out by the Biscay Chamber of Commerce in 1977. Schoolchildren were asked what they most felt themselves to be. Eliminating the 'Don't knows', the answers among native children were: 'Basque', 80 per cent; 'Spanish', 8 per cent; 'European', 12 per cent. The response from the immigrant children was: 'Basque', 48 per cent; 'Spanish', 28 per cent; 'European', 24 per cent. Among adults, it was demonstrated by the much higher than average abstention rates registered in the Basque country in the referendum held to endorse the political reform bill, and by the fact that a majority of the electorate in the Basque country failed to vote in the referendum on the constitution.* Over the years, many a son – and daughter – of immigrant parents has become involved with ETA or the network of organizations which offer it support.

ETA and its supporters were able to draw additional strength from the onset of recession in the late seventies. Its effects were particularly savage in the Basque country. This was partly because of the region's dependence on uncompetitive 'rustbelt' industries, but also partly – and ironically – because ETA's own activities were deterring investment. Between 1973 and 1979, Biscay and Guipúzcoa dropped from first and third places on the table of income *per capita* to ninth and sixth place respectively.

In retrospect, it can be seen that the late seventies were ETA's heyday. Its bloodiest year was 1980, when it was responsible for the deaths of 118 people. Since then a variety of factors have combined to reduce the level of violence – the winding-up of ETA-pm, growing cooperation between the Spanish and French governments, especially since Spain joined France in the European Union, and – partly because of that – increasingly effective police work. It has taken longer for the experience of self-government, and a modest improvement in the economic fortunes of the Basque country, to erode popular support for ETA's political apologists in Herri Batasuna.

Herri Batasuna (People's Unity) has never been the biggest party in the Basque country. The PNV and the PSOE have always been ahead of it, but its share of the vote grew with successive general elections until it peaked in 1986. Since then, it has been falling steadily, if slowly. A study published at the end of the eighties found that there had been a sharp drop in support for independence as a solution to the problems of the Basque country. By 1987 it was favoured by only 17 per cent of the population, compared with 34 per cent in 1979. The number of would-be separatists in the Basque country was actually lower than in Scotland. But while Madrid has been gradually solving the Basque question, the Basques have been quietly changing the question. Herri Batasuna has increasingly become a refuge for radical ecologists, feminists, and other rebels

---

* This was also the case in Galicia, but more because of apathy than antipathy What distinguished the Basque country, moreover, was that it was also the region with the highest 'no' vote – 23·5 per cent.

whose dissatisfaction with society is not primarily, or even minimally, nationalist in origin. Providing the people of the Basque country with an acceptable measure of home rule, therefore, does not guarantee that the problems posed by Herri Batasuna and ETA will be swiftly resolved.

In 1992, ETA was dealt the severest blow it had ever suffered with the arrest in France of its entire leadership. Yet two years later, the Spanish Interior Minister reported that it had no fewer than ten units still operating within the country. An indication of how far the organization has moved away from its roots is that, at the time of writing, one of its most wanted terrorists is the daughter of parents from Salamanca.

CHAPTER 28

The Catalans

At Barcelona's Prat airport, well-groomed executives march to and fro across the concourse with a serious, purposeful air. On your way into the city you will see that every other hoarding sports an advertisement for this or that *caixa*, or savings bank. And if you have already spent some time in Spain, it will strike you that the Catalans spend less time over their meals than other Spaniards, and that there are more self-service restaurants in Barcelona than in the other major cities. The Catalans' legendary industriousness has always meant that Barcelona has been among the most prosperous cities in Spain.

Its prosperity, taken in conjunction with its location – close by France on the shores of the Mediterranean – has also meant that it has consistently been the most cosmopolitan of Spanish cities. Most of the ideas that have shaped Spain's modern history – republicanism, federalism, anarchism, syndicalism and communism – have found their way into Spain by way of Catalonia. Fashions – whether in clothing, philosophy or art – have tended to take hold in Barcelona several years before they gained acceptance in Madrid.

In an ideal world, one feels, the Catalans would not mind swapping places with the Belgians or the Dutch. There is a poem by Catalonia's greatest modern poet, Salvador Espriu, which captures perfectly the ambivalence of his fellow-countrymen's attitude to Spain:

> Oh, how tired I am of my cowardly
> old, so savage land!
> How I should like to get away
> to the North,

where they say that the people are clean,
and decent, refined, rich, free
aware and happy! (. . .)
Yet I am destined never to realize my dream
and here I shall remain until death,
for I too am wild and cowardly.
And, what is more, I love,
with a despairing sorrow,
this my poor,
dirty, sad, hapless homeland.

It is significant, however, that Espriu ends up resigning himself to his lot. Catalan dissatisfaction has for the most part tended to be expressed as resentment, indignation and a demand for a substantial say in the running of their own affairs, rather than in terms of outright separatism. Madrid politicians are fond of saying that the difference between an ambitious Basque politician and an ambitious Catalan politician is that the first dreams of being Prime Minister of an independent *Euskadi*, whereas the second dreams of being Prime Minister of Spain.

One reason why the separatist instinct has been less pronounced in Catalonia is that the Catalans, though they tend to have somewhat fairer skin and lighter hair, would not and could not claim to be racially different from other Spaniards. But it is also a reflection of the Catalans' most highly prized virtue – *seny*. There is no exact translation of *seny*. Perhaps the nearest equivalent is the northern English term 'nous' – good old common sense. Respect for *seny* makes the Catalans realistic, earnest, tolerant and at times a bit censorious. Yet it sits uneasily with their frequently tumultuous history.

Barcelona has come under full-scale military attack by the forces of the central government on numerous occasions, usually as a consequence of uprisings and revolutions. The popularity of anarchism among the workers of Catalonia turned Barcelona into the most violent city in Europe during the early part of this century, and at the height of the civil war the Catalan capital was the scene of a bloody street war between conflicting Republican factions.

This is how the Catalan writer and academic, Victor Alba,

squares the circle: 'The opposite of *seny* is *arrauxment*: an ecstasy of violence. But *arrauxment* is seen as an ultimate consequence of *seny*. Because they [the Catalans] are convinced that when they act impetuously they are being sensible . . . When a thing is not the way it ought to be, when a situation is not "sensible", the common-sense thing to do is to oppose it abruptly, violently.' Another explanation I have seen put forward is that the Catalans fall into two very distinct groups – those who are *sorrut* (antisocial) and those who are *trempat* (spontaneous, likeable, *simpático*) – and that the violent changes of direction in Catalan political history are the product of their uneasy co-existence.

A similarly paradoxical pattern can be identified in Catalan culture. For the most part, it is rather prim and humdrum. But from time to time it throws up an outstandingly original figure. In the Middle Ages, there was Ramón Llull, the multilingual Majorcan missionary who opposed the Crusades and put forward the theory that the earth was round, and Anselm Turmeda, a renegade Franciscan who converted to Islam and is regarded as a saint in North Africa. More recently, Catalonia has produced Salvador Dalí and two architects whose works stand out like a string of beacons amid the stolidly bourgeois edifices of Barcelona – Antoni Gaudí, whose giant, eccentric cathedral, the Sagrada Familia, was started in 1882 and is likely to take until about 2020 to complete, and Ricardo Bofill, who has been responsible for, among other things, converting a cement works into an office block that looks like a medieval castle.

What unites this curiously heterogeneous and contradictory people is their language. Their pride in it is well-nigh limitless and they speak it at every opportunity. When two Catalan speakers and a Castilian speaker are talking together, the Catalans will address the Castilian speaker in Castilian, but as often as not they will address each other in Catalan – something that profoundly irritates other Spaniards.

Written down, Catalan looks like a cross between Spanish and French, but spoken it has a ruggedness which is lacking in either. It is unusually rich in monosyllabic words – to the point that Catalan poets have constructed entire poems out of them – and the syllables of multisyllabic words are particularly strongly stressed. The diphthongs 'au', 'eu' and 'iu' crop up with great frequency so that to a foreigner it sounds a bit like Portuguese.

Just about the worst gaffe you can make when speaking to a Catalan is to refer to his or her language as a dialect. Catalan is no more a dialect of Castilian than Castilian is a dialect of Catalan. Or, to put it another way, both – like French and Italian – are dialects of Latin. The first recognizably Catalan words were found in documents written in the ninth century, although the language is thought to have begun to evolve in the seventh or eighth century. It spread in the wake of Catalonia's imperial expansion to an area much bigger than the four provinces of Gerona, Lérida, Tarragona and Barcelona which comprise the Principality of Catalonia itself. It is also spoken along a 15- to 30-kilometre-deep strip of Aragonese territory bordering the Principality, in about two-thirds of the region of Valencia, throughout the Balearic Islands, in the co-Principality of Andorra and in that part of the French department of Pyrénées Orientales historically known as Roussillon. It is also spoken in Alguer, a walled town on the west coast of Sardinia, which was captured and populated by Catalans in the fourteenth century. Until the early 1950s it could still be heard in San Agustin, Florida, a town conquered by Menorcans in the eighteenth century. Catalan is the native language of something like 6,500,000 people, which makes it more widely spoken than several better-known languages such as Danish, Finnish and Norwegian.

As it spread, differences began to arise between Catalan as it was spoken in the eastern and western parts of the Catalan-speaking world. The dividing line runs from a point just to the east of Andorra to a point just to the west of Tarragona. The internal fragmentation of the language does not stop there. Both dialects can be further divided into sub-dialects – at least three within eastern Catalan (central, Roussillonaise and Balearic) and two within western Catalan (north-western and Valencian), according to the pronunciation of the first person singular of the first conjugation indicative. 'I sing' is pronounced 'cantu' in Barcelona and most of Catalonia proper, 'canti' in Roussillon, 'cant' in the Balearic Islands, 'canto' in Lérida and along the Aragonese fringe, and 'cante' in Valencia. There are even what might be called sub-sub-dialects of both Balearic and Valencian – three of them in each case corresponding to Mallorca, Menorca and Ibiza and to the northern, central and southern parts of Catalan-speaking Valencia. It is typical of the rampant localism of Spain that many of the inhabitants of the Balearic Islands and Valencia object to their language being called Catalan at all. So as not to offend local sensibilities, attempts have been made in the past to get people to call it *bacavés* (a neologism derived from the initial letters of *B*alearic, *C*atalan and *V*alencian).

Catalonia was among the most thoroughly Romanized regions of Iberia and had only the briefest contact with the Moslems. It was, moreover, the only area to be repopulated on a large scale by *reconquistadores* from outside the peninsula. The Franks' contribution to the settlement of Catalonia was only the first of the many links which were to be established between the Catalans (who were themselves originally called *francos* by other Spaniards) and the people living in what is now France. The Catalans have always been far more receptive to French ideas and attitudes than other Spaniards, who tend in fact heartily to dislike the French.

The period of Catalonia's greatest glory lasted from the twelfth to the fourteenth centuries, during which time the Catalans were allied with the Aragonese. Their confederacy was a precociously sophisticated union in which the two very different partners each allowed to retain their own laws, customs and language under the same crown. As early as the beginning of the thirteenth century, Catalonia had a Corts or parliament consisting of three chambers – one for the nobility, one for the bourgeoisie and another for the clergy. The sovereigns of the confederation subsequently undertook to call the Corts once a year and not to pass any laws without its consent. The Corts set up a committee of twenty-four members (eight from each chamber) whose job it was to collect taxes. In 1359 this body – the *Generalitat* – took over responsibility for the way the money was spent as well as the way it was collected, thus becoming what was arguably the world's first parliamentary government. As one medieval chronicler remarked, the rulers of Catalonia and Aragón were 'not the masters of their subjects, but their co-rulers'.

By the middle of the fourteenth century the Catalan–Aragonese confederation ruled not only the Balearic Islands and the city and region of Valencia, but also Sardinia, Corsica and much of present-day Greece. A member of its royal family sat on the throne of Sicily and it controlled the gold trade with the Sudan. Today the world has all but forgotten Catalonia's golden age, but the memory of her power and influence lives on in the folk-sayings of the Mediterranean. In Sicily, recalcitrant children are told to 'do what I say or I'll call the Catalans' and in Thrace you can do no worse than to wish on your enemy 'the Catalan vengeance'. A number of naval and financial terms in Castilian derive from Catalan, including probably the word *peseta*.

A banking collapse in 1381 caused by the cost of financing too many imperial wars, the rise of the Ottoman Empire and the loss of the gold trade sent Barcelona into decline even before the discovery of America shifted the geographical advantage from the Mediterranean to the Atlantic. When the city's fortunes finally took a turn for the better in the nineteenth century, it was due not so much to commerce as to industry, and in particular the cotton business.

It was during the nineteenth century that the Catalans rediscovered themselves through their language. After the unification of Spain, the ruling class throughout the country had adopted Castilian as a mark of status. Catalan became the language of the peasantry and the culture associated with it died out. But in the last century it became the medium for a literary revival which succeeded in enhancing the status of the language sufficiently for it to be re-adopted by the middle and upper classes, thereby regaining its respectability and influence.

The Catalan *Renaixença*, as it is called, began in the most curious manner. In 1833 a minor poet, Bonaventura Carles Aribau, published a poem in Catalan called 'Ode to the Fatherland'. He had intended it simply as a birthday present for his patron, another Catalan, called Gaspar Remisa i Niarous, who was at that time head of the Royal Treasury. But the poem was published in a Barcelona newspaper and made a great impact on the intellectual community. Aribau, a dedicated centralist, never again published anything of importance and spent the rest of his life working for the government and the monarchy in Madrid. But the renewed interest in Catalan which he had stimulated grew inexorably. In 1859 an annual poetry competition called the Floral Games was inaugurated and in 1877 it brought to light one of Spain's greatest modern literary figures,

Jacint Verdaguer. Several other outstanding writers emerged from Catalonia during the late nineteenth and early twentieth centuries – the playwright Angel Guimerá, the novelist Narcís Oller and the poet Joan Maragall.

The same period also saw the standardization of the language itself. In 1907 an Institut d'Estudis Catalans was founded and four years later the scientific section of the institute asked the philological section to prepare a report on how the spelling of Catalan might be standardized. This seemingly modest request begged a multitude of questions about grammar and vocabulary, many of which were resolved when the report was published in 1913 with the title of *Normes Ortográfiques*. The researcher who had made the most decisive contribution to the *Normes* was an engineer-turned-philologist called Pompeu Fabra. Soon afterwards he set about compiling a full-scale dictionary. Published in 1932, it is the cornerstone of modern Catalan.

The *Renaixença* provided the raw material and the driving force for the political movement known as Catalanism, which appeared towards the end of the last century. Catalanism was a broad church, embracing all those who believed in Catalonia's separate identity and who were keen to see it recognized, whether in the form of autonomy or nationhood. The father of Catalanism, Valentí Almirall, author of *Lo Catalanisme*, was essentially a regionalist. But within a few years his ideas were given a sharper, more nationalistic edge by Enric Prat de la Riba, who provided the movement with its first political programme and whose Catalan Union supplied it with its earliest political organization. Except during its earliest years, Catalanism was never represented by a single party. It provided the inspiration for parties of the right and the left and for parties of all classes, of which by far the most influential was the conservative upper-middle-class Lliga. But what Catalanism lacked in cohesion it more than compensated for in the depth and breadth of its appeal within the community and this point was never lost on Madrid.

The first attempt to solve 'the Catalan problem' was made shortly before the First World War when the Spanish government authorized provincial administrations to pool their functions with those of their neighbours to form *Mancomunidades*. The four Catalan provinces were the only ones in Spain to take advantage of the opportunity. The Catalan *Mancomunidad* lasted for barely a decade until it was suppressed by Primo de Rivera. It was not a particularly successful experiment. The degree of autonomy it offered was extremely limited and at one stage it had to go into debt because of a lack of financial support from the government.

In the brief period between the fall of Primo de Rivera and the resignation of Alfonso XIII, the parties of the Spanish Republican left signed a pact with the main regional nationalist parties (the so-called Pact of San Sebastián), promising that if and when they came to power they would grant home-rule statutes to Catalonia, Galicia and the Basque country. But on 14 April 1931 – two days after the local elections which persuaded the King to flee the country – nationalists in Barcelona pre-empted orderly progress towards home rule by proclaiming a Catalan Republic as part of an Iberian Federation, even though no such thing existed, nor was envisaged. They were subsequently persuaded by the leaders of the central government to change the name of the administration they had set up to the Government of the *Generalitat* in memory of the medieval institution of the same name. An assembly elected by Catalonia's town councillors later drew up a draft statute which won over-whelming endorsement in a referendum (562,691 votes for, 3,276 votes against, with 195,501 abstentions). A considerably watered-down version of the draft statute (which gave the Catalans control over health and welfare, for example, but not education) was approved by the Cortes on 9 September 1932. However, the financial powers transferred to the *Generalitat* in the ensuing months were severely restricted.

Two years later the demagogic anti-Catalanist, Alejandro Lerroux, succeeded in forcing the *Generalitat* to accept right- as well as left-wing members. This was anathema to the left, who believed that the right could not and would not support the Republic. The President of the *Generalitat*, Lluis Companys, responded by proclaiming 'the Catalan state of the Spanish Federal Republic'. The Civil Governor of Barcelona, himself a Catalan, declared war on the new government, and the offices of the *Generalitat* and the city hall both came under bombardment before Companys surrendered along with his entire government. The Cortes suspended the Catalan parliament and appointed a Governor-General to carry out the functions of the *Generalitat*. In 1935 the members of the *Generalitat* were each sentenced to thirty years in gaol, but benefited from the amnesty for political prisoners which was proclaimed when the left-wing Popular Front came to power as a result of the elections in February 1936.

The statute of autonomy was restored and, in the period immediately after the outbreak of civil war, the *Generalitat* was able to grab many of the powers which had been denied it between 1932 and 1934. As Franco and his troops steadily gained the upper hand and the Republicans were pushed back into a progressively smaller area, the capital was moved from Madrid to Valencia and then from Valencia to Barcelona, so that it was in Barcelona that the Republic met its end. Companys fled to France, only to be arrested by the Gestapo after the German invasion. They handed him over to Franco, who ordered him to be executed in secret. It later emerged that the President of the *Generalitat*'s last words – shouted out a matter of seconds before the execution squad opened fire – were '*¡Visca Catalunya!*' ('Long live Catalonia!')

Franco's victory unleashed a campaign against the Catalan language unparalleled in the region's history. Publishing houses, bookshops, and public and private libraries were searched for Catalan books and those that were found were destroyed. Pompeu Fabra's priceless collection was burned in the street. The names of villages and towns were Castilianized. The Street of the Virgin of Monserrat (the patron of Catalonia) became the Street of the Redeemer and the Library of Catalonia was renamed the Central Library. In the mid-forties permission was granted for the publication of books in Catalan and the staging of plays in Catalan. But it remained banned from radio and television, the daily press and in schools. The Institut maintained a curious half-tolerated, half-clandestine existence under Franco. It held weekly meetings, ran courses on the language, literature and history of Catalonia in private houses, gave receptions, and went as far as to publish books and pamphlets, some of which were even bought by the government for display at international exhibitions.

Throughout the first two decades of Franco's rule, Catalonia was the principal source of opposition to his regime. In 1944 the

Communists made a disastrous attempt to invade the country through the Valle de Arán, and between 1947 and 1949 the anarchists staged a bloody but futile campaign of shootings, bombings and hold-ups in Barcelona. The failure of these attempts to overthrow Franco's regime by force ushered in a period when opposition was characterized by mass public protests. Most of the more successful ones took place in Catalonia. The pattern was set in 1948 when opponents of Franco's rule succeeded in getting 100,000 people to attend a ceremony celebrating the enthronement of the Virgin of Monserrat. In 1951 the first city-wide general strike in post-war Spain was held in Barcelona, which was also the scene of mass public transport boycotts in 1951 and 1956.

But being the focus of opposition and promoting it are two very different things and the truth is that the role played by Catalan nationalists in fighting Franco was by and large a pretty tame one. There was a Catalan Liberation Front, but it never had a fraction of the support or made a hundredth of the impact of ETA. Barcelona's students were in the forefront of the search for an independent student movement but once it had been formed the leadership was exercised from Madrid. The most dramatic acts of resistance to come out of Catalonia were symbolic ones, such as when the audience at the Palau de la Música sang the unofficial national anthem of Catalonia in front of Franco when he was on a visit to the area in 1960.

The virtual absence of violent nationalism meant that the inhabitants of Catalonia were not subjected to the same relentless oppression that helped to homogenize the population of the Basque country, and so the differences between 'native' and 'immigrant' were not erased – or disguised – in Catalonia to the same extent as in the Basque country.

The growth of industry, first in and around Barcelona and then in the other provincial capitals of Catalonia, had created a demand for labour that the Catalans were quite unable to satisfy by themselves. About half the population of Catalonia today is of 'immigrant' stock and it has been estimated that there will be no 'pure' Catalans left by the year 2040.

What is more, not only did the percentage of immigrants from other parts of Spain grow, but so did the catchment area from which they were drawn. And as it grew, it took in areas which were less and less like Catalonia and whose population was therefore less and less sympathetic to Catalanism. The earliest migration was of rural Catalans to Barcelona in the early part of the last century. By the end of the nineteenth century, the immigrants came from Majorca and Valencia. At the beginning of this century, they came mostly from Aragón, with which Catalonia has close historic ties. In the 1920s, the newcomers were predominantly from Murcia, which – although Castilian-speaking – was partly conquered by Catalans. But the influx after the civil war and during the *años de desarrollo* consisted of an increasing proportion of Andalusians. Since this was by far the largest and longest 'wave', the Andalusians now form the biggest single group of 'immigrants' in Catalonia. With their gracious, passionate temperaments and their love of flamenco and bullfighting, the Andalusians are not merely not Catalan but the heirs to a very potent alternative culture.

This is only one of several reasons why it proved more difficult to assimilate the most recent wave of immigrants than it had been to integrate those who arrived before the civil war. The immigrants of the twenties arrived at a rate of between 25,000 and 35,000 a year, their numbers peaking in the period from 1927 to 1929 because of the need for labourers to complete two major public works, the Barcelona Metro and the 1929 Exposición Universal de Montjuic. At the time, it must have seemed as if they would never be absorbed. The 'Murcians' as they were all called – even though a sizeable minority originated elsewhere – were a disorderly and uncouth crowd. Crimes of passion, previously almost unknown in Catalonia, became quite common. Even after they could afford to buy better food, many stuck to the lunch of bread and onion which had sustained them in the fields of the poor south. 'Murcian' acquired a pejorative connotation – first in Catalonia and then in the rest of Spain – which it has never quite lost.

The attitudes and the behaviour of the 'Murcians' appalled the native Catalans who dubbed them *Xarnegos* (a word probably derived from *Xarnec*, a pejorative expression for someone who is half Catalan and half French) and accused them of 'coming to take the bread out of our mouths'. This wholly unfair accusation was based on the fact that a tiny minority of immigrants had been imported as strike-breakers – by Catalan businessmen. During the civil war, the denizens of the immigrant quarter of Torrasa put up a famous notice at the entrance to their suburb which read 'Catalonia stops here. This is the start of Murcia', and in one area the anarchists pre-empted Franco by putting up posters forbidding people to speak Catalan in the streets. Nevertheless, by then most of the immigrants of the twenties had begun to digest influences that would turn them into Catalans. In typically Catalan fashion, their assimilation took place by way of the language.

In the thirties it was not difficult to learn – in fact it would have been hard for a Castilian speaker not to have picked up – a working knowledge of Catalan. The immigrants came to live in districts where the shopkeepers spoke Catalan, and went to work in factories and on sites where in all probability the foreman spoke Catalan. There was Catalan on the radio and for those who could read there was Catalan in the press. Their children learnt Catalan at school. By the time a further wave of immigrants began to arrive, the 'Murcians' of the twenties were in a position to look down on the benighted newcomers from the standpoint of a common language and shared experiences. The elderly 'Murcian' whose support for Catalan nationalism was more passionate than that of any native and who had christened his eldest daughter Monserrat became a recognized stereotype in Catalan society.

The most important reason why the post-war immigrants were so difficult to assimilate was their sheer numbers – a quarter of a million in the forties, nearly half a million during the fifties and almost a million during the sixties. The tidal wave swept over Barcelona and into the rest of Catalonia. When Spain's 'economic miracle' came to an end, almost one in five of the population of the other three provinces was of immigrant stock. Because of their numbers, the immigrants of the forties, fifties and sixties often ended up in areas where only the priest, the doctor and perhaps the schoolteachers and the shopkeepers were Catalans by origin.

It is against this background that the freedom the Catalans have acquired since the return of democracy to teach and promote their language must be judged, for it has been the principal factor in making Catalonia more homogenous again.

By the time that Franco died, the Catalan language had entered a crisis. Research highlighted two specific malaises which, if allowed to continue, would sooner or later finish it off.

The first was that, since Catalan had not been taught in schools, could not be written in the press and was not used by officialdom, a lot of people who could speak Catalan were nevertheless illiterate in it. And even those Catalans who were literate in their own language were so accustomed to a world in which documents, books and newspapers were in Castilian that they found it tiring to read and write in Catalan. The second problem – which only became apparent as the result of a survey published in 1978 – was that, contrary to what one might expect, fewer people spoke Catalan at home than spoke it at work, in the shops and so on. This, the survey found, was because where a native had married an immigrant the couple almost always ended up speaking Castilian, which the Catalan-speaking partner had learned properly at school, rather than Catalan, which the Castilian-speaking partner had picked up unsystematically. It was clear that unless something was done the children of these marriages would grow up using only Castilian.

Since the restoration of the *Generalitat*, immense changes have been brought about. Catalan is to be seen on road and street signs throughout the Principality (and increasingly in the Balearic Islands and Valencia as well). It can be heard on radio and television. Catalans are free to publish newspapers and magazines in their mother tongue. And the vast majority of their children are nowadays not only taught Catalan, but taught *in* Catalan.

A comprehensive recent compilation* suggested that between 1975 and 1986, the number of Catalan-speakers in Catalonia itself had risen from 60 per cent to 64 per cent, but that in both the other Catalan-speaking areas the proportion had continued to fall – from 55 per cent to 49 per cent in Valencia, and from 75 per cent to 71 per cent in the Balearic Islands. However, the number of people who could understand Catalan was reckoned to have increased over the same period in all three regions. It was up from 80 to 90 per cent in the Principality, from 70 to 74 per cent in the Valencia region, and from 80 to 89 per cent in the Balearics.

Even so, the figures tend to understate the scale of the changes

---

* In Francesc Vallverdú, *L'ús del Català: un futur controvertit.*

which have taken place since the return of democracy. An entire generation which is more than simply bilingual has already emerged from schools in Catalonia. The young people who compose it are usually more at ease speaking, and even reading and writing, Catalan.* Their speech is frequently shot through with Castilianisms and upsets the purists, who have reproachfully dubbed it 'Catalan light'. But it is Catalan for all that, and a lot of those who speak it make frequent grammatical errors when they have to communicate in Castilian.

Nationalists pooh-pooh the idea that Catalonia is on its way to something closer to monolinguism than bilingualism. They point out that the new commercial television channels, for example, transmit exclusively in Castilian. Nevertheless, one suspects that their denials are coloured by fear of the reaction in Madrid to Catalonia's rapidly growing *de facto* separateness from the rest of Spain. It is certainly not difficult to imagine that within, say, a quarter of a century Castilian in Catalonia could occupy a position rather like that of English in Scandinavia – a second language which people are able to speak exceptionally well, but a second language nevertheless.

---

*A survey carried out for the Barcelona edition of *El País* in 1989 showed that, for the first time since figures have been recorded, a section of the population – those aged between fourteen and seventeen – preferred to read in Catalan.

CHAPTER 29

The Galicians

In 1993, Galicia – the part of Spain that juts out over Portugal – made a valiant effort to draw attention to itself. Smarting at having been left out of the previous year's festivities, the regional authorities declared 1993 to be the Año Jacobeo (or Xacobeo in the Galicians' own language). A wide range of cultural and other events was organized to capitalize on the reviving popularity of the pilgrimage to Santiago de Compostela. As a result the hotels of Santiago were packed, a lot more visitors were lured to the rest of Galicia than might otherwise have come, and Spain's tourist advertising was forced to concentrate on the region as never before.

This alone, it could be argued, made the whole costly exercise worthwhile, for in modern times Galicia – poor, damp and difficult to reach – has been among the least-known parts of Western Europe. Yet it is a region with a distinctive character whose claims to have its identity recognized are arguably just as good as those of Catalonia.

The Galicians themselves claim that the roots of their uniqueness are ethnic. Galicia, they will say, is the region of Spain in which the Celts most comprehensively swamped the indigenous population when they arrived in the peninsula around 1000 BC. Exhibit Number 1 is the *gaita*, or bagpipes – as traditional in Galicia as in Scotland or Ireland.

There is a good deal of evidence, though, to suggest that all this is a mid-nineteenth-century myth propagated by Galicia's nationalists. In ancient times, the region seems to have been no more Celtic than the rest of the peninsula, and any Celtic speech there was dead long before the end of Roman rule.

Nevertheless, Galicia does have a language of its own, which the

Galicians call *galego* and other Spaniards call *gallego*. If Catalan looks like a cross between French and Spanish, then Galician looks like a cross between Spanish and Portuguese. Once again, it needs to be stressed that Galician – like Catalan – is a language in its own right, even if a bastardized form known as *castrapo*, which is littered with Castilianisms, probably does qualify as a dialect (though as a dialect of Galician rather than Spanish). The existence of *castrapo* makes it difficult to be categoric about the number of vernacular language speakers. A Spanish government survey in 1990 put the proportion of Galicians who spoke Galician 'well' at 63 per cent, compared with a figure of 68 per cent for Catalan in Catalonia and only 26 per cent for Basque.

There are three variants: western, central and eastern, the first of which is further divided into northern and southern sub-dialects. During the seventies, attempts were made by both the Royal Galician Academy and the Galician Language Institute at the University of Santiago de Compostela to standardize the spelling and grammar. But neither succeeded in winning universal acceptance for the norms they proposed. Nevertheless, a sort of standard Galician is beginning to emerge naturally, as the language spoken in the major cities becomes more and more homogeneous. The threat to the survival of the language does not derive from its diversity but from other factors. Whereas Catalan is 'the language of the people' in the sense that it is spoken in every stratum of society, Galician is the language of the people in the sense that it is spoken by the 'masses'. With the exception of a few generally rather self-conscious intellectuals, the members of Galicia's small but influential upper and middle classes speak Spanish. There is therefore an identification in the public mind between social advancement and speaking Castilian, which, as Galicia develops and progresses, could lead its inhabitants to abandon their native tongue. Already in aspiring working-class families the children are brought up to speak Castilian.

The Galicians may not in fact share with the Irish, Welsh and Bretons a common ancestry, but they do live in a similarly wind-swept, rain-sodden land on the edge of the Atlantic, and so it is not perhaps surprising that they should have many of the characteristics associated with Celtic races – a genius for poetry, a love of music, a fascination with death and a tendency towards melancholy.

Nevertheless the last of these traits could as easily derive from the dreadful hardships to which the Galicians have been subjected during the course of their unhappy history. 'Spain's Voltaire', the Benedictine monk Benito Feijóo who visited the area in the middle of the eighteenth century, has left this account of the typical Galician peasant:

Four rags cover his body or perhaps, given the number of tears in them, it would be better to say uncover it. His accommodation is as full of holes as his clothing, to the extent that the wind and the rain enter it at will. His food consists of a bit of black bread accompanied by some kind of milk product or some sort of root vegetable, but in such tiny quantities that there are those who have scarcely ever in their life risen satisfied from the table. Add to these miseries the tough, relentless manual labour which lasts from the first rays of dawn until the onset of night and anyone will be able to see that the life of these wretched peasants is more arduous than that of the criminals whom the courts send to the galleys.

Famines were quite frequent and whenever they occurred, as the local records bear witness, the streets of the major cities echoed to the laments and entreaties of semi-naked walking skeletons.

The last great famine was in 1853–4, but even today Galicia is the scene of considerable hardship. Figures for 1992* indicated that, on the basis of purchasing power, Galicia was the poorest of Spain's seventeen Autonomous Communities, with a figure 85 per cent that of the national average. Its inland provinces of Lugo and Orense are the last places in Spain where you will see – and with disconcerting frequency – old women trudging along country lanes laden down like pack animals with crops or kindling.

Galicia is a victim of the dynamics of Spanish history. Unlike Catalonia, it was Romanized slowly and incompletely. But in common with the Catalans, the Galicians had very little contact with the Moslems. One of the earliest Asturian monarchs seems to have asserted his control over the coast in the middle of the eighth century, although it was only in the reign of his grandson in the first half of the ninth century that the whole region was finally restored to Christian rule. Thereafter, however, the attention of its rulers was drawn inexorably southwards by the desire to reconquer

* Published in the *Anuario El País, 1993*.

the peninsula. As power passed to the states to which the Asturian monarchy gave birth – first León and then Castile – the Galicians found themselves progressively more isolated from the centre of power.

The Galicians' frustration at being tied to a crown whose interests were not their own manifested itself at a very early stage in uprisings organized by the nobility and it is against this background of discontent within the region that the discovery of St James's tomb should be seen.

According to legend, it was found by a shepherd in a field to which he was guided by a star. The field became the site of a cathedral and of a city which took the name of Sant Iago (St James) de Campus Stellae (of the field of the star). An alternative etymology is offered by the fact that St James's supposed tomb lies in what had previously been a burial ground. Compostela, according to this view, derives from *composta* (burial ground) plus the diminutive *-ela*.

At all events, the discovery provided the Asturian monarchy and its successors with a reason – or perhaps a pretext – for showering gifts and privileges on the town which grew up around the tomb. Right up until the last century the Spanish monarch paid an annual sum to the city, called the *voto de Santiago*, ostensibly in return for the saint's patronage. The effect was to create within a potentially turbulent province a city which had every reason to support the central government.

As early as the fourteenth century, the Galicians were left without any representation in the Cortes. They played no part in the *Mesta*, the sheep-farming cartel whose influence brought such benefit to the farmers of the *meseta*, or in the trade with the Americas which was bestowed on the Andalusians, or in the industrial revolutions which transformed the Catalan and Basque provinces. Instead, they became a favourite target for steep taxes and military levies.

The railway from Madrid did not reach Galicia until 1883 and as the region entered the twentieth century its only industries, apart from the naval dockyard at La Bazán founded in the eighteenth century, were a modest textile industry in Corunna, a few tobacco-manufacturing and food-processing businesses and some canning. Typically, the cans came from elsewhere. The region was perhaps entitled to expect preferential treatment from Franco, who was himself a Galician from El Ferrol. But although the region undoubtedly benefited from the general increase in living standards throughout Spain during the *años de desarrollo*, during which period it acquired some important new factories (notably the Citroën plant at Vigo), the main change was a more efficient exploitation of the region's natural resources – hydroelectricity and timber. As recently as 1989, 34 per cent of the population still worked on the land – by far the highest proportion in any region of Spain.

Galicia's agriculture is woefully backward. Unlike most of the other peoples of early northern Spain, the Galicians were unable to relieve the pressure of population growth by mass migration southwards. The Asturians were able to spread into León and ultimately Estremadura. The Basques and Cantabrians were able to spread into Castile and ultimately Andalusia. The Aragonese and the Catalans had Valencia. But Galicia's southward expansion was blocked by the creation of Portugal, a state with which Galicians had no political ties. The only other people who found themselves in this predicament were the Navarrese. But unlike Galicia which was bounded by the sea, Navarre could and did expand northwards.

Hemmed in on all sides, the Galicians had no option but to divide the same amount of land into smaller and smaller plots. Today, the majority of farmers own only tiny amounts of land consisting of several isolated patches which they use for a variety of crops and livestock. Time is wasted travelling between plots, land is wasted beneath the walls that separate one plot from another, and the size of the holdings and the variety of the crops make the introduction of machinery frequently uneconomic. What you can see in Galicia today is not very different from strip-farming in the Middle Ages. Indeed, the Galician peasantry had until this century to pay feudal dues called *foros* – long after other such medieval legacies had disappeared from the rest of the country.

Any people who have been as badly treated as the Galicians are entitled to be mistrustful, and among other Spaniards they have a reputation for caution and guile. In Castilian, an ambiguous statement is a *galleguismo* (Galicianism). In this respect if in no other,

Franco was a true son of Galicia – he was famed for his cryptic remarks and always let his ministers argue out a case before he intervened.

Poverty also breeds superstition and Galicia has long been the heartland of Spanish witchcraft. The foremost textbook of Galician magic, *O antigo e verdadeiro livro de San Cipriano* – better known simply as the *Cipranillo* – has gone through countless editions. Belief in the evil eye is widespread and the region is rich in *sabias* (wise women) and *curanderos* (folk doctors). It is a legendary haunt of the werewolf, called *lobis-home* in Galician.

With its heavily indented coastline, Galicia has also long been closely associated with smuggling. Until very recently, the main commodity was tobacco. Cigarettes were unloaded from cargo ships on the high seas, whisked into shallower waters aboard high-powered speedboats, and then unloaded on to little inshore fishing-boats which could thread their way unsuspected through the *rías*. The trade still continues, but in the eighties it was joined by a vastly more profitable, dangerous and pernicious traffic in cocaine from Latin America.

It is noteworthy that the two communities in Spain where it has proved easiest to find people ready to purvey drugs have been among those historically most neglected by their fellow Spaniards – the gypsies and the Galicians. In the same way as has happened with the gypsies, drugs have brought a mixed legacy to Galicia. Cocaine has left many addicts in the communities through which it has passed. It has fostered the emergence of ruthless organized criminal gangs. But it has also undeniably brought prosperity. As early as the late eighties, indeed, there was enough evidence of conspicuous consumption to cast some doubt on the reliability of official statistics as a guide to Galicia's real wealth.

To an even greater extent than in the Basque country, women have traditionally enjoyed a high standing in society and a generous measure of influence. Galicia's national hero is a woman – María Pita, who distinguished herself by her bravery during the English siege of Corunna in 1586; and several of the region's most prominent intellectuals – the poet Rosalía de Castro, the novelist Emilia Pardo Bazán and the penal reformer Concepción Arenal – have been women. It could be just another legacy of the matriarchal society which existed in northern Spain in pre-Roman times. But it must also owe something to the fact that women in Galicia, for hundreds of years, were forced to assume responsibilities which in other societies were taken on by the men, simply because their menfolk were away in other parts of the country, at sea or abroad.

An awful lot of nonsense has been written over the years about the Galicians' propensity to emigrate. It used to be fashionable to ascribe it to their typically Celtic thirst for adventure. But as one Spanish writer remarked, 'The next time you see one of those emigrating Celts, give him a potato and you will straight away transform him into a sedentary European. What makes "the adventurous races" adventurous is lack of potatoes, lack of bread and lack of freedom.'

It has been estimated that during the past five centuries one in every three Galician males has been forced to abandon his homeland. The earliest permanent emigration was in the sixteenth century, when thousands of Galicians were settled in the Andalusian Sierra Morena in an effort to repopulate areas that had been left deserted by the expulsion of the Moslems and the Jews. Thereafter the focus shifted to the big towns of Andalusia and to those of León, Castile and Portugal, where the Galicians were only too happy to take on the menial and servile jobs that the locals spurned. Domestic servants, for example, were invariably Galician. But small-scale internal migration could only palliate the pressure on land which has always been at the root of Galicia's problems. As a people, the Galicians were blocked on land both to the south and the east. To the north and west lay the ocean, and that – in a sense – is where they finally found an outlet. For almost two centuries, beginning in the second half of the eighteenth century after the restrictions on settlement in the New World were lifted, a steady stream of Galicians set off across the Atlantic to find a new life for themselves in Argentina, Uruguay, Venezuela, Cuba and the other states of Latin America. Such was their desperation – or innocence – that in the 1850s, after the Caribbean plantation-owners had been forced to free their slaves, a Cuban of Galician extraction was able to find some 2,000 of his countrymen to take their places. In much of South America, *gallego* is synonymous with 'Spaniard'. Perhaps the most famous contemporary descendant of Galician immigrants is

Fidel Castro, whose surname derives from the Galician word for a Celtic hill-fort.

But not all the emigration was permanent. Every year, up until the early part of this century, between 25,000 and 30,000 Galicians of both sexes marched in great gangs to and from the *meseta* where they brought in the harvest. Each of these gangs was made up of a set number of reapers (*segadores*) and binders (*rapaces*), and headed by a foreman called the *maoral*. As they marched along with their sickles slung over their shoulders, these weatherbeaten nomads, who have passed into the literature of Castile as well as Galicia, must have been a fearsome sight.

The opportunities for emigration to South America dried up in the fifties at almost exactly the moment when the post-war boom in Europe began to gather momentum, creating an alternative market for cheap labour. Between 1959 and 1973 about a quarter of all the Spaniards who left to work in Europe were Galicians.

It is one of the paradoxes of Spain that Catalonia, which was independent (if fragmented) for three centuries, ranks as only a principality, while Galicia, which only enjoyed a separate existence for three brief spells totalling eleven years in the ninth and tenth centuries, is conventionally referred to as a kingdom. Galician nationalists claim to see in the popular rebellions which took place in Galicia during the later Middle Ages – and particularly the great uprising of 1467–9, organized by peasant brotherhoods called *Irmandades* – evidence of a patriotic awareness. Modern historians tend to see them more as anti-feudal outbursts, albeit impressive ones. But it is undeniable that from the earliest times there was a consciousness among Galicians of being Galician and this was recognized by Fernando and Isabel when they set up a *Junta General del Reino* composed of one representative from each of the Galician provinces to oversee the region's economic and political affairs.

The rise of Galician nationalism, like that of Catalan nationalism, coincided with a literary revival. Indeed, there was an element of imitation. The Galicians, like the Catalans, had their Floral Games – inaugurated two years later – and just as Catalonia enjoyed a *Renaixença*, so Galicia had a *Rexurdimento*. But for all that, it is arguable that Galicia's renaissance was of greater literary importance than Catalonia's. The outstanding figures of the *Rexurdimento* are the poet Eduardo Pondal, the historians Manuel Murguía and Benito Vicetto, and above all Murguía's wife, Rosalía de Castro. The illegitimate daughter of a priest, rejected by society, unhappily married and, towards the end of her life, racked by cancer, she was a quintessentially Galician figure, who suffered as much in her lifetime as her homeland has in its history. Her *Cantares Gallegos*, published in 1863, is one of the great works of Spanish literature.

It was not, however, until after the publication of Alfredo Brañas's *El Regionalismo* in 1889 that the nationalistic sentiments inherent in the *Rexurdimento* began to assume a political shape, and then only in a relatively timid form. The first truly nationalist group was the Irmandade dos Amigos da Fala, founded in Corunna in 1916 by Antonio Villar Ponte. Forced underground soon afterwards by Primo de Rivera's coup, Galician nationalism surfaced again at the start of the Republic in the form of the Partido Galleguista and it was this movement which negotiated a statute of autonomy for Galicia. The statute, which would have given the region control over agriculture, land tenure, savings institutions and social security, as well as the power to 'nationalize', was put to the vote on 28 June 1936. The turnout was almost 75 per cent and of those who voted more than 99 per cent voted 'yes'. Nineteen days later the civil war broke out and Galicia's hopes of home rule were dashed.

The vote nevertheless put the Galicians on the same footing as the Basques and Catalans as a people with a separate culture who had publicly and verifiably laid claim to self-rule, and this fact made it difficult for governments of the post-Franco era to deny them a comparable status. But for the moral authority that that vote accorded them, it is more than likely that Galicia's plaintive dirge would have been drowned by the raucous clamour for self-rule that was beginning to be heard in the other regions of Spain.

CHAPTER 30

Power to the Regions

The system of self-government which emerged from the hurly-burly of the late seventies and which the Spanish dubbed the *estado de las autonomías* was by far the most determined and comprehensive attempt ever made by the Spanish to resolve the internal tensions that have plagued their modern history.

It has been said that its defining characteristic is its 'variable geometry'. In no other country, perhaps, has a solution been applied which, while covering all the regions in that country, permits such wide variations in the nature and scope of the powers allotted to their administrations. At the outset, the constitution divided the various Autonomous Communities into three different sorts: those which reached full self-government by way of the 'fast track' set out in article 151; those which reached it via the 'slow track' set out in article 143;* and finally Navarre, which – alone of the Spanish regions – already enjoyed a measure of autonomy. In addition, substantial differences were created between the powers of the regional administrations in each of the first two categories. The Basques and the Catalans, for example, got their own police forces, whereas the Galicians and the Andalusians did not. The statutes of home rule passed for Valencia and the Canary Islands were different both from each other and from those of the other 'slow-track' Autonomous Communities. In the Basque country and Navarre, moreover, a traditional arrangement was re-established whereby the regional authorities collected the taxes and handed over to the central government sums – known in the Basque country as the *cupo* and in Navarre as the *aportación* – which notionally corres-

---

* See above, p. 44.

ponded to the services provided by Madrid. In the rest of Spain, the procedure was the reverse: Madrid collected the taxes and gave to the regional administrations what they were reckoned to need. From the very beginning, it was the 'variable geometry' of the system which aroused most controversy and disquiet.

When confusion over the UCD government's plans for the regions was at its height in 1980, Felipe González – then the leader of the biggest opposition party – had proposed a law to eliminate the ambiguities in the section of the constitution which dealt with regional government. It eventually became a reality and was given the laborious title of the Institutional Law for the Harmonization for the Autonomy Process. It soon became known by its initials, the LOAPA.

At the heart of this much debated piece of legislation was an attempt to clarify the question of whether state law should prevail over regional law. What distinguished the regions which had achieved home rule by way of article 151 from those which had attained it via article 143 was whether they were entitled to lay claim immediately to powers in certain areas which the constitution reserved in principle for the central government. But the LOAPA stipulated that, where there was a conflict between state and regional law in those areas, state law should always prevail, even after the relevant powers had been delegated to a particular region in its statute of autonomy. The nationalists of the 'historical' regions – and particularly the Basques – argued that the LOAPA was an attempt to limit the scope of their statutes without having to submit the changes to a referendum, as required by the constitution. The lines were drawn for a bitter and lengthy battle.

Nor did it end with the approval of the LOAPA by parliament in June 1982, because the law's opponents referred it immediately to the Constitutional Court. It took the Court more than a year to reach its decision, but when it was eventually delivered – in August 1983 – it was a bombshell. The judges declared that more than a third of the LOAPA was unconstitutional, including those clauses which guaranteed state law supremacy over regional law in the marginal areas where the Basques, Catalans, Galicians and Andalusians had been given powers denied to the rest.

Reservations about the 'variable geometry' of Spain's new system of self-government were inspired by more than just concern at the threat, whether perceived or real, to the country's unity. There was also a fear that disparities between the powers granted to the various regions could exacerbate the disparities which already existed between the richer and poorer parts of Spain. The Autonomous Communities given the broadest powers, the Basque country and Catalonia, were also among those with the highest GDP *per capita*, and it was argued that unless some kind of corrective mechanism could be introduced they could draw apart from the rest of the country economically as much as politically.

In 1985, therefore, a Law on the Financing of the Autonomous Communities (known as the LOFCA) was passed which, among other things, was intended to help close the gap between rich and poor regions. A pool of cash, known as the Inter-territorial Compensation Fund, was created, from which the poorer Autonomous Communities could be provided with assistance. By 1994 the annual provision for this fund had grown to some 128,845 million pesetas ($1·3 billion or £645 million).

Approval of the LOFCA meant that the last of the institutions and procedures needed to run Spain's *estado de las autonomías* had been put in place. Thereafter, attention switched to the transfer to the regional governments of the powers they had been granted in their statutes, together with the human and financial resources needed to exercise them. By the early nineties, the vast majority of the initially agreed transfers had been made. As a consequence, the share of consolidated expenditure spent by central government had fallen sharply – from 89 per cent in 1980 to 67 per cent by 1991. Of the remainder, well over half is now spent by the regional administrations whose share of the total overtook that of the local councils as far back as 1985. In 1994, it was expected that more than a fifth of overall spending would be made by the regions. That, though, understates the eventual impact of Spain's new quasi-federal arrangements.

In the case of the regions which came under article 143 of the Constitution, the transfer was conceived as a two-stage process. Though they were initially denied powers granted to the Autonomous Communities which came under article 151, they stood to acquire at least some of them once a period of a few years had elapsed. In 1992, following numerous delays, representatives from the PSOE and the PP sat down to negotiate an agreement on how many of these extra powers the 'slow-track' regions should be given. A number of new responsibilities were agreed, of which the most important was perhaps university education. As the regional governments concerned assume these new powers over the next few years, the share of overall spending accounted for by the Autonomous Communities will rise sharply.

Another effect of the 1992 deal will be to narrow the gap between the 'slow-track' and 'fast-track' regional administrations. In future, the main differences between them will be that the latter, unlike the former, will have control over the health services, and over primary and secondary education. In addition, all the article 151 regions have their own TV channels and three of them control their own police forces (though that is also true, on both counts, of an article 143 region, Valencia). The *estado de las autonomías* may not be complete, but it is possible to envisage its eventual nature and shape.

It is also the case that Spain's peculiar system of regional self-government has been in operation, albeit provisionally, for well over a decade.* So what sort of administrations has it produced? Has it narrowed or widened the gap between rich and poor regions? Has it enhanced or impaired the efficiency of government? Has it, all in all, been a success or a failure?

Such an intentionally heterogeneous set-up might have been expected to produce immense variations in the quality of regional administration. Yet that has not really been the case. Some have been better than others, to be sure. But the distance between best and worst has been relatively small (though that may reflect the limited scope of their powers until recently). A high-spending government headed by Juan Hormaechea in Cantabria was probably the most controversial, and left the region heavily indebted.

Interestingly, the 'historical nationalities'† have all opted to be

---

*The last statutes to be approved came into effect in February 1983, though a law to adapt Navarre's autonomy provisions did not reach the statute books until the following August.

† See footnote, p. 44.

governed by the right. In the first Basque and Catalan elections, it was the centre-right nationalists of, respectively, the Basque Nationalist Party (PNV) and Convergence and Union (CiU) who topped the polls. In Galicia, it was not the nationalists who came out on top, but the People's Alliance – a Madrid-based party, albeit one founded, and at that time led, by a Galician, Manuel Fraga.

In the Basque country, the first *lendakari* or president was Carlos Garaikoetxea. Following a split in the PNV, he left to lead his own slightly more radical party, Euskal Alkartasuna, and his position at the head of the Basque government was taken by José Antonio Ardanza. Ardanza projects a solid, moderate and responsible image which may go some way towards explaining why the Basque administration has been able to accumulate considerable powers without stirring too much concern in Madrid or the rest of the country. In fact, by some reckonings, the Basque country today enjoys a greater degree of self-government than any other region in the European Union.

The leadership of the Catalan *Generalitat* has been held ever since 1980 by the former banker, Jordi Pujol. Pujol, who came to power on the quintessentially Catalan slogan '*Anem per feina!*' ('Let's go to work!'), is the embodiment of many traditional Catalan values – sober, astute, conventionally Roman Catholic (his wife is the head of the local anti-abortion movement), and above all boundlessly proud of his country's language and culture. His reluctance to define whether he wants to see Catalonia autonomous or independent, though understandable in terms of local sensitivities, can raise hackles in Madrid. At the same time, he has often been criticized within Catalonia for casting the region in the role of victim in his endless disputes with the central government over the *Generalitat's* powers.

The earliest head of the Galician *Xunta* was a cultured elderly doctor, Gerardo Fernández Albor. However, day-to-day power soon came to be exercised by his conspiratorial Number 2, Xosé Luis Barreiro. In 1987, having failed in a plot to unseat Fernández Albor, Barreiro took over a small centrist party. He then linked up with the Socialists to approve a motion of censure that ousted the People's Alliance and handed the regional presidency to the PSOE's candidate, Fernando González Laxe. A year later, corruption charges were laid against Barreiro – by then re-established as the *Xunta's* Vice-President – so that it was against a background of seething controversy that the Galicians approached the regional elections due in 1989. Manuel Fraga, founder of the People's Alliance (by then re-christened the People's Party), opted to stand as its candidate, having long since accepted that his Francoist background precluded him from the premiership. The result was a landslide, with Fraga winning an absolute majority of seats in the local assembly, largely at the expense of Barreiro's party. He has since become an unlikely convert to the cause of regional autonomy, and in the early 1990s impressed nationalists like Ardanza and Pujol with a suggestion for eliminating the duplication that had grown up between regional and central government. His idea for what he called *administración única* would, in essence, mean applying to Spain the EU's principle of subsidiarity, or minimum interference from the centre.

Fraga's idea has not so far been adopted as government policy. But sooner or later action of some kind is going to need to be taken to eliminate the overlapping responsibilities and unnecessary staffing which have become a feature of Spain's administration as a result of its experiment in home rule. During the transfer of powers, two equally undesirable processes have been at work. In the first place, the central government has consistently retained more bureaucrats in each ministry or department than its remaining powers warrant. At the same time, the regional administrations have been recruiting staff of their own in addition to the personnel transferred to them by Madrid. Overall, it is the second of these problems which has been most pronounced. As was mentioned in an earlier chapter, in 1991, by which time the Autonomous Communities were responsible for 19 per cent of spending, they were employing 31 per cent of Spain's public servants.

There has also undoubtedly been a certain amount of profligacy in the new Autonomous Communities. Several of their presidents have higher salaries than the Spanish prime minister. But waste and extravagance, where it has occurred, has usually been on a relatively petty scale, and it is the problem of duplicated responsibilities which is the prime cause of the overspending and indebtedness which of late has become a worry to Madrid.

Under the terms of European economic and monetary union Spain, in common with the other EU states, is expected to control its debt. While the government can take steps to restrict its own borrowing, it cannot prevent the regional administrations – whose powers to raise taxes are severely limited – bridging their fiscal deficits by resort to the banks or the markets. Though it is understandable that the lack of control should cause anxiety in Madrid, and true that Spain's success or failure with regard to the Maastricht targets will probably be decided at the margins, the percentage of overall debt accounted for by the regions is nevertheless quite small. In 1993, debt-servicing by the Autonomous Communities was expected to account for less than 5 per cent of the nation's total repayments of capital and interest.

As a force for regional equality, Spain's system of self-government appears so far to have been a success. During the eighties, Spain's most disadvantaged regions improved their situation more than the poor regions of other EU nations. Nor does this seem to have been entirely because of the Inter-territorial Compensation Fund mentioned earlier. Research has suggested a link between the breadth of a region's powers and its rate of growth, and it should not be forgotten that two of the most backward Autonomous Communities – Galicia and Andalusia – enjoy wide powers under article 151 of the constitution. Even so, convergence between the poorest and richest regions within Spain is taking place slowly. In 1975, when Franco died, the wealthiest part of Spain was the Basque country, whose GDP *per capita* was 10 per cent above the EC average. The poorest area was Estremadura, where the figure was 53 per cent below. The span was 63 per cent. By 1989 the Balearic Islands, with a GDP *per capita* of 7 per cent above the EC average, were Spain's richest region. Estremadura was still the least prosperous, but the shortfall with respect to the EC had shrunk to 51 per cent. The overall gap was therefore 58 per cent, which was only 5 per cent less than it had been fourteen years earlier. And it remained a fact that there were some parts of Spain that were more than twice as rich as others.

It can be argued that the real success of the *estado de las autonomías* is impossible to measure in figures, or even to chronicle with events, because it is to be found in what has *not* happened rather than what has. There has not been that much fuss, and certainly no crisis. The lengthy and complex process of transferring powers to the Autonomous Communities has led to hundreds of court cases between the central and regional administrations; it has provoked the occasional furious public row between regional and national politicians. But nothing has happened that you would not expect to happen in a healthy democracy, and rarely has anyone of weight and substance in Spanish public life questioned whether the unity of the nation is at risk. This seems to me to be a remarkable tribute to the tolerance, maturity and sheer good sense of the Spanish people.

Nevertheless, it could be that the real test has yet to come, for the moment is approaching when the governments of the various Autonomous Communities will have received every last one of the powers and responsibilities delegated to them by the constitution. What will happen then? It is hard to imagine that there will be a problem in any of the 'slow-track' regions, or indeed in Andalusia, all of which will be enjoying a greater degree of self-government than at any time since at least the Middle Ages. The 'historical nationalities' – with the probable exception of Galicia – are another matter, though.

It seems unlikely that the Basque and Catalan nationalists who run the administrations of their respective Autonomous Communities will stop asking for more powers. They have never been much enamoured of a solution which granted self-government to all seventeen regions, fearing that it was a way of dodging what they regard as the central issue – recognition of the distinctive identities of the three 'historical nationalities'. The 1992 agreement, which reduced the differences between the 'fast-track' and 'slow-track' Autonomous Communities, convinced many that their fears were well founded and provided them with an incentive for re-establishing a clearer gap between the two. In any case, demanding concessions from the central government has become a way of life, a *raison d'être*, for the moderate nationalists who are under constant pressure from overtly separatist movements such as Herri Batasuna in the Basque country and Esquerra Republicana de Catalunya. If ever they were to agree that their demands had been fulfilled, there would be little except their history to distinguish the centre-right nationalists from an increasingly moderate Partido Popular.

At the same time, it seems equally unlikely that future central governments will be in much of a position to resist their demands. Ever since the 1993 election, when the Socialists failed to win an outright majority in the Chamber of Deputies, Felipe González and his ministers have been beholden to the Catalan nationalists of Convergence and Union for their survival. The same could well be true of whatever administrations succeed them. Though the fact was obscured by eleven years of Socialist majority rule, Spain's electoral system was designed to avoid giving outright power to a single party. In retrospect, it can be seen to be a formula for handing the balance of power to the nationalists.

The constitution, as has been mentioned earlier, is a vague – often deliberately vague – document, and it creates numerous grey areas where it is by no means clear whether power ought to be exercised by Madrid or by one or more of the regional administrations. So, sooner or later, the tug-of-war between the central government and the regional nationalists is going to have to be over areas where it will be a matter of opinion whether the claims made by the regional nationalists go beyond the terms of the constitution. This has already begun to happen, in fact. In 1993 Jordi Pujol demanded, and secured, the automatic allocation of a share of the income tax collected in Catalonia – a question which is not even covered, let alone settled, by the constitution. A lot of Catalans – by no means all of them fervent nationalists – talk nowadays as if a confederal solution, in which everything but foreign affairs, trade negotiations and defence would be handled by the *Generalitat*, was somehow inevitable. Such an arrangement might well be sensible and desirable. But it is not the one offered by the constitution. And it seems to me that those who speak as if it were a foregone conclusion are trying to wish away a very real problem – the constitutional role given to the armed forces. Their job is to guarantee not only Spain's 'territorial integrity', which, it could be argued, would not be threatened by even a confederal system, but also the 'constitutional arrangements' themselves.

'If Spain is the problem,' said Ortega y Gasset, 'Europe is the solution.' A lot of nationalists have seen in the continent's progress towards unification a way of squaring the circle outlined above. The idea is that European political union will involve a surrender of power 'downwards', to the regions, as well as 'upwards', to a new supra-national entity; that as national boundaries become increasingly unimportant, so the only divisions that will make sense will be those which separate Europe from the rest of the world and those which coincide with its natural, cultural and ethnic divisions. Now, this is perhaps an attractive idea, and one which might even come to fruition some time in the next century if all goes well with European unification. But in Catalonia particularly, it has been widely purveyed by the local nationalists as not just unavoidable but more or less imminent.

The reasons are not difficult to identify. Such a scenario offers the nationalists a way to profit from the popular cause of European unification, which is all about making the continent into one big unit, while keeping faith with nationalism, which is all about carving it up into smaller ones. Whether it is plausible is quite another matter, though.

I personally do not think that Europe can offer a solution – or rather, that it can offer a solution quickly enough to be of use. Instead, I suspect, the Spanish themselves are going to have to rely on their own forbearance and moderation to find a way of reconciling their constitution with their diversity. In the context of Spain's history, in which internal divisions and conflicts have played such a prominent and destructive part, it is difficult to see this as anything other than the most important challenge facing the country in the next few years. It is not, by any means, the only one.

CHAPTER 31

The New Spaniards

As the shock waves from the collapse of the Soviet Union have spread across the globe, millions of hours of air time have been spent reporting the spread of democracy through Eastern Europe and other parts of the world, just as millions of column inches in newspapers and magazines have been devoted to examining whether this or that former dictatorship can now be judged to have become a democracy. Unintentionally, the impression often given, it seems to me, is that democracy is somehow an absolute: that countries are either undemocratic or democratic, and that all that matters is that they should undergo the rites of passage needed to change them from one thing into the other. But democratization is not like circumcision. It can be undone. And there can be significant differences in the eventual results.

Spain illustrates both these points. In the 1930s, it showed that a democracy could turn into a dictatorship. Its history since the end of that dictatorship has demonstrated that democracy, like freedom and equality, is very much a matter of degree.

It has been suggested that democracy cannot be said to be properly established in a society until power has been voluntarily surrendered through the ballot box at least twice. On that reckoning, Spain still has some way to go. Indeed, it can be argued that power has not really been given up through the ballot box even once. What happened in the early eighties was that the UCD fell to pieces in office and the main opposition party, the PSOE, stepped in to fill the gap. Almost two decades after the end of Franco's dictatorship, Spaniards have still to see a fully combatant party hand over power to another, having failed to win as many votes from the electorate. Until that happens, the danger, I think, is not so much that Spain could cease to be a democracy again, but that it will remain a rather shallow, or hollow, one in which the rule of a single party is sanctioned by four-yearly votes.

In the meantime, a good deal could be done to give substance to Spanish democracy in other ways. The fact that this is not being done is largely, if not entirely, the fault of the politicians. Ordinary Spaniards have taken to democracy like ducks to water. All sorts of decisions, in schools and colleges, in offices and factories; decisions among neighbours and parents, among workmates and parishioners; decisions that would once have been settled – if at all – only by a furious row, are nowadays routinely submitted to a show of hands. The habits that go with democracy have put down equally strong roots. The respect the Spanish are prepared to extend to the views of others is nowadays virtually unlimited.

What is inadequate in Spain is not democracy in the wider sense, but democracy in the narrower sense – parliamentary democracy. The Senate, the upper house in the bicameral scheme introduced by the 1978 constitution, could scarcely occupy a more marginal position in public life. The senators themselves complain that the valuable work they do in revising the legislation sent up to them by the Chamber of Deputies is unappreciated by the public. But that is largely because no one bothers to broadcast, or even report, their proceedings, and that in turn is because the proceedings are usually extremely dull. No way has yet been found of giving the upper house a cutting edge, and for as long as the same party enjoys an effective majority in both chambers, it is unlikely that much effort will be put into the search.

If the Senate exists on the margins of Spanish public life, though, it can scarcely be said that the Chamber of Deputies is plumb in the centre. Except when it is the forum for a televised debate on the state of the nation or a motion of censure, the real political dialogue in Spain is carried on elsewhere, mainly through the press.

Until 1994, when he agreed to a British-style Prime Minister's question time, Felipe González had gone to the Chamber to which he was elected as little as possible. In the 1989–93 legislature, he attended an average of just five sessions a year. His deputies' record is even worse. Narcis Serra had not been heard to utter a word in parliament more than two years after being made deputy Prime Minister. His predecessor, Alfonso Guerra, who held the job for nine years, spoke only once. And that was when he was forced to respond to a motion accusing him of responsibility for his brother's involvement in a maze of interlocking power and money scandals.

The taint of corruption which has clung to politics in recent years will also need to be dispelled if the quality, or at least the image, of Spanish democracy is to be improved. So far, none of the scandals unearthed by the press at the end of the eighties and the start of the nineties has led to anyone being gaoled or even fined. One reason for this is that the laws regarding corruption are full of holes the government is unwilling to plug. Why this should be so is open to many different interpretations, but there is now a solid body of evidence to suggest that all of Spain's major parties, with the possible exception of the Communists, have been drawing funds from systematic graft – the charging of 'commission' to companies in exchange for either promoting, or not obstructing, their projects. Construction firms are known to have been a prime target. This is exactly the same pattern which has emerged from the investigations into Italy's system of kickbacks and payoffs.

Some Spaniards have drawn solace – or even encouragement – from the comparison, pointing out that the emergence of the *tangentopoli* ('bribesville') culture took place during a period in which Italy grew into a major economic power. This argument, though, overlooks an important point. Eventually, somebody has to pay for corruption. If the price of every public contract is to be inflated to allow for the cost of the bribe needed to secure it, then someone has to find the extra. What happened in Italy was that, year after year, these increments contributed to a whopping budget deficit which the government funded by borrowing on a grand scale. Its huge public debt is, in large part, the accumulated cost of decades of corruption. Spain cannot go down the same road – not because the markets won't allow it to, but because, like Italy, it is now committed to reducing its public debt so as to facilitate European economic and monetary union. As a result of the Maastricht Treaty, the implications of corruption have become inescapable: the greater the corruption, the higher the budget deficit; the higher the budget deficit, the less the government's scope for generating employment and prosperity, whether by cutting taxes or boosting investment.

Reducing, or at least capping, the level of corruption has thus become an important requirement for Spain's future economic growth.

In the eighties, when Spain was catching up rapidly on its European neighbours, the idea got around that it had been doing so, if only gradually, ever since the fifties. This is not, in fact, the case. Its GDP *per capita* relative to the average in the countries which make up the European Union at the time of writing has actually fluctuated quite a lot.

During the sixties and the first half of the seventies, it rose steeply, until by 1975 it was 80 per cent of the present EU average. But then it fell back sharply. Ten years later, when the recession in Spain ended, its GDP *per capita* was only 72 per cent that of the average of the Twelve. And by 1991, the year before Spain again fell prey to recession, the figure was still only 79 per cent. This is a point to which no one in government is keen to draw one's attention – that by the time the Socialists' mini-boom was over, the gap between Spain and the rest of 'Europe' was still bigger than when Franco died. Since 1991, it is quite likely that its comparative standing has deteriorated again. The recession in Spain seems to be biting deeper and lasting longer than in most of the rest of the Union.

What we have, at all events, is not straight-line convergence between Spain and its Western European neighbours, but an altogether more frustrating pattern in which the Spanish haul themselves up to a certain point before they drop back and have to start again, albeit from a higher level. It can be expected that the aid Spain is receiving from the EU will stop it from falling further, and help it to climb higher, than would otherwise be the case. But it is difficult to see this aid continuing for long after the entry into the EU of the much poorer states of the former Soviet bloc, and it may be that the Spanish are going to have to accept further changes to their way of life – even to their outlook on life – if they are to fulfil their dream of catching up with countries like Britain, France and Germany.

Their ability to act quickly and decisively when the need arises, to 'think big', take risks, and not let themselves be hidebound by rules – all these are of the essence in a successful post-industrial economy. But there are also a number of habits and attitudes to be found in Spain which act as a brake on its development, and which have scarcely changed in the almost two decades that I have been acquainted with the country: an aversion to even the most rudimentary planning, unpunctuality, procrastination, and a reluctance among many subordinates to take responsibility – a trait which goes hand-in-hand with the compulsion among many bosses to take all but the most trivial decisions.

In an age of service cultures and information technology, the difficulty a lot of Spaniards seem to have in putting themselves in the position of the other person, or of dealing with people other than face to face, must also be regarded as handicaps.

How the Spanish will deal with the political and economic challenges awaiting them is impossible to foresee. But what can be said with certainty is that they are going to have to meet these challenges against a background of renewed social change – change on a scale comparable with the migration from the countryside to the towns which so transformed Spain in the fifties and sixties. With an inevitability that only demography can assure, we are approaching a Europe in which, for the first time since at least the nineteenth century, families are going to be bigger in the north than they are in the south.* And in southern Europe, they are going to be smaller than they have ever been in northern Europe.

The effect this will have on the attitudes and lifestyles of Mediterranean Europe is potentially immense. Family affiliations, for example, are at the root of a lot of the favouritism and corruption that is characteristic of Latin societies. So it seems inevitable that, as the average size of the family shrinks, the prevalence of nepotism will recede. You can't give a job to your son-in-law if you don't have one, and you're not going to have one unless you have at least one daughter. It has been argued that the Latin propensity for putting the family first is simply a projection of egocentricity. If this is right, then the disappearance of the large, embracing, loyalty-sapping Latin family could help to kill off the sort of anti-social attitudes which are also prevalent.

* See above, p. 175.

However, if – as I have suggested in an earlier chapter – loyalty to one's relatives has become not just the central, but almost the only, value in Spanish society, the shrinkage in size and importance of the family could prove to have negative consequences that far outweigh the positive ones. One of the most interesting things over the next few decades will be to see whether Spaniards and other southern Europeans are able to transfer their loyalties and affections from the traditionally large, extended family to a much smaller, nuclear one.

At the same time, they are going to have to cope with a social environment which looks set to become increasingly multi-racial. The expulsion of, first, the Jews and subsequently the Moslems meant that for almost five centuries Spain remained ethnically unchanged. The arrival in recent years of sizeable numbers of immigrants, mainly from the Caribbean and the Maghreb, could therefore be expected to have a much more traumatic effect than in countries with a longer tradition of accommodating outsiders.

A lot of Spaniards dismiss the issue, assuring you that their society is free of racism. As any outsider can see, this is just not true. Their treatment of the gypsies, the only ethnic minority left behind after the purging of the Jews and Moslems, has been relentlessly discriminatory.

What is true is that racist attitudes in Spain are more often unconscious than conscious. Press reports about, say, a visiting American diplomat who happens to be black, will never fail to note that he is *'un hombre de color'*. Yet even the most progressively-minded journalists will look at you quizzically if you suggest that someone's skin colour should only be mentioned if relevant to the story – and that anyhow a black man is actually no more or less coloured than a 'white' one. Though the number of Africans living and working in Spain grows every year, words like 'kaffir' are cheerfully bandied about as insults by the characters in children's comic strips. And the clearly pejorative *moro* (moor) is widely used to describe not only North Africans, but also other foreigners with a dark complexion.

Despite this, though, there are real grounds for believing that Spain's racial problems could be less acute than elsewhere. The organized far right is much weaker than in France, Italy, Germany, or even Britain. What is more, the answers given to researchers and pollsters, while they confirm that racism exists, suggest a lower level of prejudice than in any other EU country. There are various possible reasons for this. One is that Spain still has a relatively small immigrant population. Another is that large numbers of Spaniards have themselves gone as emigrants to other people's countries and know what it is like to be on the receiving end of discrimination. A third reason, not necessarily exclusive of the others, is that ample tolerance to which I have returned again and again as being the single most characteristic trait of Spain and the Spaniards today.

Something I wrote in the book from which this one evolved seems to me even truer today – that the changes of recent years have not merely produced a new Spain but a new Spaniard, very different from the intolerant, intemperate figure of legend and history. Yet the new Spaniards remain Spaniards for all that. In fact, I can think of no other people I know, except possibly the Poles, who cling as tenaciously to their traditions. In 1993, it was estimated that the Spanish would spend on their village *fiestas* the equivalent of a half a *billion* pounds – roughly three-quarters of a *billion* dollars.

As important as any political, economic or social choice facing the Spanish in the coming years will be to decide how much of their culture, their identity and their way of life they are prepared to sacrifice in the interests of integration with the rest of Europe. That is not to imply that Spain's way of life is homogeneous. The Basques, Catalans, and Galicians are all going to have to make the same decision with respect to their own cultures and identities. Nevertheless, the respect for tradition is pretty much universal within Spain. Indeed, it is if anything even more intense in those areas where nationalist sentiment is strongest.

That would seem to offer a solid enough insurance against Spain's identity – or rather, its identities – being swamped. If I have a doubt, then it is because the Spanish (the Catalans excepted) tend to be conformists as well as traditionalists.

When Spaniards talk about their *individualismo*, they are not talking about what the British or Americans mean by 'individualism' (i.e. something bordering on eccentricity). What they are referring to is egocentricity – not only self-centredness, but also self-reliance.

Individualism in the Anglo-Saxon sense is quite rare in Spain and eccentricity is almost unknown. There are plenty of flamboyant, provocative and outspoken personalities in Spanish society, but almost without exception they take care to move within the limits of what is considered by the rest of society to be right, proper and decent. You could spend all day in a big Spanish city, at the height of punk fashion elsewhere, without coming across a single mohican haircut.

The fear of appearing *raro* (odd) can be obsessive. Back in the sixties, when Fraga was the Minister of Tourism, someone in his ministry thought up, or agreed to, an advertising campaign for which the slogan was 'Spain is different'. The indignation it caused has still not died away, almost thirty years later. It is understandable that it should have touched a raw nerve at the time. It seemed just a step away from saying that 'Spaniards are different', which was one of the ways that Franco had justified his dictatorship – on the assertion that, unlike other Europeans, they could not be trusted to handle their own destiny. But it is a long time since Franco died, and nobody today is claiming that the Spanish are biologically incapable of running a democracy.

Yet the phrase itself is still common currency. I have often wondered whether Fraga failed to make more headway as a democratic politician, not because of his links with Francoism, but because he is still blamed for having put out that slogan. Mention that something or other is done in another way in Spain and, if you are with a group of Spaniards, it is odds-on one of them will say defensively: 'What you mean to say is that "Spain is different".' Read the newspapers the day after a report comes out saying that Spain is, in some respect, closer to the EU average, and you can expect at least one of the stories to be headlined '*España ya no es diferente*'. Earlier I mentioned a book prepared by the researchers in the Prime Minister's office, aimed at explaining to foreigners the strides made by the country in recent years. What is Chapter 1 called? Inevitably, 'Spain is no longer so different'.

That is doubtless true. But the fact is that Spain *is* different. Some of its peculiarities have emerged in the course of this book: the home of *machismo* has one of the world's highest conscientious objection rates. The nation with the most crowded dwellings in the European

Union also has the most second homes. And the people who, overall, smoke and drink more than any other in the EU also enjoy the highest life expectancy. Spain is a country in which the bosses claim to earn less than their workers, but in which inequality has grown under a left-wing administration; a supposedly Roman Catholic state whose real abortion rate is probably higher than Britain's; a country in which the previous ruling party tore itself to pieces over a divorce law that hardly anyone uses. It now has a Socialist government which pays for the Roman Catholic Church, and a press overwhelmingly opposed to that government yet which takes much of its news from a government-run agency. Nowhere in the world is more closely associated with bullfighting, yet the evidence suggests that more Spaniards dislike than like their own *fiesta nacional*.

But it is Spain's idiosyncrasies which make it such a fascinating place, both to study and visit. Much the same could be said of Britain, France, Germany and Italy. Each, thankfully, has its own identity. And what the Spanish, in their enthusiasm for 'Europe', perhaps overlook is that to be true to themselves they may need to be different from others. For me at least, the new Spain will have reached maturity, not on the day it ceases to be different from the rest of Europe, but on the day that it acknowledges it is.

Index

Béjart, Maurice, 333, 343
Belmonte, Juan, 359n
Benabarre, 22, 23
Benavente, Jacinto, 325, 341
Benedictines, 141
Benegas, Txiki, 284
Benet, Juan, 349
Benítez, Manuel (El Cordobés), 358, 364
Berber languages, 385
Berbers, 1, 374, 385
Berganza, Teresa, 351
Berlanga, Luis García, 342, 346
Berlusconi, Silvio, 314, 315, 317
Bernabeu, Santiago, 34
Bernaola, Carmelo, 352
Bible in Spain, The, 127
Bienal (Seville flamenco competition), 356
bienes gananciales, 167
Bigas Luna, Juan José, 346
Bilbao, 6, 16, 157–8, 394
Bild Zeitung, 291
bingo, 189–90, 193
birth control see abortion; contraception
birth rate, 267–8
Biscay, 24, 388–92, 394–5, 397, 398, 401, 402, 403
Biscay Chamber of Commerce, 402
Biscayan (dialect), 388
Bishops' Conference, 138–9, 140
'black' economy, 246
black money see dinero negro
Blanco y Negro, 154
Blue Division, 93
Blueshirts, 14
Bofill, Ricardo, 351, 407
Bohigas, Oriol, 351
Bonet Correa, Antonio, 327
Bonoloto, 192
Borbón, Alfonso de (Juan Carlos's brother), 90
Borbón, Margarita de, 89
Borbón, Pilar de, 89
Borbón Dampierre, Alfonso de, 88, 94, 95–6
Borbón Dampierre, Gonzalo de, 88
Borbón Dampierre, Jaime de, 88, 94
Borbón Parma, Carlos Hugo de, 92, 94, 95, 96

Borbón Parma, Prince Javier de, 92
Borrell, José, 239
Borrow, George, 127
Bosnia, 106, 117, 169
Bourbons, 86, 379–80
Boyer, Miguel, 59–60, 61, 281
Boyer decree, 239, 281–2
Brañas, Alfredo, 427
Bravos, Los, 352
breath-testing, 202
Brigada de Investigación Social, 209
broadcasting: and PSOE, 55; and totalitarian regime, 46
brothels, 149, 166
Buero Vallejo, Antonio, 342, 346–7
bullfighting, 55, 98, 168, 187, 201, 256n, 356, 357–67, 396
bunker, 29
Buñuel, Luis, 341
BUP see Bachillerato Unificado Polivalente
bureaucracy: and cuerpos, 230–32; and Franco, 231–2, 233; inefficiency of, 233; 'reform of the clocks', 234
Burgos, 151
Bush, George, 305
Byzantines, 373

Caballé, Montserrat, 98, 351
Caballero Bonald, José María, 354
Cáceres, 345n
Cadena de Ondas Populares Españolas (COPE), 132, 140, 318, 319
Cadena Ibérica, 320
Cadena Rato, 320
Cadena SER, 318
Cádiz, 7, 354
Calatrava, Santiago, 351
Calderón de la Barca, Pedro, 8, 325
Calvinism, 127
Calviño, José María, 312
Calvo Sotelo, Leopoldo, 47, 49, 121, 183, 233
Cambio 16, 80, 105, 124, 144, 156, 295, 301, 310
Cambó, Francesc, 23
Cameroon, 180
Camino, 140

309; and trade unions, 323; and
universities, 270; and 'weak'
government, 229–30; and women's
status, 166–7; young Spaniards'
verdict on, 78; as youngest general in
Europe since Napoleon, 119
Francoism: abolition of apparatus of, 31;
fails to survive as a political
movement, 73; and Franco's death,
29; and general election (1977), 37;
and officer corps, 112, 113; and
parliamentary reform bill, 36; and
technocrats' reforms, 18
Franks, 374, 389, 409
Frederika, Queen of Greece, 91
Freemasonry, 127, 137, 141
French Revolution, 1
Frühbeck de Burgos, Rafael, 351
fruit machines, 189, 193
fueros, 391, 394–5, 397, 398
Fuerzas Eléctricas del Noroeste Sociedad
Anónima (FENOSA), 95n
Fundación Santa María, 133, 177
Fura dels Baus, 347
Fusi, Juan Pablo, 143, 198, 300

Gabilondo, Iñaki, 318
Gabon, 180
Gaceta de los Negocios, 298
Gades, Antonio, 333, 335
GAL *see* Grupos Anti-terroristas de
Liberación
Gala, Antonio, 347, 349
Galicia, 5, 22, 24, 374, 376, 434, 435,
444; agriculture, 423; Año Jacobeo
(Xacobeo), 419; and Asturian
monarchy, 421–2; Barreiro affair,
432–3; and bullfights, 366–7; coffee,
197; emigration, 425–6; first elections
(1981), 45; Fraga elected head of
regional government, 66; *Junto
General del Reino*, 426; magic, 424;
organized gangs operating from, 210;
and police, 211n; referendum on
constitution, 45, 403n; *Rexurdimento*,
426–7; Santiago de Compostela's
origin, 422; and self-government, 39,
40, 43–4, 49, 382, 412, 419, 426–7,

429; sexual equality, 424–5;
smuggling, 424; Statute of Santiago,
45
Galician (language), 375, 378, 419–20
Galician Language Institute (University
of Santiago de Compostela), 420
Gallero, Jose Luis, 345
Gallito (José Gómez), 364n
Gallup Institute, 127
gambling, 186–95, 394
gaming laws, 189
ganaderos, 362, 363, 364
Garaikoetxea, Carlos, 400, 432
Garci, José Luis, 346
García, José María, 318
García, Martina, 168n
Garrigues, Antonio, 33
Garzón, Judge Baltasar, 79
Gascon Provençal (language), 375
GATT (General Agreement on Tariffs
and Trade), 339
Gaudí, Antoni, 345, 407
gay associations, 162
gender revolution, 168–70
general elections: (1977) 27, 36–8, 77;
(1979) 44, 50, 121; (1982) 49, 50, 51;
(1986) 56, 65, 329, 403; (1989) 65–7,
309; (1993) 70–72, 218, 436
'Generation of '27', 341, 350
'Generation of '98', 341
Genet, Jean, 150
genetic engineering, 218
Geneva Conference (1975), 319
GEO *see* Grupo Especial de
Operaciones
Georgian (language), 385
Gerhardt, Roberto, 341
Gerona province, 408
gestorías administrativas, 233
Gibraltar, 1, 99, 308, 374
Gibson, Ian, 188
Gimferrer, Pere, 350
Godard, Jean-Luc, 154
Goierri, the, Guipúzcoa, 399
Golden Age, 7, 65, 244, 392
Gomá y Tomás, Cardinal Isidro, 136
Gómez, José (*Gallito*), 364n
González, Felipe, 53, 55, 63, 68, 79, 103,

Jerez, 126
Jesuits, 126, 140, 141, 269
Jews, 425, 443; anniversary of expulsion, 73; choice between exile and conversion, 1; new awareness of Jewish heritage, 3; and religious tax, 132; service of reconciliation, 3; statistics of, 127
Jiménez, Juan Ramón, 341
JOC *see* Juventud Obrera Católica
John XXIII, Pope, 136
John Paul II, Pope, 135, 138, 183
jornaleros (day-workers), 247, 248–9
José Antonio (Ruiz), 334
Joselito, 365
Journal du voleur, 150
journalism/journalists, 292, 294, 302, 303, 304
Joven Orquesta Nacional de España, 335
Joyce, James, 347
Juan Carlos I, King of Spain: and Arias, 32, 33; ascends throne, 113; character, 96–7; chooses Suárez as Prime Minister, 33–5; coup attempt (1981), 48, 86; and democracy, 85–6, 102; first year of reign, 96; and Jews, 3; 'Juan Carlos solution', 92–3; marries Sofía, 92; and media, 102–4; oath of loyalty to Franco (1969), 94–5, 113; and Operación Lucero, 93–4; relationship with Franco, 30–31; renounces privilege of being able to name bishops, 130; report of plot against (1985), 114n; possible influence of Sofía, 98–9; upbringing, 89–91
Juan de Borbón, Don, 30, 88–92, 94, 95, 96
Juana, Queen of Castile (1479–1555), 378
Juana, wife of Afonso V of Portugal, 377
judges, 219, 222
judiciary, 218–20; and constitution, 43; delays in court system, 221–5; PSOE's control, 55; and totalitarian regime, 46
JUJEM (Junta de Jefes del Estado Mayor), 120–21

Junta Superior de Orientación Cinematográfica, 152–3
juntas, 381
Juventud Obrera Católica (JOC), 137

Kent, Victoria, 226
Ketama, 353
Koplowitz, Alicia, Marchioness of Real Socorro, 59
Koplowitz, Esther, Marchioness of Casa Peñalver, 59
Kraus, Alfredo, 351
Kurdistan, 117
Kuwait, 105
Kuwait Investment Office, 59, 69

La Bazán, 422
La Caixa, 100
La Mancha, 5, 133, 344
La Rioja, 5
Labourd (Laburdi), 397
Lacruz, Mario, 348
Laguna, Ana, 351
land: hoarding, 278–9; prices, 60
Lang, Jack, 326
language(s), 170–71; expansion of Romance languages, 378; and Moslems, 375; revival of languages other than Castilian, 3; and rock/pop music, 353; and Visigoths, 373
Larva, 347
Latin America, 30, 150, 205, 210, 425
Lavilla, Landelino, 183
Law of Political Responsibilities, 74
Law of Succession to the Headship of State (1949), 89
Law on the Financing of the Autonomous Communities (LOFCA), 430
Lecturas, 301
Lee, Laurie, 372
Leguina, Joaquín, 255, 314
León, 5, 22, 65, 374, 376, 378, 389, 401, 423, 425
Lérida, 408
Lerroux, Alejandro, 412
lesbians, 162–3
Ley de Enjuiciamiento Criminal, 222

READ MORE IN PENGUIN

In every corner of the world, on every subject under the sun, Penguin represents quality and variety – the very best in publishing today.

For complete information about books available from Penguin – including Puffins, Penguin Classics and Arkana – and how to order them, write to us at the appropriate address below. Please note that for copyright reasons the selection of books varies from country to country.

In the United Kingdom: Please write to *Dept. EP, Penguin Books Ltd, Bath Road, Harmondsworth, West Drayton, Middlesex UB7 0DA*

In the United States: Please write to *Consumer Sales, Penguin USA, P.O. Box 999, Dept. 17109, Bergenfield, New Jersey 07621-0120*. VISA and MasterCard holders call 1-800-253-6476 to order Penguin titles

In Canada: Please write to *Penguin Books Canada Ltd, 10 Alcorn Avenue, Suite 300, Toronto, Ontario M4V 3B2*

In Australia: Please write to *Penguin Books Australia Ltd, P.O. Box 257, Ringwood, Victoria 3134*

In New Zealand: Please write to *Penguin Books (NZ) Ltd, Private Bag 102902, North Shore Mail Centre, Auckland 10*

In India: Please write to *Penguin Books India Pvt Ltd, 706 Eros Apartments, 56 Nehru Place, New Delhi 110 019*

In the Netherlands: Please write to *Penguin Books Netherlands bv, Postbus 3507, NL-1001 AH Amsterdam*

In Germany: Please write to *Penguin Books Deutschland GmbH, Metzlerstrasse 26, 60594 Frankfurt am Main*

In Spain: Please write to *Penguin Books S. A., Bravo Murillo 19, 1° B, 28015 Madrid*

In Italy: Please write to *Penguin Italia s.r.l., Via Felice Casati 20, I–20124 Milano*

In France: Please write to *Penguin France S. A., 17 rue Lejeune, F–31000 Toulouse*

In Japan: Please write to *Penguin Books Japan, Ishikiribashi Building, 2–5 4, Suido, Bunkyo-ku, Tokyo 112*

In South Africa: Please write to *Longman Penguin Southern Africa (Pty) Ltd, Private Bag X08, Bertsham 2013*